The
GOSPEL
of the
KINGDOM

Register This New Book

Benefits of Registering*

✓ FREE **replacements** of lost or damaged books

✓ FREE **audiobook** – *Pilgrim's Progress*, audiobook edition

✓ FREE information about new titles and other **freebies**

www.anekopress.com/new-book-registration

*See our website for requirements and limitations.

The

GOSPEL

of the

KINGDOM

A Commentary on Matthew

CHARLES H.
SPURGEON

WITH AN INTRODUCTORY NOTE BY MRS. C. H. SPURGEON

Aneko Press

www.anekopress.com

inquiries@anekopress.com

Aneko Press, Life Sentence Publishing, and our logos are trademarks of

Life Sentence Publishing, Inc.
203 E. Birch Street
P.O. Box 652
Abbotsford, WI 54405

RELIGION / Biblical Commentary / New Testament / Jesus, the Gospels & Acts

Paperback ISBN: 979-8-88936-527-3

eBook ISBN: 979-8-88936-528-0

10   9   8   7   6   5   4   3   2

Available where books are sold

Contents

Introduction to the American Edition

Goujon, the sculptor, died with chisel in hand, his eye intent upon a half-carved statue.

One who, with his graphic pen did nobler work than any mere artist or sculptor with brush or chisel, fell on the 31st of January, 1892, leaving this his last and, I think, his best work.

Charles H. Spurgeon had a rare insight into the Word of God and spiritual truth. He was a prophet of wonderfully clear vision. He saw beneath the letter to the spirit of divine truth. He was both an example and a proof that the days of anointed eyes and anointed tongue are not past, and that the *unction from the Holy One* (1 John 2:20), which confers both spiritual perception and effective utterance, was not confined to apostolic times.

This commentary on the Gospel of Matthew is the latest and ripest of his life's labors. It will be found as a tree laden with rich fruit and evidencing a soil uniquely fertile and a culture that reveals a divine husbandman. We predict for this volume a larger sale than for any of Spurgeon's previous works, partly because it is his latest and has in a sense the aroma of his dying days, and partly because it is a simple, brief, and charming memorial of the most effective popular preacher of his age. Every page is, like his sermons, full of his Master and yet sparkling with his own unique individuality. They will be found to disclose many of the secrets of his power in discerning, expounding, and applying the gospel. The reader will find himself here keeping perpetual company with one whose soul followed hard after God, and who loved the paths where his Savior had trodden before him.

May the inspiring Spirit, who guided the evangelist Matthew in the production of this narrative, become to all readers of this commentary the illuminating Spirit also; and through these pages may he who is dead still continue to speak!

     – Arthur T. Pierson

       Metropolitan Tabernacle, London, February, 1893.

Introductory Note

Few and simple should be the words that introduce this eagerly expected book to the many friends who will welcome it.

The beloved author has gone to his eternal reward, he is *the blessed of the LORD* (Isaiah 65:23) forever, but he has left with us this last precious legacy, which draws our hearts heavenward after him.

It stands alone in its sacred and sorrowful significance. It is the tired worker's final labor of love for his Lord. It is the last sweet song from lips that were ever sounding forth the praises of his King. It is the dying shout of victory from the standard-bearer, who bore his Captain's colors unflinchingly through the thickest of the fight.

Reverently, we lay it at the dear Master's feet with love, and tears, and prayers. It needs no comment. It is beyond all criticism. But His acceptance and approval will be its reward and glory.

During two previous winters in the south of France, a great part of dear Mr. Spurgeon's leisure had been devoted to the production of this commentary, and it bears much internal evidence of the brightness of the sunny shore where it was written.

On the last visit to Menton, after his terrible illness, his mental strength was apparently quite restored and this delightful service was eagerly resumed, and so eagerly, that we often feared his health would suffer from his devotion to his happy task. But it was difficult to persuade him to relax his efforts. With his Master, he could say, *My meat is to do the will of him that sent me, and to finish his work* (John 4:34), and till within a few days of the termination of his lovely and gracious life, he was incessantly occupied in expounding this portion of God's Word.

Much of the later portion of the work, therefore, was written on the very borderland of heaven, amid the nearing glories of the unseen world and almost within sight of the golden gates.

Such words acquire a solemnity and pathos with which nothing else could invest them. We listen almost as to a voice *from the excellent glory* (2 Peter 1:17).

Yet, in reading over the proof-sheets of my beloved's last work, I have been as much struck by the profound simplicity as by the tender power of the dear expositor's comments. Surely the secret of his great strength lay in this, that he was willing to say what God put in his heart, and did not seek to use *enticing words of man's wisdom* (1 Corinthians 2:4).

Although the Master's call to His faithful servant came before he could complete the revision of his manuscripts, the concluding pages have been compiled, with loving care, entirely from his own spoken and written words, by the dear friend who was most closely associated with him in all his work for God.

– Susannah Spurgeon

Westwood, Beulah Hill, Upper Norwood, January, 1893.

The Gospel
According to Matthew

Matthew 1

Matthew 1:1-17

The Pedigree of the King

1. The book of the generation of Jesus Christ, the son of David, the son of Abraham.

This verse gives us a clue to the special drift of Matthew's Gospel. He was moved of the Holy Spirit to write of our Lord Jesus Christ as King – *the son of David.* He is to be spoken of as specially reigning over the true seed of Abraham; thus He is called *the son of Abraham.* Lord Jesus, make each one of us call You my God and King! As we read this wonderful Gospel of the kingdom, may we be full of loyal obedience and pay You humble homage! You are both a King and a King's Son.

The portion before us looks like a string of names, and we might imagine that it would yield us little spiritual food, but we must not think lightly of any line of the inspired volume. Here the Spirit sets before us the pedigree of Jesus and sketches the family tree of *the King of the Jews* (Matthew 2:2). Marvelous condescension, that He should be a man and have a genealogy, even He who *was in the beginning with God* (John 1:2), and *thought it not robbery to be equal with God* (Philippians 2:6)! Let us read each line of *the book of the generation* with adoring gratitude that we have a King who is one with us in our nature – "in ties of blood with sinners one."

2. Abraham begat Isaac; and Isaac begat Jacob; and Jacob begat Judas and his brethren.

With Abraham was the covenant made that in his seed would all the nations of the earth be blessed. The line ran not in Ishmael, the offspring of the flesh, but in Isaac, who was born after the promise, and by the divine purpose it flowed in elect Jacob and not in the firstborn, Esau. Let us observe and admire the sovereignty of God. Our Lord sprang out of Judah, of which tribe nothing is said concerning the priesthood, that it might be clear that His priesthood is *not after the law of a carnal commandment, but after the power of an endless life* (Hebrews 7:16). Yet He comes from Judah's royal tribe, for He is King.

3-4. And Judas begat Phares and Zara of Thamar; and Phares begat Esrom; and Esrom begat Aram; and Aram begat Aminadab; and Aminadab begat Naasson; and Naasson begat Salmon.

Observe the dash of unclean blood that enters the stream through Judah's incest with Tamar. O Lord, You are the sinner's Friend!

5. And Salmon begat Booz of Rachab; and Booz begat Obed of Ruth; and Obed begat Jesse.

We note that two women are mentioned in this fifth verse, a Canaanite and a Moabitess. Thus Gentile blood mingled with the Hebrew strain. Our King has come to break down the partition wall. As Gentiles, we rejoice in this. Jesus is heir of a line in which flows the blood of the harlot Rahab and of the rustic Ruth. He is akin to the fallen and to the lowly, and He will show His love even to the poorest and most obscure. I, too, may have part and lot in Him.

6-9. And Jesse begat David the king; and David the king begat Solomon of her that had been the wife of Urias; and Solomon begat Roboam; and Roboam begat Abia; and Abia begat Asa; and Asa begat Josaphat; and Josaphat begat Joram; and Joram begat Ozias; and Ozias begat Joatham; and Joatham begat Achaz; and Achaz begat Ezekias.

Well may our hearts melt at the memory of David and Bathsheba! The fruit of their unholy union died, but after repentance, she who *had been the wife of Urias* became the wife of David and the mother of Solomon. Notable was the grace of God in this case that the line should be continued in this once-guilty pair; but oh, what kinship with fallen humanity does this indicate in our Lord! We will not pry into the mystery of the incarnation, but we must wonder at the condescending grace that appointed our Lord such a pedigree.

10. And Ezekias begat Manasses; and Manasses begat Amon; and Amon begat Josias.

A line of kings of a mixed character – not one of them perfect, and some of them as bad as bad could be. Three are left out altogether; even sinners who were only fit to be forgotten were in the line of this succession, and this shows how little can be made of being born of the will of man or of the will of the flesh. In this special line of descent, salvation was not of blood, nor of birth. Specially let us think of such a one as Manasses being among the ancestors of our Lord, as if to hint that, in the line that comes after Him, there would be some of the chief of sinners who would be miracles of mercy. Again we say, how near does Jesus come to our fallen race by this His genealogy!

11. And Josias begat Jechonias and his brethren, about the time they were carried away to Babylon.

Poor captives, and those who are bound with the fetters of sin, may see some like themselves in this famous ancestry. They are prisoners of hope, now that the Christ is born of a race that was once *carried away to Babylon.*

12-16. And after they were brought to Babylon, Jechonias begat Salathiel; and Salathiel begat Zorobabel; and Zorobabel begat Abiud; and Abiud begat Eliakim; and Eliakim begat Azor; and Azor begat Sadoc; and Sadoc begat Achim; and Achim begat Eliud; and Eliud begat Eleazar; and Eleazar begat Matthan; and Matthan begat Jacob; and Jacob begat Joseph the husband of Mary, of whom was born Jesus, who is called Christ.

With one or two exceptions, these are names of persons of little or no note. The later ones were persons altogether obscure and insignificant. Our Lord was *a root out of a dry ground* (Isaiah 53:2), a shoot from the withered stem of Jesse. He set small store by earthly greatness. He must needs be of human race, but He comes to a family that was of low estate and there finds His reputed father, Joseph, a carpenter of Nazareth. He is the poor man's King. He will not disdain any of us though our father's house be little in Israel. He will condescend to men of low estate.

Wonder surpassing all wonders – *the Word*, by whom all things were made, *was [himself] made flesh, and dwelt among us* (John 1:14)! He was born of a human mother, even of the lowly virgin, Mary. *Forasmuch then as the children are partakers of flesh and blood, he also himself likewise took part of the same* (Hebrews 2:14). Our hearts would anoint with sweet perfume of love and praise the blessed head of Him *who is called Christ,* the Anointed One.

> *17. So all the generations from Abraham to David are fourteen generations; and from David until the carrying away into Babylon are fourteen genera-tions; and from the carrying away into Babylon unto Christ are fourteen generations.*

The Holy Spirit led His servant Matthew to adopt a rough and simple method to help weak memories. Here are three sets of fourteen genera-tions. Let us learn from this to make ourselves familiar with our Lord's pedigree and think much of His being born into the world. Specially let us see that He was literally of the house of David and of the seed of Abraham, for many prophecies in the Old Testament pointed to this fact. He is truly the Messiah, the Prince, who was to come.

Matthew 1:18-25

The Birth of the King

> *18. Now the birth of Jesus Christ was on this wise: When as his mother Mary was espoused to Joseph, before they came together, she was found with child of the Holy Spirit.*

A word or two sufficed to describe the birth of all the kings whose names we have read, but for our Lord Jesus Christ there is much more to be said. The evangelist Matthew girds himself up for his solemn duty and writes, *Now the birth of Jesus Christ was on this wise.* It is a deep, mysterious, and delicate subject, fitter for reverent faith than for speculative curiosity. The Holy Spirit worked in the chosen virgin the body of our Lord. There was no other way of His being born, for had He been born of a sinful father, how would He have possessed a sinless nature? He was born of a woman, that He might be human, but not by man, so that He might not be sinful. See how the Holy Spirit cooperates in the work of our redemption by preparing the body of our Lord!

19. Then Joseph her husband, being a just man, and not willing to make her a public example, was minded to put her away privily.

Mary was betrothed to him, and he was saddened and perplexed when he learned that she would become a mother before they had been actually married. Many would have thrust her away in indignation and put her to open shame, but Joseph was of a royal mind as well as a royal race. He would not expose what he thought to be the sin of his betrothed wife, although he felt that she must be put away, but he would do it quietly. When we have to do a severe thing, let us choose the most tender manner. Maybe we shall not have to do it at all.

20. But while he thought on these things, behold, the angel of the LORD *appeared unto him in a dream, saying, Joseph, thou son of David, fear not to take unto thee Mary thy wife: for that which is conceived in her is of the Holy Spirit.*

He could not but feel very anxious and no doubt he prayed about these things both day and night. God would not leave the honor of the chosen virgin mother without protection. Soon Joseph had the best of guidance.

From heaven, he had the assurance that Mary had not sinned, but had been favored of the Lord. Joseph is reminded of his royal rank, *thou son of David,* and is told to cast away his fear. How he must have been comforted by the Lord's *fear not!* He was to take Mary under his tender care and be a foster father to the Son who would be born of her.

Mary must have been in great anxiety herself as to whether her story of angelic visitation would be believed, for it looked improbable enough. We doubt not that faith sustained her, but she needed much of it. Every great favor brings a great trial with it as its shadow and becomes thus a new test of faith. The Lord very graciously removed all suspicion from Joseph's mind and thus provided for the honor of the mother and for the comfort of the holy child. If Jesus is born in our hearts, we shall have trouble, but the Lord will witness that Christ is ours and He will surely bear us through.

21. And she shall bring forth a son, and thou shalt call his name JESUS: for he shall save his people from their sins.

The Lord of glory is born the Son of Man, and is named by God's command and by man's mouth, Jesus the Savior. He is what He is called. He saves us from the punishment and the guilt of sin, and then from the ill effect and evil power of sin. This He does for *his people*, even for all who believe in Him. It is His nature to do this, as we see in the fact that His very name is Jesus – Savior. We still call Him by that name, for He still saves us in these latter days. Let us go and tell out His name among men, for He will save others.

22-23. Now all this was done, that it might be fulfilled which was spoken of the Lord by the prophet, saying, Behold, a virgin shall be with child, and shall bring forth a son, and they shall call his name Emmanuel, which being interpreted, God with us.

Who would have thought that the prophecy contained in Isaiah 7:14 could have referred to our Lord? One of these days, we shall discover a great deal more in the inspired Word than we can see today. Perhaps it is necessary to our understanding a prophecy that we should see it actually fulfilled. What blind eyes we have!

It is pleasant to mark that, according to this verse and the twenty-first verse, *Emmanuel* and *Jesus* mean the same thing. *God with us* is our Savior. He is with us as God on purpose to save us. The incarnation of Jesus is our salvation.

To cheer up Joseph and resolve his mind, Holy Scripture is brought to his remembrance, and truly, when we are in a dilemma, nothing gives us such confidence in going forward as the sacred oracles impressed upon the heart. How conversant was Joseph with the prophets to have their words before him in a dream! Lord, whether I read Your Word when awake or have it brought to my memory in my sleep, it is always precious to me! But You, Lord Jesus, God with us, are dearer still, and the written Word is especially precious because it speaks of You, the incarnate Word.

24-25. Then Joseph being raised from sleep did as the angel of the Lord had bidden him, and took unto him a wife: and knew her not till she had brought forth her firstborn son: and he called his name JESUS.

Joseph was not disobedient to the heavenly vision in any respect. He did not delay, but as soon as he rose he *did as the angel of the Lord had bidden him.* Without delay, protest, or reservation, he obeyed. What holy awe filled his heart as he welcomed the favored virgin to his home, to be respectfully and affectionately screened from all evil! What must he have thought when he saw the Son of the Highest lying on the bosom of her whom he had married! He was happy to render any service to the newborn King. Since he accepted Mary as his betrothed wife, her child was the heir of Joseph and so of David, and thus was by right the King of the Jews. Our Lord Jesus had a birthright by His mother, but His right on the father's side was, by Joseph's act and deed, also put beyond dispute.

Let us leave this wonderful passage worshipping the Son of God, who condescended to be born the Son of Man. Thus our God became our brother, bone of our bone, and flesh of our flesh. The nearer He comes to us, the more humbly let us adore Him. The more true the kinship of our King, the more enthusiastically let us crown Him Lord of all!

Matthew 2

Matthew 2:1-23

The King Appearing and the King Attacked

1-2. Now when Jesus was born in Bethlehem of Judaea in the days of Herod the king, behold, there came wise men from the east to Jerusalem, saying, Where is he that is born King of the Jews? for we have seen his star in the east, and are come to worship him.

The King is born and now He must be acknowledged. At the same moment He will be attacked. His birth was in the days of another king, of Edomite stock, who had usurped the throne of David. The world's kingdom is opposed to that of our Lord: Where Jesus is born there is sure to be a Herod in power. It is a marvelous thing that magi from afar would know that a great king was born and would come from so great a distance to do Him homage, for the world's wise men are not often found bowing at the feet of Jesus. When wise men seek our King, they are wise indeed. These were devout men to whom the stars spoke of God. An unusual star was understood by them to indicate the birth of the coming Man for whom many in all lands were looking. Stars might guide us if we were willing to be led. Lord Jesus, make everything speak to me concerning You and may I be truly led till I find You!

The wise men were not content with having *seen his star;* they must see Himself, and seeing, they must adore. These were not in doubt as to His Godhead. They said, *We . . . are come to worship him.* Lord, I pray You, make all the wise men to worship You!

3. When Herod the king had heard these things, he was troubled, and all Jerusalem with him.

Herod is expressly called *Herod the king*. In that capacity, he is the enemy of our King. They are in a sad state to whom the Savior is a trouble. Some, like Herod, are *troubled* because they fear that they shall lose position and honor if true religion makes progress, and many have an undefined dread that the presence of Jesus will deprive them of pleasure or call them to make unwilling sacrifices. O You who are the King of heaven, You do not trouble me. You are my joy!

See the influence of one man. Herod's trouble infects *all Jerusalem*. Well it might, for this cruel prince delighted in shedding blood, and the darkness of his brow meant death to many. Unhappy Jerusalem, to be *troubled* by the birth of the Savior! Unhappy people, to whom true godliness is a weariness!

4. And when he had gathered all the chief priests and scribes of the people together, he demanded of them where Christ should be born.

When the earthly king dabbles in theology, it promises no good to truth. Herod among priests and scribes is Herod still. Some men may become well-instructed in their Bibles and yet be all the worse for what they have discovered. Like Herod, they make ill use of what they learn, or like these scribes, they may know much about the Lord Jesus and yet have no heart towards Him.

5-6. And they said unto him, In Bethlehem of Judaea: for thus it is written by the prophet, And thou Bethlehem, in the land of Juda, art not the least among the princes of Juda: for out of thee shall come a Governor, that shall rule my people Israel.

They were right in their conclusion, though somewhat cloudy in their quotation. Jesus was to be born in the city of David, in *Bethlehem*, which is, being interpreted, "the house of bread." Though the city was but a little one, His birth therein made it famous. Jesus ennobles all that He touches. These scribes knew where to find the text about the Savior's birth, and they could put their finger upon the spot in the map where He would be born, and yet they knew not the King, nor cared to seek Him out. May it never be my case, to be a master of scriptural geography, prophecy, and theology, and yet to miss Him of whom the Scripture speaks!

With joy would we note the name of *Governor,* here given to Jesus. We are of the spiritual Israel if He rules us. Oh, that the day may soon come when the literal Israel shall behold the government laid upon His shoulder!

7. Then Herod, when he had privily called the wise men, enquired of them diligently what time the star appeared.

We delight in anxious inquirers, but here was one of a very evil sort. Many pry into holy things so that they may ridicule or otherwise oppose them. What an evil diligence is this! When very private inquiries are made, we may suspect that something is wrong, and yet it is not always so.

However, truth fears not the light. Whether men inquire secretly or not, we are ready to give them information about our Lord and about everything that concerns Him.

8. And he sent them to Bethlehem, and said, Go and search diligently for the young child; and when ye have found him, bring me word again, that I may come and worship him also.

Crafty wretch! Murder was in his heart, but pious façades were on his tongue. May none of us be Herodians in hypocrisy! To promise to worship, and to intend to destroy, is a piece of trickery very usual in our own days.

Observe that the wise men never promised to return to Herod. They probably guessed that all this eager zeal was not quite so pure as it seemed to be, and their silence did not mean consent. We must not believe everybody who makes loud professions, nor do all that they ask of us, lest we aid them in some evil design.

9-10. When they had heard the king they departed; and, lo, the star, which they saw in the east, went before them, till it came and stood over where the young child was. When they saw the star, they rejoiced with exceeding great joy.

Yes, *they departed,* and were wise to get out of Herod's vile company. They made no compact with him. They heard his false professions and they went their way. The star appeared when the tyrant disappeared.

The star, which having shone long enough in the western heavens to guide them to Judea, then ceased to be visible, but shone forth again as they left Jerusalem. We must not always expect to have visible signs to cheer us, but we are very glad for them when the Lord grants them to us. We seek not the star of inward feelings or outward signs, but Jesus Himself. Yet have we great joy when heavenly comfort shines into our souls. Lord, *shew me a token for good* (Psalm 86:17). This will make me glad. Show me Yourself and I will rejoice *with exceeding great joy.*

See how the stars above as well as the men below pay their homage to the newborn King! My soul, be not slow to adore your Savior! The star moved *till it came and stood over where the young child was.* So will my heart never rest till it finds the Lord.

> *11. And when they were come into the house, they saw the young child with Mary his mother, and fell down, and worshipped him: and when they had opened their treasures, they presented unto him gifts; gold, and frankincense and myrrh.*

Those who look for Jesus will see Him. Those who truly see Him will worship Him. Those who worship Him will consecrate their wealth to Him. The gold and spices were *presented* not to Mary, but *unto him.* The wise men kept their caskets closed till they saw Jesus and then they *opened their treasures.* Let us keep our love and our holy service for our Lord's eye and never wish to expose them to the world's gaze. The wise men's gifts were royal, with a touch of the priestly in them: *Gold, and frankincense and myrrh.* These choice offerings, especially the gold, would help Joseph and Mary to provide for the Royal Child, who was so soon to be exiled. God brought providers from the Far East to supply the needs of His Son. "Remember that Omnipotence has servants everywhere." Before the babe starts for Egypt, Eastern scholars must pay His charges.

Lord, You shall have my worship and my gifts, for You are the sole Monarch of my soul, and I will aid Your missionary cause, so that when You go into Africa with Your gospel, my gifts may go with You.

> *12. And being warned of God in a dream that they should not return to Herod, they departed into their own country another way.*

Probably, they half suspected Herod already, and the Lord by a dream led their thoughts further in the same direction. Wise men need to be *warned of God.* When they are, they alter their minds at once. Though they had planned to return by one route, they took another. They did not linger, but *departed into their own country another way.* Oh, that I may never be disobedient to a hint from the throne! *Thou shalt guide me with thy counsel* (Psalm 73:24).

13. And when they were departed, behold, the angel of the Lord appeareth to Joseph in a dream, saying, Arise, and take the young child and his mother, and flee into Egypt, and be thou there until I bring thee word: for Herod will seek the young child to destroy him.

Angels were busy in those days, for they had special charge of their Royal Master. Joseph's high office, as guardian of the young child and His mother, involved him in care and made him an exile from his country. We cannot expect to serve the Lord and yet have an easy time of it. We must cheerfully journey across a desert if we have a charge to keep for our God, and we must wait in banishment, if need be, and never venture to come back till the Lord sends us our passports. Our orders are, *Be thou there until I bring thee word.* The Lord's servants must wait for the Lord's word before they make a move, whether it be to go abroad or to come home. Waiting is hard work, especially waiting in Egypt, but it is safe to wait till we have our marching orders.

14-15. When he arose, he took the young child and his mother by night, and departed into Egypt: and was there until the death of Herod: that it might be fulfilled which was spoken of the Lord by the prophet, saying, Out of Egypt have I called my son.

Night journeys, both actual and spiritual, may fall to the lot of those who carry Jesus with them. Even the Son of God, who is preeminent above all others, must depart into Egypt like the rest of the family, and must only come out of it when He is called. Let us not wonder if we also have to go down to Egypt, and go in a hurry, and go by night, and are allowed to stay there for many a day. We, too, shall be called out in due time by Him whose call is effective. The angel who leads us into Egypt will bring us word to come forth from it, for all our times are in the Lord's hands. Let us never forget that the chosen may have to go into Egypt, but they must be brought out of it, for the rule is of universal bearing: *Out of Egypt have I called my son.*

How the prophecies mark out our Lord's way from the beginning! The King of Israel comes out of Egypt, even as Moses did, who in his day *was king in Jeshurun* (Deuteronomy 33:5).

> *16. Then Herod, when he saw that he was mocked of the wise men, was exceeding wroth, and sent forth, and slew all the children that were in Bethlehem, and in all the coasts thereof, from two years old and under, according to the time which he had diligently inquired of the wise men.*

Herod, with all his craftiness, misses his mark. He thinks that he has been made a fool of, though the wise men had no such intention. Proud men are quick to imagine insults. He is furious. He must kill this newborn King lest He claim his crown, and therefore he orders the death of every two-year-old child in Bethlehem, taking good margin so that none might escape through error in the age. What did it matter to him if a few babes were needlessly slain? He must make sure that the little King is made an end of, and he imagines that a speedy and indiscriminate slaughter of all who have reached their second year will put him beyond all fear of this reputed rival. Men will do anything to be rid of Jesus. They care not how many children, or men, or women are destroyed, so that they can but resist His kingdom and crush His holy cause in its infancy. Yet vain is their rage. The holy child is beyond their jurisdiction and their sword.

> *17-18. Then was fulfilled that which was spoken by Jeremiah the prophet, saying, In Rama was there a voice heard, lamentation, and weeping, and great mourning, Rachel weeping for her children, and would not be comforted, because they are not.*

Our Prince steps along a pathway paved with prophecies. Yet see what trouble accompanies His early days! The weeping prophet foretells the wailing over the innocents. He is the innocent cause of the death of many innocents. Men say that religion has been the cause of cruelty and bloodshed. Honesty should compel them to admit that not religion, but opposition to religion, has done this. What! Blame Jesus because Herod sought to murder Him and therefore made so many mothers weep over their dead babes? What three drops of gall are these: *Lamentation, and weeping, and great mourning*! The triple mixture is all too common.

Our Rachels still weep, but holy women who know the Lord Jesus do not now say concerning their little ones that *they are not*. They know that their children are, and they know where they are, and they expect to meet them again in glory. Surely, if these women had but known, they might have been comforted by the fact that though their little ones were slain, the children's Friend had escaped and still lived to be the Savior of all who die before committing actual transgression.

> *19-20. But when Herod was dead, behold, an angel of the Lord appeareth in a dream to Joseph in Egypt, saying, Arise, and take the young child and his mother, and go into the land of Israel: for they are dead which sought the young child's life.*

Angels again! Yes, and they are still busy around *the beloved of the LORD* (Deuteronomy 33:12). Joseph still watches over his honored charge, even as Joseph of old watched over Israel in Egypt. See the order in which the family is arranged – *the young child and his mother*. The Lord is placed first. It is not here, as in Rome, "the Virgin and child." The angel loathed to mention Herod's name, but said, *They are dead*. Such a wretch did not deserve to be named by a holy angel. Herod had gone to his own place and now the Lord brings back His banished ones to their own place. Instead of making Jesus to die, the tyrant is dead himself. Sword in hand, he missed the young child, but without a sword, that child's Father struck home to his heart. It is a relief to the world when some men die. It was certainly so in the case of Herod. Those who keep our King out of His own are not likely to live long. My soul, ponder the lessons of history concerning the King's adversaries!

> *21-22. And he arose, and took the young child and his mother, and came into the land of Israel. But when he heard that Archelaus did reign in Judaea in the room of his father Herod, he was afraid to go thither: notwithstanding, being warned of God in a dream, he turned aside into the part of Galilee.*

Joseph obeyed without question. *He arose*; that is to say, as soon as he was awake he set about doing as he was bidden. At once he made the journey and came into the land of Israel. So should we hasten to obey. He had his fears about Judea, yet he did not follow his fears, but only went as his guide from heaven directed him. This Joseph was a dreamer like his namesake of old, and he was also a practical man and turned his dreams to wise account. He *came into the land of Israel,* but he was allowed to go into that part of it that was under a gentler sway than that of Archelaus, who was no improvement upon his father. Galilee, a despised country, a land where Gentiles mixed with the Jews, a dark and ignorant part, was to be the land of our Lord's early days. He was of the common people and He was educated in a rustic region, in *the part of Galilee,* among a plain folk who had none of the fine manners of the towns. Blessed King, the days of Your minority were not spent at court, but among the common multitude, whom still You delight to bless! I pray You, turn aside into the parts of this Galilee and abide with me.

23. And he came and dwelt in a city called Nazareth: that it might be fulfilled which was spoken by the prophets, He shall be called a Nazarene.

Our Lord was called Netzar, which means "branch." Probably this is the prophecy referred to, for *Nazareth* signifies sprouts or shoots. Possibly some unrecorded prophecy, often repeated by the prophets and known to all the people, is here alluded to. Certainly He has long been called a Nazarene, both by Jews and violent unbelievers. Spitting on the ground in disgust, many a time has His fierce adversary hissed out the name *Nazarene,* as if it were the climax of contempt. Yet, O Nazarene, You have triumphed! Jesus of Nazareth, the greatest name among men. O Lord, my King, as You are dishonored by Your foes, so shall You be adored among Your friends, with all their heart and all their soul. While others call You Nazarene, we call You Jesus – Jehovah, King of Kings, and Lord of Lords.

Matthew 3

Matthew 3:1-12

The Herald of the King

The King has been in concealment long enough and it is time for His herald to appear and proclaim His coming. This chapter tells us of the champion who came in advance of the King.

1-2. In those days came John the Baptist, preaching in the wilderness of Judaea and saying, Repent ye: for the kingdom of heaven is at hand.

While Jesus still remained at Nazareth, His kinsman, the Baptizer, made his appearance. The morning star is seen before the sun. John came not to the court, but to solitary wildernesses, places left to sheep and a handful of rural folk. The mission of Christ Jesus is to the moral wastes and to the desolate places of the earth. To them the Lord's harbinger makes his way, and there he fitly preaches the command, *Repent ye.* Give up your thorns and briars, O you wildernesses, for your Lord is coming to you! See how John announces the coming kingdom, how he bids men to make ready for it, and how he urges them to be speedy in their preparation, *for the kingdom of heaven is at hand.* Let me be ready for my Lord's coming and put away all that would grieve His Holy Spirit!

3. For this is he that was spoken of by the prophet Esaias, saying The voice of one crying in the wilderness, Prepare ye the way of the Lord, make his paths straight.

Matthew keeps to his custom of quoting from the Old Testament. The prophets described not only the King, but also His forerunner. They mention the character of this harbinger. He was a *voice* (Jesus is *the Word* [John 1:1]); his tone was *crying;* his place was *in the wilderness;* and his message, which was one of announcement, in which he required preparation for the coming King, was: *Prepare ye the way of the Lord.* Men's hearts were like a wilderness, where there is no way; but as loyal subjects throw up roads for the approach of beloved princes, so were men to welcome the Lord, with their hearts made right and ready to receive Him.

O Lord, I would welcome You if You would come to me. I have great need of Your royal presence, and therefore I would prepare a way for You. Into my heart my desires have made for You a path most short and smooth. Come, Lord, and delay not! Come into my wilderness nature and transform it into a garden of the Lord.

4. And the same John had his raiment of camel's hair, and a leathern girdle about his loins; and his meat was locusts and wild honey.

He was rough and stern, like Elijah. His garments indicated his simplicity, his sternness, and his self-denial. His food, the product of the desert where he dwelt, showed that he cared nothing for luxuries. His whole bearing was symbolic, but it was also fit and suitable for his office. The plainest of food is best for body and mind and spirit, and, moreover, it fosters manliness. Lord, let not my meat, or drink, or garments hinder me in Your work!

5-6. Then went out to him Jerusalem, and all Judaea, and all the region round about Jordan, and were baptized of him in Jordan, confessing their sins.

The people were expecting a Messiah and so they went *en masse* to John as soon as his shrill voice had startled the solitudes. Baptism, or the washing of the body in water, most fitly accompanied the cry, *Repent ye.* The *confessing their sins,* which went with baptism in the river Jordan, gave it its meaning. Apart from the acknowledgment of guilt, it would have been a mere bathing of the person without spiritual significance, but the confession that went with it made it an instructive sign. John must have inwardly wondered at seeing the multitudes come, but his chief thought ran forward to his coming Lord. He thought more of Him than of *all Judaea.*

7. But when he saw many of the Pharisees and Sadducees come to his baptism, he said unto them, O generation of vipers, who hath warned you to flee from the wrath to come?

It was strange to see the proud Separatists and the skeptical Moralists coming to be baptized, and therefore, as a test, John addressed them with scorching words. He saw that they were serpentine in their motives and viperish in their tempers, and so he calls them a *generation of vipers.* Thus would he see whether they were sincere or not. He asks who suggested to them to flee from that wrath of which he was the forerunner, according to the closing words of the Old Testament. This inquiry was not complimentary, but it is no business of the Lord's servants to make themselves pleasing. They must be faithful and especially so to the great and learned. Thus, faithful was John the Baptist and he was honored for it by Him that sent him.

8. Bring forth therefore fruits meet for repentance.

Act as a change of mind would lead you to do. Above all, quit the pride in which you envelop yourselves and leave the serpent motives that now activate you. Lord, save us from a fruitless repentance, which would be only an aggravation of our previous sins.

9. And think not to say within yourselves, We have Abraham to our father: for I say unto you, that God is able of these stones to raise up children unto Abraham.

Do not imagine that God needs you in order to fulfill His promise to His servant Abraham, for He can make each stone in Jordan into an heir of grace. Do not presume upon your ancestry and think that all the blessings of the coming kingdom must be yours because you are of the seed of the father of the faithful. God can as easily make sons of *stones* as of a *generation of vipers.* He will never be short of means for fulfilling His covenant, without bowing His gospel before the whim of conceited men. He will find a people in the slums if His gospel is rejected by the respectable. Let none of us, because we are orthodox or exceedingly scriptural in our religious observances, dream that we must, therefore, be in the favor of God, and that we are under no necessity to repent. God can do without us, but we cannot do without repentance and the works that prove it true. What a blessing that He can transform hearts of stone into filial spirits! Wonders of grace to God belong!

10. And now also the axe is laid unto the root of the trees: therefore every tree which bringeth not forth good fruit is hewn down, and cast into the fire.

He means the King is come – the Cutter-down of every fruitless tree has arrived. The Great Woodsman has thrown down His axe at *the root of the trees.* He lifts the axe. He strikes. The fruitless tree is felled. It is cast into the fire. The sketch is full of life. The Baptizer sees forests falling beneath the axe, for He whom he heralds will be the Judge of men and the Executioner of righteousness. What an announcement he had to make! What a scene his believing eye beheld! Our vision is much the same. The axe is still at work. Lord, cut me not down for the fire. I know that the absence of good fruit is as fatal as the presence of corrupt fruit. Lord, let me not be a mere negative, lest I be *hewn down, and cast into the fire.*

11. I indeed baptize you with water unto repentance: but he that cometh after me is mightier than I, whose shoes I am not worthy to bear: he shall baptize you with the Holy Spirit, and with fire.

John could plunge the repentant ones into water, but a greater-than-he must baptize men into the Holy Spirit and into fire. Repentance is well attended by washing in water, but the true baptism of the believer by the Lord Jesus Himself brings us into spiritual floods of holy fire. John considered himself to be nothing more than a household slave, unworthy of the office of removing his Master's sandals; and his baptism in water was as much inferior to the Spirit-baptism as a slave is to his lord. Jesus is the divine Lord who covers us with the fiery influences of the Holy Spirit. Do we know this baptism? What is water-baptism without it? What are all the Johns in the world, with their baptisms in water, when compared with Jesus and His baptism into fire?

12. Whose fan is in his hand, and he will thoroughly purge his floor, and gather his wheat into the garner; but he will burn up the chaff with unquenchable fire.

He sets forth his Lord under another figure – that of a Husbandman. This time He holds in His hand not the axe, but the winnowing shovel. Pharisees, Sadducees, and all the rest lie on *his floor*. It is with them he deals, in saying, *He will thoroughly purge his floor*. If they do not wish to be purified by Him, they should not be there. But there they are, and He deals with them. His *fan is in his hand*. He throws up the heap to the breeze that He may test and divide. His wheat He gathers, for this He seeks. *The chaff* is blown farther off to the place where a fire is burning, and so it is consumed out of the way by what he tells us is *unquenchable fire*. Our Lord's teaching would act like a great winnowing fan, leaving the true by themselves and driving off the false and worthless to utter destruction. It was so in the life of our Lord; it is so every day where He is preached. He is the Great Divider. It is His Word that separates the sinners from the saints and gathers out a people for Himself.

Thus, the herald prepared the people for the King, who would be the Cleanser, the Hewer, and the Winnower. My soul, behold your Lord under these aspects and reverence Him!

Matthew 3:13-17

The King Designated and Anointed

It was fitting that there should be some public recognition of the King, some pointing out of Him by a truthful witness among men, and some indication from the Father in heaven that He was indeed His beloved Son.

13. Then cometh Jesus from Galilee to Jordan unto John, to be baptized of him.

In due time, when all was prepared, the Prince left His obscurity. Putting Himself in a lowly place, He did not summon the Baptizer to come to the Sea of Galilee, but went down the country along the banks of the Jordan to him, seeking baptism. Should any of the servants neglect what their Lord so heartily attended to? Do any say, "It is not essential"? Was it essential to our Lord Jesus? He said, *It becometh us* (verse 15), and what was becoming in Him is not unbecoming in His followers. If it should cost us a journey, let us pay attention to the command that is binding on all believers.

14. But John forbad him, saying, I have need to be baptized of thee, and comest thou to me?

This was very natural. John knew Jesus to be eminently more holy than himself, and therefore he protested against appearing to be His purifier. John was strong in this protest: He *forbad him.* It seemed to him to be out of order for him to baptize one so supremely good. Although he was not yet assured from heaven that Jesus was the Messiah (for he had not yet seen the Spirit descending and resting upon Him), yet he shrewdly guessed that Jesus was indeed the Christ. He knew Him to be a very special favorite of heaven, superior to himself, and he therefore expected that sign by which he had been assured the Christ would be known.

John never shirked a duty, but he declined an honor. He would not even seem to be of any consequence as compared with his Lord. Blessed Jesus, teach us the same humility!

15. And Jesus answering said unto him, Suffer it to be so now: for thus it becometh us to fulfil all righteousness. Then he suffered him.

Jesus answered John so completely that he ceased his opposition at once. It was suitable both in John and in Jesus that our Lord should be baptized of him. This assurance satisfied the Baptist so far that, still under protest, *he suffered him.* Baptism was suitable even in our Lord, who needed no personal purification, for He was the Head over all things to His church, and it was suitable that He should be as the members should be. Baptism beautifully sets forth our Lord's immersion in suffering, His burial, and His resurrection. Thus, typically, it fulfills *all righteousness.* The ordinance is most full of meaning when rightly observed, and it is to be most reverently regarded, since our Lord Himself submitted to it. Shall I refuse to follow my Lord? Shall I think that there is nothing in an ordinance of which He said, *Thus it becometh us to fulfil all righteousness*?

16-17. And Jesus, when he was baptized, went up straightway out of the water: and, lo, the heavens were opened unto him, and he saw the Spirit of God descending like a dove, and lighting upon him: and lo a voice from heaven, saying, This is my beloved Son, in whom I am well pleased.

Our Lord went down into the water, and then He *went up straightway out of the water.* He did not wait in the river, but when He had fulfilled one duty, He *straightway* went on His way to carry out another. In baptism, our Lord was openly attested and sealed as the *beloved Son,* both by the Word of God and the Spirit of God. What more witness is needed? It is often so with His people. Their sonship is made clear during an act of obedience, and the Word and the Spirit bear witness with their consciences.

Our Lord Jesus had now to enter on His public lifework, and He did so in the best manner. The world was opening before Him, and *the heavens were opened unto him.* As His need appeared, His source of supply was set open before Him. On Him also the divine anointing descended. Like a swift-winged, pure, and quiet dove, *the Spirit of God* came, and found a resting place in Him. When He had been immersed into the element of water, He was immediately surrounded by the divine element of the Spirit. Then, also, was His ear charmed with the Father's audible acknowledgment of Him, and with the expression of that good pleasure that the Lord God had always felt in Him. It was a glorious moment. Our King was now proclaimed and anointed. Would not His next step be to take the kingdom? We shall see.

Our Lord and King is now fully before us. He has been preceded, predicted, and pointed out by John the Baptist. He has been dedicated to His work in baptism. He has been anointed by the Spirit and confessed by the Father, and therefore He has fairly entered upon His royal work. May none of us in the service of the Lord run before our time or go forward without a sense of the Father's approval, and without that spiritual fervor that is from above!

O my Lord, let me be anointed and approved in my measure, even as You were in Yours. For the purpose of this, I would behold Your anointing of the Spirit with the full belief that I am anointed in You, as the body receives spiritual fervor in the anointing of the Head.

Matthew 4

Matthew 4:1-11

The King Begins His Reign by a Combat with the Prince of Darkness

1. Then was Jesus led up of the Spirit into the wilderness to be tempted of the devil.

No sooner was He anointed than He was attacked. He did not seek temptation, but was *led up of the Spirit.* The time selected was immediately after His sonship had been attested, when we might have thought that He was least likely to be attacked upon that point. Times of holy enjoyment verge on periods of temptation. Our Lord was led *into the wilderness.* The place was one of great solitude, where He would be alone in the conflict. The devil himself came to the spot and plied his diabolical craftiness upon the Man ordained to be his Destroyer.

Let me be ever on my watchtower and particularly during seasons of great enjoyment, for then is Satan most likely to attack me. Lord Jesus, be with me in the hour of my testing, for You know how to help the tempted.

2. And when he had fasted forty days and forty nights, he was afterward an hungered.

Throughout the long fast, He was miraculously sustained, but at the close of it, hunger began to test Him. We are more in danger when our labor or suffering is over than during the time of its continuance. Now that the Lord is drained dry by His long fast and is made faint by hunger, the Enemy will be upon Him. The devil is a great coward and takes a mean advantage of us.

Lord, make me a match for the Enemy!

3. And when the tempter came to him, he said, If thou be the Son of God, command that these stones be made bread.

He adapted the temptation to the circumstances: he tempted a hungry man with bread. He put it very cunningly. Only one single word, and the hard stone of the desert would be a biscuit. Let Him undertake to be His own provider and use His miraculous power as *Son of God* to spread a table for Himself. The tempter begins his suggestion with an *if*, an *if* about his sonship. This is his usual fashion. He bids the Lord prove His sonship by catering for Himself, and yet that would have been the surest way to prove that He was not the Son of God. A true son will not doubt his father and undertake to provide his own bread; he will wait to be fed by his father's hand. The Evil One would have the only begotten Son cease to depend on God and take matters into His own hands. Temptations to unbelieving self-help are common enough, but are very dangerous.

4. But he answered and said, It is written, Man shall not live by bread alone, but by every word that proceedeth out of the mouth of God.

Out flashed the sword of the Spirit. Our Lord will fight with no other weapon. He could have spoken new revelations, but He chose to say, *It is written.* There is a power in the Word of God that even the devil cannot deny.

Our life and its sustenance are not dependent upon the visible, though the visible is ordinarily used for our support. We do *not live by bread alone*, though it is the usual means of our support. He who sustained the Savior fasting for forty days could still keep Him alive without bread. The secret influence of the word of the Omnipotent could keep the vital forces in action even without bread. Bread owes its power to nourish our bodies to the secret agency of God, and that divine agency could work as surely without the usual means as with them. The word of the Lord that made the heavens can assuredly support all that it has made. Our Lord Jesus, in fact, told the tempter that He would not distrust the providence of God, but would await His Father's time for feeding Him and would by no means be driven to an act of unbelief and self-reliance.

5-6. Then the devil taketh him up into the holy city, and setteth him on a pinnacle of the temple, and saith unto him, If thou be the Son of God, cast thyself down: for it is written, He shall give his angels charge concerning thee: and in their hands they shall bear thee up, lest at any time thou dash thy foot against a stone.

This second temptation is a cunning one. He is persuaded rather to believe too much than too little. He is not now to take care of Himself, but recklessly to presume and trust His Father's promise beyond its meaning. The place was cunningly chosen. Temple pinnacles are not safe standing. High and holy places are open to temptation. The posture was advantageous to the tempter, for nature feels a tendency to fall when set *on a pinnacle.* The aim of the fiery dart was at our Lord's sonship: *If thou be the Son of God.* If the Enemy could have hurt our Lord's filial confidence, he would have gained his objective.

Satan borrowed our Lord's weapon and said, *It is written,* but he did not use the sword lawfully. It was not in the nature of the false fiend to quote correctly. He left out the necessary words, *in all thy ways;* thus, he made the promise say what in truth it never suggested, and then boldly prescribed a course that the Law of God would condemn, saying, *Cast thyself down.* We are to be kept in our ways, but not in our follies. The omission of a word may spoil the meaning of a Scripture. Verbal inspiration makes accurate quotation to be a duty, as the omission of a word or two entirely alters the sense. What reliable inspiration can there be except that which suggests words as well as ideas?

Hear how the devil talks about angels, their Lord, their charge, their care, and their diligence. A man may handle holy subjects with great familiarity and yet be himself unholy. It is wrong to talk of angels and yet to act like devils.

See how the fiend passes from a temptation about humble bread to one of an ambitious and daring character. He hopes by a sudden change to catch the Lord in one way, even if He escaped from him in another. But our Lord was ready for him. His sword was on guard for all kinds of strokes. May His grace keep us in the same manner well-armed against the foe! Though the Enemy alters his tactics, we must not cease our resistance or change our weapon.

7. Jesus said unto him, It is written again, Thou shalt not tempt the Lord thy God.

It is written again. One text must not be looked at alone and magnified out of proportion, as if it were the whole Bible. Each utterance of the Lord must be taken in connection with other parts of Scripture. There is a balance and proportion in divine truth. *It is written* is to be set side by side with, *It is written again.*

How short and decisive was the stroke of our Lord upon the great Enemy! He meets a falsely quoted promise with a plain precept, forbidding us to presume. *Thou shalt not* from the mouth of God is the shield of conscience against a foul temptation. Our rule of action is neither a promise nor a providence, but the clear command of the Lord. Presumption is a tempting of God, and to *tempt the Lord* is not to be thought of for a moment. Remember, believer, He is *thy God* to be trusted, not to be tempted. The second time, the adversary was so completely baffled that he made no reply, but changed his line of warfare.

Lord, permit me not to sin presumptuously, nor to act rashly! I see that faith is for ways of obedience, not for flights of delusion. Let me not cast myself down and so throw myself out of the range of Your promised keeping.

8-9. Again, the devil taketh him up into an exceeding high mountain, and sheweth him all the kingdoms of the world, and the glory of them; and saith unto him, All these things will I give thee, if thou wilt fall down and worship me.

Wretched traitor! None of these kingdoms were really his own. They were in truth the rightful heritage of the Lord to whom he pretended he could give them. How he opened his mouth and said, *All these things will I give thee*! A poor *all* after all, and it would only have been a stolen gift had he bestowed it. Yet it would have been to any of us a very dazzling and fascinating sight, for the glories of even one kingdom make hearts beat and eyes glisten and feet slip. The bait is sweet, but the hook lies under it. The glittering glory would be bought too dear by that demand – *Fall down and worship me.* If Jesus would have adopted carnal means, He would soon have had *the kingdoms of the world* at

His feet. A little tampering with truth and a little flattery of prejudice, and He might have had many men around Him, irresistible in their fanaticism. By their enthusiastic effort, He would soon have been able to wield a mighty power, before which Rome would have fallen. Our holy Lord disdained to use the help of evil, though the master of wickedness promised Him success. How could He bow down before the devil? It was the height of disrespect for the false fiend to invite worship from the perfect One. Christ at the devil's feet! It reminds us of religion supported by theatricals and raffles. What gift of the foul fiend could tempt the Son of God to be the servant of evil? The tempter does not dare to mention sonship in this case, for that would have laid the blasphemous suggestion too bare. No son of God can worship the devil.

O Lord, grant that if ever we should hunger and be in poverty, like our Lord, we may never yield to the temptation to do wrong to gain wealth and honor or even the supply of pressing need! May Your church never yield to the world with the idea of setting up the kingdom of Christ in a more easy and rapid manner than by the simple preaching of the gospel!

10. Then said Jesus unto him, Get thee hence, Satan: for it is written, Thou shalt worship the Lord thy God, and him only shalt thou serve.

The Lord spoke strongly to the tempter. Satan had betrayed his own character and now he gets his proper name and is ordered into his proper place. How that word staggered him – *Get thee hence*! This was the final word that banished him from the Lord's presence. How he slunk away. He hastened off ashamed, like a dog who is sent home.

Our Lord gave him a parting stroke with the sword of the Spirit. Again, He said, *It is written.* God's command, which demands all worship and service for Jehovah the covenant God only, was a word for Satan to remember when he dived hastily into the nether deep to hide his head in confusion at his complete defeat. He, too, is under law to God and cannot cast away His cords from him. Oh, that we may acknowledge the power of this precept and have nothing to do with the pursuit of the vain things of this world and temporary glory it offers, but are to give our entire lives to the service of the one Lord! Idolatry of the creature withers under the scorching heat of this imperative law of the Highest. We must not pay even a shade of deference to evil, though the whole world should be the reward of a single act of sinful submission to it. *Him only shalt thou serve.* Ours it is to choose Jehovah for our God and then to live alone for His praise and service.

It is noteworthy that all the passages quoted by our Lord are from the book of Deuteronomy, which book has been so severely attacked by the destructive critics. Thus did our Lord put special honor upon that part of the Old Testament that He knew would be most attacked. The past few years have proved that the devil does not like Deuteronomy. He would rather avenge himself for the wounds it caused him on this most memorable occasion.

11. Then the devil leaveth him, and, behold, angels came and ministered unto him.

The Enemy left Him when he had shot his last bolt, but even then he left Him only for a season, intending to return at the first opportunity. Only when he has tried his utmost will the tempter let a child of God alone, and even then, he will watch for another opportunity.

So soon as the Evil One had departed, angels appeared to fulfill a ministry for which they eagerly longed, but which the presence of the devil hindered. No doubt they had been hovering near, waiting for their opportunity. These holy beings might not come upon the scene while the battle was being fought, lest they should seem to divide the honors of the day; but when the duel was ended, they hastened to bring food for the body and comfort for the mind of the champion King. It was a battle royal, and the victory deserved to be celebrated by the courtiers of the heavenly King. Let us *behold* these angels, learn from their example, and believe that they are also near to all the warriors of the cross in their hour of conflict with the fiend.

O tempted but triumphant King, Your servants worship You and ask permission and grace to minister to You as angels did!

Matthew 4:12-25

The King Setting Up His Kingdom Openly

12. Now when Jesus had heard that John was cast into prison, he departed into Galilee.

The history is not consecutive, for it was not Matthew's design to make it so. He leaves out much that others record, because it is not suitable for his purpose. Possibly John was put in prison more than once. It seems that the imprisonment of John called our Lord away from the immediate scene of persecution to the more rustic region of Galilee. He became the more publicly active when His forerunner was laid aside. As the morning star is hidden, the sun shines out the more brightly. His departure was not caused by fear, nor by desire of self-pleasing, but He moved under the guidance of the Lord God who sent Him.

13-16. And leaving Nazareth, he came and dwelt in Capernaum, which is upon the sea coast, in the borders of Zabulon and Nephthalim: that it might be fulfilled which was spoken by Esaias the prophet, saying, The land of Zabulon, and the land of Nephthalim, by the way of the sea, beyond Jordan, Galilee of the Gentiles; the people which sat in darkness saw great light; and to them which sat in the region and shadow of death light is sprung up.

Note how the movements of our King are all ordered according to diving prophecy. *Leaving Nazareth, he came and dwelt in Capernaum* to fulfill a passage in the book of Isaiah. There was an ancient program that settled from of old the track of His royal progressions. He went where the foreknowledge and predestination of Jehovah had declared His way.

He went, moreover, where He was needed, even to *the borders of Zabulon and Nephthalim.* The *great light* encountered the great darkness. The far-off ones were visited by Him who gathers together the outcasts of Israel.

Our Lord courts not those who glory in their light, but those who languish in their darkness. He comes with heavenly life, not to those who boast of their own life and energy, but to those who are under condemnation, and who feel the shades of death shutting them out from light and hope.

Great light is a very suggestive figure for the gospel, and *[sitting] in the region and shadow of death* is a very graphic description of men bowed under the power of sin and paralyzed by fear of condemnation. What a mercy that to those who appear out of the reach of the usual means, to those who dwell *by the way of the sea, beyond Jordan, Galilee of the Gentiles,* Jesus comes with power to enlighten and revive!

If I feel myself to be an out-of-the-way sinner, Lord, come to me and cause me to know that *light is sprung up* even for me!

17. From that time Jesus began to preach, and to say, Repent: for the kingdom of heaven is at hand.

He continued the warning that John the Baptist had given: *Repent: for the kingdom of heaven is at hand.* The King exceeds His herald, but He does not differ from him as to His message. Happy is the preacher whose word is such that his Lord can endorse it! Repentance is the demand of the law, of the gospel, and of John the Baptist, who was the connecting link between the two. Immediate repentance is demanded because the theocracy is established. The kingdom demands turning from sin. In Christ Jesus, God was about to reign among the sons of men, and therefore men were to seek peace with Him. How much more ought we to repent who live in the midst of that kingdom! What manner of persons ought we to be who look for His Second Advent! *The kingdom of heaven is at hand.* Let us be as men that look for their Lord. O my gracious King and Savior, I pray You, accept my repentance as to past rebellions as a proof of my present loyalty!

18-19. And Jesus, walking by the sea of Galilee, saw two brethren, Simon called Peter, and Andrew his brother, casting a net into the sea: for they were fishers. And he saith unto them, Follow me, and I will make you fishers of men.

Our Lord not only preached the kingdom, but He now also began to call one and another into its service and privilege. He was *walking by the sea,* and there and then He began His converting, calling, and ordaining work. Where He found Himself living, there He put forth His power. Our sphere is where we are.

Jesus had a special eye for fishermen. He summoned to His side the fishing brothers whom He had chosen from of old. He had previously called them by grace, and now He calls them into the ministry. They were busy in a lawful occupation when He called them to be ministers. Our Lord does not call idlers but fishermen. His word was sovereign – *Follow me.* His work was appropriate to their occupation as fishermen. It was full of royal promise – *I will make you fishers of men,* and it was eminently instructive, for an evangelist and a fisherman have many points of likeness. From this passage we learn that nobody can make a man-fisher but our Lord Himself, and that those whom He calls can only become successful by following Him.

Lord, as a winner of souls, cause me to imitate Your spirit and method, that I may not labor in vain!

20. And they straightway left their nets, and followed him.

The call was effective. No nets can entangle those whom Jesus calls to follow Him. They come *straightway.* They come at all cost. They come without a question. They come to leave old haunts. They come to follow their Leader without stipulation or reserve.

Lord, cause me ever to be Your faithful and unhesitating follower as long as I live! May no nets detain me when You call me!

21-22. And going on from thence, he saw other two brethren, James the son of Zebedee, and John his brother, in a ship with Zebedee their father, mending their nets; and he called them. And they immediately left the ship and their father, and followed him.

Our Lord delighted in fishermen; possibly their bold, hearty, and outspoken character fitted them for His service. At any rate, these would be the briars upon which He could graft the roses of His grace. Some He calls to preach when casting their nets, and some while *mending* them, but in either case they are busy. We shall need both to cast and mend nets after we are called to our Lord's work. Note how our Lord again calls *two brethren.* Two together are better far than one and one acting singly. The Lord knows that our nature seeks companionship. No companion in work is better than a brother.

This second pair of brothers *left their father* as well as their fishery.

The first left their nets, but these *left the ship.* The first have no relatives mentioned, but these left father and mother for Christ's sake, and they did it as unhesitatingly as the others. It did not seem much of a prospect, to follow the houseless Jesus, but an inward attraction drew them and they followed on, pleased to obey the voice divine. Zebedee may have thought his sons' going was a great loss to him, but it is not recorded that he expressed any objection to their doing so. Perhaps he gladly gave up his boys for such a service. We feel sure that their mother did. In the service of Jesus, we are not to be restrained by ties of kindred. He has a higher claim than father or husband.

Lord, call me, and my brother, and all my family into Your grace, if not into Your ministry!

23. And Jesus went about all Galilee, teaching in their synagogues, and preaching the gospel of the kingdom, and healing all manner of sickness and all manner of disease among the people.

Our Lord was ever on the move – *Jesus went about all Galilee.* The Great Itinerant made a province His parish. He taught *in their synagogues,* but He was equally at home in their streets. He cared nothing for consecrated places. *Teaching* and *preaching* go well with *healing.* Thus, soul and body are both taken care of. Our Lord's great power is seen in the universality of His healing energy, *healing all manner of sickness and all manner of disease.* Dwell on those words: *All manner.* But our Lord was not content with miracles for the body; He had the gospel for the soul, that gospel that lies in His own person as King, in His promise of pardon to believers, and in His rule of love over those who are loyal to Him. He preached *the gospel of the kingdom,* a true royal gospel, which made men kings and priests. To this gospel the miracles of healing were so many seals to its truth. To this day, the healing of souls is an equally sure seal of God upon the gospel.

Lord, I know the truth and certainty of Your gospel, for I have felt Your healing hand upon my heart. May I feel the rule and power of Your kingdom and joyfully yield myself to Your sway!

24. And his fame went throughout all Syria: and they brought unto him all sick people that were taken with divers diseases and torments, and those

which were possessed with devils, and those which were lunatick, and those
that had the palsy; and he healed them.

Of course, men told one another about the great prophet. Even the
regions beyond began to hear of Him. Syria heard again that there was
a God in Israel who could heal a man of his leprosy. Now the worst
cases are brought to Him – epileptics, the possessed, and the mad were
led to Him, and were not led in vain. What a bill of diseases we find
in this verse!

Diseases, torments, devils, lunacy, palsy, and so forth. And what
a receipt at the foot: *And he healed them*! Oh, that men were eager to
bring their spiritual ailments to the Savior! It would lead to the same
result. In every case we should read, *he healed them.*

Our King surrounded Himself with the spiritual pomp of gratitude
by displaying His power to bless the afflicted. Some kings have pretended
to heal by their touch, but Jesus really did so. Never king or prophet
could work such marvels as He did. Well might *his fame* be great!

25. And there followed him great multitudes of people from Galilee, and from
Decapolis, and from Jerusalem, and from Judaea, and from beyond Jordan.

Such a teacher is sure to have a following. Yet how small His spiritual
following compared with the *great multitudes* who outwardly came
to Him! Our King has many nominal subjects, but few there are who
know Him as their Lord, so as to be renewed in heart by the power of
His grace. These alone enter truly into His kingdom, and it is foolish
and wicked to talk of including any others in His spiritual domain. Yet
is it a hopeful sign when there is a great inquiry after Jesus, and every
region and city yields its quota to the hearing throng.

Now we shall hear more from the blessed lips of Him who was King
in Jerusalem and also Preacher to the people.

Matthew 5

Matthew 5:1-16

The King Promulgates the Laws of His Kingdom

This is the natural order of royal action. The King is anointed, He comes among the people to show His power, and afterwards He acts as a legislator and sets forth His statutes.

1. And seeing the multitudes, he went up into a mountain: and when he was set, his disciples came unto him.

For retreat, fresh air, and wide space, the King seeks the hillside. It was suitable that such elevated ethics should be taught from a mountain. A natural hill suited His truthful teaching better than a pulpit of marble would have done. Those who desired to follow Him as disciples gathered closely around the seated Rabbi, who occupied the throne of instruction in their midst; and then in outer circles *the multitudes* stood to listen.

2. And he opened his mouth, and taught them, saying.

Even when His mouth was closed, He was teaching by His life, yet He did not withhold the testimony of His lips. Earnest men, when they address their fellows, neither mumble, nor stumble, but speak distinctly, opening their mouths. When Jesus opens His mouth, let us open our ears and hearts.

3. Blessed are the poor in spirit: for theirs is the kingdom of heaven.

The King's first statutes are benedictions. He begins His teaching with an abundance of blessings. The Old Testament ended with *a curse* (Malachi 4:6). The New Testament opens here with *Blessed.* This word is by some rendered "happy," but we like *blessed* best. Our Lord brings to men true beatitudes by His teaching and by His kingdom.

Spiritual poverty is both commanded and commended. It is the basis of Christian experience. No one begins aright who has not felt poverty of spirit. Yet even to this first sign of grace is the kingdom given in present possession: *Theirs is the kingdom of heaven.* The question in heaven's kingdom is not, "Are you a prince?" but, "Are you poor in spirit?" Those who are of no account in their own eyes are of the royal blood of the universe. These alone have the principles and the qualifications for the heavenly kingdom. May I be such!

4. Blessed are they that mourn: for they shall be comforted.

These seem worse off than the merely *poor in spirit,* for *they mourn.* They are a stage higher, though they seem to be a stage lower. The way to rise in the kingdom is to sink in ourselves. These men are grieved by sin and tested by the evils of the times, but for them a future of rest and rejoicing is provided. Those who laugh shall lament, but those who sorrow shall sing. How great a blessing is sorrow, since it gives room for the Lord to administer comfort! Our griefs are blessed, for they are our points of contact with the divine Comforter. The beatitude reads like a paradox, but it is true, as some of us know full well. Our mourning hours have brought us more comfort than our days of mirth.

5. Blessed are the meek: for they shall inherit the earth.

They are lowly minded and are ready to give up their portion in the earth; therefore, it shall come back to them. They neither boast, nor contend, nor exult over others, yet they are heirs of all the good that God has created on the face of the earth. In their meekness, they are like their King, and they shall reign with Him. The promised land is for the tribes of the meek; before them the Canaanites shall be driven out. He has the best of this world who thinks least of it and least of himself.

6. Blessed are they which do hunger and thirst after righteousness: for they shall be filled.

They are not full of their own righteousness, but long for more and more of that which comes from above. They long to be right themselves both with God and man, and they long to see righteousness have the upper hand all the world over. Such is their longing for goodness, that it would seem as if both the appetites of *hunger and thirst* were concentrated in their one passion for righteousness. Where God works such an insatiable desire, we may be quite sure that He will satisfy it; yes, fill it to the brim.

In contemplating the righteousness of God, the righteousness of Christ, and the victory of righteousness in the latter days, we are more than filled. In the world to come, the satisfaction of the "man of desires" will be complete. Nothing here below can fill an immortal soul, and since it is written, *they shall be filled,* we look forward with joyful confidence to a heaven of holiness with which we shall be satisfied eternally.

7. Blessed are the merciful: for they shall obtain mercy.

They forgive and they are forgiven. They judge charitably and they shall not be condemned. They help the needy and they shall be helped in their need. What we are to others, God will be to us. Some have to labor hard with their stinginess in order to be kind, but the blessing lies not only in doing a merciful act, but also in being merciful in disposition. Followers of Jesus must be men of mercy, for they have found mercy and mercy has found them. As we look for *mercy of the Lord in that day* (2 Timothy 1:18), we must show mercy in this day.

8. Blessed are the pure in heart: for they shall see God.

Foul hearts make dim eyes Godward. To clear the eye, we must cleanse the heart. Only purity has any idea of God or any true vision of Him. It is a great reward to be able to *see God,* and on the other hand, it is of great help towards being *pure in heart* to have a true sight of the thrice-Holy One. There are no pure hearts on earth unless the Lord has made them so, and none shall see God in heaven who have not been purified by grace while here below. Lord, create in me a clean heart, that I may behold You both now and forever!

9. Blessed are the peacemakers: for they shall be called the children of God.

They are not only passively peaceful, like the meek who keep the peace, but they are also actively peaceful by endeavoring to end wars and contentions, and so make peace. These not only are the children of the peace-loving God, but they also come to be *called* so, for men are struck by their likeness to their Father. Hereby is our sonship known to ourselves and others. Men of peace are the children of the God of peace, and their Father's blessing rests on them.

This seventh beatitude is a very high and glorious one. Let us all endeavor to obtain it. Never let us be peacebreakers, forever let us be *peacemakers.* Yet must we not cry, *Peace, peace; where there is no peace* (Jeremiah 6:14; 8:11)? The verse before this speaks of purity and this verse speaks of peace. First pure, then peaceable. This is God's order and it should be ours.

10. Blessed are they which are persecuted for righteousness' sake: for theirs is the kingdom of heaven.

This is the peculiar blessing of the elect of God and it stands high up in the list of honor. The only homage that wickedness can pay to righteousness is to persecute it. Those who in the first blessing were poor in spirit are here despised as well as poverty-stricken, and in this they get a new royal charter, which for the second time ensures to them *the kingdom of heaven.* Yes, they have the kingdom now. It is theirs in present possession. Not because of any personal fault, but simply on account of their godly character, the Lord's Daniels are hated, but they are blessed by that which looks like a curse. Ishmael mocks Isaac, but nevertheless, Isaac has the inheritance and Ishmael is cast out. It is a gift from God to be allowed to suffer for His name. So may we be helped to rejoice in Christ's cross when we are honored by being reviled for His name's sake.

11-12. Blessed are ye, when men shall revile you, and persecute you, and shall say all manner of evil against you falsely, for my sake. Rejoice, and be exceeding glad: for great is your reward in heaven: for so persecuted they the prophets which were before you.

Persecution of the tongue is more common but not less cruel than that of the hand. Slander is corrupt and indulges in accusations of every kind – *all manner of evil* is a comprehensive phrase. No crime is too vile to be laid at the door of the innocent, nor will the persecutor have any hesitation as to the vileness of the charge. The rule seems to be, "Throw plenty of mud and some of it will stick." Under this very grievous trial, good men are to be more than ordinarily happy, for thus are they elevated to the rank of the prophets, upon whom the storm of falsehood beats with tremendous fury. *So persecuted they the prophets.* This is the heritage of the Lord's messengers. They killed one and stoned another. The honor of suffering with the prophets, for the Lord's sake, is so great that it may well reconcile us to all that it involves. There is an inquisitorial succession of persecutors: *For so persecuted they the prophets which were before you,* and there is a prophetical succession of saints, ordained to glorify the Lord in the fires. To this succession it is our high privilege to belong, and we are happy that it is so. Our joy and gladness are to exceed all ordinary bounds when we are honored with the decoration of the iron cross and the collar of S. S., or "savage slander."

> *13. Ye are the salt of the earth: but if the salt have lost his savour, wherewith shall it be salted? it is thenceforth good for nothing, but to be cast out, and to be trodden under foot of men.*

Thus, He speaks to those whom He enrolls in His kingdom. In their character there is a preserving force to keep the rest of society from utter corruption. If they were not scattered among men, the race would putrefy. But if they are Christians only in name and the real power is gone, nothing can save them, and they are of no use whatever to those among whom they mingle. There is a secret something, which is the secret of the believer's power. That something is *savour.* It is not easy to define it, but yet it is absolutely essential to usefulness. A worldling may be of some use even if he fails in certain respects, but a Christian who is not a Christian is bad all-around; he is *good for nothing,* and utterly useless to anybody and everybody. Utter rejection awaits him. He will *be cast out, and trodden under foot of men.* His religion makes a footpath for fashion or for scorn, as the world may happen to take it.

In either case, it is no preservative, for it does not even preserve itself from contempt.

How this teaches the necessity of final perseverance! For if the savor of divine grace could be altogether gone from a man, it could never be restored. The text is very clear and positive upon that point. What unscriptural nonsense to talk of a man's being born again and yet losing the divine life, and then getting it again. Regeneration cannot fail. If it did, the man must be forever hopeless. He could not be born again, and again, and again. His case would be beyond the reach of mercy, but who is hopeless? Are there any whom it is impossible to restore? If so, some may have altogether fallen from grace, but not else. Those who speak of all men as within the reach of grace may not scripturally or logically believe in total apostasy, since *it is impossible to renew them again unto repentance* (Hebrews 6:4-6) if any have really apostatized.

The great lesson is, that if grace itself fails to save a man, nothing else can be done for him. *If the salt have lost his savour, wherewith shall it be salted?* You can salt meat, but you cannot salt salt. If grace fails, everything fails. Gracious Master, do not permit me to try any experiments as to how far I may lose my savor, but ever keep me full of grace and truth.

14-15. Ye are the light of the world. A city that is set on an hill cannot be hid. Neither do men light a candle, and put it under a bushel, but on a candlestick; and it giveth light unto all that are in the house.

We are to remove the darkness of ignorance, sin, and sorrow. Christ has lighted us so that we may enlighten the world. It is not ours to lie in concealment as to our religion. God intends His grace to be as conspicuous as a city built on the mountain's brow. To attempt to conceal His Spirit is as foolish as to put a lamp *under a bushel.* The lamp should be seen by *all that are in the house,* and so should the Christian's graces. Household devotion is the best of devotion. If our light is not seen in the house, depend upon it, we have none. Candles are meant for parlors and bedrooms. Let us not cover up the light of grace. Indeed, we *cannot be hid* if once the Lord has built us on the hill of His love, and neither can we dwell in darkness if God has lighted us and set us *on a candlestick.*

Lord, let me be zealous to spread abroad the light I have received from You, even throughout the world! At least let me shine in my own home.

16. Let your light so shine before men, that they may see your good works, and glorify your Father which is in heaven.

The light is ours, but the glorification is for our *Father which is in heaven*. We shine because we have light, and we are seen because we shine. By good works, we best shine before men. True shining is silent, but yet it is so useful that men, who are too often very bad judges, are yet forced to bless God for the good that they receive through the light that He has kindled. Angels glorify God whom they see, and men are forced to glorify God whom they do not see, when they mark the *good works* of His saints. We need not object to be seen, although we are not to wish to be seen. Since men will be sure to see our excellences, if we possess any, be it ours to see that all the glory is given to our Lord, to whom it is entirely due. *Not unto us, O LORD, not unto us, but unto thy name give glory* (Psalm 115:1).

Matthew 5:17-20

Our King Honors His Father's Law

He took care to revise and reform the laws of men, but the Law of God He established and confirmed.

17. Think not that I am come to destroy the law, or the prophets: I am not come to destroy, but to fulfil.

The Old Testament stands in all its parts, both as to *the law* and *the prophets*. The Lord Jesus knew nothing of *destructive criticism*. He establishes in its deepest sense all that is written in Holy Scripture and puts a new fullness into it. This He says before He proceeds to make remarks upon the sayings of men of old time. He is Himself the fulfillment and substance of the types and prophecies and commands of the law.

18. For verily I say unto you, Till heaven and earth pass, one jot or one tittle shall in no wise pass from the law, till all be fulfilled.

Not a syllable is to become degraded. Even to the smallest letters – the dot of every *i,* and the crossing of every *t* – the law will outlast the creation. The Old Testament is as sacredly guarded as the New Testament. *The word of the Lord endureth for ever* (1 Peter 1:25). Modern critics have set themselves an impossible task in their endeavor to get rid of the inspiration of the whole sacred volume, or of this book, or that chapter, or that verse; for the whole shall come forth of their furnace *as silver purified seven times* (Psalm 12:6).

19. Whosoever therefore shall break one of these least commandments, and shall teach men so, he shall be called the least in the kingdom of heaven: but whosoever shall do and teach them, the same shall be called great in the kingdom of heaven.

Our King has not come to abolish the law, but to confirm and reassert it.

His commands are eternal, and if any of the teachers of it should through error break His law, and teach that its least command is nullified, they will lose rank and will sink into the lowest place. The peerage of His kingdom is ordered according to obedience. Not birth, knowledge, nor success will make a man great, but humble and precise obedience, both in word and in deed, will.

Whosoever shall do and teach is the man who *shall be called great in the kingdom of heaven.* Hence, the Lord Jesus does not set up a milder law, nor will He allow any one of His servants to presume to do so. Our King fulfills the ancient law, and His Spirit works in us *to will and to do of his good pleasure* (Philippians 2:13), as set forth in the fixed statutes of righteousness.

Lord, make me of this Your kingdom a right loyal subject and may I both *do and teach* according to Your Word! Whether I am little or great on earth, make me great in obedience to You.

20. For I say any unto you, That except your righteousness shall exceed the righteousness of the scribes and Pharisees, ye shall in no case enter into the kingdom of heaven.

We cannot even *enter into the kingdom* and begin to be the Lord's without going beyond the foremost of the world's religionists. Believers are not to be worse in conduct, but far better than the most precise legalists. In heart, and even in act, we are to be superior to the law-writers and the law-boasters. The kingdom is not for rebels, but for the exactly obedient.

It not only requires of us holiness, reverence, integrity, and purity, but it also works all these in our hearts and lives. The gospel does not give us outward liberty to sin because of the superior excellence of a supposed inner sanctity, but rather it produces outward sanctity through working in our inmost soul a glorious freedom in the law of the Lord.

What a King we have in Jesus! What manner of persons ought we to be who declare ourselves to be in His holy kingdom! How conservative ought we to be of our Father's revealed will! How determined to allow no trifling with the law and the prophets!

Matthew 5:21-48

The King Corrects Traditional Law

It was necessary for the Lord Jesus to clear away human traditions to make room for His own spiritual teaching.

> *21. Ye have heard that it was said by them of old time, Thou shalt not kill; and whosoever shall kill shall be in danger of the judgment.*

Antiquity is often pleaded as an authority, but our King makes short work of *them of old time.* He begins with one of their alterations of his Father's law. They added to the sacred oracles. The first part of the saying that our Lord quoted was divine, but it was dragged down to a low level by the addition about the human court and the murderer's liability to appear there. It thus became rather a proverb among men than an inspired utterance from the mouth of God. Its meaning, as God spoke it, had a far wider range than when the offense was restrained to actual killing, such as could be brought before a human judgment seat. To narrow a command is basically to annul it. We may not do this even with antiquity for our warrant. Better the whole truth newly stated than an old falsehood in ancient language.

22. But I say unto you, That whosoever is angry with his brother without a cause shall be in danger of the judgment: and whosoever shall say to his brother, Raca, shall be in danger of the council: but whosoever shall say, Thou fool, shall be in danger of hell fire.

Murder lies within anger, for we wish harm to the object of our wrath, or even wish that he did not exist, and this is to kill him in desire. Anger *without a cause* is forbidden by the command that says, *Thou shalt not kill* (Exodus 20:13), for unjust anger is killing in intent. Such anger without cause brings us under higher judgment than that of Jewish police courts. God takes cognizance of the emotions from which acts of hate may spring, and calls us to account as much for the angry feeling as for the murderous deed. Words also come under the same condemnation. A man shall be judged for what he *shall say to his brother.* To call a man *Raca,* or a worthless fellow, is to kill him in his reputation; and to say to him, *Thou fool,* is to kill him as to the noblest characteristics of a man. Hence, all this comes under such censure as men distribute in their councils, yes, under what is far worse, the punishment awarded by the highest court of the universe, which dooms men to *hell fire.* Thus, our Lord and King restores the law of God to its true force and warns us that it denounces not only the overt act of killing, but also every thought, feeling, and word that would tend to injure a brother or annihilate him by contempt.

What a sweeping law is this! My conscience might have been easy as to the command, *Thou shalt not kill,* but if anger without just cause be murder, how shall I answer for it? *Deliver me from bloodguiltiness, O God, thou God of my salvation* (Psalm 51:14).

23-24. Therefore if thou bring thy gift to the altar, and there rememberest that thy brother hath ought against thee; leave there thy gift before the altar, and go thy way; first be reconciled to thy brother, and then come and offer thy gift.

The Pharisee would declare, as a cover for his malice, that he brought a sacrifice to make atonement; but our Lord will have forgiveness rendered to our brother first, and then the offering presented. We ought to worship God thoughtfully, and if in the course of that thought we remember that our brother *hath ought against* us, we must stop. If we have wronged another, we are to pause, cease from the worship, and hasten to seek reconciliation. We easily remember if we have something against our brother, but now the memory is to be turned the other way. Only when we have remembered our wrongdoing, and have made reconciliation, can we hope for acceptance with the Lord. The rule is – first peace with man and then acceptance with God. The holy must be traversed to reach the Holiest of all. Peace being made with our brother, then let us conclude our service towards our Father, and we shall do so with a lighter heart and truer zeal.

I would anxiously desire to be at peace with all men before I attempt to worship God, lest I present to God the sacrifice of fools.

25-26. Agree with thine adversary quickly, whiles thou art in the way with him; lest at any time the adversary deliver thee to the judge, and the judge deliver thee to the officer, and thou be cast into prison. Verily I say unto thee, Thou shalt by no means come out thence, till thou hast paid the uttermost farthing.

In all disagreements, be eager for peace. Leave off strife before you begin.

In lawsuits, seek speedy and peaceful settlements. Often, in our Lord's days, this was the most profitable way, and usually it is so now. Better to lose your rights than to get into the hands of those who will only fleece you in the name of justice, and hold you fast so long as a semblance of a demand can stand against you, or another penny can be extracted from you. In a country where *justice* meant robbery, it was wise to be robbed and to make no complaint. Even in our own country, a lean settlement is better than a fat lawsuit. Many go into the court to get wool, but come out closely shorn. Carry on no angry suits in courts, but make peace with the utmost promptitude.

27-28. Ye have heard that it was said by them of old time, Thou shalt not commit adultery: but I say unto you, That whosoever looketh on a woman to lust after her hath committed adultery with her already in his heart.

In this case, our King again sets aside the façades of men upon the commands of God, and makes the law to be seen in its vast spiritual breadth. Whereas tradition had confined the prohibition to an overt

47

act of unchastity, the King shows that it forbade the unclean desires of the heart.

Here the divine law is shown to refer not only to the act of criminal conversation, but even to the desire, imagination, or passion that would suggest such a disgrace. What a King is ours, who stretches His scepter over the realm of our inward lusts! How sovereignly He puts it: *But I say unto you!* Who but a divine being has authority to speak in this fashion? His word is law. So it ought to be, seeing He touches evil at the fountainhead and forbids uncleanness in the heart. If sin were not allowed in the mind, it would never be made manifest in the body. This, therefore, is a very effective way of dealing with evil. But how searching, how condemning! Irregular looks, unchaste desires, and strong passions are the very essence of adultery, and who can claim a lifelong freedom from them? Yet these are the things that defile a man. Lord, purge them out of my nature and make me pure within.

29. And if thy right eye offend thee, pluck it out, and cast it from thee: for it is profitable for thee that one of thy members should perish, and not that thy whole body should be cast into hell.

That which is the cause of sin is to be given up as well as the sin itself. It is not sinful to have an eye or to cultivate keen perception, but if the eye of speculative knowledge leads us to offend by intellectual sin, it becomes the cause of evil and must be shamed. Anything, however harmless, which leads me to do, or think, or feel wrongly I am to get rid of as much as if it were in itself an evil. To be done with it involves deprivation, yet it must be dispensed with, since even a serious loss in one direction is far better than the loss of the whole man. Better a blind saint than a quick-sighted sinner. If abstaining from alcohol caused weakness of body, it would be better to be weak than to be strong and fall into drunkenness. Since vain speculations and reasonings land men in unbelief, we will have none of them. To *be cast into hell* is too great a risk to run, merely to indulge the evil eye of lust or curiosity.

30. And if thy right hand offend thee, cut it off, and cast it from thee: for it is profitable for thee that one of thy members should perish, and not that thy whole body should be cast into hell.

The cause of offense may be rather active as the *hand* than intellectual as the eye, but we had better be hindered in our work than drawn aside into temptation. The most dexterous hand must not be spared if it encourages us in doing evil. It is not because a certain thing may make us clever and successful that therefore we are to allow it. If it should prove to be the frequent cause of our falling into sin, we must bring it to an end, and place ourselves at a disadvantage for our lifework, rather than ruin our whole being by sin. Holiness is to be our first object; everything else must take a very secondary place. Right eyes and right hands are no longer right if they lead us wrong. Even hands and eyes must go, so that we may not offend our God by them. Yet, let no man read this literally and therefore mutilate his body, as some foolish fanatics have done. The real meaning is clear enough.

Lord, I love You better than my eyes and hands. Let me never hesitate for a moment to the giving up of all for You!

31-32. It hath been said, Whosoever shall put away his wife, let him give her a writing of divorcement: but I say unto you, That whosoever shall put away his wife, saving for the cause of fornication, causeth her to commit adultery: and whosoever shall marry her that is divorced committeth adultery.

This time our King quotes and condemns a permissive enactment of the Jewish State. Men were accustomed to bidding their wives, "Depart," and a hasty word was thought sufficient as an act of divorce. Moses insisted upon *a writing of divorcement,* so that angry passions might have time to cool, and that the separation, if it must come, might be performed with deliberation and legal formality. The requirement of a writing was to a certain degree a check upon an evil habit, which was so engrained in the people that to refuse it altogether would have been useless and would only have created another crime. The law of Moses went as far as it could practically be enforced. It was because of the hardness of their hearts that divorce was tolerated. It was never approved.

But our Lord is more heroic in His legislation. He forbids divorce except for the one crime of infidelity to the marriage vow. She who commits adultery does by that act and deed in effect sever the marriage bond, and it ought then to be formally recognized by the State as being severed. But for nothing else should a man be divorced from his wife.

Marriage is for life and cannot be loosed, except by the one great crime that severs its bond, whichever of the two is guilty of it. Our Lord would never have tolerated the wicked laws of the modern age, which allows married men and women to separate on the barest pretext. A woman divorced for any cause but adultery, and marrying again, is committing adultery before God, whatever the laws of man may call it. This is very plain and positive, and thus a sanctity is given to marriage that human legislation ought not to violate. Let us not be among those who take up novel ideas of wedlock and seek to distort the marriage laws under the pretense of reforming them. Our Lord knows better than our modern social reformers. We had better let the laws of God alone, for we shall never discover any better ones.

> *33-37. Again, ye have heard that it hath been said by them of old time, Thou shalt not forswear thyself, but shalt perform unto the Lord thine oaths: but I say unto you, Swear not at all; neither by heaven; for it is God's throne: nor by the earth; for it is his footstool: neither by Jerusalem; for it is the city of the great King. Neither shalt thou swear by thy head, because thou canst not make one hair white or black. But let your communication be, Yea, yea; Nay, nay: for whatsoever is more than these cometh of evil.*

False swearing was forbidden of old, but every kind of swearing is forbidden now by the word of our Lord Jesus. He mentions several forms of oath and forbids them all, and then prescribes simple forms of affirmation or denial as all that His followers should employ. Notwithstanding much that may be advanced to the contrary, there is no evading the plain sense of this passage, that every sort of oath, however solemn or true, is forbidden to a follower of Jesus. Whether in court of law, or out of it, the rule is, *Swear not at all.* Yet, in this "Christian" country, we have swearing everywhere and especially among lawmakers. Our legislators begin their official existence by swearing. By those who obey the law of the Savior's kingdom, all swearing is set aside, so that the simple word of affirmation or denial, calmly repeated, may remain as a sufficient bond of truth. A bad man cannot be believed on his oath, and a good man speaks the truth without an oath. To what purpose is the superfluous custom of legal swearing preserved? Christians should not yield to an evil custom, however great the pressure put upon them;

but they should abide by the plain and unmistakable command of their Lord and King.

38. Ye have heard that it hath been said, An eye for an eye, and a tooth for a tooth.

The law of *an eye for an eye,* as administered in the proper courts of law, was founded in justice, and worked far more equitably than the more modern system of fines, for that method allows rich men to offend with comparative impunity. But when the *lex talionis* ("an eye for an eye") came to be the rule of daily life, it fostered revenge, and our Savior would not tolerate it as a principle carried out by individuals. Good law in court may be a very bad custom in common society. He spoke against what had become a proverb and was heard and said among the people: *Ye have heard that it hath been said.* Our loving King would have private dealings ruled by the spirit of love and not by the rule of law.

39. But I say unto you, That ye resist not evil: but whosoever shall smite thee on thy right cheek, turn to him the other also.

Nonresistance and forbearance are to be the rule among Christians. They are to endure personal ill-usage without coming to blows. They are to be as the anvil when bad men are the hammers, and thus they are to overcome by patient forgiveness. The rule of the judgment seat is not for common life, but the rule of the cross and the all-enduring Sufferer is for us all. Yet how many regard all this as fanatical, utopian, and even cowardly. The Lord, our King, would have us bear and forbear, and conquer by mighty patience. Can we do it? How are we the servants of Christ if we have not His spirit?

40. And if any man will sue thee at the law, and take away thy coat, let him have thy cloak also.

Let him have all he asks and more. Better lose a suit of cloth than be drawn into a suit in law. The courts of our Lord's day were vicious, and His disciples were advised to suffer wrong sooner than appeal to them. Our own courts often furnish the surest method of solving a difficulty by authority, and we have known them resorted to with the view of preventing strife. Yet even in a country where justice can be had, we are not to resort to law for every personal wrong. We should rather endure to be put upon than be forever crying out, "I'll bring an action!"

At times this very rule of self-sacrifice may require us to take steps in the way of legal appeal, and to stop injuries that would fall heavily upon others; but we ought often to forego our own advantage, yes, and always when the main motive would be a proud desire for self-vindication.

Lord, give me a patient spirit, so that I may not seek to avenge myself, even when I might righteously do so!

41. And whosoever shall compel thee to go a mile, go with him twain.

Governments in those days demanded forced service through their petty officers. Christians were to be of a yielding temper and bear a double exaction rather than provoke ill words and anger. We ought not to evade taxation, but stand ready to render to Caesar his due. *Yield* is our watchword. To stand up against force is not exactly our part; we may leave that to others. How few believe the long-suffering, nonresistant doctrines of our King!

42. Give to him that asketh thee, and from him that would borrow of thee turn not thou away.

Be generous. A miser is no follower of Jesus. Discretion is to be used in our giving, lest we encourage idleness and poverty; but the general rule is, *Give to him that asketh thee.* Sometimes a loan may be more useful than a gift. Do not refuse it to those who will make right use of it. These precepts are not meant for fools. They are set before us as our general rule, but each rule is balanced by other scriptural commands, and there is the teaching of a philanthropic common sense to guide us. Our spirit is to be one of readiness to help the needy by gift or loan, and we are not exceedingly likely to err by excess in this direction; hence, the boldness of the command.

43. Ye have heard that it hath been said, Thou shalt love thy neighbor, and hate thine enemy.

In this case, a command of Scripture had a human antithesis fitted onto it by depraved minds, and this human addition was mischievous. This is a common method – to append to the teaching of Scripture a something that seems to grow out of it or to be a natural inference from it, which something may be false and wicked. This is a sad crime against the Word of the Lord. The Holy Spirit will only father His own words. He owns the precept, *Thou shalt love thy neighbor,* but He hates the parasitical growth of *hate thine enemy.* This last sentence is destructive of that out of which it appears legitimately to grow, since those who are here called enemies are, in fact, neighbors. Love is now the universal law, and our King, who has commanded it, is Himself the pattern of it. He will not see it narrowed down and placed in a setting of hate. May grace prevent any of us from falling into this error!

> *44-45. But I say unto you, Love your enemies, bless them that curse you, do good to them that hate you, and pray for them which despitefully use you, and persecute you; that ye may be the children of your Father which is in heaven: for he maketh his sun to rise on the evil and on the good, and sendeth rain on the just and on the unjust.*

Ours it is to persist in loving, even if men persist in enmity. We are to render blessing for cursing, prayers for persecutions. Even in the cases of cruel enemies, we are to *do good to them and pray for them.* We are no longer enemies to any, but friends to all. We do not merely cease to hate and then abide in a cold neutrality, but we love where hatred seemed inevitable. We bless where our old nature bids us to curse, and we are active in doing good to those who deserve to receive evil from us. Where this is practically carried out, men wonder, respect, and admire the followers of Jesus. The theory may be ridiculed, but the practice is reverenced and is counted so surprising that men attribute it to some godlike quality in Christians and acknowledge that they are *the children of your Father which is in heaven.* Indeed, he is a child of God who can bless the unthankful and the evil, for in daily providence the Lord is doing this on a great scale and none but His children will imitate Him. To do good for the sake of the good done, and not because of the character of the person benefited, is a noble imitation of God. If the Lord only sent the fertilizing shower upon the land of the saintly, drought would deprive whole leagues of land of all hope of a harvest. We also must do good to the evil or we shall have a narrow sphere, our hearts will grow constricted, and our sonship towards the good God will be rendered doubtful.

46. For if ye love them which love you, what reward have ye? do not even the publicans the same?

Any common sort of man will love those who love him; even tax-gatherers and the scum of the earth can rise to this poor, starving virtue. Saints cannot be content with such a flinching style of things. Love for love is manlike, but love for hate is Christlike. Shall we not desire to act up to our high calling?

47. And if ye salute your brethren only, what do ye more than others? do not even the publicans so?

On a journey, or in the streets, or in the house, we are not to confine our friendly greetings to those who are near and dear to us. Courtesy should be wide and nonetheless sincere because generally, we should speak kindly to all, and treat every man as a brother. Anyone will shake hands with an old friend, but we are to be cordially courteous towards every being in the form of man. If not, we shall reach no higher level than mere outcasts. Even a dog will salute a dog.

48. Be ye therefore perfect, even as your Father which is in heaven is perfect.

Or, *You shall be perfect.* We should reach after completeness in love – fullness of love to all around us. Love is the bond of perfectness, and if we have perfect love, it will form in us a perfect character. Here is that which we aim at – perfection like that of God. Here is the manner of obtaining it – namely, by abounding in love. And this suggests the question of how far we have proceeded in this heavenly direction and also the reason why we should persevere in it even to the end, because as children we ought to resemble our Father. Scriptural perfection is attainable; it lies rather in proportion than in degree. A man's character may be perfect and entire, lacking nothing, and yet such a man will be the very first to admit that the grace that is in him is at best in its infancy, and though perfect as a child in all its parts, it has not yet attained to the perfection of full-grown manhood.

What a mark is set before us by our perfect King, who, speaking from His mountain throne, says, *Be ye therefore perfect, even as your Father which is in heaven is perfect.* Lord, give what You command, then both the grace and the glory will be Yours alone.

Matthew 6

Matthew 6:1-18

The King Contrasts the Laws of His Kingdom with The Conduct of Outward Religionists in the Matters of Alms and Prayer

1. Take heed that ye do not your alms before men, to be seen of them: otherwise ye have no reward of your Father which is in heaven.

Our King sets men right as to almsgiving (charity). It is taken for granted that we give to the poor. How could we be in Christ's kingdom if we did not?

Charity may be given publicly, but not for the sake of publicity. It is important that we have a right aim, for if we obtain the result of a wrong aim, our success will be a failure. If we give to be seen, we shall be seen, and there will be an end of it: *Ye have no reward of your father which is in heaven.* We lose the only reward worth having. But if we give to please our Father, we shall find our reward at His hands. To the matter of our intent and goal, we must *take heed,* for nobody does right without carefully aiming to do so. Our giving of charity should be a holy duty, carefully performed, not for our own honor, but for God's pleasure. Let each reader ask himself how much he has done in the way the King prescribes.

2. Therefore when thou doest thine alms, do not sound a trumpet before thee, as the hypocrites do in the synagogues and in the streets, that they may have glory of men. Verily I say unto you, They have their reward.

We must not copy the loud charity of certain conceited persons. Their character is hypocritical, their manner is ostentatious, their aim is to be seen of men, and their reward is in the present. That reward is a very poor one and is soon over. To stand with a penny in one hand and a trumpet in the other is the posture of hypocrisy. *Glory of men* is a thing that can be bought, but honor from God is a very different thing. This is an advertising age and too many are saying, "Behold my liberality!" Those who have Jesus for their King must wear His garb of humility and not the scarlet trappings of a purse-proud generosity, which blows its own trumpet not only in the streets, but also in the synagogues. We cannot expect two rewards for the same action: If we have it now, we shall not have it hereafter. Unrewarded charity will alone count in the record of the last day.

3-4. But when thou doest alms, let not thy left hand know what thy right hand doeth: that thine alms may be in secret: and thy Father which seeth in secret himself shall reward thee openly.

Seek secrecy for your good deeds. Do not even see your own virtue. Hide from yourself that which you yourself have done that is commendable, for the proud contemplation of your own generosity may tarnish all your charity. Keep the thing so secret that even you yourself are hardly aware that you are doing anything at all praiseworthy. Let God be present, and you will have enough of an audience. He will reward you, reward you *openly,* reward you as a father rewards a child, reward you as one who saw what you did and knew that you did it wholly unto Him.

Lord, help me, when I am doing good, to keep my left hand out of it, that I may have no sinister motive and no desire to have a present reward of praise among my fellow man.

5. And when thou prayest, thou shalt not be as the hypocrites are: for they love to pray standing in the synagogues and in the corners of the streets, that they may be seen of men. Verily I say unto you, They have their reward.

Prayer also is taken for granted. No man can be in the kingdom of heaven who does not pray.

Those around our Lord knew what He meant when He alluded to the *hypocrites,* for they had often seen the proud member of a sect standing in public places repeating his prayers, and very likely they had up to this time felt bound to hold such in repute for superior sanctity. By our Lord's words, these *hypocrites* are unmasked and made to seem what they really are. Our King was wonderfully plainspoken, and called both things and persons by their right names. These religionists were not seekers of God, but seekers after popularity – men who twisted even devotion into a means for self-aggrandizement. They chose places and times that would render their saying of prayers conspicuous. *The synagogues and the corners of the streets* suited them admirably, for their aim was *that they may be seen of men.* They were seen. They had what they sought for. This was their reward, and the whole of it.

Lord, let me never be so profane as to pray to You with the intent of getting praise for myself.

> *6. But thou, when thou prayest, enter into thy closet, and when thou hast shut thy door, pray to thy Father which is in secret; and thy Father which seeth in secret shall reward thee openly.*

Be alone. Enter into a little room into which no other may intrude. Keep out every interloper by shutting the door, and there and then, with all your heart, pour out your appeal. *Pray to thy Father.* Prayer is mainly to be addressed to God the Father and always to God as *our* Father. Pray to your Father who is there present, to your Father who sees you, and specially takes note of that which is evidently meant for Him only, seeing it is done *in secret,* where no eye can see but His own. If it be indeed to God that we pray, there can be no need for anyone else to be present, for it would hinder rather than help devotion to have a third person for a witness of the heart's private intercourse with the Lord.

As the very soul of prayer lies in communion with God, we shall pray best when all our attention is confined to Him, and we shall best reach our end of being accepted by Him when we have no regard for the opinion of anyone else. Secret prayer is truly heard and *openly* answered in the Lord's own way and time. Our King reigns *in secret.* There He sets up His court and there He will welcome our approaches. We are not where God sees when we court publicity and pray to obtain credit for our devotion.

> *7-8. But when ye pray, use not vain repetitions, as the heathen do: for they think that they shall be heard for their much speaking. Be not ye therefore like unto them: for your Father knoweth what things ye have need of, before ye ask him.*

To repeat a form of prayer a very large number of times has always seemed to the ignorantly religious to be a praiseworthy thing, but assuredly it is not so. It is a mere exercise of memory and of the organs of noisemaking, and it is absurd to imagine that such a parrot exercise can be pleasing to the living God. The Muslims and Roman Catholics keep to this heathenish custom, but we must not imitate them.

God does not need us to pray for His information, for He *knoweth what things ye have need of,* nor to repeat the prayer over and over for His persuasion, for as our Father, He is willing to bless us. Therefore, let us not be superstitious and dream that there is virtue in *much speaking.* In the multitude of words, even in prayer, there lacks not sin.

Repetitions we may have, but not *vain repetitions.* Counting beads and reckoning the time occupied in devotion are both idle things. Christians' prayers are measured by weight and not by length. Many of the most prevailing prayers have been as short as they were strong.

9. After this manner therefore pray ye: Our Father which art in heaven, Hallowed be thy name.

Our Lord, having warned us against certain vices that had connected themselves with prayer as to its place and spirit, now gives us a model upon which to fashion our prayers. This delightful prayer is short, devout, and full of meaning. Its first three petitions are for God and His glory. Our chief prayers to God are to be for His glory. Do we thus begin with God in prayer? Does not the daily bread often come in before the kingdom?

We pray as children to a Father and we pray as brothers, for we say, *Our Father. Our Father* is a familiar name, but the words, *which art in heaven* suggest the reverence due unto Him. Our Father and yet in heaven – in heaven and yet our Father. May His name be treated reverently, and may all that is about Him – His Word and His gospel – be regarded with the deepest awe! It is for us so to walk before the Lord in all lowliness, that all shall see that we reverence the character of the thrice Holy One. Then can we truly pray, *Hallowed be thy name,* when we hallow it ourselves.

10. Thy kingdom come, Thy will be done in earth, as it is in heaven.

Oh, that You may reign over all hearts and lands! Men have thrown off their allegiance to our Father, God; and we pray with all our might that He may, by His almighty grace, subdue them to loyal obedience. We long for the coming of King Jesus, but meanwhile we cry to our Father, *Thy kingdom come.* We desire for the supreme will to *be done in earth,* with a cheerful, constant, universal obedience like that of *heaven.* We would have the Lord's will carried out, not only by the great physical forces that never fail to be obedient to God, but also by lovingly active spirits; by men once rebellious, but graciously renewed. Oh, that all who say this prayer may display on earth the holy willingness of obedience that is seen in the happy, hearty, united, and unquestioning service of perfect saints and angels before the throne. Our heart's highest wish is for God's honor, dominion, and glory.

11. Give us this day our daily bread.

We pray for providential supplies for ourselves and others – *Give us.* We ask for our food as a gift – *Give us.* We request no more than bread or food necessary for us. Our petition concerns the day and asks only for a daily supply, bread enough for this day. We ask not for bread that belongs to others, but only for that which is honestly our own – *our daily bread.* It is the prayer of a lowly and contented mind, of one who is so sanctified that he waits upon God even for his daily food, and of one who lovingly links others with himself in his sympathy and prayer.

Give me, Lord, both the bread of heaven and of earth, that which feeds my soul and sustains my body. For all I look to You, my Father.

12. And forgive us our debts, as we forgive our debtors.

No prayer of mortal men could be complete without confession of sin. Prayer that does not seek for pardon will fail, as the Pharisee's prayer did. Let proud men boast as they please; those who are in Christ's kingdom will always pray, *Forgive us our debts.* Our Lord knew that we would always have debts to own and therefore would always need to cry, *Forgive!* This is the prayer of men whom the Judge has absolved because of their faith in the Great Sacrifice, for now to their Father they come for free forgiveness, as children. No man may pass a day without praying, *Forgive,* and in his pleading he should not forget his fellow sinners, but should pray, *Forgive us.* The writer ventures to pray, "Lord, forgive me and my brother over yonder, who says he is perfect."

This pardon we can only obtain as we freely pass over the offenses of others against ourselves, *as we forgive our debtors.* This is a reasonable, no, a blessed requirement, which it is a delight to fulfill. It would not be safe for God to forgive a man who will not forgive others.

Lord, I most heartily forgive all who may have done me wrong. I am lenient with those who are indebted to me, and now, with a hopeful heart, I pray You, forgive me, as surely as I now forgive all who are in any sense my debtors.

13. And lead us not into temptation, but deliver us from evil: For thine is the kingdom, and the power, and the glory, for ever. Amen.

In the course of providence, the Lord tests our graces and the sincerity of our profession, and for this purpose He does *lead us into temptation.* We entreat Him not to test us too severely. Lord, let not my joys or my sorrows become temptations to me. As I would not run into temptation of myself, I pray You, do not lead me where I must inevitably meet it.

But if I must be tested, Lord, deliver me from falling into evil, and specially preserve me from that Evil One, who, above all, seeks my soul, to destroy it. Temptation or trial may be for my good, if I am delivered from evil. Lord, do this for me, for I cannot preserve myself.

The prayer finishes with a doxology. That devotion that begins with prayer ends in praise. All rule, and might, and honor belong to God, and to Him let them forever be ascribed. His is *the kingdom,* or the right to rule; *the power,* or the might to uphold His authority; and *the glory,* or the honor that comes out of His government. Our whole heart delights that the Lord is thus supreme and glorious, and therefore we say, *Amen.*

How perfect is this model of prayer! So fit for man to pray, so suitable to be laid before the throne of the Majesty on High. Oh, that we may have grace to copy it all our days! Jesus, our King, will not refuse to present a prayer that is of His own drawing-up and is directed to the Father whom He loves to glorify.

14-15. For if ye forgive men their trespasses, your heavenly Father will also forgive you: but if ye forgive not men their trespasses, neither will your Father forgive your trespasses.

This enforces Christian action by limiting the power of prayer according to our obedience to the command to forgive. If we would be forgiven, we must forgive. If we will not forgive, we cannot be forgiven. This yoke is easy; this burden is light. It may be a blessing to be wronged, since it affords us an opportunity of judging whether we are indeed the recipients of the pardon that comes from the throne of God. Very sweet is it to pass by other men's offenses against ourselves, for thus we learn how sweet it is to the Lord to pardon us.

16. Moreover when ye fast, be not, as the hypocrites, of a sad countenance: for they disfigure their faces, that they may appear unto men to fast. Verily I say unto you, They have their reward.

Having dealt with prayer, our King now instructs us as to fasting. Fasting took a leading place in devotion under the Law, and it might profitably be more practiced even now under the gospel. The Puritans called it soul-fattening fasting, and so many have found it. We must, by order of our King, avoid all attempt at display in connection with this form of devotion. Hypocrites went about with faces unwashed and sorrowful, so that all might say, "See how rigidly those men are fasting. What good men they must be!" To look miserable in order to be thought holy is a wretched piece of hypocrisy, and as it makes fasting into a trick to catch human admiration, it thereby destroys it as a means of grace. We cannot expect to get a reward both from the praise of our fellows and the pleasure of God. We have our choice, and if we snatch at the minor reward, we leave the major. May it never be said of us, *They have their reward.*

17-18. But thou, when thou fastest, anoint thine head, and wash thy face; that thou appear not unto men to fast, but unto thy Father which is in secret: and thy Father, which seeth in secret, shall reward thee openly.

Use diligence to conceal what it would be foolish to parade. Leave off no outward act of personal cleanliness or adornment; *anoint thine head, and wash thy face.* If your fasting is unto God, keep it for Him. Act in seasons of extraordinary devotion as you do at other times, that those with whom you come in contact may not know what special devotion you are practicing. You may fast, and that fasting may be discovered, but let it be no intent of yours that you should *appear unto men to fast.* Fast from vanity, ambition, pride, and self-glorification. Fast in secret before the Seer of secrets. Secret fasting shall have an open reward from the Lord, but that which is done out of mere flamboyance shall never be reckoned in the books of the Lord. Thus our King has taught us both how to give alms, how to pray, and how to fast; and He will now proceed to legislate for the concerns of daily life.

Matthew 6:19-34

The King Gives Commands As to the Cares of This Life

He would not have His servants seeking two objects and serving two masters. He calls them away from anxieties about this life to a restful faith in God.

> *19. Lay not up for yourselves treasures upon earth, where moth and rust doth corrupt, and where thieves break through and steal.*

Lay not out your life for gathering wealth. This would be degrading to you as servants of the heavenly kingdom. If you accumulate either money or clothing, your treasures will be liable to *moth and rust,* and of both you may be deprived by dishonest men. That earthly things decay, or are taken from us, is an excellent reason for not making them the great objects of our pursuit. Hoard not for *thieves,* gather not for *corruption.* Accumulate for eternity and send your treasures into the land where you are going. To live for the sake of growing rich is a gilded death in life.

> *20. But lay up for yourselves treasures in heaven, where neither moth nor rust doth corrupt, and where thieves do not break through nor steal.*

Let our desires and efforts go after heavenly things. These are not liable to any decay within themselves, nor can they be taken from us by force or fraud. Does not wisdom bid us to seek such sure possessions? Out of our earthly possessions, that which is used for God is laid up *in heaven.* What is given to the poor and to the Lord's cause is deposited in the Bank of Eternity. To heaven we are going; let us send our treasures before us. There they will be safe from decay and robbery, but in no other place may we reckon them to be secure.

Lord, let me be rich towards You. I had better send on to my treasury in heaven more of my substance than I have already sent. I will at once remember the church and its missions, orphans, aged saints, and poor brethren. These are Your treasury boxes and I will bank my money there.

21. For where your treasure is, there will your heart be also.

This is a grand moral motive for keeping our desires above cringing objects. The heart must and will go in the direction of that which we count precious. The whole man will be transformed into the likeness of that for which he lives. Where we place our treasures, our thoughts will naturally fly. It will be wise to let all that we have act as magnets to draw us in the right direction. If our very best things are in heaven, then our very best thoughts will fly in the same direction; but if our choicest possessions are of the earth, then our heart will be earthbound.

22-23. The light of the body is the eye: if therefore thine eye be single, thy whole body shall be full of light. But if thine eye be evil, thy whole body shall be full of darkness. If therefore the light that is in thee be darkness, how great is that darkness.

The motive is the eye of the soul, and if it be clear, the whole character will be right, but if it be polluted, our whole being will become defiled. The eye of the understanding may also be understood here. If a man does not see things in a right light, he may live in sin and yet imagine that he is doing his duty. A man should live up to his light, but if that light is itself darkness, what a mistake his whole course will be! If our religion leads us to sin, it is worse than irreligion. If our faith is presumption, our zeal selfishness, our prayer formality, our hope a delusion, and our experience infatuation, then the darkness is so great that even our Lord holds up His hands in astonishment and says, *How great is that darkness*!

Oh, for a single eye to God's glory, a sincere consecration unto the Lord! This alone can fill my soul with light.

24. No man can serve two masters: for either be will hate the one, and love the other; or else he will hold to the one, and despise the other. Ye cannot serve God and mammon.

Here our King forbids division of aim in life. We cannot have two master passions. If we could, it would be impossible to serve both. Their interests would soon come into conflict and we would be forced to choose between them. God and the world will never agree, and however much we may attempt it, we shall never be able to serve both. Our danger is that in trying to gain money or in the pursuit of any other object, we should put it out of its place and allow it to get the mastery of our mind. Gain and godliness cannot both be masters of our souls. We can serve *two*, but not *two masters*. You can live for this world or live for the next, but to live equally for both is impossible. Where God reigns, the lust of gain must go.

Oh, to be so decided, that we may pursue one thing only! We would *hate* evil and *love* God, *despise* falsehood and *hold to* truth! We need to know how we are affected both by righteousness and sin, and when this is ascertained to our comfort, we must stand to the right with uncompromising firmness. Wealth is the direct opposite of God as much today as in past ages, and we must loathe its greed, its selfishness, its oppression, and its pride, or we do not love God.

> *25. Therefore I say unto you, Take no thought for your life, what ye shall eat, or what ye shall drink; nor yet for your body, what ye shall put on. Is not the life more than meat, and the body than raiment?*

Therefore, in order that our one Master may be served, we must cease from serving self and from the burdensome care that self-seeking involves. Read the passage this way: *Be not anxious for your life.* Though we may *take* but anxious, burdensome care, we must not *know* it. Our most pressing bodily needs are not to engross our minds. Our life is more important than the food we eat or the clothes we wear. God who gives us life will give us bread and clothing. We should much more care about how we live than how we eat. The spiritual should go before the bodily, and the eternal before the temporal. What we wear is of very small importance compared with what we are. Therefore, let us give our chief care to that which is chief, yes, our sole thought to the one all-absorbing object of all true life – the glory of God.

> *26. Behold the fowls of the air: for they sow not, neither do they reap, nor*

gather into barns; yet your heavenly Father feedeth them. Are ye not much better than they?

The birds are fed by God; will He not feed us? They are free from the fret that comes of hoarding and trading. Why should we not be? If God feeds *the fowls of the air* without sowing, or reaping, or storing, surely He will supply us when we trustfully use these means. For us to rely upon these means and forget our God would be folly indeed. Our King would have His subjects give their hearts to His love and service, and not worry themselves with cringing anxieties. It is well for us that we have these daily needs, because they lead us to our heavenly Father; but if we grow anxious, they are turned from their purpose and made into barriers to shut us out from the Lord. Oh, that we would be as good as the birds in trustfulness, since in dignity of nature we are so *much better than they*!

27. Which of you by taking thought can add one cubit unto his stature?

It is a small matter whether we are tall or short, and yet all the worry in the world could not make us an inch taller. Why, then, do we give way to caring about things that we cannot alter? If fretting were of any use, it would have some excuse; but as it does no good, let us cease from it.

28-29. And why take ye thought for raiment? Consider the lilies of the field, how they grow; they toil not, neither do they spin: and yet I say unto you, That even Solomon in all his glory was not arrayed like one of these.

Clothes must not be made much of, for in our finest array, flowers far excel us. We must not be anxious about how we shall be clad, for the *lilies of the field,* not under the gardener's care, are as glorious as the most pompous of monarchs, and yet they enjoy life free from labor and thought. Lovely lilies, how you rebuke our foolish nervousness! The array of lilies comes without fret. Why do we kill ourselves with care about that which God gives to plants that cannot care?

My Lord, I wish to grow to Your praise as the lily does, and be content to be what You make me to be, and wear what You give me.

30. Wherefore, if God so clothe the grass of the field, which to day is, and to morrow is cast into the oven, shall he not much more clothe you, O ye of little faith?

It is not merely that lilies grow, but that God Himself also clothes them with surpassing beauty. These lilies, when growing, appear only as *the grass,* commonplace enough, but Solomon could not excel them when God has put them in their full array of cloth of gold. Will He not be sure to take care of us, who are precious in His sight? Why should we be so slightly trustful as to have a doubt upon that point? If that which is so very short-lived is yet so adorned of the Lord, depend upon it, He will guard immortal minds and even the mortal bodies with which they are associated.

Little faith is not a little fault, for it greatly wrongs the Lord and sadly grieves the fretful mind. To think that the Lord who clothes lilies will leave His own children naked is shameful. O little faith, learn better manners!

31. Therefore take no thought, saying, What shall we eat? or, What shall we drink? or, Wherewithal shall we be clothed?

"Be not anxious" is the right interpretation. Think, so that you may not have to be anxious. Do not forever be following the world's trinity of cares. The questions in this verse are taken out of the worldling's catechism of distrust. The children of God may quietly work on from day to day, and cast all ominous cares from themselves.

32. (For after all these things do the Gentiles seek:) for your heavenly Father knoweth that ye have need of all these things.

We are to excel those who are aliens and foreigners. Things that *Gentiles seek* are not good enough for the Israel of God. The men of the world seek after earthly things and have no mind for anything beyond. We have a *heavenly Father* and therefore we have higher aims and aspirations. Moreover, as our Father knows all about our necessities, we need not be anxious, for He is quite sure to supply all our needs. Let the Gentiles hunt after their many carnal objects, but let the children of the Lord leave their temporal desires with the Lord of infinite grace, and then let them follow after the one thing that is necessary.

Lord, enable me to be a nonanxious one. May I be so eager for heavenly things, that I altogether leave my earthly cares with You!

33. But seek ye first the kingdom of God, and his righteousness; and all these things shall be added unto you.

Seek God first and the rest will follow in due course. As for *all these things,* you will not need to seek them; they will be thrown in as a matter of course. God who gives you heaven will not deny you your bread on the road there. *The kingdom of God* and the *righteousness* suitable to that kingdom – seek these first and foremost, and then all that you can possibly need shall be your portion. To promote the reign of Christ and to practice righteousness are but one object, and may that be the one aim of our lives! Let us spend life on the one thing and it will be well spent. As for the twenty secondary objects, they also will be ours if we pursue the one thing only.

34. Take therefore no thought for the morrow: for the morrow shall take thought for the things of itself. Sufficient unto the day is the evil thereof.

Understand the former verses as the argument to this *therefore.* Anxiety cannot help you (verse 27). It is quite useless. It would degrade you to the level of the heathen (verse 32), and there is no need for it (verse 33); therefore, do not anticipate sorrow by being anxious as to the future. Our business is with today. We are only to ask bread day by day, and that only in sufficient abundance for the day's consumption. To import the possible sorrows of tomorrow into the thoughts of today is an excess of unbelief. When the morning brings sorrow, it will bring strength for that sorrow. Today will require all the vigor we have to deal with its immediate evils; there can be no need to import cares from the future. To load today with trials not yet arrived would be to overload it. Anxiety is evil, but anxiety about things that have not yet happened is altogether without excuse.

> "Cast foreboding cares away,
> God provideth for today."

O my heart, what rest there is for you if you will give yourself up to your Lord and leave all your own concerns with Him! Mind you your Lord's business, and He will see to your business.

Matthew 7

Matthew 7:1-12

The King Continues to Regulate the Behavior of His Subjects

He deals with matters in which we come into contact with our fellow man, as He had formerly set in order our personal devotion towards God and our private business for ourselves.

1-2. Judge not, that ye be not judged. For with what judgment ye judge, ye shall be judged: and with what measure ye mete, it shall be measured to you again.

Use your judgment, of course. The verse implies that you will *judge* in a right sense. But do not indulge the criticizing power upon others in a hypercritical manner, or as if you were set in authority and had a right to dispense judgment among your fellows. If you accredit motives and pretend to read hearts, others will do the same towards you. A hard and hypercritical behavior is sure to provoke reprisals. Those around you will pick up the peck measure you have been using and measure your corn with it. You do not object to men forming a fair opinion of your character, and neither are you forbidden to do the same towards them; but as you would object to their sitting in judgment upon you, do not sit in judgment upon them. This is not the day of judgment, neither are we his Majesty's judges, and therefore we may not anticipate the time appointed for the final judicial inquest, nor usurp the prerogatives of the Judge of all the earth.

Surely, if I know myself aright, I need not send my judgment upon circuit to try other men, for I can give it full occupation in my own Court of Conscience to try the traitors within my own bosom.

3-5. And why beholdest thou the mote that is in thy brother's eye, but considerest not the beam that is in thine own eye? Or how wilt thou say to thy brother, Let me pull out the mote out of thine eye; and, behold, a beam is in thine own eye? Thou hypocrite, first cast out the beam out of thine own eye; and then shalt thou see clearly to cast out the mote out of thy brother's eye.

The judging function is best employed at home. Our tendency is to spy out splinters in other men's eyes and not to see the beam in our own. Instead of beholding, with gratified gaze, the small fault of another, we should act reasonably if we apologetically considered the greater fault of ourselves. It is *the beam that is in [our] own eye* that blinds us to our own wrongdoing, but such blindness does not suffice to excuse us, since it evidently does not shut our eyes to the little error of our brother. Meddling pretends to play the optometrist, but in very truth it plays the fool. Imagine a man with a beam in his eye pretending to deal with so tender a part as the eye of another, and attempting to remove so tiny a thing as a *mote* or splinter! Is he not a *hypocrite* to pretend to be so concerned about other men's eyes and yet he never attends to his own? Jesus is gentle, but He calls that man a *hypocrite* who fusses about small things in others, and pays no attention to great matters at home in his own person. Our reformations must begin with ourselves, or they are not true and do not spring from a right motive. Sin we may rebuke, but not if we indulge it. We may protest against evil, but not if we willfully practice it. The Pharisees were great at judging, but slow at amending. Our Lord will not have His kingdom made up of hypocritical theorists. He calls for practical obedience to the rules of holiness.

After we are ourselves sanctified, we are bound to be eyes to the blind and correctors of unholy living, but not till then. Till we have personal devoutness, our preaching of godliness is sheer hypocrisy. May none of us provoke the Lord to say to us, *Thou hypocrite*!

6. Give not that which is holy unto the dogs, neither cast ye your pearls before swine, lest they trample them under their feet, and turn again and rend you.

When men are evidently unable to perceive the purity of a great truth, do not set it before them. They are like mere *dogs,* and if you set holy things before them, they will be provoked to *turn again and rend you.* Holy things are not for the profane. *Without are dogs* (Revelation 22:15). They must not be allowed to enter the holy place. When you are in the midst of the vicious, who are like *swine,* do not bring forth the precious mysteries of the faith, for they will despise them and *trample them under their feet* in the mire. You are not needlessly to provoke attack upon yourself or upon the higher truths of the gospel. You are not to judge, but you are not to act without judgment. Count not men to be dogs or swine, but when they declare themselves to be such, or by their conduct act as if they were such, do not put occasions in their way for displaying their evil character. Saints are not to be simpletons. They are not to be judges, but also, they are not to be fools.

Great King, how much wisdom Your precepts require! I need You, not only to open my mouth, but also at times to keep it shut.

7-8. Ask, and it shall be given you; seek, and ye shall find; knock, and it shall be opened unto you: for every one that asketh receiveth; and he that seeketh findeth; and to him that knocketh it shall be opened.

To men you may not always speak of heavenly things, but to God you may.

Ask, seek, knock. Let your prayer be adapted to the case. Let it increase in intensity. Let it advance in the largeness of its object. To receive a gift is simple, to find a treasure is more enriching, to enter into a palace is best of all. Each form of prayer is prescribed, accepted, and rewarded in a manner suitable to its character. The promise is universal to all who obey the precept. The commands are in opposition to the methods of burdensome care, which have been denounced in the former chapter; and they are encouragements to the precepts of giving and nonresistance set forth previously, since he that can have of God for the asking may well give to men who ask, and even yield to those who unjustly demand. With such boundless stores at command, we should not be either stingy or contentious. Lord, help me to have no further concern with fretting and to abound in asking, seeking, and knocking. So shall I soon overflow with thanksgiving.

9-10. Or what man is there of you, whom if his son ask bread, will he give him a stone? Or if he ask a fish, will he give him a serpent?

In worldly things we make blunders and ask for that as bread that we think to be so, when in truth it is a stone. We mistake a serpent for an eel and beg for it as for a fish. Our heavenly Father will correct our prayer and give us not what we ignorantly seek, but what we really need. The promise to give what we ask is here explained and set in its true light. This is a gracious correction of the folly that would read the Lord's words in the most literal sense, and make us dream that every whim of ours had only to put on the dress of prayer in order to see its realization. Our prayers go to heaven in a revised version. It would be a terrible thing if God always gave us all we asked for. Our heavenly Father Himself *knows how to give* far better than we know how to ask.

11. If ye then, being evil, know how to give good gifts unto your children, how much more shall your Father which is in heaven give good things to them that ask him?

We, although ourselves evil, correct our children's blunders in their requests to us, and much more will our all-wise and good heavenly Father correct in His giving the errors of our requests. He will give the good that we did not ask and withhold the ill that we so unwisely requested. We know our children and know for our children, and yet we are poor, evil creatures. Shall not the perfectly good Father, who knows all things, arrange His gifts most graciously? Yes, we are sure He will. *How much more!* says our Lord, and He does not say how much more, but leaves that to our meditations. We know not what we should pray for as we ought, but He knows how to give as suits His perfection, and He will do so. He will give *good things,* and especially His Holy Spirit, who is all good things in one. Lord, I would think more of You than of my own prayer, more of Your Son than of my own faith, and more of Your Holy Spirit than of all good gifts beside.

12. Therefore all things whatsoever ye would that men should do to you, do ye even so to them: for this is the law and the prophets.

Everything that has gone before leads up to this and argues for it, and so He says, *Therefore.* It will be instructive to look back and think this out. Let my reader set about it.

In this place our King gives us His Golden Rule. Put yourself in another's place and then act towards him as you would wish him to act towards you under the same circumstances. This is a very royal rule, a precept always at hand, always applicable, always right. Here you may be a judge, and yet not be judging others, but judging *for* others. This is the sum of the Decalogue, the Pentateuch, and the whole sacred Word.

Oh, that all men acted on it and then there would be no slavery, no war, no sweating, no striking, no lying, no robbing, but all would be justice and love! What a kingdom is this which has such a law! This is the code of Christian ethics. This is the summary of all that is right and generous. We adore the King out of whose mouth and heart such a law could flow. This one rule is a proof of the divinity of our holy religion. The universal practice of it by all who call themselves Christians would carry conviction to Jew, Muslim, and infidel, with greater speed and certainty than all the apologies and arguments that the wit or devotion of men could produce.

Lord, teach it to me! Write it on the fleshy tablets of my renewed heart! Write it out in full in my life!

Matthew 7:13-23

The King Teaches His Servants to Discern and to Distinguish

13-14. Enter ye in at the strait gate: for wide is the gate, and broad is the way, that leadeth to destruction, and many there be which go in thereat: because strait is the gate, and narrow is the way, which leadeth unto life, and few there be that find it.

Be up and on your journey. Enter in at the gate at the head of the way and do not stand hesitating. If it be the right road, you will find the entrance somewhat difficult and exceedingly *narrow,* for it demands self-denial and calls for strictness of obedience, and watchfulness of spirit. Nevertheless, *enter ye in at the strait gate.* Whatever its drawbacks of fewness of pilgrims or narrowness of entrance, yet choose it and use it. True, there is another road, *broad* and much frequented, but it *leadeth to destruction.* Men go to ruin along the turnpike road, but the way to heaven is a bridle path. There may come other days when the many will crowd the *narrow* way, but at this time, to be popular one must be broad – broad in doctrine, in morals, and in spirituality. But those on the *narrow* road shall go straight to glory, and those on the *broad* road are all abroad. All is well that ends well. We can afford to be narrowed in the right way rather than enlarged in the wrong way, because the first ends in endless life and the second hastens down to everlasting death.

Lord, deliver me from the temptation to be *broad,* and keep me in the *narrow* way though few find it!

15. Beware of false prophets, which come to you in sheep's clothing, but inwardly they are ravening wolves.

We have need of our judgments and we must test the spirits of those who profess to be sent of God. There are men of great gifts who are *false prophets.* These affect the look, language, and spirit of God's people, while really they long to devour souls, even as wolves thirst for the blood of sheep. *Sheep's clothing* is all very fine, but we must look beneath it and spy out the *wolves.* A man is what he is *inwardly.* We need to *beware.* This precept is timely at this hour. We must be careful not only about our way, but also about our leaders. They come to us. They come as prophets. They come with every outward commendation, but they are very much Balaams and will surely curse those they pretend to bless.

16. Ye shall know them by their fruits. Do men gather grapes of thorns, or figs of thistles?

Their teaching, their living, and their effect upon our minds will be a sure test to us. Every doctrine and doctrinaire may thus be tested. If we *gather grapes* from them, they are not *thorns.* If they produce nothing but thistledown, they are not fig trees. Some object to this practical method of testing, but wise Christians will carry it with them as the ultimate touchstone. What is the effect of modern theology upon the spirituality, the prayerfulness, the holiness of the people? Has it any good effect?

17-18. Even so every good tree bringeth forth good fruit; but a corrupt tree bringeth forth evil fruit. A good tree cannot bring forth evil fruit, neither can a corrupt tree bring forth good fruit.

Every man produces according to his nature. He cannot do otherwise.

Good tree, good fruit; corrupt tree, evil fruit. There is no possibility of the effect being higher and better than the cause. The truly good does not bring forth evil. It would be contrary to its nature. The radically bad never rises to produce good, though it may seem to do so. Therefore, the one and the other may be known by the special fruit of each. Our King is a great teacher of prudence. We are not to judge, but we are to *know,* and the rule for this knowledge is as simple as it is safe. Such knowledge of men may save us from great mischief that would come to us through associating with bad and deceitful persons.

19. Every tree that bringeth not forth good fruit is hewn down, and cast into the fire.

Here is the end to which evil things are tending. The axe and the fire await the ungodly, however fine they may look with the leafage of profession. Only let time enough be given, and every man on earth who bears no good fruit will meet his doom. It is not merely the wicked, the bearer of poison berries, that will be cut down, but the neutral, the man who bears no fruit of positive virtue must also be cast into the fire.

20. Wherefore by their fruits ye shall know them.

It is not ours to hew or to burn, but it is ours to know. This knowledge is to save us from coming under the shadow or influence of false teachers. Who wants to build his nest upon a tree that is soon to be cut down? Who would choose a barren tree for the center of his orchard?

Lord, let me remember that I am to judge myself by this rule. Make me a true fruit-bearing tree.

21. Not every one that saith unto me, Lord, Lord, shall enter into the kingdom of heaven; but he that doeth the will of my Father which is in heaven.

No verbal homage will suffice. *Not every one that saith.* We may believe in our Lord's deity and we may take great pains to affirm it over and over again with our *Lord, Lord,* but unless we carry out the commands of the Father, we pay no true homage to the Son. We may acknowledge our obligations to Jesus and so call Him *Lord, Lord,* but if we never practically carry out those obligations, what is the value of our admissions? Our King receives not into His kingdom those whose religion lies in words and ceremonies, but only those whose lives display the obedience of true discipleship.

22-23. Many will say to me in that day, Lord, Lord, have we not prophesied in thy name? and in thy name have cast out devils? and in thy name done many wonderful works? And then will I profess unto them, I never knew you: depart from me, ye that work iniquity.

An orthodox creed will not save if it stands alone, neither will it be sure to do so if accompanied by official position and service. These people said, *Lord, Lord,* and in addition, pleaded their prophesying or preaching in His name. All the preaching in the world will not save the preacher if he does not practice. Yes, and he may have been successful – successful to a very high degree, *and in thy name have cast out devils,* and yet, without personal holiness, the caster-out of devils will be cast out himself. The success boasted of may have had about it surprising circumstances of varied interest – *and in thy name done many wonderful works,* and yet the man may be unknown to Christ. Three times over the person is described as doing all *in thy name,* and yet the Lord, whose name he used so freely, so boldly, knew nothing of him and would not permit him to remain in His company. The Lord cannot endure the presence of those who call Him *Lord, Lord,* and then work iniquity. They professed to Him that they knew Him, but He will *profess unto them, I never knew you.*

How solemn is this reminder to me and to others! Nothing will prove us to be true Christians but a sincere doing of the Father's will! We may be known by all to have great spiritual power over devils and men, and yet our Lord may not acknowledge us in that great day, but may drive us out as impostors whom He cannot tolerate in His presence.

Matthew 7:24-29

The King Sums Up His Discourse

24-25. Therefore whosoever heareth these sayings of mine, and doeth them, I will liken him unto a wise man, which built his house upon a rock: and the

rain descended, and the floods came, and the winds blew, and beat upon
that house; and it fell not: for it was founded upon a rock.

We are to *hear* our Lord and by this, of course, it is intended that
we are to accept what He says as authoritative. This is more than some
do at this time, for they sit in judgment upon the teachings of the Lord.
But hearing is not enough, we must *do these sayings.* There must be
practical godliness or nothing is right within us. The doing hearer has
built a house with a stable foundation, the wisest and safest, but it is
the most expensive and toilsome thing to do. Trials come to him. His
sincerity and truthfulness do not prevent his being tested. From above,
and from beneath, and from all sides, the trials come – *rain, floods,* and
winds. No screen is interposed. All these *beat upon that house.* It is a
substantial structure, but the tests become so severe that nothing can
save the building unless it be the strength of its foundation. Because the
chief support is so immovable, the entire structure survives. *It fell not.*
It may have suffered damage here and there, and it may have looked
very weather-beaten, but *it fell not.* Let the Rock of Ages be praised if,
after terrible tribulation, it can be said of our faith, *It fell not: for it was*
founded upon a rock.

> *26-27. And every one that heareth these sayings of mine, and doeth them not,*
> *shall be likened unto a foolish man, which built his house upon the sand:*
> *and the rain descended, and the floods came, and the winds blew, and beat*
> *upon that house; and it fell: and great was the fall of it.*

The mere hearer is in a poor plight. He, too, is a housebuilder. The
hearing of the Lord's sayings sets him upon work and work that is
designed to afford him shelter and comfort. He *built his house.* He was
practical and persevering, and did not begin and leave off before comple-
tion. Yet though he was industrious, he was *foolish.* No doubt he built
quickly, for his foundation cost him no severe labor. His excavations
were soon made, for there was no rock to remove. He *built his house*
upon the sand. But trials come even to insincere professing persons.
Are we not all born to trouble? The same kind of afflictions come to
the foolish as come to the wise, and they operate in precisely the same
way, but the result is very different.

It fell. These are solemn words. It was a fine building and it promised to stand for ages, but *it fell.* There were minor faults in the fabric, but its chief weakness was underground, in the secret place of the foundation. The man *built his house upon the sand.* His fundamentals were wrong.

The crash was terrible. The sound was heard afar. *Great was the fall of it.* The overflow was final and irretrievable. Many heard the fall and many more saw the ruins, as they remained a perpetual memorial of the result of that folly that is satisfied with hearing and neglects doing.

28-29. And it came to pass, when Jesus had ended these sayings, the people were astonished at his doctrine: for he taught them as one having authority, and not as the scribes.

The sermon is over. What has come of it? Never was there so great a Preacher and never did He deliver a greater discourse. How many were the repentant ones? How many the converts? We do not hear of any. Divine truth, even when preached to perfection, will not of itself affect the heart to conversion. The most overpowering *authority* produces no obedience unless the Holy Spirit subdues the hearer's heart.

The people were astonished. Was this all? It is to be feared that it was. Two things surprised them – the substance of His teaching and the manner of it. They had never heard such *doctrine* before. The precepts that He had given were quite new to their thoughts. But their main astonishment was at His manner. There was certainly a power, a weight about it, such as they had never seen in the ordinary professional instructors. He did not raise questions, nor speak with hesitation; neither did He cite authorities, and hide His own responsibility behind great names. *He taught them as one having authority.* He spoke royally. The truth itself was its own argument and demonstration. He taught prophetically, as one inspired from above. Men felt that He spoke after the manner of one sent of God. It was no fault on their part to be astonished, but it was a grave crime to be *astonished* and nothing more.

My Savior, this was a poor reward for Your true royal discourse – *The people were astonished.* Grant to me that I may not care to astonish people, but may I be enabled to win them for You, and if, with my utmost endeavors, I do astonish them and nothing more, may I never complain, for how should the disciple be above his Lord?

Matthew 8

Matthew 8:1-18

The King, Having Spoken in Wisdom, Works with Power

1. When he was come down from the mountain, great multitudes followed him.

Curiosity drew the crowd. Our Lord was popular, but He never prized this popularity for its own sake. He was too wise to think much of that which is so fickle a thing. Yet we are glad to see multitudes gathered to hear the Word, for good may come of it. Jesus *came down* to lift the *multitudes* up.

2. And, behold, there came a leper and worshipped him, saying, Lord, if thou wilt, thou canst make me clean.

This verse begins with a *behold.* It was not wonderful that great multitudes came to Jesus, but it was a marvel that *a leper* should believe that He could remove an incurable disease. The leper rendered to Christ divine homage, and if Jesus had been merely a good man, and nothing more, He would have refused the worship with holy indignation. Those who call Jesus *Lord,* and do not worship Him, are more diseased than the leper was. His was a high degree of faith, for, so far as we know, no one had previously believed in Jesus in this fashion. Leprosy breeds great despair, but this poor creature rose superior to all doubt. If Jesus willed it, even he might be healed.

He did not doubt the Savior's will when he said, *Lord, if thou wilt.* No, rather, he so believed in our Lord's power, that he felt that he had but to exercise His will and the cure would be effected at once. Have we as much faith as this? Are we convinced that the mere will of Jesus would make us whole?

Lord, I can and do go as far as this and farther still.

3. And Jesus put forth his hand, and touched him, saying, I will; be thou clean. And immediately his leprosy was cleansed.

Anyone else would have been defiled by touching a leper, but the healing power in Jesus repelled pollution. He touches us by the finger of His humanity, but He is not thereby defiled. His touch proves His condescension, His sympathy, His fellowship. It was no accidental touch: *Jesus put forth his hand.* Our Lord has come to us by His own act and effort. He was determined to come to us in all our loathsomeness and pollution. After the touch came the words, *I will.* One has well observed that Jesus is never recorded saying, "I will not." He wills, and it is done. *Be thou clean* was the royal word of One conscious of abundant power. What a work, to cleanse a leper! Yet it is easy enough to our King, seeing He is divine, otherwise unbelief would be most reasonable.

With what pleasure Jesus spoke! With what joy the leper heard! With what curiosity the bystanders looked on! They did not have to wait. The miracle followed the word without a moment's delay. The cure was instantaneous. He spoke and it was done. Our King's having left His throne to stand side by side with the leper was the greatest of all miracles, and after that we wonder not that other miracles sprang out of it.

4. And Jesus saith unto him, See thou tell no man; but go thy way, shew thyself to the priest, and offer the gift that Moses commanded, for a testimony unto them.

Our Lord would not increase His own reputation. He sought no honor of men and He did not wish to swell the crowds, which, even now, made it almost impossible for Him to go about His work. He sought usefulness and not fame. It would have been hard for the leper to have held his tongue, but he ought to have done so when bidden. Be it ours to speak, or to be silent, as our Lord requires.

The old law stood and our Lord would have it honored while it lasted. Therefore the healed leper must go to the priest, present his offering, and get from the proper official a certificate of health. Besides, he would thus be bearing witness to the nation that there was One among them who could cure the leprosy. The man was clean and yet he must go to be ceremoniously cleansed. After we have the thing signified by an ordinance, we are not, therefore, to forego the sign, but rather to attend to it with care. How prudent was it on the part of our Lord not to remove ancient regulations till the full time had come for the introduction of the new!

> *5-7. And when Jesus was entered into Capernaum, there came unto him a centurion, beseeching him, and saying, Lord, my servant lieth at home sick of the palsy, grievously tormented. And Jesus saith unto him, I will come and heal him.*

A Gentile approaches our King – a soldier, one of Israel's oppressors – and our Lord receives him with an *I will*, even as He had received the leper. This Roman officer came about his slave-boy. It is good for masters to be concerned for their servants, especially when they are sick. It is best of all when they go to Jesus about their servants, as this centurion did. The boy was at his master's house. He had not packed him off because he was ill. The kind master watched his servant's bed and he sympathetically describes what he had seen. He seeks a cure, but does not prescribe to the Lord how or where He shall work it. In fact, he does not put his request into words, but pleads the case and lets the sorrow speak. That the youth is *grievously tormented* is mentioned as an argument to move our Lord to pity. One does not often see palsy and acute pain united, but the watchful centurion had marked these symptoms, and he pleads them with Jesus. Not merit, but misery, must be our plea with the Savior.

Our Lord needed very little imploring. He promptly said, *I will come and heal him.* Lord, say this to us concerning those for whom we lovingly intercede!

> *8-9. The centurion answered and said, Lord, I am not worthy that thou shouldest come under my roof: but speak the word only, and my servant shall be healed. For I am a man under authority, having soldiers under me: and I say to this man, Go, and he goeth; and to another, Come, and he cometh; and to my servant, Do this, and he doeth it.*

He would not put the Lord Jesus to so much trouble as to come to his house. He felt unworthy to be served at such a cost by such a Lord. He argues that a word will do it all. He was *under authority* himself and thus he had power to exercise authority over others. He believed that the Lord Jesus had a commission also from the supreme power and that this would gird Him with command over all the minor forces of the universe, a command that He could exercise from a distance with a single word. If soldiers would come and go at a centurion's bidding, much more would diseases fly at the word of the Lord Jesus. It was a thoughtful argument, but it was fair and conclusive. May we also know Jesus under authority, Jesus with authority, and ourselves under authority to Jesus! May we also believe in the omnipotence of the divine word and go forth and prove its power in the hearts of men! O Lord, who are our King, display Your royal power!

10. When Jesus heard it, he marvelled, and said to them that followed, Verily I say unto you, I have not found so great faith, no, not in Israel.

Jesus marveled to see any man believe, for men are skeptical by nature. He rejoices to see a far-off one believe, for, alas! the favored hearers are slow to trust Him. He marvels at a soldier, an officer, having so much faith. Jesus did not praise the centurion to his face, but after he spoke, he *said to them that followed.* Avoid flattering young converts. Learn, from what our Lord said, that He looks for faith, that He looks for it among hearers of the Word, that He usually does not find it, but that, when He does, it may be so great as to astonish Him. Great faith may grow where there is little soil, and no faith where everything seems to promise and promote it. Great faith is very dear to the Lord Jesus, but He marvels when He sees it, for it is so rare.

11-12. And I say unto you, That many shall come from the east and the west, and shall sit down with Abraham, and Isaac, and Jacob, in the kingdom of heaven. But the children of the kingdom shall be cast out into outer darkness: there shall be weeping and gnashing of teeth.

Heaven will be filled. If the likely ones will not come, the unlikely ones shall do so. Many beloved ones are there already, a sort of nucleus to which we gather, even as Israel gathered to *Abraham, and Isaac, and Jacob. From the east and the west,* great multitudes shall come, undeterred by distance, and these shall share the same heaven as do the patriarchs of old. How sad to think that the descendants of those patriarchs shall be *cast out* like refuse, thrown behind the wall in the dark, and left in the cold to gnash their teeth in anguish! What a turning of things upside down! The nearest cast out and the furthest made near! How often is this the case! The centurion comes from the camp to Christ and the Israelite goes from the synagogue to hell. The harlot bows at Jesus' feet in repentance, while the self-righteous Pharisee rejects the great salvation. Oh, that this incident may sweetly persuade us to believe greatly and may none of us doubt the power of the incarnate Son of God!

13. And Jesus said unto the centurion, Go thy way; and as thou hast believed, so be it done unto thee. And his servant was healed in the selfsame hour.

In the words, *Go thy way,* we see that, oftentimes, a return to our usual duties and our habitual calm of mind may be the best proof that our faith has recognized the promised blessing. Why should he linger who has obtained all he sought? Rather let him go home and enjoy the fruit of his success in prayer. The Lord often gives in proportion to faith. *As thou hast believed, so be it done unto thee* is a word by which we are allowed to bring our own measure and set the standard of blessing that we would possess. Our Lord spoke the word as the centurion desired. The result was immediate and complete; not only was life spared, but health was also restored. Many a time prolonged prayer is but muttering unbelief, but to go about one's business would be to take the Lord at His word and honor His truthfulness.

Lord, grant me faith enough to go about my business, having prayed the prayer of faith. In the selfsame hour in which I believe You, be pleased to work the miracle I seek.

14. And when Jesus was come into Peter's house, he saw his wife's mother laid, and sick of a fever.

It was a feverish place. Devoutness does not make unsanitary places healthy.

Peter had a wife. Let the so-called successors of Peter remember that fact. His wife's mother had a fever. Holiness does not secure immunity from disease. This mother-in-law was a specially good woman, for she was allowed to live with her son-in-law, and he was anxious to have her restored to health. The Lord Jesus *saw* the sick one, for He was not put away in a back room, and He was not careful to keep away from the contagious disorder. Jesus feared no fever. Our Lord sees all our sick ones and herein lies our hope for their recovery.

15. And he touched her hand, and the fever left her: and she arose, and ministered unto them.

Our Lord was entreated by her friends and therefore took her hand, and by a touch recovered her. The first miracle in this chapter was by a touch, the second by a word, and now this by a touch again. It is all one to Jesus. The cure was instantaneous. It was a very complete cure. We expect to read that the fever left her very weak, but our Lord's cures are always perfect ones. She felt active enough to rise, energetic enough to work, and we need hardly add, grateful enough to wait upon her Physician and all His friends. No proof of recovery from the fever of sin is more sure than the holy earnestness of the healed ones to do works fitting for thankfulness towards Him who has restored them.

16. When the even was come, they brought unto him many that were possessed with devils: and he cast out the spirits with his word, and healed all that were sick.

Our Lord made long days. The setting of the sun was not the setting of His power. Wise persons brought their sick within the circle of His presence as soon as the Sabbath was ended. His power flowed forth at once. He lived in a hospital and it was a hospital of incurables, which contained *many* distressing cases. Yet in no case was He overmatched. He dispossessed the devils who possessed poor men and women, not only calling them out, but also casting them out with a divine violence. As for sicknesses, nothing came amiss to Him. He *healed all that were sick*. The Kingly One battled with legions of foes and readily overcame them all. What were demons or diseases to the omnipotent Lord? His Word is still almighty.

17. That it might be fulfilled which was spoken by Esaias the prophet, saying, Himself took our infirmities, and bore our sicknesses.

His deeds of healing proved His living sympathy with men. Becoming man, He reckoned man's infirmities to be His infirmities. He looked on men's illnesses as if they were His own and did not delay a moment to remove them.

Moreover, the cure cost Him much as to His bodily frame, which was loaded with the burden of human woe. Virtue, as it went forth from Him, made a drain upon His system and thus, while His strength went forth to men, their weaknesses seemed to come back upon Himself. He bowed His back beneath our burden and thus raised it from those shoulders that had been crushed to the earth by it.

O Lord, let me never forget what a brother You are and how surely Your helping us proves that You do truly share our griefs!

18. Now when Jesus saw great multitudes about him, he gave commandment to depart unto the other side.

He ran away from popularity. Having healed all that were sick, the royal Physician sought to begin practice on fresh ground. He saw the crowds becoming dangerous and perhaps too enthusiastic, and so He took ship for the farther shore to be away from their rash acts. Too often we invite the notoriety that our Lord avoided. Is it not because we are swayed by inferior motives, which had no power over Him? We ought not to keep to the side where we get flattery, but we should *depart unto the other side* to begin fresh work. Moreover, *the other side* may be the side that needs us most, and it is right even to leave a multitude that have had their share of privilege to go to a smaller company who have had no time of gracious opportunity.

Lord, command me *to depart unto the other side*! Go with me and I will start at once.

Matthew 8:19-22

Our King Discerning His True Followers

19-20. And a certain scribe came, and said unto him, Master, I will follow thee whithersoever thou goest. And Jesus saith unto him, The foxes have holes, and the birds of the air have nests; but the Son of man hath not where to lay his head.

Was this scribe pleased by what he heard and saw of our Lord? We think so. In a sudden fit of enthusiasm, he calls Him *Master.* He had probably hurried around the shore after Jesus and he declares he will always follow Him, let the Master go where He may. His is an unreserved discipleship that knows no time or place: *I will follow thee whithersoever thou goest.* His was an unasked-for following, for the Lord had not said to him, "Follow Me." It was the best fruit of nature, but not the result of grace. Our King soon tests this loudly expressed loyalty by telling the new convert that he was so poor a master that beasts of the fields and *birds of the air* were better off for lodgings than Himself. If the Leader fared so badly, there was a poor outlook for the follower. How great was the humiliation of our Lord and King! He had no palace and no silken canopy. He who was our Head had nowhere to lay His own head.

Did this scribe have his name inscribed among the poor scholars of a homeless teacher? We do not know. How does it stand in our case? Can we follow a penniless cause? Can we proclaim a despised doctrine?

21. And another of his disciples said unto him, Lord, suffer me first to go and bury my father.

The first man was too fast, the second was too slow. This person was a disciple. Jesus sent him on a mission. He was not ready to start. He must do something else *first.* That something had to do with a dead relative. It was a grave fault to put the sepulcher before the Savior. His father would be sure to be buried by some other member of the family, but no other could obey the command of Christ that this disciple had received. We may leave work that another can do when our Lord appoints us a peculiar personal service. It must be Christ first and father next. Living commands must take precedence over duties to the dead. Soldiers cannot be excused from war on account of domestic claims.

22. But Jesus said unto him, Follow me; and let the dead bury their dead.

Our Lord repeated His command, *Follow me.* Others could *bury the dead.* It was for the disciple to obey His orders. Men who are unrenewed are dead, and they are quite able to attend to such dead business as a funeral. Much of the concerns of politics, party tactics, committee meetings, social reforms, innocent amusements, and so forth may be very suitable, described as burying the dead. Much of this is very necessary, proper, and commendable work, but is still only such a form of business as unregenerate men can do, as well as the disciples of Jesus. Let them do it, but if we are called to preach the gospel, let us give ourselves wholly to our sacred calling. Let not the higher worker entangle himself with what worldlings can do quite as well as he can. *Follow me* is a precept that will need all our powers to carry it out, but by grace we will obey.

Matthew 8:23-27

Our King Ruling the Sea

23. And when he was entered into a ship, his disciples followed him.

They were wise to follow Him and safe in so doing, but they were not therefore secure from trial. In the boat with Jesus is a happy place, but storms may come even when we are there.

24. And, behold, there arose a great tempest in the sea, insomuch that the ship was covered with the waves: but he was asleep.

This inland lake was subject to sudden squalls and tempests, where the wind raged so as to lift the boat fairly out of the water. This was an unusually bad storm. The little ship seemed lost. The wing of the tempest covered it. The comfort was that Christ was in the vessel and His presence covered the boat, as surely as did the waves. Yet the presence of our great Lord will not prevent our being tossed by *a great tempest.*

25. And his disciples came to him, and awoke him, saying, Lord, save us: we perish.

He was not worried. His trust in His great Father was so firm that, rocked in the cradle of the deep, He slept peacefully. Winds howled and waters dashed over Him, but He slept on. His disciples caused Him more anxiety than the storm. They *awoke him* with their cries. They were mistrustful and ready to rebuke Him with indifference. Little faith prayed, *Save us.* Much fear cried, *We perish.* Men in a storm cannot be very select in their language, but they learn to be very earnest and eager. The appeal of these disciples may suit many. Here was reverence for Jesus – *Lord*, an intelligent supplication – *save us*, and an overwhelming argument – *we perish.*

> *26. And he saith unto them, Why are ye fearful, O ye of little faith? Then he arose, and rebuked the winds and the sea; and there was a great calm.*

He spoke to the men first, for they were the most difficult to deal with; wind and sea could be rebuked afterwards. He questions the disciples.

Alas, they had questioned Him in an unworthy sense! There is no reason for our unbelief. That *Why?* is unanswerable. If we are right in having any faith, we must be wrong in having any fear. Little faith, from one point of view, is most precious, but under another aspect, it is most unjustifiable. Why *little faith* in a great God? It is well that it is faith, it is bad that it is little.

See the Lord rise from His hard couch. In royal dignity, He lifts up Himself. A word makes a calm. As it was a great tempest, now He gives *a great calm.* There was nothing little in the whole business, except the disciples' faith. When our Lord rebuked the winds, He did in the best manner also rebuke their unbelief. He has very happy ways of correcting us by the greatness of His mercy to us.

My soul, you know what that *great calm* is. From this point on, exercise a great faith in the great Peacemaker. Be sure to have that faith when you are caught in a great tempest.

> *27. But the men marvelled, saying, What manner of man is this, that even the winds and the sea obey him!*

It was well that they wondered, but it would have been better had they adored. If Christ had been only man, the wonder about Him would have been beyond all wonderment. He was divine, and therefore, to His royal word all nature yielded. This is the end of the wonder of the intellect, but it is the beginning of the worship of the heart. In this case, our glorious King for the moment unveiled His glory and commanded obedience from the most boisterous of the elements. In our own cases, how often have we had to cry out, *What manner of man is this!* How grandly has He brought us through terrible storms! How easily has He calmed the surges of our souls! Blessed be His name! Still *the winds and the sea obey him.*

Matthew 8:28-34

The King Driving Legions before Him

28. And when he was come to the other side into the country of the Gergesenes, there met him two possessed with devils, coming out of the tombs, exceeding fierce, so that no man might pass by that way.

Did they come out to oppose Him? As He steps on the shore, did Satan mean to drive Him back by this double legion of demons? The tombs were Satan's castle. He used the madness of these afflicted men as his weapons of war. They had driven away everybody else; will they stop the advance of the Lord Jesus? They were *exceeding fierce.* Will they fright Him to flight?

29. And, behold, they cried out, saying, What have we to do with thee, Jesus, thou Son of God? art thou come hither to torment us before the time?

This is the old cry: "Mind your own business! Do not interfere with our trade! Let us alone and go elsewhere!" Devils never like to be interfered with. But if devils have nothing to do with Jesus, He has something to do with them. His presence is torment to them. They know that a time is coming when they shall fully receive their hell, but that time seems to be anticipated when the Lord Jesus invades their solitary lurking-place among the tombs. The devils here spoke and compelled the lips of the men thus to plead against themselves. How very like is this to the swearer's case, whose mouth is used to invoke a curse upon himself! The devils acknowledged Him as the *Son of God,* for even they are not so vile as to deny His deity. The demons confessed that He was not under their rule: *What have we to do with thee?* They also expressed their dread of His almighty power and feared the torment they deserved.

30-31. And there was a good way off from them an herd of many swine feeding. So the devils besought him, saying, If thou cast us out, suffer us to go away into the herd of swine.

Jews had no right to be feeding herds of swine, for they were unclean to them. The devils began to tremble before Jesus had said a word, *saying, If thou cast us out.* They cannot bear to go to their own place and so they beg to go into a herd of pigs. Devils would sooner dwell inside swine than be in the presence of Jesus. If they cannot do mischief to men, they would sooner destroy pigs than be without doing mischief. Devils cannot, however, even afflict hogs without permission from Christ. Think of these demons in their pride begging Jesus and begging Him for so small a favor as to be allowed to enter into a herd of swine. Truly the Son of God is King! The laments of a legion of devils admit His sovereignty.

32. And he said unto them, Go. And when they were come out, they went into the herd of swine: and, behold, the whole herd of swine ran violently down a steep place into the sea, and perished in the waters.

Our Lord never wastes words on devils: *He said unto them, Go.* The less we say to bad men the better. One word is enough for such dogs as these tormenting spirits were. The devils soon went from the lunatics to the hogs. From a madman to a beast was a short removal for a foul spirit.

Swine prefer death to wickedness, and if men were not worse than swine, they would be of the same opinion. They run hard whom the devil drives. The devil drives his hogs to a bad market. Those who pursue a downward path without consideration will come to destruction in the end. The swine *perished in the waters,* but the devils are reserved for the judgment of eternal fire. We need not dread the powers of hell. They fly pell-mell before our Lord.

33. And they that kept them fled, and went their ways into the city, and told every thing, and what was befallen to the possessed of the devils.

Well might the swine herds flee! When evil men perish at the last, their wicked pastors will have a hard time with it.

How vividly they told their story! No item was left out! *They told every thing.* Probably all the details were brought out into exaggerated relief. Thus would they excuse their own loss of the swine that they were set to keep but had seen lost before their very eyes. Their employers, the owners of the herd, must have greatly lamented their loss, but they must have trembled as they saw the hand of God in it. What a crushing misfortune for the swine-keepers of Gadara! Who pities them, since their trade was unlawful? The story of the healing of the demoniacs was mentioned by the reporters as a secondary matter, but indeed, it was the central point of the narrative. To some men, souls are secondary to swine. The healing of the two demoniacs added to the wonder and set every ear tingling throughout the city. Yet the result on the people was not what one would have expected.

> 34. *And, behold, the whole city came out to meet Jesus: and when they saw him, they besought him that he would depart out of their coasts.*

A rare occurrence: a whole city meeting Jesus and that city unanimous in their appeal to Him. Alas, it was the unanimity of evil! Here was a whole city at a prayer meeting, praying against their own blessing. Think of having the Lord among them, healing the worst of diseases, and yet entreating Him to go away from them! They would be rid of the one glorious Being who alone could bless them. Horrible was their prayer, but it was heard, and Jesus *depart[ed] out of their coasts.* He will not force His company on any. He will be a welcome guest or He will be gone. What a mercy that our Lord does not hear every prayer of this sort! How would it fare with swearers if their curses were fulfilled?

O Lord, I thank You that You did not go away from me when I, in my unregenerate condition, wished You to let me alone!

Matthew 9

Matthew 9:1-8

The King Continues to Display His Royal Power

1. And he entered into a ship, and passed over, and came into his own city.

Many times He crossed the Sea of Galilee, but this time, more in sadness than in anger, He left a people behind Him who had prayed for Him to depart. He had made Capernaum his own city by the privileges with which He had exalted it. What a name! *His own city.* It was its highest honor that He came sailing into its port, even He who was Lord High Admiral of all seas. Yet the favored city refused Him and knew not its day. May none of us be thus favored and prove thus unworthy!

2. And, behold, they brought to him a man sick of the palsy, lying on a bed: and Jesus seeing their faith said unto the sick of the palsy; Son, be of good cheer; thy sins be forgiven thee.

Here our King displays His power over weakness. The man is sad and paralyzed. The weight of sin is on his conscience and his body is in bonds. Yet he has good friends who band themselves together, and four of them carry him up to the roof of the house where our Lord is preaching, and let him down, in his bed, by ropes. They have faith in Jesus and so has he, and the Lord answers to *their faith* with a cheering word, in which He called him *son.* How sweet a word for a young man and for one so feeble! His mental distress was the hardest to suffer, and our Lord removed it with a word. Perhaps the youth's sin had some connection with his palsy and thus his double distress. None but Jesus could pardon sin, but with a royal word He pronounced effective forgiveness. This He gave first, because it was the greatest blessing, because the evil it removed lies at the root of every other, and because He thus unveiled His majesty and had an opportunity to instruct opposers. How the youth's face must have brightened as he felt the comfort of that effective forgiveness! He could not as yet walk, but he felt happier than tongue could tell: *Thy sins be forgiven thee* is a note that never fails to bring *good cheer* to the saddest heart.

3. And, behold, certain of the scribes said within themselves, This man blasphemeth.

They were afraid to speak out, but *said within themselves.* Each one of these law-writers felt a bitter feeling towards the Lord Jesus, and by their looks they conspired in the charge against Him. They did not call Him *man.* The word is in italics in our version. They did not know what to call Him even in their hearts. They meant *this* – this upstart, this nobody, this strange being, who is so great that we fear Him, so good that we hate Him. They were blaspheming Him by their agnosticism and yet these blasphemers charged the Lord with blasphemy. Yet, supposing our Lord to be only a man, they were right. Pardon of sin is the sole prerogative of God. Who dares to usurp it?

I know that none but God can forgive, yet Jesus has forgiven me and in so doing He did not blaspheme, for He is most truly God.

4. And Jesus knowing their thoughts said, Wherefore think ye evil in your hearts?

He is the great thought-reader. Just now we met with the expression, *seeing their faith* (verse 2), and now we read, *knowing their thoughts.* He puts the questioners to the question. His *whys* and *wherefores* go to the root of the matter. We are responsible for secret thoughts, and the Lord will one day call us to account concerning them. Accusations against Jesus are always unreasonable, and when fairly faced are put to silence. It would be well if many of our Lord's enemies today could be brought to ponder the question, *Wherefore think ye evil in your hearts?* What is the cause of it? What is the good of it? Why not cease from it?

5. For whether is easier, to say, Thy sins be forgiven thee; or to say, Arise, and walk?

He answers their evil thoughts by a question that was to them unanswerable. Surely the two things are equally beyond human power to work. But *to say, Thy sins be forgiven thee* is the easier to all appearance, because no apparent result is expected to follow by which the reality of the speech can be tested. Thousands have pretended to absolve a man from sin, who would not have dared to command a disease to disappear. The difference in merely *saying* is all in favor of the first speech. If we compare the two miracles, it would be long before one could arrive at an answer as to which is the easier, for they are both impossible with men. In some respects, the pardon of sin is the greater work of the two, for its accomplishment requires the whole apparatus of incarnation and atonement. Our Lord worked both miracles and thus confirmed His claim of power by a visible sign that none could question.

He that can pardon my soul can heal my body, for that would seem to be the easier of the two deeds of mercy. I may bring both forms of malady to Jesus and He will deal with them. Lord, heal my spirit and cure my flesh! Yes, You will do this work most effectively by raising my body incorruptible as Your own.

6. But that ye may know that the Son of man hath power on earth to forgive sins, (then saith he to the sick of the palsy,) Arise, take up thy bed, and go unto thine house.

The second part of the miracle was for the silencing of those muttering scribes: *That ye may know.* Did they ever come to this knowledge? The case was made clear for them, but they would not see it. Jesus, *the Son of man,* was yet *on earth,* but in His lowly condition He had authority and power to forgive sins against God, for He was God. He would prove that He had *power on earth* by healing the paralytic. By exerting what they thought was the greater power, He would prove His possession of the less. He told the man, *Arise,* or stir himself up. He further said, *take up thy bed,* or roll up your mat and lift it to your shoulders. Thus would the obedient patient, by the free use of his limbs, prove himself to be wholly recovered. This was a great word to speak, but he, who had already received pardon from our Lord's lips, felt no difficulty in believing it, and he found his faith justified. If sin be forgiven, nothing is impossible. Surely it follows that if Jesus had power on earth to forgive sins, He can abundantly pardon now that we see Him as the Son of God, enthroned in heaven.

7. And he arose, and departed to his house.

His limbs had received strength and he did what Jesus told him do at once. Faith grasped the Savior's command and obeyed it. There was no delay, no deviation from orders, no failure in the performance. It must have seemed hard to leave one to whom he owed so much and go at once to the retreat of *his house,* but he did as he was bidden and in that respect he is an example to us all. He did not go to the temple with the Sacramentarian, nor to the theater with the man of the world. He went to his home. His palsy had made his house sad and now his healing would cheer his family. A man's restoration by grace is best seen in his own house. Lord, let it be seen in mine. Whether I carry my bed or my bed carries me, may I do all to Your glory!

8. But when the multitude saw it, they marvelled, and glorified God, which had given such power unto men.

It was openly seen by *the multitude.* Crowds heard of the marvel. It was town talk. It was evidently no delusion. The hopelessly palsied had been assuredly healed, for he had carried off his mattress and had gone home. The common people did not complain, but they wondered and then they trembled, and were overawed, and driven to the adoration of God. So far so good, but it did not go far enough, nor last long enough. Men may see, marvel, and even in words *glorify God,* and yet may not accept His Son as their Lord. The multitudes had common sense enough to give the glory of such a work to God and to be struck with surprise that He should *give such power unto men.* Evidently they viewed Jesus as a man on whom God had bestowed special gifts, a prophet who had received miraculous power, and used it on the behalf of men. They went as far as they knew. We wish we could say the same of many who, in this day, refuse to give our Lord the divine honors that He claims and abundantly deserves. If *the Son of man* (verse 6) had all this power, how can we limit Him as the Son of God? Let us not leave the narrative till we have glorified God for all the many ways in which He gives power to those who have no strength, raises believers out of the paralysis of sin, and makes them blessings to others.

Matthew 9:9-13

The Grace of the Kingdom

9. And as Jesus passed forth from thence, he saw a man, named Matthew, sitting at the receipt of custom: and he saith unto him, Follow me. And he arose, and followed him.

Thus our evangelist speaks of himself as *a man, named Matthew.* He says that the Lord *saw* him. What a seeing is meant here! Reader, may the Lord see you, whatever your name may be! Was Matthew at all like the man *sick of the palsy*? Does he mention his conversion here to suggest a parallel? His old name had been Levi. Was Matthew his new name or was it that which he had taken when he had degraded himself into a publican? At any rate, it is a beautiful name, meaning "given." He was a gift of Jehovah. To us he has been a true Theodore, which means "gift of God," by being the author of this Gospel. He was an official of a kingdom and therefore all the more fit to write this *gospel of the kingdom* (Matthew 4:23). He was at this time busy *taking,* but he was called to a work that is essentially *giving.* He was sitting in one place *at the receipt of custom,* but he was now to go about with his Lord doing good. Two words sufficed for his conversion and obedience: *Follow me.* They are very full and pregnant words. Like the palsied man, he did precisely what he was told to do: *He arose, and followed him.* Matthew describes his own conduct from personal knowledge, but he does not use a superfluous word. He acted with great decision and promptness. No doubt he saw his accounts settled, or it may be, he had just sent them in and he could leave at once without causing confusion in the customhouse. At any rate, he did there and then follow Jesus as a sheep follows its shepherd.

Lord, let my obedience towards You be as the echo to the voice.

10-12. And it came to pass, as Jesus sat at meat in the house, behold, many publicans and sinners came and sat down with him and his disciples. And when the Pharisees saw it, they said unto his disciples, Why eateth your Master with publicans and sinners? But when Jesus heard that, he said unto them, They that be whole need not a physician, but they that are sick.

In Matthew's house, the Savior *sat at meat.* The new convert most naturally called in his old friends so that they might have the advantage of our Lord's teaching. They would come to a supper more readily than to a sermon, and so he gave them a feast, and thus attracted them to the place where Jesus was. We may use all lawful means to bring others under the sound of the Word. A lot of the riffraff came. *Sinners* by occupation, as well as sinners by character, ventured in to the publican's house and dared to sit *with him and his disciples,* as if they had been members of his society. Probably they had been Matthew's favorable companions, and now he wished them to become his brothers in Christ.

Our Lord willingly accepted Matthew's hospitality, for He desired to do good to those who most needed to be uplifted. He allowed persons of ill-fame to *sit down with him and his disciples.* Here was a fine opportunity for the sneering Pharisees. They insinuated that the Lord Jesus could be but a sorry person, since He drew such a rabble around Him and even allowed them to be His table companions. They were very careful of their company when anyone saw them, for they thought that their superior holiness would be debased by allowing sinners to sit with them, and now they have a handy stone to throw at Jesus while He eats *with publicans and sinners.*

The Pharisees were cowardly enough to speak their complaint *unto his disciples* rather than to the Master, but the Leader put Himself in the front and soon baffled the adversaries. His reasoning was overwhelming and His justification ample. Where should a physician be but among the sick? Who should come to a doctor's house but those who are diseased? Thus our Lord was more than justified in being the center to which the morally sick should gather for their spiritual healing.

Lord, grant that if ever I am found in the company of sinners, it may be with the purpose of healing them, and may I never become myself infected with their disease!

13. But go ye and learn what that meaneth, I will have mercy, and not sacrifice: for I am not come to call the righteous, but sinners to repentance.

Our Lord, having gloriously defended Himself from the insinuations of the proud Pharisees, now carries the war into the enemies' territory. He says to them, *Go ye and learn,* and this alone would be distasteful to men who thought they knew everything already. They were to learn *the meaning* of a Scripture in Hosea 6:6 (*For I desired mercy, and not sacrifice; and the knowledge of God more than burnt offerings*), and this would teach them that to *have mercy* upon sinners is a work more pleasing to God than the presenting of expensive sacrifices or the performing of religious exercises. They would learn that He would rather do mercy Himself and have them do mercy to others, than accept their most formal observances.

The Lord Jesus also gave them a clear word as to His object in coming among men. He came not to be served by the good, but to save the evil. He had come to call to repentance those who needed repentance and not those just ones who required no correction, if such there were. This was a very just satire upon the Pharisees' self-opinionated notions, but at the same time, it was, and is, and forever will be a grand consolation for those who acknowledge their guilt. Our Savior King has come to save real sinners. He deals not with our merits, but with our demerits. There would be no need to save us if we were not lost. The Son of God does no unnecessary work, but to those who need repentance He has come to bring it.

Lord, I am one who needs Your call, for surely if anyone needs to repent, I am that one. Call me with Your effective call. *Turn thou me, and I shall be turned* (Jeremiah 31:18).

Matthew 9:14-17

The Joy of the Kingdom

14. Then came to him the disciples of John, saying, Why do we and the Pharisees fast oft, but thy disciples fast not?

The disciples of John, like their leader, were ascetics and therefore, like *the Pharisees,* abounded in fasts. They were scandalized because the disciples of Jesus were seen at feasts and were not known to fast. They did not murmur in secret like the scribes, but had the matter out face-to-face. They *came to Him.* Like honest friends, who felt hurt, they came to the headquarters and asked the Lord Himself. This open expression prevented later dissension and it was therefore wise. When good men differ, it is well to refer the matter to the Lord Himself. To agree to differ may be all very well, but to have the difference removed by explanation is far better.

> *15. And Jesus said unto them, Can the children of the bridechamber mourn, as long as the bridegroom is with them? but the days will come, when the bridegroom shall be taken from them, and then shall they fast.*

Here our Lord answered the second part of their inquiry. The first part they must answer on their own account. They knew, or ought to have known, why they and the Pharisees fasted. Why His disciples did *not* fast He proceeds to explain. He is *the Bridegroom* who came to woo and win His bride. Those who followed Him were the guests, the Bridegroom's best men and attendants. It was for them to rejoice while the Bridegroom headed their company, for sorrow is not suitable for wedding feasts. Our Lord is that Bridegroom of whom Solomon sang in the Song of Solomon, and we who enjoy His fellowship are one with Him in His joy. Why should we fast while He is near? Can we allow little things to kill our great joy? Can we, in consistency with reason and in harmony with respect for our Lord, *mourn as long as the Bridegroom is with us?*

But Jesus was to go away. He says Himself, *The Bridegroom shall be taken from them.* Here first He speaks about His death. Did His disciples note the warning word? When their Beloved was gone, they would have enough fasting. How true was this! Sorrows crowded in upon them when He was gone. It is the same with us. Our Lord is our joy. His presence makes our banquet. His absence is our fast, black and bitter. All ritualistic fasting is the husk. The reality of fasting is known only to the child of the bridechamber when his Lord is no more with him. This is fasting indeed, as some of us know full well.

There is no wedding without a bridegroom, no delight without Jesus. In His presence is fullness of joy. In His absence is depth of misery. Let but the heart rest in His love and it desires nothing more. Take away a sense of His love from the soul, and it is dark, empty, and near unto death.

16. No man putteth a piece of new cloth unto an old garment, for that which is put in to fill it up taketh from the garment, and the rent is made worse.

Jesus came not to repair Israel's worn clothes, but to bring new robes. Even if a mere mending had been aimed at, it could not have been effected through His disciples copying old ways. *New cloth* that has been unshrunk is not fit to be used as a patch to mend *an old garment,* fully shrunk by many washings. His disciples must act consistently and not join untimely fasting to their enjoyment of His company. They were not the kind of persons to repair the old religion of Judaism, which had become worn out. They were *new* men, unshrunk by the spirit of tradition, and to try to enclose them within the clothes of legal ritualistic religion would not tend to unity, but the reverse. Genuine believers had better not attempt fellowship with ceremonialists. They will soon find themselves out of place. Jesus did not come to patch up our old outward religiousness, but to make a new robe of righteousness for us. All attempts to add the gospel to legalism will only make the tear worse. It may be added that rash attempts to unite the various churches by comprehending all their errors within the pale of supposed truth, will only increase the present lamentable divisions and postpone real unity to a distant day.

17. Neither do men put new wine into old bottles: else the bottles break, and the wine runneth out, and the bottles perish: but they put new wine into new bottles, and both are preserved.

His teaching and spirit could not be associated with the Pharisaic order of things. Judaism in its degenerate condition was an old skin bottle that had seen its day, and our Lord would not pour the *new wine* of the kingdom of heaven into it. John's disciples were trying to emulate the Pharisees and make common cause with them to save the old church. Jesus would have nothing to do with this project. He would have a new church for His new doctrine and for His new spirit. There was to be no amalgamation. Christianity was not to be an outgrowth of rabbinism. There was to be a severance between Jesus and the scribes and their school of thought, for He who had come was resolved to make all things new. There is rare teaching here and guidance for the present crisis. Compromises are often proposed, and we have good people, like John's disciples, who would have us conform to what they think to be good in things established, but we had better act consistently and begin *de novo* ("anew"). The old cloth will always be tearing, and tearing all the worse because of our new pieces; therefore, let us leave the old garment to those who prefer antiquity to truth.

The mixing of wedding feasts and funeral fasts, the patching of old cloth with pieces unfurled and unshrunk, and the putting of new wine into old bottles are all pictures of those mixtures and compromises that cannot, in the nature of things, serve any good and lasting purpose. If we follow the rejoicing Bridegroom, let us not try to keep in with the fasting Pharisees or the Sacramentarian legalists of the day. Let the scientific doubters also go, for faith is not of their mind. Let us be done with the doubts that make us fast, and let us hold high festivity while the Bridegroom is still with us by His Spirit.

We would follow nothing beside Jesus, Jesus crucified.

Matthew 9:18-26

The King's Dominion over Disease and Death

18-19. While he spake these things unto them, behold, there came a certain ruler, and worshipped him, saying, My daughter is even now dead: but come and lay thy hand upon her, and she shall live. And Jesus arose, and followed him, and so did his disciples.

Our Lord had better work to do than to be talking about meats and drinks, feastings and fastings. He is soon clear of that debate. The battle of life and death was raging and He was needed in the fray.

Sorrow comes even to the families of the excellent of the earth. *A certain ruler* of the synagogue and a believer in Jesus has such sickness come upon his daughter that she is at death's door and is probably by this time actually dead. But the father has a grand faith. Even if she be dead, Jesus can restore her with a touch. Oh, that He would but come! He worships the Lord and pleads with Him, *Come and lay thy hand upon her, and she shall live.* Have we such faith as this? After centuries of manifestation, is Jesus as well trusted as in the days of His flesh? Have we not those among us who have not yet learned the happy blend that we see in the ruler's conduct? He came to Jesus, he worshipped Him, he prayed to Him, he trusted in Him.

Our King, in whom is vested the power of life and death, yields at once to the petition of faith and sets out for the ruler's house. The Lord *follows* believers, for believers follow their Lord. Such is the order of verse 19. Jesus does as we pray and we follow as He leads. The Preacher steps down from His pulpit and becomes a visiting Surgeon, taking His rounds. From discussing church questions, our great Rabbi very readily turns aside to go and see a sick, no, a dead girl. He is more at home in doing good than in anything else.

> *20-21. And, behold, a woman, which was diseased with an issue of blood twelve years, came behind him, and touched the hem of his garment: for she said within herself, If I may but touch his garment, I shall be whole.*

This is an incident on the road, a wonder by the way. While the Lord is moving towards the chamber of the ruler's dying daughter, He works a miracle without a word. He was intent on His plan to raise a girl, but without planning it, He cures an older woman. The very spillings and overflowings of Christ's power are precious.

Note the word *behold.* Here we have a notable circumstance. This afflicted woman had suffered from a weakening hemorrhage for *twelve years,* and had found no cure, but now she beheld the great Miracle Worker and with a timid courage she pushed into the crowd, and *touched the hem of his garment.* Great fear kept her from facing Him. Great faith led her to believe that a touch of His robe *behind him* would cure her. She was ignorant enough to think that healing went from Him unconsciously, but yet her faith lived despite her ignorance, and triumphed despite her bashfulness. It was her own idea to make a dash for it and steal a cure. *She said within herself.* It was her wisdom that at once she carried out her resolve. Poor soul! It was her only chance and she would not lose it. It happened that our Lord's garment was drawn backward by the throng, and she was able with her finger to reach its hem. She believed that this would be enough and so it proved. Oh, that we were as eager to be saved as she was to be healed! Oh, that we had such confidence in Jesus as to be sure that if we come into contact with Him, even by the least promise and the smallest faith, He can and will save us!

My soul, when you are in urgent need, be brave to come near unto your Lord, for if a touch of His garment will heal, what virtue must lie in His own self!

> *22. But Jesus turned him about, and when he saw her, he said, Daughter, be of good comfort; thy faith hath made thee whole. And the woman was made whole from that hour.*

We have not all the story here. It will be well to read it in Mark 5 and Luke 8. Jesus knew all that was going on behind Him. If His back be towards us now, it need not always be, for He *turned him about.* Even when fear would hide from Jesus, He spies out the trembling one. His eye found her speedily, for He knew where to look. *He saw her.* His voice cheered her with joyful tones of acceptance. He did not chide the blundering of her ignorance, but He commended the bravery of her faith and consoled her trembling heart. A piece of fringe and a finger sufficed to form a contact between a believing sufferer and an almighty Savior. Along that line faith sent its message and love returned the answer. She *was made whole,* and she knew it, but she feared when she was found out lest she should lose the blessing and earn a curse. This fear soon vanished. Jesus called her *daughter.* He fathered her because He had created faith in her. He gave her *good comfort* because she had good faith. It was His garment that she touched, but it was *her faith* that had touched it; therefore, our Lord said, *Thy faith hath made thee whole,* and thus He put the crown upon the head of her faith, because her faith had already set the crown on His head. The moment we touch Jesus, we are *made whole,* yes, *from that hour.* May we touch Him now and may this hour be as memorable to us as that hour was to her!

> *23-24. And when Jesus came into the ruler's house, and saw the minstrels*

and the people making a noise, he said unto them, Give place: for the maid is not dead, but sleepeth. And they laughed him to scorn.

The funeral wailing had already begun. *The minstrels* had commenced their hideous discords. Mistrustful friends are eager to bury us before the due time, and we are ourselves too apt to fall into the same error about others. Unbelief calls in the undertakers and the hired mourners to bury those who will yet live for years. We give over to hopelessness those whom Jesus will save, or we begin *making a noise* where a gracious, silent work would be far better.

Jesus will have the death-music quieted, for it is premature and even false in its significance. He says to the minstrels, *Give place.* Many things have to give place when Jesus comes on the scene, and He takes care that they shall give place, for He puts them out of the room. To Him the maid is asleep rather than dead, for He is about to call her back to life. He sees the future as well as the present, and to Him in that light, *the maid is not dead, but sleepeth.* The Lord Jesus wants not pipers, flute players, and wailers. His own still voice is more fit for work in the death chamber with a young girl. Jesus is going to do wonders, and the hired performances of those who mimic woe are not in tune with that.

When Jesus tells the hired performers that there will be no need to proceed with the funeral, for the girl will live, they answer with scoffs, for they are sure that she is dead. It is a shameful thing to laugh at Christ. Yet He *endured such contradiction of sinners against himself* (Hebrews 12:3), and was not angry. We need not be dismayed when we are ridiculed, for *they laughed him to scorn.* Nor may we stop our working because of derision, for Jesus went on with His resurrection work despite the mockers.

25. But when the people were put forth, he went in, and took her by the hand, and the maid arose.

It was not fitting that a crude throng should behold the majestic mystery of resurrection. They must be *put forth.* Moreover, the hideous noise of the funeral wailers was not a fit accompaniment to the Savior's word of power. The people were turned out and then the Lord *went in* to work His miracle. He loves to work quietly. There are directions in modern church life in which noise and popular excitement will have to come to an end before much is done by the Lord.

When we read, *he took her by the hand*, it reminds us of His touching Peter's wife's mother. He shows a sacred familiarity with those whom He saves. He is not said in this Gospel to have spoken, and thus the contrast between empty noise and His mighty silence is brought out clearly. Life was gone from the maiden, but the result was the same as in the case of Peter's relative who was still alive: she *arose*. How much had taken place before a dead girl could rise! This is the first case of resurrection by our Lord. It was that of one who had but just died, and it is typical of the giving of spiritual life to persons who have not yet come to the stage of corruption that necessitates carrying them out, like the widow's son, or of actual decay, which has led to burial, as in the case of Lazarus. In each case, the miracle was the same, but the surroundings greatly differed, so that the instruction varied.

Lord, take our dear young children by the hand and raise them up to everlasting life while they are children!

26. And the fame hereof went abroad into all that land.

The news of the raising of the dead was sure to spread, especially since it was the daughter of the ruler of the synagogue. Where new life is bestowed, there will be no fear of its being unobserved. Jesus will have *fame* if we have life, and we should take care that it is so.

Matthew 9:27-31

The King's Touch Healing the Blind

27. And when Jesus departed thence, two blind men followed him, crying, and saying, Thou son of David, have mercy on us.

No sooner does Jesus move, than fresh candidates for His bounty appear. The blind seek sight from Him. Two sightless men had become companions in affliction. They may have been father and son. They were in downright earnest, for they *followed him, crying, and saying, have mercy on us.*

Persevering, vehement, yet intelligent was their appeal. They were of one mind in reference to Jesus and therefore they went one way and used one prayer, to one and the same person. Our Lord is here called by His royal name, *Thou son of David.* Even the blind could see that He was a king's son. As son of David, He is entreated to show mercy and act according to His royal nature. It is mercy that gives us our faculties, and mercy alone can restore them.

This prayer suits us when we perceive our own darkness of mind. When we cannot see our way into truth, let us appeal to the Lord for gracious instruction, ever remembering that we have no claim except that which originates in His mercy.

> 28. *And when he was come into the house, the blind men came to him: and Jesus saith unto them, Believe ye that I am able to do this? They said unto him, Yea, Lord.*

They were most eager for the help. They gave Him no leisure. They pressed *into the house* where He had neither privacy nor rest. They *came to him,* even to Jesus Himself. The Lord would have them express their faith, and so He makes inquiry of them as to what they believe about Him. Jesus makes no inquiry about their eyes, but only about their faith. This is ever the vital point. They could not see, but they could believe, and they did so. They had a specific faith as to the matter about which they prayed, for our Lord put it plainly: *Believe ye that I am able to do this?* They had also a clear view of the character of Him to whom they made an appeal, for they had already styled Him, *son of David,* and now they called Him *Lord.*

> 29. *Then touched he their eyes, saying, According to your faith be it unto you.*

Again, He arouses their faith and this time He throws the whole responsibility upon their confidence in Him: *According to your faith be it unto you.* He touched them with His hand, but they must also touch Him with their faith. The word of power in the last sentence is one upon which He acts so continually that we may call it, as to many blessings, a rule of the kingdom. We have the measuring of our own mercies; our faith obtains less or more according to its own capacity to receive. Had these men been mere pretenders to faith, they would have remained blind. If we will not in absolute truth trust our Lord, we shall die in our sins.

30. And their eyes were opened; and Jesus straitly charged them, saying, See that no man know it.

They both saw. The double miracle was worked at the same moment. Comrades in the dark, they are now companions in the light. It was unusual that for two souls there should thus be one destiny! It was a peculiar double fact and deserved to be made widely known, but our Lord had wise reasons for requiring silence. He *straitly charged them.* He left them no option. He demanded complete silence. He that opened their eyes closed their mouths. Jesus did not desire fame, He wanted less crowding. He wished to avoid excitement and therefore He was explicit and peremptory in His order, *See that no man know it.*

31. But they, when they were departed, spread abroad his fame in all that country.

They most industriously published what they were bidden to conceal, till *all that country* rang with the news. In this, they erred greatly and probably caused the Savior so much inconvenience by the pressure of the crowd that He had to remove Himself from the town. We may not hope that we are doing right if we disobey our Lord. However natural disobedience may appear to be, it is disobedience, and it must not be excused. Even if the results turned out to be advantageous, it would not make it right to break the command of our Lord. Silence is more than golden when our King commands it. He does not seek applause, *nor causes his voice to be heard in the street* (Isaiah 42:2), that He may be known to be doing a great work. His followers do well to copy His example.

We do not wonder that our Lord's name became famous when there were such persons to advertise it. How earnestly and eloquently would the two formerly blind men tell the story of how He opened their eyes! We are not forbidden, but exhorted, to make known the wonders of His grace. Let us not fail in this natural, this necessary, this useful duty. More and more let us *spread abroad his fame.*

Matthew 9:32-35

The King and Those Possessed with Devils

32. As they went out, behold, they brought to him a dumb man possessed with a devil.

As a pair of patients leave the surgery, another poor creature comes in.

Note the *behold.* The case is striking. He comes not freely or of his own accord: *They brought* him. Thus should we bring men to Jesus. He does not cry for help, for he is *a dumb man.* Let us open our months for the dumb. He is not himself, but he is *possessed with a devil.* Poor creature! Will anything be done for him?

33. And when the devil was cast out, the dumb spake: and the multitudes marvelled, saying, It was never so seen in Israel.

Our Lord does not deal with the symptoms, but with the source of the disorder, even with the evil spirit. *The devil was cast out,* and it is mentioned as if that were a matter of course when Jesus came on the scene. The devil had silenced the man, and so, when the Evil One was gone, *the dumb spake.* How we would like to know what he said! Whatever he said it matters not. The wonder was that he could say anything. The people confessed that this was a wonder quite unprecedented, and in this they only said the truth: *It was never so seen in Israel.* Jesus is great at surprises. He has novelties of gracious power. The people were quick to express their admiration, yet we see very little trace of their believing in our Lord's mission. It is a small thing to marvel, but a great thing to believe.

O Lord, give the people around us the ability to see such revivals and conversions as they have never known before!

34. But the Pharisees said, He casteth out devils through the prince of the devils.

Of course, they had some bitter sentence ready. Nothing was too bad for them to say of Jesus. They were hard-pressed when they took to this statement, which our Lord in another place so easily answered. They hinted that such power over demons must have come to Him through an unholy compact with *the prince of the devils.* Surely this was going very near to the unpardonable sin.

35. And Jesus went about all the cities and villages, teaching in their synagogues, and preaching the gospel of the kingdom, and healing every sickness and every disease among the people.

This was His answer to the blasphemous slanders of the Pharisees. A glorious reply it was. Let us answer defamation by greater zeal in doing good.

Small places were not despised by our Lord. He went about the *villages* as well as the *cities.* Village devotion is of the utmost importance and has a close relation to city life. Jesus turned old institutions to good account. The *synagogues* became His seminaries. Threefold was His ministry – expounding the old, proclaiming the new, healing the diseased.

Observe the repetition of the word *every* as showing the breadth of His healing power. All this stood in relation to His royalty, for it was *the gospel of the kingdom* that He proclaimed. Our Lord was *the Great Itinerant. Jesus went about preaching and healing.* His was a medical mission as well as an evangelistic tour. Happy are people who have Jesus among them! Oh, that we might now see more of His working among our own people!

Matthew 9:36-38

The King Pitying the Multitudes

36. But when he saw the multitudes, he was moved with compassion on them, because they fainted, and were scattered abroad, as sheep having no shepherd.

A great crowd is a demand upon compassion, for it suggests so much sin and need. In this case, the great need was instruction, *because they fainted* for lack of comfort. They *were scattered abroad* for lack of guidance. They were eager to learn, but they had no fit teachers. *Sheep having no shepherd* are in a bad situation. Unfed, unfolded, unguarded – what will become of them? Our Lord was stirred with a feeling that agitated

His inmost soul. *He was moved with compassion.* What He saw affected not His eye only, but also His heart. He was overcome by sympathy. His whole frame was stirred with an emotion that put every faculty into forceful movement. He is even now affected towards our people in the same manner. *He* is moved with compassion if *we* are not.

> *37-38. Then saith he unto his disciples, The harvest truly is plenteous, but the labourers are few; pray ye therefore the Lord of the harvest, that he will send forth labourers into his harvest.*

His heavy heart sought solace among *his disciples,* and He spoke to them. He mourned the scantiness of workers. Pretenders were many, but real *labourers* in the harvest were few. The sheaves were spoiling. The crowds were ready to be taught, even as ripe wheat is ready for the sickle, but there were few to instruct them, and where could more teaching men be found?

God only can thrust out or *send forth labourers.* Man-made ministers are useless. Still are the fields encumbered with gentlemen who cannot use the sickle. Still the real ingatherers are few and far between. Where are the instructive, soul-winning ministries? Where are those who labor in birth for their hearers' salvation? Let us plead with the Lord of the harvest to care for His own harvest and send out His own men. May many a true heart be moved by the question, *Whom shall I send, and who will go for us?* and to answer, *Here am I; send me* (Isaiah 6:8).

Matthew 10

Matthew 10:1-15

The King Commissioning His Officers

1. And when he had called unto him his twelve disciples, he gave them power against unclean spirits, to cast them out, and to heal all manner of sickness and all manner of disease.

See the way of making apostles. They were first *disciples* and afterwards teachers of others. They were specially His and then they were given to be a blessing to men. They were *called unto him* and thus their higher call came to them. In the presence of their Lord, they received their equipment, and *he gave them power.* Is that so with us in our own special duty? Let us come to Him that we may be clothed with His authority and girded with His strength.

Their power was miraculous, but it was an imitation of their Lord's, and the words applied to it are very much the same as we have seen in use about His miracles of healing. The twelve were made to represent their Lord. We, too, may be enabled to do what Jesus did among men. Oh, for such an endowment!

2. Now the names of the twelve apostles are these; The first, Simon, who is called Peter, and Andrew his brother; James the son of Zebedee, and John his brother.

The Holy Spirit does not object to truthful statistics. There were *twelve apostles.* This was a complete number, neither too many nor too few, and a number that linked the spiritual Israel with the nation that had typified it. The Holy Spirit has no love for the anonymous or for the use of initials, as some have in these days. He gives the names, and why not? Order is observed in this muster roll. *The first,* for he generally put himself first and was by his energy and ability most fittingly the leader, *Simon, who is called Peter, a stone* (John 1:42), and a very solid stone he came to be. With him is *Andrew his [manly] brother.* It is well when brothers in the flesh are brothers in spirit. Then come *James and John,* the two *sons of thunder* (Mark 3:17), one of them so early to be a martyr, the other so inexpressibly dear to the Lord Jesus.

3. Philip, and Bartholomew; Thomas, and Matthew the publican: James the son of Alphaeus, and Lebbaeus, whose surname was Thaddaeus.

It seems probable that *Bartholomew* is Nathanael, whom *Philip* led to Jesus. They are well put together. Bartholomew is never mentioned without an *and.* He was a kind of man to work with other people. It is also likely that *Lebbaeus* is Jude, or *Judas . . . not Iscariot* (John 14:22). There may have been some link between him and James. A man may have an alias and yet not be an alien. Observe how *Matthew* keeps us in mind that he had been a *publican.* With holy gratitude, he thus records his former estate that the grace that called him might be the more conspicuous. *Thomas* was as truly called by the Lord as any of them, though he was one whose mind entertained distressing questions.

4. Simon the Canaanite, and Judas Iscariot, who also betrayed him.

Thus they go two and two, till the traitor brings up the rear. *Simon the Zealot* is cooled down by the calculating prudence of *Judas Iscariot.* Judas was probably the best financier of the company, and he comes at the end with the bag. This quality rendered him useful, but it was perverted to his ruin, for he sold his Master for silver. What a description to follow a name – *who also betrayed him.* God grant it may never be set after the name of any one of us! The apostolic number fitly represents the twelve tribes of Israel, and for practical purposes the twelve form a workable band of leaders, a sufficient jury, and a competent company of witnesses.

5-6. These twelve Jesus sent forth, and commanded them, saying, Go not into the way of the Gentiles, and into any city of the Samaritans enter ye not: but go rather to the lost sheep of the house of Israel.

This was a mission to the Jews only, meant for the general arousing of the chosen nation. It is an example of a special mission, and it gives authority for missions to special characters, but it must not be made into an example by which the Lord is supposed to prescribe a cast-iron rule for all missions. The people at that time were favorably disposed to our Lord, and thus His apostles might expect treatment of a more generous kind than can be looked for in these times. Certain of these regulations were altered on a subsequent mission, when the people were less favorably disposed. This was a mission from Israel to *Israel.* It was not for *the Gentiles,* but it was to be strictly confined to *the house of Israel.* Even the people most like the Jews were not to be visited: *Into any city of the Samaritans enter ye not.* It was a search for *the lost sheep of the house of Israel,* in the pastures near the fold. We may occasionally have class-services for workingmen, etc., but the standing orders are not so, but rather, *Go ye into all the world, and preach the gospel to every creature* (Mark 16:15).

7. And as ye go, preach, saying, The kingdom of heaven is at hand.

Their first work was proclaiming the coming kingdom and preparing the way for the coming King. Those Israelites who were willing might become subjects of this heavenly kingdom and therefore were they informed of its near approach.

8. Heal the sick, cleanse the lepers, raise the dead, cast out devils: freely ye have received, freely give.

Having ministered to souls, they were to bless the bodies of men and thus they would confirm their message by their miracles. These deeds of mercy are on the ascending scale – note the steps. All was to be done without fee or reward. Their powers had not been purchased. Their miracles were not to be sold.

9-10. Provide neither gold, nor silver, nor brass in your purses, nor scrip for your journey, neither two coats, neither shoes, nor yet staves: for the workman is worthy of his meat.

They would not need to pay for food or lodging. The people would entertain them freely and therefore they required no form of money, not even a copper coin. They did not need to carry a wallet, for meals would be generously offered them by those whom they instructed and healed. They were not to load themselves with extra clothing, for if the weather should require it, the people would supply it. Even if their shoes wore out, their hearers would see them shod. When a ministry is really acceptable, the preacher will not be left to suffer lack as to the absolute necessities of life. They needed not even wait to find a staff, for if one was required and they set off without it, one would be given. Among a willing people, such a mission is not only possible, but it is also in the highest degree suitable. It is but right and just that people should support materially those who minister to them spiritually, and it is right that plans should be adopted that cast this duty upon them, as in this case. The preacher is to preach freely, but those who are benefited are also freely to find meat for him. Such a mission as this is not a mission to the heathen in any sense. Its methods are good for itself, but they would not be possible among hostile tribes. In the case of work among opponents, our Lord's command under other circumstances is to be followed. See Luke 22:36: *He that hath a purse, let him take it.* Different modes of procedure are to be adopted at different times. Oh, that some of our very spiritual brethren had a little common sense! We offer the prayer with very faint heart.

11. And into whatsoever city or town ye shall enter, enquire who in it is worthy; and there abide till ye go thence.

Seek out people fit to be associated with you in holy service. Whatever their circumstances may be, regard chiefly their character. For the best work, seek out the best men. Do not compromise your Master by lodging with persons of evil repute. But do not shift your quarters, or run from one to another, lest you seem as mere beggars, going from door to door. Keep to those good people with whom your mission begins. It may be that richer people will turn up, but never forget the *worthy* men and women who first entertained you. Wise rules are these. This is not the method to be followed among the heathen, where none can be called *worthy*. There we seek the sinful and feel ourselves sent to the most degraded.

12. And when ye come into an house, salute it.

Say, *Peace be to this house* (Luke 10:5). Be very courteous openly and very benevolent inwardly. You come *as* a benediction, so come *with* a benediction. We ought never to enter a house without wishing it good, nor to leave it without having endeavored to make it better.

13. And if the house be worthy, let your peace come upon it: but if it be not worthy, let your peace return to you.

Think well of all till they prove by their conduct that your good opinion is an error. Bless the house, and if it be *worthy,* the Lord will make your blessing effective, and peace shall dwell there, but if the house be *not worthy,* the blessing shall, by your Lord's ordinance, *return to you,* and that will enable you to bear the rebuff without being discouraged. *We* cannot judge of worthiness, but *the Lord* will do so. We are to hope well of all. We shall get good even if we fail to do good. If the failure be through no fault of ours, it will be no failure to us.

14. And whosoever shall not receive you, nor hear your words, when ye depart out of that house or city, shake off the dust of your feet.

Disclaim all fellowship with those who will not have fellowship with your Lord. Be not angry. Do not denounce with bitterness. Just *shake off the dust of your feet,* and go elsewhere. Don't depart in order to rail at the people in private, but let them know that you left them because they refused your message. Do this openly and in the most solemn and instructive manner, hoping that your departing act may be remembered. It is to be feared that we treat rejectors of Christ in a sadly tolerating manner and do not hold up their rejection of our King to the loathing it deserves. We ought to let unrepentant sinners know that we consider them out of our fellowship. If they will not hear, we must make them see that we disown them and count them to be unclean, because they refuse Christ Jesus. How little of this is done by the smooth-tongued preachers of today! Men may refuse their gospel and still be the close friends of those who preach to them. Yes, they try even from the pulpit to cheer them in their unrepentance by the dream of a larger hope.

15. Verily I say unto you, It shall be more tolerable for the land of Sodom and Gomorrha in the day of judgment, than for that city.

The accursed cities of the plain may look for a fearful doom, but their portion will not be so unbearable as that of those to whom the gospel comes in freest fashion and yet they will not receive its messengers, nor even hear their words. With what solemnity do these threatenings surround both the preaching and the hearing of the kingdom! Our Lord seals His terrible prophecy with a *Verily* and with that solemn introduction, *I say unto you.*

Here our ever-blessed King sends forth His royal ambassadors under orders to summon the Jewish nation to acknowledge their sovereign Lord, and He supports them in their errand by a tremendous threat of doom to those who will not receive them or listen to their words.

Matthew 10:16-25

The King's Messengers May Expect to Be Mistreated

16. Behold, I send you forth as sheep in the midst of wolves: be ye therefore wise as serpents, and harmless as doves.

Behold. Our Lord calls for special attention and then sets before His sent ones, both then and now, what would be the future of their crusade. What He was doing was very wonderful, thus the *Behold.*

It would be foolhardy to go if Jesus did not say, *I send you.* When Jesus sends forth *sheep,* they may go fearlessly into the very *midst of wolves.* He sends them not to fight with wolves, nor to drive them out of their havens, but to transform them. The disciples were sent to fierce men to convince them, and therefore they must be wise to convert them, and therefore they must be gentle. The weapons of Christians are that they are weaponless. They are to be prudent, discreet, and *wise as serpents,* but they are also to be loving, peaceful, and *harmless as doves.* The Christian missionary will need to be wary to avoid receiving harm, but he must be of an honest mind so that he does no harm. We are called to be martyrs, not maniacs. We are to be simplehearted, but we are not to be fools.

After all, the mission of sheep to wolves is a hopeful one, since we see in the natural world that the sheep, though so feeble, by far outnumber the wolves who are so fierce. The day will come when persecutors will be as scarce as wolves and saints as numerous as sheep.

Lord, in my work for You, so teach me that I may display the wonderful blend of serpent and dove, which You do here commend to Your ministers. Never allow me to become to others like a wolf, but may I conquer by the meekness of a lamb!

17-18. But beware of men: for they will deliver you up to the councils, and they will scourge you in their synagogues; and ye shall be brought before governors and kings for my sake, for a testimony against them and the Gentiles.

Beware of men. Do not rely upon them or regard them as fellow helpers in setting up the kingdom of heaven, nor attempt to soften down your testimony to suit their taste. Do not invite their approval or place any great value upon their favor. They will not shelter you, but will *deliver you up.* They will not arrange for your entertainment, but for your accusation before *councils.* They will not load you with decorations, but will lash you with scourges in their places of public assembly. Thus would Israelites treat Israelites. The cruelty described by the words, *scourge you in their synagogues,* must surely have been a refinement of malice, yet with some men persecution is a part of religion.

The malice of the Jews would call in the interference of *Gentile* magistrates and monarchs. These also would become persecutors, and before their tribunals saints would have to plead for their lives; but as this would be *for Christ's sake,* they would thus be enabled to bear witness *for* their Lord and *against* His foes. In this way only would heathen *governors and kings* be likely to hear their testimony and therefore they were to welcome the summons to appear before earthly rulers.

Our attitude must be one of caution towards men. We must not commit ourselves to them, nor rely on their patronage, but we must at the same time make use of every opportunity to testify for our Lord before them. Our Protector and Lord is in heaven.

19. But when they deliver you up, take no thought how or what ye shall speak: for it shall be given you in that same hour what ye shall speak.

When you are before the judge, or about to be there, do not worry yourself about *what you shall speak.* Be not anxious as to your manner or matter when on your defense. If you are the Lord's true servant, you are the spokesman of the Holy Spirit. He will work in you a peaceful frame of mind and suitable words *shall be given you.* He will speak in you and through you. The Father Himself will put into your mouth, at the moment, the most fitting reply to your adversaries. This has been wonderfully true in former ages in the cases of martyrs for the truth's sake, and bold defenders of the faith still receive the same kind of guidance. Simple peasants have made great philosophers cringe, and humble women have put learned religious leaders in a quandary.

20. For it is not ye that speak, but the Spirit of your Father which speaketh in you.

All along, men of God are simply instruments for God. Our Lord Jesus claimed to speak, not of Himself, but from the Father; and to this He conforms His faithful witnesses. They speak and yet they speak not. God is silent and yet He speaks by them.

21. And the brother shall deliver up the brother to death, and the father the child: and the children shall rise up against their parents, and cause them to be put to death.

Unnatural hatreds have sprung out of religious bitterness. The old Serpent not only endeavors to poison the relationship of the creature to the Creator, but also that of child to parent, and parent to child. Brothers can become unbrotherly and all other relationships unnatural, when under the dominion of religious bigotry. In times of persecution, we may not expect love to ourselves from those who love not God. It might have seemed impossible that blood relations should be willing to assist in bringing about the death of each other, but history has abundantly shown that our Lord's words were none too strong. He knew the hearts of men and forewarned His disciples of the pitiless tempest that would beat upon them in consequence of human enmity to the truth.

22. And ye shall be hated of all men for my name's sake: but he that endureth to the end shall be saved.

These are heavy words, but true. If we are faithful, we shall of necessity make enemies. Jesus as good as says, "The classes and the masses will turn against you because of the name, the doctrine, and the rule of your Master. Sometimes the monarch and sometimes the mob will rage against you, but either from one or other, or both, shall the opposition arise." *Ye shall be hated of all men for my name's sake* was the storm-signal by which successive persecutions were announced. That signal may again be displayed in the order of Divine Providence. Happy are they who can bear persecution and hold on and hold out even *to the end* of the trial – the close of life or the termination of the dispensation. Such *shall be saved* indeed, but those who can be overcome by opposition are lost.

May the Lord prepare us to bear up under the utmost unkindness and hold on till the day of judgment comes, or till He makes even our enemies to be at peace with us!

23. But when they persecute you in this city, flee ye into another: for verily I say unto you, Ye shall not have gone over the cities of Israel, till the Son of man be come.

They were to keep to their work and preach in all the cities of Israel, but they might flee from danger in one city, and move to another. They were not to stop in a town and contend with the magistrates, and create confusion and disorder, but were to quickly move off when they were cruelly opposed. It is to the last degree foolish to attempt to force religion upon men. It advances by gentleness and not by violence. If a town is up in arms against the preacher, let him go where he will be less opposed.

There would always remain cities that needed the light. They would not be forced to cease their labors because certain towns closed their gates against them. Much wasteland needed reclaiming; let them hasten to fresh fields and raise harvests there.

While they were to change their place, they were to keep to their plan. Their mission to Israel was to be a quick work altogether, for the Lord would soon visit the land in judgment, and they would hardly have time to traverse the whole country before Israel's day of mercy as a nation, dwelling in her own land, would come to a close. The persecution that they felt in one city should hasten their pace in going to another, and so promote the rapid visitation of the whole country. They were not to delay over a hopeless town, for they had no time to spare. In some such diligent manner ought we to evangelize the world, believing that we have not an hour in which to loiter, for *the Son of man [may] come* all of a sudden. If His second coming were very speedily to happen, it would come before all tribes and peoples had heard His gospel, and this must not be. Many should run to and fro and spread the knowledge of His cross. If we do not do this willingly, it may be that we shall be driven to it. Persecution has often been a stimulus to the church. Let us be diligent in our holy calling and preach the gospel while we can do so in peace, for perilous times may be upon us or the Lord Himself may appear before we think He will.

> *24-25. The disciple is not above his master, nor the servant above his lord. It is enough for the disciple that he be as his master, and the servant as his lord. If they have called the master of the house Beelzebub, how much more shall they call them of his household?*

The scholar is not more excellent than the teacher, nor the servant than his master. Who would wish to see such a violation of all order and rule? Therefore, even if we had not had so much respect paid to us as to our Lord, we ought to have been well content. If we receive the same treatment as our Master, we have enough honor and more than we have a right to expect. What then? If the Master of the family is likened to *Beelzebub,* the lord of flies of the Philistines, and named after the prince of demons, by what names will they call us? Doubtless malice will invigorate the mind, and sarcasm will invent words that pierce as daggers and cut like knives. Thank God, they may *call* us what they like, but they cannot make us evil. They can, and will, cast out our names as evil, for they call good evil and evil good. God was slandered in Paradise and Christ on Calvary. How can we hope to escape? Instead of wishing to avoid bearing the cross, let us be content to endure dishonor for our King's sake. Let it be our ambition to be as our Master in all things. Since we are *of his household,* let us rejoice to share with *the master of the house.* It is so great an honor to be of the royal household, that no price is too high to pay in consequence. Close conformity to the image of their Lord is the glory of saints. To *be as his master* is to every true servant the climax of his ambition.

O Lord Jesus, our Savior King, we see how You were treated and we joyfully enter into the fellowship of Your sufferings! Grant us grace never to shrink in our loyalty to You, cost whatever it may.

Matthew 10:26-42

The King Cheering His Champions

26. Fear them not therefore: for there is nothing covered, that shall not be revealed; and hid, that shall not be known.

The King gives reasons for courage, saying, *Fear them not therefore.* Have no fear of slander. Your Lord and Master bore the full blast of that pitiless storm. Have no fear of misrepresentation, for the great God will right our characters before long. You and your betrayers will alike be shown up in the colors of truth. Though you should be *covered* with bad repute, your integrity shall be *revealed.* Though your true value is *hid,* it shall yet be *known.* Secret evil and secret virtue will alike be set in the full blaze of day. Anticipate the future and be not overwhelmed by the present.

27. What I tell you in darkness, that speak ye in light: and what ye hear in the ear, that preach ye upon the housetops.

God is the great revealer and you should imitate Him by publishing the truth to men. Go on, true believers, with your proper work, as mouths for God. Tell out what your Master tells you. Receive a message from Him in your quiet meditation and then make it known everywhere. Hear it like a whisper *in your ear* and then sound it forth as the eastern town crier, who gets to the highest point in the village and makes all the people hear from *the housetops.* Keep the study and the closet out of sight and there in secret meet with Jesus, and then set the pulpit of testimony in as conspicuous a place as you can find. If plunged *in darkness* of sickness, trouble, or distress, listen to Him whose voice is heard in the thick darkness, and then *speak ye in light* the profitable lessons ye have learned.

Lord, let no one of us speak till You speak to us, and then let us not be silent. May all Your disciples present to You their opened ears and then use for Your cause their fire-touched tongues!

28. And fear not them which kill the body, but are not able to kill the soul: but rather fear him which is able to destroy both soul and body in hell.

This, following upon the former verse, forbids us to hold back our testimony out of fear of men. We should not say less or more because of the opposition of the foe. A mighty argument against fear is the comparative weakness of the Enemy. Men can only wound our inferior part, the body, *but are not able to kill the soul.* But if we disobey God, the Supreme Lord of life and death has power even to destroy both parts of our being by casting them both into the death and darkness of *Gehenna,* or hell. Let us fear the Greater One and we shall not fear the lesser. There is no cure for the fear of man like the fear of God.

29-31. Are not two sparrows sold for a farthing? and one of them shall not fall on the ground without your Father. But the very hairs of your head are all numbered. Fear ye not therefore, ye are of more value than many sparrows.

Here is a sermon against fear, and *sparrows* are the text. Those birds are of little worth, and you are of far greater consideration than many of them. God observes the death of a sparrow and He much more notes the lives and deaths of His people. Even the least part of His children's bodily frame has been registered. *The very hairs of [their] head* are counted and catalogued, and to the most minute circumstance, all their lives are under the arrangement of the Lord of love. Chance is not in our creed; the decree of the Eternal Watcher rules our destiny and love is seen in every line of that decree.

Since we shall not suffer harm at the hand of men by their arbitrary conduct, apart from the will and permission of *our Father,* let us be ready to bear with holy courage whatever the wrath of man may bring upon us. God will not waste the life of one of His soldiers, no, nor a hair of his head. If we die in God's battle, we live in the grandest sense, for by loss of life we gain life.

32-33. Whosoever therefore shall confess me before men, him will I confess also before my Father which is in heaven. But whosoever shall deny me before men, him will I also deny before my Father which is in heaven.

Because divine providence rules over all, the destiny of believers is secure beyond fear of harm, and they must not shrink from the boldest declaration of their faith because of anxiety to preserve their lives. Our business is to *confess [Christ] before men.* In Him the truth we acknowledge begins, centers, and ends. Our confession of faith is a confession of Christ. He is our theology or Word of God. What a joy to *confess* Him now! What a reward to be confessed by Him hereafter in the glory-world! It will be a high offense against the great God, whom Jesus twice calls *my Father which is in heaven,* if we fail to confess His Son on earth.

It is clear that in this passage to *deny* Jesus means to not confess Him. What a grave warning is this for the cowardly believer! Can a nonconfessing faith save? To live and die without confessing Christ before men is to run an awful risk. Actually to recant and give up Christ must be a dreadful crime, and the penalty is fearful to contemplate. Disowned by Jesus before His Father who is in heaven! What hell can be worse?

Lord, let me never blush to acknowledge You in all companies! Work in me a bold spirit by Your Holy Spirit. Let me confess Your truth whatever the spirit of the age may be; let me uphold Your church when she is most despised; let me obey Your precepts when they cost me most dearly; and let me glory in Your name when it is most dishonored.

34-36. Think not that I am come to send peace on earth: I came not to send peace, but a sword. For I am come to set a man at variance against his father, and the daughter against her mother, and the daughter in law against her mother in law. And a man's foes shall be they of his own household.

Peace will be the ultimate outcome of our Lord's coming, but at the first, the Lord Jesus sends *a sword* among men. He wars against war and contends against contention. In the act of producing the peace of heaven, He arouses the rage of hell. Truth provokes opposition, purity excites enmity, and righteousness arouses all the forces of wrong.

During the process of fermentation, in which the right works for mastery, natural relationships go for nothing as preservatives of peace. The coming of Christ into a house is often the cause of discord between the converted and the unconverted. The more loving the Christian is, the more he may be opposed. Love creates a tender zeal for the salvation of friends, and that very zeal frequently calls forth resentment. We are to expect this and not to change course by it when it occurs. Animosities on account of religion often excite the fiercest of hostilities, and nearness of kin inflames rather than quenches the hostility. We are to press on in confessing the Lord Jesus, come what may of it. Even if our house becomes a den of lions to us, we must stand up for our Lord. The peace-at-any-price people have no portion in this kingdom.

Lord, teach us how to behave in these trying circumstances.

37. He that loveth father or mother more than me is not worthy of me: and he that loveth son or daughter more than me is not worthy of me.

Christ must be first. He herein claims the highest place in every human breast. Could He have done so had He not been divine? No mere prophet would talk in this fashion. Yet we are not sensible of the slightest egotism in His speech, and neither does it occur to us that He goes beyond His line. We are conscious that the Son of God has a right to speak thus and only He.

We must earnestly beware of making idols of our dearest ones, by loving them more than Jesus. We must never set them near the throne of our King. We are *not worthy* to dwell with Christ above, nor even to be associated with Him here, if any earthly object is judged by us to be worthy to rival the Lord Jesus.

Father and mother, son and daughter – we would do anything to please them, but as opposed to Jesus, they stand nowhere and cannot for an instant be allowed to come in the way of our supreme loyalty to our Lord.

38. And he that taketh not his cross, and followeth after me, is not worthy of me.

Here our Lord, for the second time in this Gospel, brings in His death. At first He spoke of being taken from them, but now He speaks of the *cross*. There is a cross for each one of us that we may regard as *his cross*. It may be that the cross will not take us up, but we must *take it up,* by being willing to endure anything or everything for Christ's sake. We are not to drag the cross after us, but to *take* it up. "Dragged crosses are heavy; carried crosses grow light." Bearing the cross, we are to *followeth after* Jesus. To bear a cross without following Christ is a poor affair. A Christian who shuns the cross is no Christian, but a crossbearer who does not follow Jesus equally misses the mark. Is it not peculiar that nothing is so essential to make a man worthy of Christ as crossbearing in His track? Yet it is assuredly so. Lord, You have laid a cross upon me; do not permit me to shirk it or shrink from it.

39. He that findeth his life shall lose it: and he that loseth his life for my sake shall find it.

If to escape from death he gives up Christ and so *findeth* a continuance of this poor mortal life, by that very act, *he loses* true *life.* He gains the temporal at the expense of the eternal. On the other hand, he who *loses life* for Christ's sake does in the highest sense *find life* – life eternal, life infinitely blessed. He makes the wisest choice who lays down his life for Jesus and finds life in Jesus.

40. He that receiveth you receiveth me, and he that receiveth me receiveth him that sent me.

What blessed union and holy communion exist between the King and His servants! The words before us are especially true of the apostles to whom they were first addressed. Apostolic teaching is Christ's teaching. To *receiveth* the twelve is to receive their Lord Jesus, and to receive the Lord Jesus is to receive God Himself. In these days, certain teachers despise the Epistles, which were written by apostles, and they are themselves worthy to be despised for so doing. This is one of the surest tests of soundness in the faith. *He that knoweth God heareth us,* says John (1 John 4:6). This bears hard on modern critics who in a hypocritical manner pretend to receive Christ and then reject His inspired apostles.

Lord, teach me to receive Your people into my heart, that thus I may receive You; and as to the doctrine that I hold, be pleased to establish me in the apostolic faith.

41. He that receiveth a prophet in the name of a prophet shall receive a prophet's reward; and he that receiveth a righteous man in the name of a righteous man shall receive a righteous man's reward.

Men may *receiveth a prophet* as a patriot or a poet, but that is not the point in hand. The prophet must be received in his highest character, *in the name of a prophet,* and for the sake of his Lord, and then the Lord Himself is received and He will reward the receiver in the same way in which His prophet is rewarded. If we cannot do all the good deeds of *a righteous man,* we can yet partake in his happiness by having fellowship with him and by uniting with him in vindicating the faith and comforting his heart.

To receive into our homes and our hearts God's persecuted servants is to share their reward. To maintain the cause and character of good men is to be numbered with them in God's account. This is all of grace, since the deed is so little and the recompense so large.

> *42. And whosoever shall give to drink unto one of these little ones a cup of cold water only in the name of a disciple, verily I say unto you, he shall in no wise lose his reward.*

He looked away from the apostles to some of the least and youngest of those who followed Him, and He declared that the very least kindness shown to them would have its recompense. There may be a sea of warm love in *a cup of cold water.* Much loyalty to the King may be expressed by little kindnesses to His servants, and perhaps more by kindness to the *little ones* among them than by friendship with the greater sort. To love a poor and despised child of God for Christ's sake shows greater love to Christ than if we love the honorable, and amiable, and rich members of His church.

Acts of love are divinely estimated rather by motive than by measure. *A cup,* and that *of cold water,* may mean as much from one as a banquet from another. Cold water has a special value in a hot climate, but this text makes it precious anywhere. Giving refreshment may be made a choice means of fellowship with holy men, if we give it because they are disciples and specially so when persecuting governments make it penalizing to help the saints in any way.

Though every kind deed is its own reward, yet the Lord promises a further recompense. What we give for Christ's sake is insured against loss by the promise of the text, by the *verily I say unto you,* which confirms it, and by the use of the negative *in no wise,* which shuts out all possibility of its being otherwise.

Matthew 11

Matthew 11:1-19

The King Supports His Messengers by His Own Appearing

1. And it came to pass, when Jesus had made an end of commanding his twelve disciples, he departed thence to teach and to preach in their cities.

He arranged their missionary tour and then followed in their wake. It was His plan to send them two by two through the cities of Israel, and then to follow them up in person and sustain their testimony by His own instruction, for He came *to teach and to preach*. We are to do our best for men and then to hope that our Lord will condescend to certify and confirm our teaching by His own coming to men's hearts. The term *their cities* sounds rather singular. Had our Lord given those cities to the twelve? It would seem so. In a spiritual sense, we go first and take possession of the souls entrusted to us, and then the King Himself comes in and takes His own at our hands. Lord, give me many souls that may be Yours in the day of Your appearing. To this end, I would gladly go at Your bidding and preach Your Word, trusting that I may hear the sound of my Master's feet behind me.

The King Vindicates and Cheers His Herald

2-3. Now when John had heard in the prison the works of Christ, he sent two of his disciples, and said unto him, Art thou he that should come, or do we look for another?

Here we begin quite another story. The first verse ought to have gone with the preceding chapter, to which it belongs. John the Baptist was in prison. He did not make a good caged bird – he of the wilderness and the river – and his faith began to wilt. So some think. Was it so? Or was this embassy sent to our Lord for the sake of John's disciples? Were they wavering so much that John could not reassure them without the aid of Jesus? Or was it that John would indicate to our Lord that there were doubts abroad that would be met by a further proclamation of His mission? Was this all that John now thought himself able to do – namely, to call upon the Lord to state His claims in the most decisive manner? Did John resolve to draw from our Lord a very clear statement, that his disciples might thus be readily transferred to Jesus? The question as to our Lord's having a mission was surely not for John's sake. He knew full well that Jesus was the Son of God. But when he heard of all that Jesus did, he may have wondered that he himself was left in prison, and he may have thought that possibly *another* was yet to come before all things could be rectified. Dark thoughts may come to the bravest when confined in a narrow cell. It was well that John's question was put, that it might receive a distinct reply, reassuring for himself, and instructive for us.

> *4-5. Jesus answered and said unto them, Go and shew John again these things which ye do hear and see: the blind receive their sight, and the lame walk, the lepers are cleansed, and the deaf hear, the dead are raised up, and the poor have the Gospel preached to them.*

Our Lord makes no assertion, but sets clear evidence before the eyes of John's delegates. He based the evidence of his messiahship upon His miracles. Why is it that, in these days, it is said that the miracles are rather a trial of faith than a support of it? An unbelieving generation turns even food into poison. What John had heard in prison, his messengers were to see for themselves and then to tell to their imprisoned master. Prison walls cannot shut out news of Jesus, but good news comes best through friends who are personal witnesses.

The messengers received the command: *Go and shew John again those things which ye do hear and see.* Of hearing and seeing, they had more than they could fully report and more than enough to make them see for themselves that Jesus was the Christ. The cures worked were all beneficial, superhuman, and of a kind foretold by the prophets as signaling the coming of Messiah. The proof was cumulative. The argument increased in power. The last two proofs are evidently placed as the climax of the argument: *The dead are raised up, and the poor have the Gospel preached to them.* These two wonders are placed side by side. There is as much of the miraculous in the poor man's gospel as in the dead man's resurrection.

John's disciples had come at a right time when our Lord's work was in full swing and all these wonderful works were following each other rapidly. Jesus is His own proof. If men would have arguments for the gospel, let them hear and see what it is and what it does. Let us tell to souls in the prison of doubt what we have seen Jesus do.

6. And blessed is he, whosoever shall not be offended in me.

That man is blessed who so believes, that his faith cannot be stumbled. A hint for John: John had not fallen, but very possibly he had stumbled. He had been a little put to it, through a sense of nondeliverance in time of need, and therefore he had asked the question. Blessed is he who can be left in prison, can be silenced in his testimony, can seem to be deserted of his Lord, and yet can shut out every doubt. John speedily regained this blessedness and fully recovered his serenity.

Lord, grant me to be firmly settled in my convictions, that I may enjoy the blessedness that flows from unstaggering faith. May nothing about You ever cause me to stumble upon You!

7. And as they departed, Jesus began to say unto the multitudes concerning John, What went ye out into the wilderness to see? A reed shaken with the wind?

Our Lord will sooner or later bear testimony to the man who has faithfully testified of Him. John honors Jesus, and in due time, Jesus honors John. Our Lord asks His hearers what they thought of John. You went to see John. You even *went out into the wilderness* to have a look at him. What did you see? A vacillating orator? A man who felt the influence of his times and bowed before its spirit, like a bulrush in the breeze? No, truly John was no time-server, no flattering courtier, no pleaser of the great. The Baptist had not sent to Jesus because he was weak, but because he was honestly outspoken and so anxious for absolute certainty that he could not endure the shadow of a doubt. John sent to headquarters to make assurance doubly sure, by a new declaration from Christ's own lips.

8. But what went ye out for to see? A man clothed in soft raiment? behold, they that wear soft clothing are in kings' houses.

Did you see a man of courtly manners, costly dress, pompous speech, and delicate expressions? Was John a court preacher, fit to flatter royal ladies? If so, how came he to be in the wilderness? *Behold, they that wear soft clothing are in kings' houses.* John was hated for his plain rebukes, and revenge against him burned in the heart of one near the throne because he knew not how to be silent in the presence of royal sin. John the Baptist was not in the palace. He had been promoted to the prison. His style had grated on the ear of a shameless princess, for he knew not how to speak soft words like those who are *clothed in soft raiment.* Thus does our Lord bear witness to John who came to be His witness.

9-10. But what went ye out for to see? A prophet? yea, I say unto you, and more than a prophet. For this is he, of whom it is written, Behold, I send my messenger before thy face, which shall prepare thy way before thee.

John was all that the very greatest of the prophets had been, and he came nearer to Jesus than all the rest. His Master's steps were close upon his heel. He shone like Milton's star:

"Fairest of stars, last in the train of night,
   If better thou belong'st not to the dawn."

He was almost a gospel-preacher, and failing to reach that point, he was chief among the prophets, *yea, and more than a prophet.* In the book of Malachi, the Lord God had promised to send a messenger before Messiah, and now the Messiah Himself quotes the prophecy with a change of persons not to be understood except as we believe in the Trinity in unity. He who is *Me* is also *Thee,* according to the aspect in which He is regarded or the person who speaks. John was the messenger of God to prepare the way of the Lord Jesus, and our Lord recognizes him in that honored capacity. Jesus is not ashamed of His forerunner because he is in prison, but rather He speaks the more openly of him. John had confessed his Lord and now his Lord confesses him. This is a rule with our King.

11. Verily I say unto you, Among them that are born of women there hath not risen a greater than John the Baptist: notwithstanding he that is least in the kingdom of heaven is greater than he.

Jesus sets John in a very high position and we know that His judgment is true. Up till the coming of our Lord, John was the greatest of woman born, but the new dispensation was on a higher plane, for *the kingdom of heaven* was set up. As we may say, as a rule, that the darkest day is lighter than the brightest night, so John, though first of his own order, is behind the last of the new or gospel order. The least in the gospel stands on higher ground than the greatest under the law. How privileged are we who, by virtue of entering into the kingdom of heaven by faith, are made to see and hear and enjoy those things that even the prophet of prophets could not enter upon! We may rest assured that there is nothing better to be discovered or revealed than that heavenly kingdom into which our Lord and King has brought us.

12. And from the days of John the Baptist until now the kingdom of heaven suffereth violence, and the violent take it by force.

John had aroused an unusual earnestness that had not died out. Men were eager for the glories of *the kingdom of heaven.* Though they misinterpreted it, they were on fire to seize it. John himself, in his excess of eagerness, had sent his two disciples to our Lord with an impatient question. Our Savior does not blame his intense inquiry, but says that so it must be. A holy violence had been introduced by John and they had just seen it in his question, and our Lord would have all those who would obtain the kingdom capture it by the same passionate eagerness. The time was come to end indifference and put on a holy resolution as to the things of God.

Thus the King sets forth the spirit demanded in these who would take part and lot in His great cause and kingdom. Lord, wake us up! Permit us not to be using dead formality, where living violence can alone avail.

13. For all the prophets and the law prophesied until John.

God left not Himself without witness all along. John ended the chain of foreseers and foretellers, and now the Lord Himself appears. Our Lord draws a line at John by saying, *Until John.* Henceforth the kingdom is set up.

14. And if ye will receive it, this is Elias, which was for to come.

John was the Elijah for whom they looked. Would people believe it? Would they obey his command to repent? Then he would be to them a true Elijah and make straight for them the way of the Lord. Even a man sent of God is to his hearer very much what that hearer chooses to make of him. No doubt, many a great blessing has been missed by men failing to accept it. *If ye will receive it,* a minister may be the channel of salvation, or the means of spiritual edification, or of surpassing joy; but if not received, he may become a weariness or as meaningless *as sounding brass, or a tinkling cymbal* (1 Corinthians 13:1).

15. He that hath ears to hear, let him hear.

This matter is worthy of earnest heed. If you can hear anything, hear this truth. This call to attention needs to be often repeated. Through the hearing ear, the divine blessing comes to the soul. Therefore, hear, and your soul shall live. Our Lord and King, who made the ear, has a right to demand its attention to His voice. Some men have no ears to hear truth, but have quick ears for falsehood. We should be grateful if the Lord has given us spiritual perception, for *the hearing ear, and the seeing eye* are from the Lord (Proverbs 20:12).

16-19. But whereunto shall I liken this generation? It is like unto children sitting in the markets, and calling unto their fellows, and saying, We have piped unto you, and ye have not danced; we have mourned unto you, and ye have not lamented. For John came neither eating nor drinking, and they say, He hath a devil. The Son of man came eating and drinking, and they say, Behold a man gluttonous, and a winebibber, a friend of publicans and sinners. But wisdom is justified of her children.

Our Lord condemns the folly of the age in which He lived. The people would not listen to the messenger of God, whoever he might be, but raised childish objections. Therefore, the Lord likens them to *children sitting in the markets,* who were asked to play by their fellows, but they could never agree upon the game. If some of the children would imitate a wedding and began to *pipe,* the others would not *dance.* And when they proposed a funeral and began to *mourn,* the others would not *lament.* They were disagreeable, sullen, and critically resolved to reject every offer.

Such was the foolish manner of men in our Lord's time. John was an ascetic. He must be out of his mind and under the influence of a demon. Jesus is a man among men and goes to their feasts. He is accused of eating and drinking to excess and associating with the sordid and the wicked. There was no pleasing them. Thus it is at this hour. One preacher, who speaks with elegant speech, is too flowery, and another, who uses plain speech, is vulgar. The instructive preacher is dull and the earnest preacher is far too excitable. There is no suiting some people. Even the great Lord of all finds His wise arrangements met with discontent.

Yet *wisdom,* after all, gave forth her teachings by rightly chosen ambassadors. She *is justified of her children.* Her children recognized the fitness of her messengers, and her messengers, who were also her children, were a credit to her choice, and justified her selection and preparation of them. The all-wise God is a better judge of what a minister should be than any of us are. Well did George Herbert write:

"Judge not the preacher, he is thy judge."

The varied orders of preachers are all necessary, and if we would but know it, they are all ours, whether Paul or Apollos, or Cephas, and it is ours not to carp at them, but to give earnest heed to their proposals.

Lord, deliver us from a critical, faultfinding spirit, for if we begin objecting, we are apt to keep on at it. If we will not hear one preacher, we may soon find ourselves quite weary of a second and a third, and before long it may come to pass that we cannot hear any minister to profit.

Matthew 11:20-30

The King's Warnings, Rejoicings, and Invitations

The wonderful portion of Scripture that makes up the rest of this chapter deals with three things, about which there has been great disputing, namely, the responsibility of man, the sovereign election of God, and the free invitations of the gospel. They are all here in happy combination.

20. Then began he to upbraid the cities wherein most of his mighty works were done, because they repented not.

Some cities were more favored with the Lord's presence than others, and therefore He looked for more from them. These cities ought to have repented, or Christ would not have rebuked them – repentance is a duty. The more men hear and see of the Lord's work, the greater is their obligation to repent. Where most is given, most is required. Men are responsible for the way in which they treat the Lord Jesus and *his mighty works.*

There is a time for rebuke: *Then began he.* The most loving preacher will see cause for complaining of His unrepentant hearers; He rebukes, even He who also wept. Repentance is what we who are preachers drive at, and where we do not see it, we are sorely troubled. Our trouble is not that our hearers did not applaud our ability, but *because they repented not.* They have enough to repent of, and without repentance, woe is upon them, and therefore we mourn that they do not repent.

21. Woe unto thee, Chorazin! woe unto thee, Bethsaida! for if the mighty works, which were done in you, had been done in Tyre and Sidon, they would have repented long ago in sackcloth and ashes.

Jesus knew what the doom of certain Jewish towns would be, and He knew what certain heathen cities would have done if they had been placed in their favorable circumstances.

He spoke infallibly. Great privileges were lost on *Chorazin* and *Bethsaida,* but would have been effective had they been granted to *Tyre and Sidon.* According to our Lord's declaration, God gave the opportunity where it was rejected, and it was not given where it would have been accepted. This is true, but how mysterious! The practical point was the guilt of these favored cities, in that they remained unmoved by visitation that would have converted the heathen Sidonians, yes, and would have made them repent quickly *long ago* and in the most humiliating manner: *In sackcloth and ashes.* It is a sad fact that our unrepentant hearers treat with contempt a grace that would have brought cannibals to the Savior's feet!

22. But I say unto you, It shall be more tolerable for Tyre and Sidon at the day of judgment, than for you.

Terrible as the hell of these two sinful cities will be, their punishment will be *more tolerable* than the sentence passed on the cities of Galilee where Jesus taught and worked miracles of love. The sin is in proportion to the light.

Those who perish with salvation sounding in their ears perish with a vengeance. Assuredly the day of judgment will be notable for surprises. Who would have thought to see Bethsaida sink lower than Sidon? Believers will not in *the day of judgment* be surprised, for they will remember in that day our Lord's words: *I say unto you.*

23. And thou, Capernaum, which art exalted unto heaven, shalt be brought down to hell: for if the mighty works, which have been done in thee, had been done in Sodom, it would have remained until this day.

The warning to *Capernaum* is, if possible, still more emphatic, for *Sodom* was actually destroyed by fire from heaven. Capernaum, His own city, the headquarters of the army of salvation, had seen and heard the Son of God. He had done in it that which even Sodomites would have felt, and yet it remained unmoved. Those foul sinners of the accursed Sodom, had they beheld the miracles of Christ, would have so forsaken their sins that their city would have been spared. Jesus knew that it would have been so, and therefore He mourned to see Capernaum remain as hardened as ever. Because of this rejection of special privilege, the city that had been *exalted unto heaven* would be brought as low in punishment as it had been raised high in privilege. May none of our favored English race perish in the same condemnation! Alas, how much we fear that millions of them will do so!

24. But I say unto you, That it shall be more tolerable for the land of Sodom in the day of judgment, than for thee.

What *Sodom* will endure when the great Judge of all appoints the doom of the wicked, we may not try to realize, but it will be somewhat less than the penalty inflicted upon those who have sinned against the light and rejected the testimony of the Lord from heaven. To reject the gospel of the Son of God is to create for oneself a sevenfold hell. Here, again, our Lord speaks from His own full authority with, *I say unto you.* He speaks what He knows. He will Himself be the Judge.

So far our Lord spoke in heaviness of heart, but His brow cleared when He came to the glorious doctrine of election in the next verse.

25-26. At that time Jesus answered and said, I thank thee, O Father, Lord of heaven and earth, because thou hast hid these things from the wise and prudent, and hast revealed them unto babes. Even so, Father: for so it seemed good in thy sight.

He turned to the other side of truth: *Jesus answered.* One doctrine answers to another – sovereign grace is the answer to abounding guilt. With rejoicing spirit, Jesus sees how sovereign grace meets the unreasonable abundance of human sin and chooses out its own, according to the good pleasure of the Father's will. Here is the spirit in which to regard the electing grace of God: *I thank thee.* It is cause for deepest gratitude. Here is the author of election: *O Father.* It is the Father who makes the choice and reveals the blessings. Here is His right to act as He does – He is *Lord of heaven and earth.* Who shall question the good pleasure of His will? Here we see the objects of election, under both aspects – the chosen and the passed-over. *Babes* see because sacred truths are revealed to them and not otherwise. They are weak and inexperienced. They are simple and unsophisticated. They can cling and trust, and cry, and love, and to such the Lord opens up the treasures of wisdom. The objects of divine choice are such as these. Lord, let me be one among them! The truths of the heavenly kingdom are *hid,* by a judicial act of God, from men who, in their own esteem, are *the wise and prudent.* They cannot see, because they trust their own dim light and will not accept the light of God.

Here we see also the reason of election, the divine will: *So it seemed good in thy sight.* We can go no further than this. The choice seemed good to Him who never errs and therefore it is good. This stands to the children of God as the reason that is above all reason. *Deus vult* ("God wills it") is enough for us. If God wills it, so must it be and so ought it to be.

27. All things are delivered unto me of my Father: and no man knoweth the Son, but the Father; neither knoweth any man the Father, save the Son, and he to whomsoever the Son will reveal him.

Here we have the channel through which electing love works towards men: *All things are delivered unto me of my Father.* All things are put into the Mediator's hands – fit hands both towards God and towards man, for He alone knows both to perfection. Jesus reveals the Father to the babes whom He has chosen. Only the Father can fill the Son with blessing, and only through the Son can that blessing flow to any one of the race of men. Know Christ and you know the Father, and know that the Father Himself loves you. There is no other way of knowing the Father but through the Son. In this our Lord rejoiced, for His office of Mediator is dear to Him, and He loves to be the way of communication between the Father whom He loves and the people whom He loves for the Father's sake.

Observe the intimate fellowship between the Father and the Son, and how they know each other as nobody else ever can. Oh, to see all things in Jesus by the Father's appointment and so to find the Father's love and grace in finding Christ.

My soul, there are great mysteries here! Enjoy what you cannot explain.

28. Come unto me, all ye that labor and are heavy laden, and I will give you rest.

Here is the gracious invitation of the gospel in which the Savior's tears and smiles were blended, as in a covenant rainbow of promise.

Come. He drives none away. He calls them to Himself. His favorite word is *Come*, not "Go to Moses," but *Come unto me.* To Jesus Himself we must come by a personal trust. Not to doctrine, ordinance, or ministry are we to come first, but to the personal Savior. *All laboring and laden* ones may come. He does not limit the call to the spiritually laboring, but every working and wearied one is called. It is well to give the largest sense to all that mercy speaks. Jesus calls me. Jesus promises *rest* as His gift. His immediate, personal, effective rest He freely gives to all who come to Him by faith.

To come to Him is the first step, and He entreats us to take it. In Himself, as the great sacrifice for sin, the conscience, the heart, and the understanding obtain complete rest. When we have obtained the rest He *gives,* we shall be ready to hear of a further rest that we *find.*

29-30. Take my yoke upon you, and learn of me; for I am meek and lowly in heart: and ye shall find rest unto your souls. For my yoke is easy, and my burden is light.

Take my yoke and learn. This is the second instruction. It brings with it a further rest that we *find.* The first rest He gives through His death. The second we *find* in copying His life. This is no correction of the former statement, but an addition thereto. First, we *rest* by faith in Jesus, and next we *rest* through obedience to Him. Rest from fear is followed by rest from the turbulence of inward passion and the drudgery of self. We are not only to bear *a* yoke, but also *His* yoke; and we are not only to *submit* to it when it is laid upon us, but we are also to *take it upon us.* We are to be workers and *take* His yoke, and at the same time we are to be scholars and *learn* from Him as our Teacher. We are to learn *of* Christ and also to learn Christ. He is both teacher and lesson. His gentleness of heart suits Him to teach, to be the illustration of His own teaching, and to work in us His great design. If we can become as He is, we shall rest as He does. We shall not only rest from the guilt of sin – this He gives us – but we shall also rest in the peace of holiness, which we find through obedience to Him. It is the heart that makes or mars the rest of the man. Lord, make us *lowly in heart,* and we shall be restful of heart.

Take my yoke. The yoke in which we move *with* Christ must of necessity be a happy one, and the burden that we carry *for* Him is a blessed one. We rest in the fullest sense when we serve, if Jesus is the Master. We are unloaded by bearing His burden. We are rested by running on His errands.

Come unto me is thus a divine prescription, curing our ills by the pardon of sin through our Lord's sacrifice, and causing us the greatest peace by sanctifying us to His service.

Oh, for grace to be always coming to Jesus and to be constantly inviting others to do the same! Always free, yet always bearing His yoke. Always having the rest once given, yet always finding more – this is the experience of those who come to Jesus always and for everything. Blessed heritage and it is ours!

Matthew 12

Matthew 12:1-13

Our King As Lord of the Sabbath

1-2. At that time Jesus went on the sabbath day through the corn; and his disciples were an hungred, and began to pluck the ears of corn and to eat. But when the Pharisees saw it, they said unto him, Behold, thy disciples do that which is not lawful to do upon the sabbath day.

They were probably on their way to the synagogue. They were allowed by law to take ears of corn as they passed along, but the objection of the Pharisees was to their doing so *on the Sabbath.* Plucking was reaping, and rubbing the grain from the husk was threshing, to their hypercritical minds. Their traditions and notions they regarded as a code of law, and according to this, the disciples were doing *that which is not lawful to do upon the sabbath day.* They came to Jesus Himself with their grave complaints. For once they plucked up courage to deal with the Leader, for they felt very strongly on the Sabbath question and they thought it fair to lay the faults of the disciples at the door of their Teacher.

We incidentally learn from this story that our Lord and His disciples were poor, and that He who fed the multitudes did not use His miraculous power to feed His own followers, but left them till they did what poor men are forced to do to supply a little sustenance for their stomachs. Our Lord bribes none into following Him. They may be His apostles and yet be hungry on a Sabbath.

Why did not these Pharisees give them bread and so prevent their doing that to which they objected? We might also fairly ask, How came they to see the disciples? Did they not break the Sabbath by setting a watch over them?

3-4. But he said unto them, Have ye not read what David did, when he was an hungred, and they that were with him; how he entered into the house of God, and did eat the shewbread, which was not lawful for him to eat, neither for them which were with him, but only for the priests?

He speaks to his learned opponents as if they had not read the law that they professed to uphold. *Have ye not read?* The example of David served the Son of David well. It was clear from his example that necessity has no law. The tabernacle law was broken by David when he and his band were pressed with hunger, and that breach of law touched Jewish ritual in a very special and tender point, and yet he was never rebuked for it. To have eaten the holy bread out of profanity, or bravado, or flippancy might have involved the offender in the judgment of death, but to do so in urgent need was not blameworthy in the case of David. As men excuse any breach of manners necessitated by the pressure of hunger, so does the Lord permit any ceremonial point of law to give way to His mercy and to man's evident necessity. The law of the Sabbath was never meant to compel starvation to hungry men, any more than the law of *the house of God* and *the shewbread.* Works of necessity are lawful on the Sabbath.

5-6. Or have ye not read in the law, how that on the sabbath days the priests in the temple profane the sabbath, and are blameless? But I say unto you, That in this place is one greater than the temple.

This instance is absolutely to the point. *The priests* worked hard on the Sabbath in offering sacrifice and in other appointed ways, but they were to be honored rather than censured for so doing, seeing they had the approval of the temple law. But in the case of Christ's disciples, that which they did had the sanction of the temple's Lord, who is far *greater than the temple.* Work done for God on the Sabbath is no real violation of the Sabbath, though it may seem to be so to those whose religion lies wholly in external observances. If we work *with* Jesus and *for* Jesus, we care not for the criticisms of formalists. As the substance is greater than the shadow, so is our Lord greater than the temple or any or all ceremonial laws, and His sanction overrules all the interpretations of the law that religiousness or superstition may thrust upon us. Works of devotion are lawful on the Sabbath.

7. But if ye had known what this meaneth, I will have mercy, and not sacrifice, ye would not have condemned the guiltless.

Our Lord had galled the Pharisees by saying twice, *Have ye not read?* Did He imagine that they had left any part of the Psalms or Law unread? Now He attacks them again with the charge of ignorance of the meaning of a passage from the prophets: *If ye had known what this meaneth.* Then He quotes from Hosea 6:6, which He had used against them before (see Matthew 9:13): *I will have mercy, and not sacrifice.* There must be very much in this word of the prophet to make it so great a favorite with our Lord. God preferred that His priests should rather give the consecrated shewbread to David as an act of mercy, than keep it sacred to its use. He would rather that the disciples should spend a few minutes in plucking ears of corn for their hunger than suffer faintness in order to preserve the sanctity of the day. Having thus the permission of the Lord Himself, those who allowed the merciful act of removing hunger were guiltless and ought not to be condemned. Indeed, they would not have been condemned had their critics been better instructed. Works of mercy are lawful on the Sabbath.

8. For the Son of man is Lord even of the sabbath day.

This sets the whole matter beyond further question. *The Son of man,* Christ Jesus, being in union with the Godhead, *is Lord* of everything that lies in the range of that law that concerns God and man, seeing He is Mediator, and therefore He may arrange and dispose of Sabbaths as He pleases. He has done so and has interpreted the sabbatical law, not with license, but with a sweet reasonableness that the more rigid of religionists do not exhibit. From His example and teaching we learn that the Sabbath is not profaned by works of necessity, devotion, or mercy, and that we need not care for the sharp speeches of hypercritical formalists who strain the sabbatical law and make a bondage of that which was intended to be a season of holy rest.

9. And when he was departed thence, he went into their synagogue.

The time arrived when the Sabbath question came up again in reference to our Lord's own work among the sick and diseased.

Jesus set the example of attending public worship. The synagogues had no divine appointment to authorize them, but in the nature of things it must be right and good to meet for the worship of God on His own day, and therefore Jesus was there. He had nothing to learn, yet He went up to the assembly on the day that the Lord God had consecrated.

10. And, behold, there was a man which had his hand withered. And they asked him, saying, Is it lawful to heal on the sabbath days? that they might accuse him.

The incident was noteworthy and therefore it is mentioned with a *behold.* It was remarkable that so very soon a case occurred to bring up again the matter in dispute. Did the Pharisees bring the *man which had his hand withered* into the synagogue so as to raise the question in a practical form? They went to the synagogue to indulge their bigotry and not to worship. It is to be feared that many in these days imitate them. Before our Lord made any motion towards a miracle, they were at Him with what they hoped would prove an entangling question: *Is it lawful to heal on the sabbath days?* He had claimed to be Lord of the Sabbath, and now they, with much show of fairness, submit a difficulty to Him, but it was with a bad purpose. In the moral character of questioning, everything depends upon the motive. They did not ask so that they might learn from Him, but *that they might accuse him.* They were on the catch, yet they took nothing by their malicious craftiness.

11-12. And he said unto them, What man shall there be among you, that shall have one sheep, and if it fall into a pit on the sabbath day, will he not lay hold on it, and lift it out? How much then is a man better than a sheep? Wherefore it is lawful to do well on the sabbath days.

He answers their question with another. He propounds a case and makes them to be judges in it. If a poor man, with *one sheep,* saw it *fall into a pit,* or become cast on its back *on the sabbath day,* would he not *lay hold on it, and lift it out,* and set it on its feet? Of course he would, and he would be right in so doing. *How much then is a man better than a sheep?* Therefore, it is and must be right to help a man. Alas, some act as if a man were not better than an animal, for their dogs and horses are better housed than their laborers, and they are more indignant about the killing of a fox than about the starving of a pauper.

Our Lord's argument was overwhelming. One form of human kindness being proved to be right, the whole class of benevolent actions is admitted, and *it is lawful to do well on the sabbath days.* One wonders that anybody ever thought otherwise. But zeal for externals and hatred of spiritual religion, when united, create a narrow bigotry as cruel as it is ridiculous. Our Lord has set us free from the rabbinical yoke, and we find rest to our souls in a true spiritual Sabbath. Let none, however, from this liberty, infer a license and treat the Lord's Day as if it were their own and might be spent for their own purposes. They best keep the Sabbath who on the seventh day, and always, rest from their own works, as God did from His; but how can a man rest until he knows the finished work of God in Christ Jesus?

13. Then saith he to the man, Stretch forth thine hand. And he stretched it forth; and it was restored whole, like as the other.

Thus our Lord practically carried out His own teaching. He that could work a miracle of this sort was divine and could rightly interpret His own law. The man was sitting down and Jesus told him to stand up so that all might observe him, and then He further told him to hold up his hand so that all could see its lifeless condition. It does not appear that his arm was withered, as some have supposed, but he was able, by the use of his arm, to hold out his hand to public view. This being done, the Lord restored it at once, before the whole synagogue, and before the judgmental Pharisees. The man stretched out each finger perfectly restored to its natural vigor.

The poor man had hidden his hand when it was dried up, but when it was restored, it was fitting that it should be seen by all in the synagogue. By that restored hand, made whole on the Sabbath, all men knew that Jesus would work deeds of mercy on the Sabbath. Let us pray for Him to do the same in our assemblies. Oh, that the hands that have been useless for holy purposes may at His bidding become whole! Oh, that those who are bidden to believe and live would cease from questioning, and obey, as this man did, then would His healing surely come to them, as it did to the obedient man!

Matthew 12:14-21

Our King in the Majesty of His Peacefulness

14. Then the Pharisees went out, and held a council against him, how they might destroy him.

The synagogue was too hot for the Pharisees and so they *went out.* Utterly defeated, they withdrew from public gaze, hating the Man who had so completely baffled them. They could not silence Him and so they would kill Him. Those who begin with seeking to accuse the Lord soon come seeking to *destroy him.* It was not easy to touch one who lived so much in the esteem of the people, and so they consulted together as to the safest method of procedure. Their killing of Jesus was indeed the result of premeditated malice, for they deliberately planned their cruel deed. Men at this hour still take counsel *against him.* Why and for what reason? Let their own consciences answer, if they have any. The present cool, calculating attacks of skeptics upon the gospel have a special degree of crime in them.

15-16. But when Jesus knew it, he withdrew himself from thence: and great multitudes followed him, and he healed them all; and charged them that they should not make him known.

Their secret counsels were all discerned by His omniscience. *Jesus knew it.* He acted accordingly. He came not to contend with quarrelers, and therefore *he withdrew himself* from the scene of their perpetual disputes. But He could not get alone. The crowd flocked after Him, and His love could not refuse to bless them with healing. He did not want to create an excitement, and so, when the people gathered in multitudes, He commanded them not to advertise His presence. To Him popularity became a hindrance in His work and He shunned it. In this avoidance of notoriety, He fulfilled an ancient prophecy.

We are under no charge to conceal His gracious wonders, and therefore we would joyfully enlarge upon that glorious record, *He healed them all.* What an encouragement to sin-sick souls to trust in Him!

17-19. That it might be fulfilled which was spoken by Esaias the prophet, saying, Behold my servant, whom I have chosen; my beloved, in whom my soul is well pleased: I will put my spirit upon him, and he shall shew judgment to the Gentiles. He shall not strive, nor cry; neither shall any man hear his voice in the streets.

It is in Isaiah 42:1-4 that we read words that are quoted in their full sense, if not literally, by the evangelist Matthew. The *servant* of God, elect, beloved, and delightful to the Lord, clothed with the Spirit of God, would come forth and reveal the Lord's mind to the nations, but it would not be with tumult and turmoil, noise and clamor.

To avoid contention and ostentation, our Lord quieted those whom He had healed, or at least charged them not to make Him known. Our Lord did not aim at raising Himself in the esteem of the multitude by successfully contending with the Pharisees, for His method was of another sort. The names given to the Savior here are exceedingly precious and worthy of our careful meditation, and especially so in connection with the passage in Isaiah. Jesus is the *chosen* of Jehovah, ordained to be His Servant, *beloved* in that capacity, and *well-pleasing* to His Father. The power of this beloved Servant of God would lie in the divine Spirit, in the doctrine that He would teach, and in the law that He would proclaim, with His whole life being a judging and condemnation of sin before the eyes of all men. Not by might, nor by power, but by the Spirit of the Lord and the force of truth would He prevail. The wrath of man in hot controversy, the frenzy of wild rhetoric, the torrent of popular speech – all these He left to mere pretenders. He disdained such weapons in establishing His kingdom. Certain of His followers have taken an opposite course and are much enamored by outspoken and blatant methods. In this they will yet find that they are not well-pleasing to the Lord.

20. A bruised reed shall he not break, and smoking flax shall he not quench, till he send forth judgment unto victory.

He left the *bruised reed* of Pharisaic presence to prove its own impotence – it was not at that time worth His while to break it. And the *smoking flax* of a nominal religiousness He passed by and left all dealing with it till another day, when the hour should come to end its offensiveness. He will in the end victoriously judge those hypocrites who were as useless as bruised reeds and as offensive as smoking flax, but He would not do this during His first mission to men. He is in no haste to destroy every petty opposition.

This I take to be the exact sense of the words in this connection, but as the passage is popularly received, it is equally true and much richer in consolation. The feeblest are not disdained by our Lord Jesus, though apparently useless as a bruised reed or even actually offensive as a smoking flax. He is gentle and exercises no harsh severity. He bears and is patient with those who are unlovely in His eyes. He longs to bind up the broken reed and fan the smoking flax into flaming life. Oh, that poor sinners would remember this and trust Him!

21. And in his name shall the Gentiles trust.

Because He is so kind, the despised Gentile dogs shall come and crouch at His feet and love Him as their Master. He shall be the hope of those who were left as hopeless. Our Lord's desire for quiet, and His avoiding antagonism, thus proved Him to be the Messiah of the prophets. Shall we not more and more trust in the Anointed of the Lord? Yes, Gentiles as we are, we do *trust in His name.* In us is this prophecy fulfilled, yet how unlikely it seemed that Gentiles would do so when Israel refused Him.

Matthew 12:22-37

Our King and the Powers of Darkness

22. Then was brought unto him one possessed with a devil, blind, and dumb: and he healed him, insomuch that the blind and dumb both spake and saw.

It is well when men take to bringing others to Jesus – good is sure to come of it. An extraordinary case exhibited a novel form of the handicraft of Satan. The evil spirit had secured himself by stopping up the windows and the door of the soul. The victim was *blind and dumb.* How could he escape? He could not see his Savior, nor cry to Him. But the double evil vanished when, in an instant, Jesus dislodged the demon:

The blind and dumb both spake and saw. When Satan is dethroned, the spiritual faculties begin to work at once. Nothing baffles our Lord. Men who neither see their sin, nor cry for mercy, His grace can save.

Lord, be with us when we preach and cast out devils by Your Word; then shall moral inability be succeeded by gracious health.

23. And all the people were amazed, and said, Is not this the son of David?

Again and again we have noticed their astonishment, and here a question was asked that may have been the footfall of coming faith in many. Our Revised Standard Version very properly leaves out the *not.* It was natural for the translators to put it in, for it looks as if many must have seen the true Solomon in this great Wonder-worker. But as it is not in the original, we must not allow the *not;* and then the question shows how strangely unbelieving they were, and yet how some conviction forced itself on them. "Is He? He cannot be. He must be, but is He? *Is not this the Son of David?*" There were various voices, yet the people were one in their astonishment, and *all the people were amazed.*

24. But when the Pharisees heard it, they said, This fellow doth not cast out devils, but by Beelzebub the prince of the devils.

This was their former concoction. It was old and stale, yet for lack of a better or more bitter suggestion, they stick to it. Our Lord was too busy to reply to the vile slander on its first appearance (Matthew 9:34), or perhaps He so loathed it that He would not touch it, but left the abominable thing to poison itself with its own venom. Now they bring it out again and come to a more minute detail of lying by mentioning *Beelzebub* as the name of *the prince of the devils,* with whom He was thought to be in league. Lies grow as they move on. Those who doubt God's work in the conversion of sinners soon advance in vigor and ascribe the blessed change to hypocrisy, self-interest, madness, or some other evil influence.

25-26. And Jesus knew their thoughts, and said unto them, Every kingdom divided against itself is brought to desolation; and every city or house divided against itself shall not stand: and if Satan cast out Satan, he is divided against himself; how shall then his kingdom stand?

The Thought-reader meets them with an argument in the highest degree conclusive, overwhelming them by reducing their statement to absurdity.

Imagine Satan divided against Satan and his kingdom thus torn with civil war! No, whatever faults the devils have, they are not at strife with each other; that fault is reserved for the servants of a better Master. Oh, that divisions in the church were not so many and so desolating as they are! It would be a very hopeful circumstance if we could hear of divisions among the powers of darkness, for then would Satan's kingdom fall. No, you cunning Pharisees, your slanderous suggestion is too manifestly a lie, and reasonable men are not to be entrapped by it!

27. And if I by Beelzebub cast out devils, by whom do your children cast them out? therefore they shall be your judges.

Our Lord here used an argument suitable for the men he dealt with. It was not so forcible in itself as the former one, but as an argument *to them* it would come home with singular force. Some of the disciples of the Pharisees, and probably some of *[their] children*, acted as exorcists, and whether truly or falsely, professed to cast out devils. If Jesus worked this marvel by Beelzebub, and the Pharisees had made that discovery, how could they have learned it better than from their own sons? Did their sons have dealings with the demon-prince? This would impale them on the horns of a dilemma and prevent their uttering that malicious invention again, for the sake of their own friends.

28. But if I cast out devils by the Spirit of God, then the kingdom of God is come unto you.

Our Lord in effect says, "*If I cast out devils by the Spirit of God,* then is a new era begun. The divine power has come into distinct conflict with the Evil One and is manifestly victorious. In My Person is *the kingdom of God* inaugurated and you are placed in a position of gracious advantage by My being among you. But if the devils be not cast out by the Spirit of God, the throne of God is not among you and you are tragic losers."

The overthrow of evil is a clear proof that the kingdom of grace has come.

Note that, though our Lord had power all His own, He honored the

Spirit of God and worked by His energy, and mentioned the fact that He did so. What can we do without that Spirit? Lord God the Holy Spirit, teach us to wait on You!

29. Or else-how can one enter into a strong man's house, and spoil his goods, except he first bind the strong man? and then he will spoil his house.

The devil is the *strong man,* the giant robber. He holds men in possession as a warrior holds his property. There is no getting *his goods* from him without first encountering him. The bare idea of spoiling him while you are his friend, or he is unsubdued, is ridiculous. Our Lord, when His work began, bound Satan. The presence of God in human flesh was a restraint upon man's foe. Having bound the Enemy, He now takes out of *his house* those spoils that otherwise had been forever in his possession. There is no deliverance for us except by our Lord's victory over our powerful tyrant. Glory be to His name, He has bound the mighty and He takes from him his prey! This was our Lord's fair and self-evident explanation of the matter concerning which the Pharisees theorized so badly.

30. He that is not with me is against me; and he that gathereth not with me scattereth abroad.

Our Lord had made no compromise with Satan. Satan was *not with* Him but *against* Him. He meant to be equally decisive in His dealings with all other parties. Men must either come to His side or be reckoned as His opponents. There can be no middle course. Jesus meant war with the great Enemy and with all who sided with evil. Men would of necessity practically take sides. Their actions would tend to gather men to Him or to scatter them from Him. Jesus is the one and only possible center of human unity, and whatever teaching does not unite men in Him, disperses them through selfishness, pride, hate, and a thousand other disintegrating forces. Our King has thrown down the gauge of battle and He will never accept truce or compromise. Lord, let me never hesitate, but *be* with You and *gather* with You.

31. Wherefore I say unto you, All manner of sin and blasphemy shall be forgiven unto men: but the blasphemy against the Holy Spirit shall not be forgiven unto men.

Here is a solemn warning for these slanderous Pharisees. The sin of reviling the Spirit of God and attributing His work to Beelzebub is a very great one, and in fact, it so hardens the heart that men who are guilty of it never repent and consequently are never forgiven. Our Lord let His opponents see where they were drifting. They were on the verge of a sin for which no pardon would be possible. We must be very tender in our conduct towards *the Holy Spirit,* for His honor has a special guard set around it by such a solemn text as this.

32. And whosoever speaketh a word against the Son of man, it shall be forgiven him: but whosoever speaketh against the Holy Spirit, it shall not be forgiven him, neither in this world, neither in the world to come.

Why should a word be spoken against Jesus? Yet many words are so spoken and He forgives. But when it comes to willfully confounding the Holy Spirit with the evil spirit, the offense is rank and heinous, and most hardening to the heart. In no state of the divine economy was it ever possible to extend forgiveness to one who willfully regarded God Himself as in league with the devil. This is spiritual death, no, rottenness and corruption of the most putrid kind. It is no error, but a wicked, willful blasphemy of *the Holy Spirit* that dares to attribute His works of grace and power to diabolical agency. He who is guilty of this outrageous crime has sinned himself into a condition in which spiritual feeling is dead and repentance has become morally impossible.

33. Either make the tree good, and his fruit good; or else make the tree corrupt, and his fruit corrupt: for the tree is known by his fruit.

Still he argues with the Pharisees, and He as good as says, "Be consistent. Accept Me and My works, or reject Me and My works, for by My works only can you judge Me. But do not admit the work to be a good one and then charge Me with being in league with the devil in the doing of it. If I were in league with the devil, I would do works such as the devil does and not works that shake his kingdom." The objection is most powerful, because it is founded in righteousness. We judge a tree by its fruits and a man by his actions, and there is no other truthful mode of judging.

Read the words out of their connection and they teach the great general truth that the inner and the outer life must correspond.

34-35. O generation of vipers, how can ye, being evil, speak good things? for out of the abundance of the heart the mouth speaketh. A good man out of the good treasure of the heart bringeth forth good things: and an evil man out of the evil treasure bringeth forth evil things.

Our Lord accuses them of *being evil.* He repeats John's words: *O generation of vipers.* They had spoken evil. How could they do otherwise when their hearts were so full of malice towards Him? They had gone to the utmost extreme of malevolence in charging Him with being in league with Satan, and that only showed what a *treasure* of evil lay within their hearts. They threw evil forth with energy of temper and with lavishness of falsehood, because they had such a fullness of it within. That which is in the well comes up in the bucket. The heart betrays itself through the mouth. Had they been good, their words would have been good, but such was their corruption of heart that they could not *speak good things.* Thus our Lord carried the war into their own territory and flashed holy indignation in their faces.

36-37. But I say unto you, That every idle word that men shall speak, they shall give account thereof in the day of judgment. For by thy words thou shalt be justified, and by thy words thou shalt be condemned.

They might think that they had done no great wrong when they scattered their wicked phrases among the people. They had only given their opinion with more or less of flippancy; at the worst, they had only spoken *idle words.* Thus they would make light of what they had done now that the Lord had most completely crushed them. But our Lord drives them out of this retreat. He deals strictly with such gross offenders. *Words* are to be accounted for at the last great day. Words prove men just or worthy of condemnation. Their very works may be judged by their words. There is something very heart-revealing about men's language and especially about those words that spring from deep-seated passion. We may, when we are convicted of unjust speech, shield ourselves behind the notion that our bark was worse than our bite, and that we merely said so-and-so, and hardly meant it to be taken so seriously; but the plea will not avail us. We must mind what we say about godly men and especially about their Lord, for libelous words will live and will be swift witnesses against us *in the day of judgment,* when we shall find that they were all recorded in the Book of God.

Surely this business of charging the Lord Jesus with being in league with Satan was never likely to be heard of again while He lived! He had silenced that form of slander once and for all, as far as the Pharisees were concerned.

Dear Master, help me to bridle my tongue so that I will not be found guilty of *idle words,* and teach me when to speak so that I may keep equally clear of idle silence.

Matthew 12:38-42

Our King Challenged to Give a Sign

38-39. Then certain of the scribes and of the Pharisees answered, saying, Master, we would see a sign from thee. But he answered and said unto them, An evil and adulterous generation seeketh after a sign; and there shall no sign be given to it, but the sign of the prophet Jonas.

The Pharisees change their manner, but they are in pursuit of the same object. How hopeless had the religionists of that age become! Nothing would convince them. They manifest their hate of the Lord Jesus by ignoring all the wonders He had worked. What further signs could they seek than those He had already given? Pretty inquirers these! They treat all the miracles of our Lord as if they had never occurred. Well might the Lord call them *evil and adulterous,* since they were so given to personal vulgarity and were spiritually so untrue to God. We have those among us now who are so uncandid as to treat all the achievements of evangelical doctrine as if they were nothing, and talk to us as if no result had followed the preaching of the gospel. There is need of great patience to deal wisely with such.

40. For as Jonas was three days and three nights in the whale's belly; so shall the Son of man be three days and three nights in the heart of the earth.

The great sign of our Lord's mission is His resurrection and His preparing a gospel of salvation for the heathen. His life story is well symbolized by that of Jonah. They cast our Lord overboard, even as the sailors did the man of God. The sacrifice of Jonah calmed the sea for the mariners. Our Lord's death made peace for us. Our Lord was awhile in the heart of the earth as Jonah was in the depth of the sea, but He rose again and His ministry was full of the power of His resurrection. As Jonah's ministry was certified by his restoration from the sea, so is our Lord's ministry attested by His rising from the dead. The man who had come back from death and burial in the sea commanded the attention of all Nineveh, and so does the risen Savior demand and deserve the obedient faith of all to whom His message comes.

41. The men of Nineveh shall rise in judgment with this generation, and shall condemn it: because they repented at the preaching of Jonas; and, behold, a greater than Jonas is here.

The heathen of Nineveh were convinced by the sign of a prophet restored from burial in the sea, and moved by that convincement, they repented at his preaching. Without complaint or delay they put the whole city in mourning and pleaded with God to turn from His anger. Jesus came with a clearer command of repentance and a brighter promise of deliverance, but He spoke to callous hearts. Our Lord reminds the Pharisees of this, and since they were the most Jewish of Jews, they were touched to the heart by the fact that heathens perceived what Israel did not understand, and that Ninevites repented while Jews were hardened.

All men will rise at the judgment: *The men of Nineveh shall rise.* The lives of repentant ones will condemn those who did not repent. The Ninevites will condemn the Jews *because they repented at the preaching of Jonas* and the Jews did not. Those who heard Jonah and repented will be swift witnesses against those who heard Jesus and refused His testimony.

The standing witness to our Lord is His resurrection from the dead. God grant that every one of us, believing that unquestionable fact, may be so assured of His mission that we may repent and believe the gospel.

Resurrection is one proof. In fact, it is *the sign,* although, as we shall see, it is supplemented by another. The two will convince us or condemn us.

42. The queen of the south shall rise up in the judgment with this generation, and shall condemn it: for she came from the uttermost parts of the earth to hear the wisdom of Solomon; and, behold, a greater than Solomon is here.

The second sign of our Lord's mission is His kingly wisdom. As the fame of Solomon brought *the queen of the south from the uttermost parts of the earth,* so does the doctrine of our Lord command attention from the utmost isles of the sea. If Israel perceives not His glorious wisdom, Ethiopia and Seba shall hear of it and come bowing before him. The queen of Sheba will rise again and will *rise up* as a witness against unbelieving Jews, for she journeyed far to hear Solomon, while they would not hear the Son of God Himself who came into their midst. The superlative excellence of His wisdom stands for our Lord as a sign that can never be effectively disputed. What other teaching meets all the needs of men? Who else has revealed such grace and truth? He is infinitely greater than Solomon, who from a moral point of view exhibited a sorrowful littleness. Who but the Son of God could have made known the Father as He has done?

Matthew 12:43-45

Our King Unveiling the Tactics of the Archenemy

Our Lord was mindful to deal a finishing stroke to the notion of His being aided by satanic cooperation, by returning to His parable (verse 29), and declaring that even if the contingency should occur of the evil spirit leaving a man of its own accord, the man would be none the more a subject of hope, for the Enemy would return before long.

43. When the unclean spirit is gone out of a man, he walketh through dry places, seeking rest, and findeth none.

Well is the devil named *the unclean spirit.* He loves that which is foul and makes the man in whom he dwells filthy in heart. In the incident described above, the devil has been in possession *of a man* and he *is gone out* for purposes of his own. He has left the man of his own accord, without conflict of any kind. This is a case that frequently occurs. The devil does in this way leave the madly immoral to become decent and orderly. The crafty spirit takes the key of the house with him, for he means to return. He has left occupancy, but has not given up ownership. He has gone out so that he might not be turned out. Who can understand the subtlety of the old Serpent?

The evil spirit is, however, uneasy when he is not ruling a human mind. He wanders *seeking rest, and findeth none;* he finds nothing to cheer him on this earth, or in heaven, or in hell. These are all *dry places* to him. Within the sinful heart he was at home and found some little content, but outside in nature, he finds a desert for his unclean desires.

> "Every prospect pleases
> And only man is vile!"

And hence only man affords a suitable lodging for the vile spirit.

> *44. Then he saith, I will return into my house from whence I came out; and when he is come, he findeth it empty, swept, and garnished.*

The foul fiend calls the man *my house.* His audacity is amazing. He did not build or buy that house and he has no right to it. He speaks of his leaving the man as a mere coming out: *I came out.* He says, as if it were an easy matter, *I will return.* Evidently he considers that he has the freehold of man's nature and can come and go at his pleasure. If Satan leaves a man of his own will, he is sure to return just when it suits his purpose. Only the divine force that ejects him can secure his non-return. Reformations that are not the work of conquering grace are usually temporary and often lead up to a worse condition in later years.

The unclean spirit carries out his resolve. He returns, *and when he is come, he findeth it empty.* No one else has taken possession and so no one hinders his entrance into his own residence. It is true that it is *swept* from certain grosser sins and *garnished* with some pretty moralities, but the Holy Spirit is not there and no divine change has been worked, and therefore the unclean spirit is as much at home there as ever he was. The parable needs no further explanation. Temporary reformation is well pictured. The devil has no objection to his house being swept and furnished, for a moralist may be as truly his slave as the man of debauched habits. So long as the heart is not occupied by his great foe and he can use the man for his own purposes, the adversary of souls will let him reform as much as he pleases.

45. Then goeth he, and taketh with himself seven other spirits more wicked than himself, and they enter in and dwell there: and the last state of that man is worse than the first. Even so shall it be also unto this wicked generation.

He takes another walk. He is so pleased with his elegant mansion that he calls upon other demons and invites them to his furnished home. The evil ones join him and the inhabitants of the house are as eight to one of their former number. They *enter in and dwell there.* They take the fullest possession and make a permanent stay. Their residence is secured beyond future likelihood of removal, and now the man is *worse than at the first,* for the unclean spirits are more numerous and *more wicked.* The sinful man becomes more proud and more unbelieving, or he becomes more vicious and more blasphemous than at the beginning. So much for a hopeful reformation, which indeed from the very first was hopeless, because Jesus was not there and the Holy Spirit had no hand in it. Cunningly the unclean spirit submits to an apparent giving up of power that he may establish his dominion the more firmly. No doubt, relapses into sin are, like relapses in disease, even more dangerous than the original malady.

In Christ's day, the Pharisees and others were in this situation. The spirit that led the Jews to idolatry was gone, but the true God was not spiritually loved nor even known, and so the demon power held them still in possession. In the future, even in that *wicked generation,* in the form of hatred to Christ, and fanatical contempt of other nations, the evil spirit that had depraved Judaism would yet display itself in a still more hideous shape, as it did from our Lord's day and onward till the destruction of Jerusalem, when the race seemed to have gone fairly mad, under a diabolical influence that made them *hateful, and hating one another* (Titus 3:3). We may fear that our present age of culture and advancement will go onward till it reaches a similar goal. It is progressing towards infidelity, and advancing towards absurdity, while at the same time worldliness is rampant and holiness is ridiculed.

Matthew 12:46-50

Our King and His Earthly Relatives

46. While he yet talked to the people, behold, his mother and his brethren stood without, desiring to speak with him.

The members of His family had come to take Him, because they thought Him beside Himself. No doubt the Pharisees had so represented His ministry to His relatives that they thought they had better restrain Him, lest He should procure His own destruction by His zealous preaching. Friends may be a good man's greatest hindrance. They intruded upon His holy service *while he yet talked to the people.* A mark of wonder is put before this record: *Behold.* How dare they act in this manner? By the request of *his mother and his brethren,* He is called away from the pressing engagement of teaching the people, which was His urgent lifework, but the call had no power over Him. What ailed Mary that she joined in this transaction? Many a nervous mother has been ready to hold back her consecrated son when his courage has defied danger. Our Lord did not allow His love to His mother to turn Him aside.

47. Then one said unto him, Behold, thy mother and thy brethren stand without, desiring to speak with thee.

A meddling person reported the errand of the family: *One said unto him, Behold, thy mother and thy brethren stand without.* It is hard when interruptions come from our own flesh and blood, for strangers are sure to back them up. Ignorantly or willfully, the reporting person lent himself to the design of the relatives by representing that they were *desiring to speak with [Him],* though, indeed, they desired to take Him. He who would not permit a disciple to neglect his duty on the plea of burying his father, how will He act now that His mother comes to hinder Him? He will do the right thing. We may always find the rule of our conduct by asking the question, "What would Jesus do?"

48-49. But he answered and said unto him that told him, Who is my mother? and who are my brethren? And he stretched forth his hand toward his disciples, and said, Behold my mother and my brethren!

He does not reject the tender ties of His human nature, but He exhibits their true position as secondary to the spiritual bonds that united Him to the spiritual family. Those who were related to Him by the bonds of discipleship had in this the truest union with Him. He pointed to *his disciples, and said, Behold my mother and my brethren!* All believers in Jesus are of the royal family, princes of the blood, brothers of the Christ. See how He acknowledges the affinity and bids all to know it. *He is not ashamed to call them brethren* (Hebrews 2:11). In this instance, His method of acknowledging them was singularly striking. He even set them before His earthly mother and brethren.

Lord, let us know and enjoy our nearness to Yourself. Help us also to care for You as a mother for her son, and to love You as a man should love his own brother.

> *50. For whosoever shall do the will of my Father which is in heaven, the same is my brother, and sister, and mother.*

He enlarges upon the truth. Every doer of the Father's will is thereby proved to be a true disciple, and he is to Jesus as near as a brother, as dear as a sister, and as much cared for as a mother. According to our condition and capacity, let us act towards our Lord the part of *brother* in help, of *sister* in sympathy, and of *mother* in tender love, for all these relationships act in both ways and involve giving as well as receiving. What a blessed *whosoever* is this! It is not for ministers only or for persons set apart to special service, but all who *do the will of [their] Father* in any position of life are enveloped in the family circle of the Lord Christ.

Our Lord Jesus had a little while before He cut Himself adrift from the bands of formality by routing the scribes and Pharisees, and now the knife goes deeper, and all that is of the flesh at its very best is divided from that which is of the spirit. From this point on, it is clear that after the flesh He knows no man anymore, neither can we hope to know Him by birthright membership or anything else that is of blood, or birth, or the will of the flesh. The inner life that is akin to God and shows itself in holiness is that which gives us union with our Lord. Oh, to feel its influence more and more!

Matthew 13

Matthew 13:1-53

Our King Sets Forth Seven Parables of His Kingdom

1. The same day went Jesus out of the house, and sat by the sea side.

He was not afraid of being seized by His family, but freely went abroad. How serene was His behavior. He *sat by the sea side.* This must have been a great relief to Him. He ceased from the controversy of the house and the street, and came into restful communion with nature. On the beach, in the open air, He gave greater play to His imagination and left the sermonic style for the allegorical.

2. And great multitudes were gathered together unto him, so that he went into a ship, and sat; and the whole multitude stood on the shore.

Great multitudes longed to hear His teaching and see His miracles. These pressed upon Him so eagerly that there was danger of His being pushed into the sea and the more so because it was not a scattered crowd, but they *were gathered together unto him* – pressing around His person. The ship became His pulpit, and the little space between it and the shore gave Him breathing space and enabled more people to hear Him. The shelving beach and the blue sky would make a grand auditorium, with room for *the whole multitude,* a finely comprehensive expression. The Teacher *sat* and the people *stood.* We would have less sleeping in congregations if this arrangement still prevailed.

3. And he spake many things unto them in parables, saying, Behold, a sower went forth to sow.

He had much instruction to give and He chose to convey it *in parables.*

What wonderful pictures they were for us, as well as for those who heard them! This parable of the sower is a mine of teaching concerning the kingdom, for the seed was *the word of the kingdom* (see verse 19).

Behold. Every word is worthy of attention. Maybe, the Preacher pointed to a farmer on the shore, who was beginning to sow one of the terraces. *A sower;* read *The Sower.* Jesus, our Lord, has taken up this business of the Sower at His Father's bidding. *The sower went forth.* See Him leaving the Father's house with this one purpose upon His heart: *To sow.*

> 4. *And when he sowed, some seeds fell by the way side and the fowls came and devoured them up.*

When he sowed, some seeds fell by the way side. Even when the Chief Sower is at work, some seed fails. We know He sows the best of seed and in the best manner, but some of it falls on the trodden path and so lies uncovered and unaccepted by the soil. That soil was hard and beaten down with traffic. There, too, on the wayside, we meet with dust to blind, settlements of mud to foul, and birds to pilfer. It is not a good place for good seed. No wonder, as the seeds lay all exposed, that *the fowls came and devoured them up.* If truth does not enter the heart, evil influences soon remove it.

> 5-6. *Some fell upon stony places, where they had not much earth: and forthwith they sprung up, because they had no deepness of earth: and when the sun was up, they were scorched; and because they had no root, they withered away.*

Among the rocks or on the shallow soil, with the unbroken rock-pan underneath, the seed fell, for if the sower had altogether avoided such places he might have missed some of the good ground. In these stony places, the seed speedily *sprung up* because the rock gave it all the heat that fell on it and so hastened its germination. But soon up, soon down. When the time came for the sun to put forth its force, the rootless plants instantly languished and died. *They had no deepness of earth* and *no root.* What could they do but *wither* completely *away?* Everything was hurried with them. The seeds had no time to root themselves and so in hot haste the speedy growth met with a speedy death. No trace remained.

7. And some fell among thorns; and the thorns sprung up, and choked them.

The ground was originally a thorn-brake and had been cleared by *the thorns* being cut down; but speedily the old roots sent out new shoots and other weeds came up with them, and the tangled beds of thistles, thorns, nettles, and whatnot strangled the feeble up-shootings of the wheat. The native plants *choked* the poor stranger. They would not permit the intrusive corn to share the field with them. Evil claims a monopoly on our nature.

Thus we have seen three sets of seeds come to an untimely end.

8. But other fell into good ground, and brought forth fruit, some an hundredfold, some sixtyfold, some thirtyfold.

This would repay all losses, especially at the highest rate of increase here quoted. To the bird, the weather, and the weeds, three sets of seeds have gone, yet, happily, one remains to increase and fill the barn. The sowing of good seed can never be a total failure: *Other fell into good ground.*

The harvest was not equally great on every spot of fertile soil. It varied from *an hundredfold* to *thirtyfold.* All good ground is not alike good, and besides, the situation may differ. Harvests are not all alike in the same farm, in the same season, and under the same farmer, and yet each field may yield a fairly good harvest.

Lord, if I cannot reach to a hundredfold, let me at least prove to be good ground by bearing thirtyfold.

9. Who hath ears to hear, let him hear.

It reminds one of the officer saying to his men, *"Attention!" He* speaks, who, as Lord of all, has a right to be heard. Ears are for hearing. Use them most when He speaks who made the ear.

10. And the disciples came, and said unto him, Why speakest thou unto them in parables?

Perhaps the crowd had complained to the disciples that they could not see what their Master was driving at. The apostles may have felt unable to reply. As the matter perplexed them, they did well to inquire of their infallible Teacher, rather than to invent an explanatory theory, which might have been altogether a mistake.

11. He answered and said unto them, Because it is given unto you to know the mysteries of the kingdom of heaven, but to them it is not given.

The usual reasons for the use of parables would be to make truth clear, to arrest attention, and to impress teaching upon the memory. But in this instance our Lord was, by His parabolic speech, fulfilling the judicial sentence that had been long before pronounced upon the apostate nation among whom He received such unworthy treatment. They were doomed to have the light and to remain willfully in the dark. To His own disciples our Lord would explain the parable, but not to the outside unbelieving throng. If anyone among the multitude became sincerely anxious to know the Lord's meaning, he would become His disciple and then he would be taught *the mysteries of the kingdom of heaven;* but those who rejected the Messiah would, while listening to parables, hear and not hear, see and not perceive.

To hear the outward word is a common privilege; *to know the mysteries* is a gift of sovereign grace. Our Lord speaks the truth with much boldness: *It is given unto you, but to them it is not given.* Solemn words.

Humbling truths. Salvation, and the knowledge by which it comes, are given as the Lord wills. There is such a thing as distinguishing grace after all. Let the modernists revile the doctrine as they may.

12. For whoever hath, to him shall be given, and he shall have more abundance: but whosoever hath not, from him shall be taken away even that he hath.

Those who had some understanding of spiritual truth would come to yet clearer light, but those who lived willfully in the dark would, in the presence of light, become more and more bewildered and would gain nothing but the discovery that they did not know what they thought they knew. An ignorant man going into a museum, or hearing a learned lecture, only feels himself a greater fool. He learns nothing, because he is not able to comprehend the elementary terms of the science. It is just so with carnal men. Spiritual truth rather blinds them than enlightens them.

13. Therefore speak I to them in parables: because they seeing see not; and hearing they hear not, neither do they understand.

This was His reason for *speaking to them in parables*. They could not understand spiritual things and therefore He gave them no naked doctrine, for then they would not have listened at all. They did not really see what they saw, nor hear what they heard. The plainer the teaching, the more they were puzzled by it. They had become so morally and spiritually diseased that the only thing they would notice was the attractive dress of a truth; for the truth itself they had no liking and no perception. To this day, marvels of creation, works of grace, deeds of providence, and ordinances of religion are all as voiceless music or painted suns to carnal men. They hear not their teaching, they feel not their power.

14. And in them is fulfilled the prophecy of Esaias, which saith, By hearing ye shall hear, and shall not understand; and seeing ye shall see, and shall not perceive.

That wonderful sixth chapter of Isaiah is constantly being quoted in the New Testament. How clearly it sets forth the doom of guilty Israel! Those who refuse to see are punished by becoming unable to see. The penalty of sin is to be left in sin. The Jews of our Lord's day would trifle with what they heard and so they were left to hear without understanding. Even the Messenger of the Covenant would speak in vain to them.

15. For this people's heart is waxed gross, and their ears are dull of hearing, and their eyes they have closed; lest at any time they should see with their eyes and hear with their ears, and should understand with their heart, and should be converted, and I should heal them.

They had deadened their own faculties. Perversity in sin had made them heartless, and deaf, and blind to all spiritual things. Thus, they blocked up the way of salvation against themselves and used their utmost diligence to prevent their own conversion. It was but just that the truth should reach them in a manner that would condemn rather than convert. If it had come in any other form but the parabolic, they would not even have stooped to listen to it. In that form, truth would have been more clearly seen than in any other, if they had been willing to see it; but as they were unwilling, the emblem became a dark lantern shutting the light from them. If men will willfully close their eyes, the very light shall blind them. Thus, when the Lord passes any by, it is due to their sin, but when He chooses any, it is not because they *are* better, but that He may *make* them better.

This passage teaches that the possession of faculties is a small thing unless we appropriately use them. Men should *see with their eyes and hear with their ears, and should understand with their heart.* If they turn to Christ He will heal them, even of impure hearts, and *dull ears,* and *closed eyes.* But alas! there is a generation that will not be *converted,* for they are proud of their blindness and foulness.

> *16-17. But blessed are your eyes, for they see: and your ears, for they hear. For verily I say unto you, That many prophets and righteous men have desired to see those things which ye see, and have not seen them; and to hear those things which ye hear, and have not heard them.*

Happy men to be chosen to such a privilege! Grace has opened your eyes and ears. *Blessed are your eyes, for they see.* What wonders, treasures, and revelations do they see! Eyes are blessed that gaze upon the mysteries of divine love. *Blessed are your ears, for they hear.* You hear something sweeter than the song of angels, even the voice of everlasting love from the heart of Jesus. You have learned the great secret. The counsel of the Lord has been revealed to you and you are *blessed.* You, under the gospel, are made to know what the greatest and best of men under the law could not discover. The shortest day of summer is longer than the longest day in winter, and you, you humble ones, under the gospel dispensation see more of truth in Jesus than the best of saints could see before He came. There is no doubt about this, for Jesus sets the seal of *verily I say unto you* upon the statement. Favored above all others are those whose regenerated faculties both see and hear the truth of God. Are we among this blessed number? If so, let us praise the Lord for so great a blessing. Truly *to hear* the gospel and *to see* its blessings is a high favor. The love and gratitude that we show in return should be great indeed!

18. Hear ye therefore the parable of the sower.

Because you see behind the curtain and have grace given to discern the inner meaning through the outer metaphor, come and *hear* the explanation of *the parable of the sower.*

> *19. When any one heareth the word of the kingdom, and understandeth it not, then cometh the wicked one, and catcheth away that which was sown in his heart. This is he which received seed by the way side.*

The gospel is *the word of the kingdom.* It has royal authority in it. It proclaims and reveals King Jesus and it leads men to obedience to His influence. To hear but not to understand is to leave the good seed on the outside of your nature and to not take it into yourself. Nothing can come of such hearing to anyone.

Satan is always on the watch to hinder the Word: *Then cometh the wicked one,* even at the moment when the seed fell. He is always afraid to leave the truth even in hard and dry contact with a mind, and so he *catcheth it away* at once and it is forgotten or even disbelieved. It is gone, at any rate, and we have not in our hearer's mind a cornfield, but a highway, hard and much frequented. The man was not an opposer, for he *received seed;* but he received the truth as he was, without the soil of his nature being changed, and the seed remained as it was, till the foul bird of hell took it off the place and there was an end of it. So far as the truth *was sown in his heart,* it was in his natural, unrenewed heart, and therefore it took no living hold. How many such hearers we have! To these we preach in vain, for what they learn they unlearn, and what they receive they reject almost as soon as it comes to them.

Lord, allow none of us to be impenetrable to Your royal Word, but whenever the smallest seed of truth falls on us, may we open our soul to it!

> *20-21. But he that received the seed into stony places, the same is he that heareth the word, and anon with joy receiveth it; yet hath he not root in himself, but dureth for a while: for when tribulation or persecution ariseth because of the word, by and by he is offended.*

Here the seed was the same and the sower the same, but the result was somewhat different. In this case there was earth enough to cover the seed and heat enough to make it grow quickly. The convert was attentive and easily persuaded. He seemed glad to accept the gospel at once. He was even eager and enthusiastic, joyful and demonstrative. *He heareth the word, and anon with joy receiveth it.* Surely this looked very promising! But the soil was essentially evil, hard, barren, and superficial. The man had no living entrance into the mystery of the gospel, no root in himself, no principle, no hold of the truth with a renewed heart, and so he flourished hurriedly and showily for a season, and only for a season. It is tersely put: He *dureth for a while.* That *while* may be longer or shorter according to circumstances. When matters grow hot with Christians, either through affliction from the Lord or persecution from the world, the temporary believer is so sapless, so rootless, so deficient in moisture of grace, that he dries up and his profession withers. Thus, again, the sower's hopes are disappointed and his labor is lost. Till stony hearts are changed it must always be so. We meet with many who are soon hot and as soon cold. They receive the gospel *anon* ("immediately"), and leave it *by and by.* Everything is on the surface and therefore is hasty and unreal. May we all have broken hearts and prepared minds that when truth comes to us it may take root in us and abide.

> 22. *He also that received seed among the thorns is he that heareth the word; and the care of this world, and the deceitfulness of riches, choke the word, and he becometh unfruitful.*

This class of hearers we know by personal acquaintance in this busy age. They *heareth the word,* they are affected by the gospel, they take it as *seed* into their minds, and it grows well for a season; but the heart cannot belong to two absorbing objects at the same time, and therefore these men cannot for long yield themselves up to the world and Christ too. A man needs to be careful of getting money, covetousness, trickery, and sins that come from hastening to be rich, or else pride, luxury, oppression, and other sins that come from having obtained wealth prevent the man from being useful in religious matters, or even sincere to himself, *and he becometh unfruitful.* He keeps his profession. He occupies his place, but his religion does not grow; in fact, it shows sad signs of being choked and checked by worldliness. The leaf of outward religiousness is there, but there is no dew on it. The ear of promised fruit is there, but there are no kernels in it. The weeds have outgrown the wheat and smothered it. We cannot grow thorn and corn at the same time. The attempt is fatal to a harvest for Jesus.

See how wealth is here associated with *care, deceitfulness,* and *unfruitfulness.* It is a thing to be handled with care. Why are men so eager to make their thorn-brake more dense with briars?

Would not a good husbandman root out the thorns and brambles? Should we not, as much as possible, keep free from the care to get, to preserve, to increase, and to hoard worldly riches? Our heavenly Father will see that we have enough. Why do we fret about earthly things? We cannot give our minds to these things and to the kingdom also.

> *23. But he that received seed into the good ground is he that heareth the word, and understandeth it; which also beareth fruit, and bringeth forth, some an hundredfold, some sixty, some thirty.*

Here is the story of the Word's success. This fourth piece of land will repay all charges. Of course, no one parable teaches all truth, and therefore we have no mention here of the ploughing that always precedes a fruitful harvest. No heart of man is good by nature. The good Lord had made this plot into *good ground.* In this case, both thought and heart are committed to the heavenly message, and the man *heareth the word, and understandeth it.* By being understood lovingly, the truth gets into the man, and then it roots, it grows, it fruits, and it rewards the sower. We must aim at the inward apprehension and comprehension of the Word of God, for only in this way can we be made fruitful by it.

Be it ours to aim to be among those who bear fruit *an hundredfold!* Ah! we would give our Lord ten thousandfold if we could. For every sermon we hear we should endeavor to do a hundred gracious, charitable, or self-denying acts. Our divine Sower, with such heavenly seed, deserves to be rewarded with a glorious harvest.

> *24. Another parable put he forth unto them, saying, The kingdom of heaven is likened unto a man which sowed good seed in his field.*

Still to give us often the keynote of this gospel, our Lord speaks of *the kingdom of heaven,* and to continue His method of making truth so clear that only the willfully blind should fail to see it, He brings forth another plain and compelling simile. We know right well that *man which sowed good seed in his field.* Right well He sowed it. He sowed it in His own chosen ground, *his field,* and right good was the seed He sowed. He is gone within His heavenly house and has left His field to the care of His servants. Alas! that care is by no means what it should be!

> 25. But while men slept, his enemy came and sowed tares among the wheat, and went his way.

The servants are all too apt to sleep. There is a season when nature requires them to do so, and there are other times when sinful sloth persuades them to the same indulgence. Good, easy men, they cannot believe that anyone would do harm to their master's field; besides, watching and driving away trespassers is unpleasant work. *Heresy-hunting* is the nickname for watchfulness. *Rigid Puritanism* is the contemptuous title for careful discipline. *Bigotry* is the title by which faithfulness is described. *While men slept* could any cultured person resist the spirit of the times and stay awake?

His enemy came. We know who the enemy is. His time for work is in the night. He sleeps not when watchmen are steeped in slumber, but then is he specially active. Quietly, cunningly, without observation, that malicious one sowed the darnel, the bastard wheat – a something so like wheat that no one could tell the difference till it began to ripen. He brought in those who loved modern thought and worldly amusements, who were by their talk Christian and by their boasts profoundly spiritual, and having introduced them cunningly, he departed. He might have been suspected had he lingered upon the scene of his craft, and so he *went his way* to do the same elsewhere. His dear children all declared that he did not exist, but it was a mere myth, and as he had gone away, many concluded that they were right. Satan is not omnipresent, but this he cunningly turns into an advantage, for he can often do more by his absence than by his presence. A known devil is only half a devil.

> 26. But when the blade was sprung up, and brought forth fruit, then appeared the tares also.

Good seed grows and alas! evil seed is equally full of the power to increase. Satan's principles have a terrible vitality and rigor in them.

Both seeds were for a while hidden, but when one *sprung up,* the other *appeared also.*

The darnel is up as soon as the wheat is, and it looks so like it that it appears to be the selfsame thing. The field is ruined. Its yield is poisoned by the mixture of a dangerous plant. What had the enemy gained for himself? Nothing. It was enough for him that he had injured the man he hated.

27. So the servants of the householder came and said unto him, Sir, didst not thou sow good seed in thy field? from whence then hath it tares?

Now they wake up. It would have been better to have stayed awake. They see the evil growth, though they did not see the evil sowing. Overwhelmed with the sight of the spoiled field, they hastened to tell their lord, wondering much how such a state of things could have come about. What a question to ask of their master: *From whence then hath it tares?* They were sure that he sowed *good seed,* and nothing else, and they evidently thought that he would know who sowed the horrible wheat. We, too, wonder how so much evil can have entered into a region where Christ has set His ministers, and we cry out in astonishment, *From whence then hath it tares?* The question is best left with the Master, but the asking it is a confession that we have been asleep.

28. He said unto them, An enemy hath done this. The servants said unto him, Wilt thou then that we go and gather them up?

The householder had not slept. He knew who had done the cruel wrong. He who is the enemy of God and man, and he only, had perpetrated this piece of malice. It may have seemed to be a learned doctor, or a clever poet, or a treacherous orator who scattered doubt among the people and introduced skeptics into the church; but the worker behind the scenes, the real author of the mischief, is always the devil himself.

The servants were eager to undo the mischief at once in the first way that suggested itself. Out with the false wheat and let the true wheat grow! A thing more easy to propose than to do, but one that would naturally occur to all true servants who were sorry for their neglect and eager to set matters right. Had there been weeds in the corn, the hoe could have removed them, but this darnel grew on the wheat and was like the wheat, and thus was the true picture of those in the church and in the world who are nominal Christians and fair moralists, but who know nothing of the life of God. We cannot get rid of these and yet how often we wish we could!

29. But he said, Nay; lest while ye gather up the tares, ye root up also the wheat with them.

The darnel was so plentiful, had become so intermixed with the corn, and was so much like it, that it would not be possible to cut up the one without pulling up the other also. In fact, there was a false wheat that grew upon the true corn, and to part these would be perilous to the crop.

Hasty disciplinarians have often cast out the best and retained the worst. Where evil is clear and open, we may not hesitate to deal with it, but where it is questionable, we had better hold our hand till we have fuller guidance.

30. Let both grow together until the harvest: and in the time of harvest I will say to the reapers, Gather ye together first the tares, and bind them in bundles to burn them: but gather the wheat into my barn.

Allow the two seeds to remain together for a season, that they may be the more effectively separated later on. It is true that the evil will hinder and hamper the good, but even this will be better than that you should cast out the good by mistake. A separation time will come and that will be *in the time of harvest,* when both will be fully developed. That will be a suitable season, when the division can be made and no harm done thereby. *The reapers* then employed will do the work correctly, efficiently, universally, and finally. For the false wheat, there will be burning in bundles. For the true wheat, there will be ingathering into the Lord's own storehouse. This will be a perfect separation and we are bidden to wait for it. Our Lord's *I will say to the reapers* may very well keep us from making any hasty speeches to the elders of the churches or to the magistrates of the land, so as to excite them to hurried and stingy discipline. Thorns and thistles they can root up, but the darnel is another matter. Magistrates and churches may remove the openly wicked from their society. The outwardly good who are inwardly worthless they must leave, for the judging of hearts is beyond their sphere.

Our Lord declares that the doom of the false wheat, the horrible professors, is terrible. *Bind them in bundles;* put like with like, sinner with like sinner, to burn them. No words can be more suggestive of terrible destruction. After this, what a quiet, peaceful tone we hear in the words, *Gather the wheat into my barn.* All gathered, all recognized as the Lord's own, all housed in His storehouse.

> *31-32. Another parable put he forth unto them, saying, The kingdom of heaven is like to a grain of mustard seed, which a man took, and sowed in his field: which indeed is the least of all seeds: but when it is grown, it is the greatest among herbs, and becometh a tree, so that the birds of the air come and lodge in the branches thereof.*

Mustard seed is the least of all seeds in proportion to that which comes of it, but it has a peculiar life in it and therefore it produces so great a growth. The man in the parable we know. His field is the church or the heart. He *takes* the seed that perhaps others neglect because they think it is so small. He sows the living seed in his own field and watches over it. It grows and grows, till at length it becomes *the greatest among herbs* and is like to *a tree.* The results of the divine life in the soul are by no means little, but great graces, great projects, and great deeds are produced by it. The work of grace in the church and in the individual is so apparent, that persons who know as little about heavenly things as finches and sparrows, come and find shelter beneath the holy and kind influences and institutions that are its outgrowth.

We could not have guessed that our Lord and His twelve apostles would produce the myriad churches of Christendom. We cannot even now tell to what end a humble effort to do good may grow. We know not what our own inner life will come to. It has an expanding power within it, and it will burst every bond, and grow to a thing that will cast a shadow, yield fruit, and lend shelter. If the Lord has planted the incorruptible seed within, its destiny is a great one.

Good Master, hasten this blessed development. We have seen nearly enough of the mustard seed. Now let us see the tree.

> *33. Another parable spake he unto them; The kingdom of heaven is like unto leaven, which a woman took, and hid in three measures of meal, till the whole was leavened.*

Many expositors argue that this relates to the power of evil in the church or in the heart. On this interpretation we see why *a woman took the leaven,* and why she was so secret about it, that it is said she *hid* it.

According to the rule that is observed in the use of this symbol, leaven must be taken as the type of evil, and if the rule must be applied in this case, the teaching is obvious and valuable. The leaven soon began its corrupting influence in the church, and it continues, in one form or another, working still.

But the connection does not lead us so to interpret. The parable begins with the same words as the other: *The kingdom of heaven is like,* and there is not a word to warn us that the theme is changed and that our Lord is not now speaking of the kingdom itself, but of evil in the kingdom. Moreover, our Lord does not say, "shall be like," but *is like,* referring, therefore, to something then in operation, and we really fail to see that the woman had then hidden the leaven, much less hidden it *in three measures of meal,* that is to say, in a large church. Is not leaven here used simply as another picture of an influence that appears feeble, but turns out to be active, conquering, and at length all-pervading? This, though hidden in obscurity, in the midst of nations comparable to *three measures of meal,* worked with a mysterious rapidity and will still continue to work in the whole mass of the world, and subdue the nations to itself. Let our friends take their choice of the two interpretations and learn a good lesson from either or both. From evil leaven, may the Lord preserve us. By holy influences, may we all be worked upon!

34-35. All these things spake Jesus unto the multitude in parables; and without a parable spake he not unto them: that it might be fulfilled which was spoken by the prophet, saying, I will open my mouth in parables; I will utter things which have been kept secret from the foundation of the world.

That prophet was David or Asaph. Psalm 78 begins with, *Give ear, O my people, to my law.* By whom could this be spoken but by God? And yet in the third verse this same person speaks of *our fathers,* and therefore he must be a man. Here, then, in this seventy-eighth psalm, is the sacred person who is both God and man, and to our Lord Jesus Christ the language is most suitably applied by the evangelist. Our Lord speaks hidden things and sets forth *secret* things in an open parable, which is understood by those who have had the eyes of their understanding opened, while those who are self-blinded perceive not His meaning. These parables contain ancient secrets and deep mysteries, and maybe there is more of prophecy in them than we have yet perceived.

36. Then Jesus sent the multitude away, and went into the house: and his disciples came unto him, saying, Declare unto us the parable of the tares of the field.

Possibly, they had figured out the mustard seed and the leaven, but the *tares* remained a puzzle to them. We are not sorry for this, since, through their ignorance, we obtain our Lord's own interpretation. We would certainly have missed our way without it.

37. He answered and said unto them, He that soweth the good seed is the Son of man.

He came to this world on purpose to sow the kingdom of heaven in it. All the grace and truth and spiritual life among us is of His sowing.

38. The field is the world; the good seed are the children of the kingdom; but the tares are the children of the wicked one.

The field is the world, including the church, but the field is not the church exclusively. For *the good seed,* or *the children of the kingdom,* is much the same as the church, and the evil seed is persons who mingle with the people of God and live together with them in necessary association in the great field of the world. Church fellowship is not particularly aimed at here, though it is encompassed by the terms used. Bigots have tried to eradicate heretics, and national churches have even forbidden unsound thinkers to remain in the country, but all attempts at securing any region from having infidels or heretics residing in it have soured into persecution. Nowhere on earth can we maintain a settlement of saints alone. In many cases, the cruel treatment of the very best of men has been produced by the notion that they were erroneous teachers and therefore ought not to be tolerated. To contend earnestly against error by spiritual means is right and necessary, but to use carnal weapons and other remedies of force is absolute folly and wickedness. This world is now a field of mingled growths, and so it must be till the end comes.

39. The enemy that sowed them is the devil; the harvest is the end of the world; and the reapers are the angels.

The devil is the sower of evil men. There were none such till he came into Paradise, but now they are everywhere, not only in the field of the world, but also in the garden of the church. Now is the time of growing. The harvest hastens on and the reapers are already chosen by the great householder. We may rejoice that angels, and not men, are *the reapers.* At what hour *the consummation of the age* (Amplified Bible, Classic Edition) shall come we do not know, but it is surely drawing nigh.

40-42. As therefore the tares are gathered and burned in the fire; so shall it be in the end of this world. The Son of man shall send forth his angels, and they shall gather out of his kingdom all things that offend, and them which do iniquity; and shall cast them into a furnace of fire: there shall be wailing and gnashing of teeth.

What a description! The gathering out of *all things that offend,* and of all persons who cause others to stumble and who work evil, will be a consummation devoutly to be wished. Not only the outwardly wicked, but also the false pretenders, the mock wheat, shall be removed. This will be the purging not of the church, but of *out of his kingdom,* which at that time will include the whole field of the world. We could not effect this clearance, but the Lord's own angels can and will. This shall be *in the end of this world,* the finale and climax of this dispensation. The fate of these ungodly ones will be *fire,* the most terrible of punishments, but this will not annihilate them, for they shall exhibit the surest tokens of a living woe: *Wailing and gnashing of teeth.* Sooner or later, this is what must come of evil men. Though in this world they flourish in the same field with believers, and can hardly be discerned from them, they shall be removed from such honorable association and be cast, with the rubbish of the universe, into that great *furnace of fire,* whose smoke goes up forever and ever. This *the Son of man* will do with authority. The angels are simply the executioners of the wrath of the Lamb.

43. Then shall the righteous shine forth as the sun in the kingdom of their Father. Who hath ears to hear, let him hear.

Relieved of the cloud created by compulsory association with mere pretenders, *the righteous shall shine forth.* The *kingdom* always was *their Father's*, and now shall they be seen to be His heirs and in consequence, inheritors of His glory and joy. Till then they must be, to a great extent, concealed by those who intrude their unworthy presence and keep them in a measure of darkness through the world-mixture. With the intruders being removed by the angelic executioners, *the righteous* will gain a distinct manifestness of character, which will cause their excellence to be as clearly seen as the sun at noonday. This is good hearing for them, and as they have *ears to hear,* let them hear it with delighted attention.

> *44. Again, the kingdom of heaven is like unto treasure hid in a field; the which when a man hath found, he hideth, and for joy thereof goeth and selleth all that he hath, and buyeth that field.*

Still the theme is *the kingdom of heaven.* The man lighted upon *treasure hid in a field,* perhaps while he was ploughing or digging. He was not looking for it, yet he *found* it. Is it not written, *I am found of them that sought me not* (Isaiah 65:1)? To obtain a right to the treasure trove, the finder must buy the field, and to do this he parts with *all that he hath.* So do men act when they discover the riches of the gospel. So did Jesus Himself, at the utmost cost, buy the world to gain His church, which was the treasure that He desired. The special application of the parable we leave to the reader. Practically he will do well to become the chief actor in a similar incident. Gladly may he part with all that he has to make sure of the kingdom of heaven.

> *45-46. Again, the kingdom of heaven is like unto a merchant man, seeking goodly pearls: who, when he had found one pearl of great price, went and sold all that he had, and bought it.*

Observe that in this instance the precious thing was not met with by accident, but discovered after an intelligent search for it. The first parable is descriptive of the ordinary man, to whom the gospel comes when he is following his calling and is by no means earnest after spiritual things. He turns up a crock of gold while ploughing, and having enough sense to prefer gold to clods, he buys the field and the treasure. In the present parable, the actor is not a ploughman, but *a merchant man,* dealing in precious things. This man is a superior person, aware of the value of jewels, and seeking them as the business of his life. He is a thoughtful, earnest individual, anxious for the best things, and therefore he reads, he hears, he considers and searches, even as a jeweler would do who is *seeking goodly pearls.* He discovers the gospel and rightly judges *the kingdom of heaven* to be the pearl of pearls, and therefore sacrifices all things else that he may have it in his own possession. In both cases, all was sold to win the prize, and so in any case, however our conversion takes place, we must give up all for Christ, not of compulsion, but willingly. It must be a pleasure to us to make sacrifices; indeed, we must consider them to be no sacrifices, just as those two men were eager and anxious to sell all their property to get possession of the one treasure that would make them rich for life.

> *47-48. Again, the kingdom of heaven is like unto a net, that was cast into the sea, and gathered of every kind: which, when it was full, they drew to shore, and sat down, and gathered the good into vessels, but cast the bad away.*

Here, among men, the *kingdom of heaven* is as a seine or a drawnet. It encompasses a great area of water, and entangles within it all kinds of creatures that move in the sea. The net-casting is a success, for the net *gathered* and *was full.* Yet the success may not be so great as it seems, for the contents of the net are varied. It *gathered of every kind.* So long as it is in the water, it contains *bad* and *good,* of necessity. It cannot be otherwise, and it would be vain to set about sorting the things that it encompasses while yet in the sea. On the shore will be the place for separation. The worthless, useless, and corrupt will be castaways, even though they were once in the net, but the truly precious will be taken from the net and presented to their Lord. We must now stand and fish, casting the net, and waiting for a haul. Not till the end shall we *[sit] down* and sort out our takings. Many are trying to do the last thing first.

> *49-50. So shall it be at the end of the world: the angels shall come forth, and sever the wicked from among the just, and shall cast them into the furnace of fire: there shall be wailing and gnashing of teeth.*

The separation between *the wicked* and *the just,* who are in the kingdom, will be at the close of the dispensation. It will be accomplished by the messengers of God, the appointed *angels*. It will be done infallibly, readily, fully, and finally. The doom of the wicked is described in terms that are terrible to the last degree. Those who would have us think lightly of the punishment of the ungodly have no support for this in the teachings of the Lord Jesus. Neither does the idea that fire causes annihilation find any support from the metaphor here employed, for *in the furnace of fire there shall be wailing and gnashing of teeth.*

51. Jesus saith unto them, Have ye understood all these things? They say unto him, Yea, Lord.

This is a very important question. To understand truth is essential, to understand it *all* is desirable. The mere letter or parable, without a sense of the meaning, will neither revive nor sanctify. As food must be eaten, digested, and assimilated, so must truth be taken up and taken in by the mind. Could *we* say, *Yea, Lord,* if He were to inquire of us? Do we even understand the seven parables that He has here given us? Did those who said, *Yea, Lord,* comprehend the Master's teaching as they might have done? Probably their view of their own understanding was not so lowly as it might have been.

52. Then said he unto them, Therefore every scribe which is instructed unto the kingdom of heaven is like unto a man that is an householder, which bringeth forth out of his treasure things new and old.

Our first desire should be that we ourselves may be *instructed unto the kingdom of heaven* – a remarkable phrase. This done, we are each one appointed to be like a *householder* and are made responsible for using our knowledge as food for all in our house. What we understand, we must teach. What we have received into our *treasure* we must *bringeth forth*. If the Lord has instructed us unto His kingdom, it is for the sake of others. Toward these we must act as one who keeps house and brings out provisions for the family. Some things have been laid up to ripen, and these the steward fetches out in due season. Others are the better for being fresh from the garden and these he serves up at once. He keeps back nothing, but he does not confine his provision to one single thing. He is not weary of the *old*. He is not afraid of the *new*. Old truth is made new by a living experience. New views of truth, if indeed it be truth, are only the old in a fresh light. We must, in our instruction of others, cultivate variety, but we must not aim at it by poisoning the children with deadly drugs for the sake of giving them new dishes. Only things worth putting into a treasury are worth bringing forth to the household. That *scribe* needs to be well instructed who has to keep on handing out a variety of precious truths throughout a long life.

Lord, make us sufficient for these things. Instruct us that we may instruct our household. May we make no reserve for self, but bring out for Your people all of that which You have put in our charge. Oh, to be accepted of You in the day of Your return, because we were found faithful to our trust!

53. And it came to pass, that when Jesus had finished these parables, he departed thence.

He stayed so as not to overdo what had been so well done. When He *had finished,* He left off. When He had completed His ministry in a place, *he departed thence.*

Matthew 13:54-58

The King in His Own Country

54. And when he was come into his own country, he taught them in their synagogue, insomuch that they were astonished, and said, Whence hath this man this wisdom, and these mighty works?

With what emotion did our Lord return to His native place! How ready He was to associate with former friends, for *he taught them in their synagogue.* How eagerly they came together to hear their young countryman, who had made so great a stir! How amazed they were at the masterly way in which He touched great subjects and worked great deeds!

Astonishment led to inquiry. They began to ask how it could be. The question, *Whence hath this man this wisdom, and these mighty works?* might have been brought forward reverently and have led to their obtaining a most instructive reply; but some flavored their question with impertinent unbelief and this cost them dearly.

Lord, grant that my questions may never savor of skepticism. Give me to be astonished at what You do and yet not to be astonished that You should be able to do such mighty works.

55-56. Is not this the carpenter's son? is not his mother called Mary? and his brethren, James, and Joses, and Simon, and Judas? And his sisters, are they not all with us? Whence then hath this man all these things?

His pedigree seemed to them to be of the lowliest. He had sprung from among themselves. His reputed father was a village craftsman. His mother was plain *Mary* and His relatives were commonplace parties enough. This ought to have gratified and encouraged them, but it did not. They grew sarcastic, and harped upon the family names of *James, and Joses, and Simon, and Judas.* They hinted that He could not have learned much wisdom in a *carpenter's* shop, and as He had not been among the rabbis to obtain a superior education, He could not really know much. How could He have attained to such eminence? He was a mere nobody. Why, they knew Him when His parents lost Him when they went up to the feast at Jerusalem! They could not listen to the talk of *the carpenter's son.*

57. And they were offended in him. But Jesus said unto them, A prophet is not without honour, save in his own country, and in his own house.

They stumbled at that which should have been a stepping stone for them. Poor souls! How like to many in these days, who must have glitter and superiority or they think nothing of the profoundest wisdom! If they can understand a sermon, they conceive that it cannot be a good one. If a man acts simply and naturally, he cannot in their eyes be worthy of much notice. Still is it commonly the case that, where a man is known, his neighbors find it hard to think that he can be really great. Distance lends enchantment – a cloud increases the apparent size. This is folly.

58. And he did not many mighty works there because of their unbelief.

Unbelief bound His hands. Why should He spend His sacred energy among a people who would not be profited thereby? Where He would have chosen to do the most, He was forced to do the least, because He saw that all He did would be wasted on them. The Lord save us from such a state of mind!

Give us, O Lord, faith to the full, that for us and in us and by us, You may be able to do *many mighty works* of grace!

Matthew 14

Matthew 14:1-12

The King's Herald Slain

1-2. At that time Herod the tetrarch heard of the fame of Jesus, and said unto his servants, This is John the Baptist; he is risen from the dead; and therefore mighty works do shew forth themselves in him.

When the whole country was moved, *at that time Herod the tetrarch heard of the fame of Jesus.* Then, but not till then, the fame of Jesus reached this wretched prince, who was too absorbed in self and lust to hear much about spiritual matters. The peasant heard of Jesus before the prince. The Word of God may enter the palace, but it forces its way slowly. Herod spoke to his servants about this famous person, for he was so alarmed that he could not conceal his fears. A guilty conscience is haunted by a misdeed. *John* was written on the tyrant's memory, and now that he is startled by a rumor of wonders being done, he cries out, *This is John the Baptist; he is risen from the dead.* Herod was a Sadducee by profession, but his terror made his skeptical creed crumble to dust. For John at least, he believes that there is a resurrection. Great superstition often underlies a surface of professed unbelief. Herod Antipas had a quarter of his father's kingdom and less than a quarter of his ability, but in selfish cruelty he was a true cub of the old wolf. He had enough conscience to scare him, though not enough to change him. Note how he believed in the power of a risen man: *Therefore mighty works do shew forth themselves in him.* If from mere hearsay Herod attributed such power to our Lord on earth, shall we not believe in the almighty power of our risen Lord upon His throne in glory?

3-4. For Herod had laid hold on John, and bound him, and put him in prison for Herodias' sake, his brother Philip's wife. For John said unto him, It is not lawful for thee to have her.

Of course it was *not lawful* for him to take to himself *his brother Philip's wife* while Philip was yet living, and while his own wife was living also. While he was the guest of Philip at home, he became ensnared by Herodias, and the guilty pair, who, in addition to their being already wedded, were by birth too near of kin for lawful marriage, came back to Galilee as if they were man and wife. It was bravely spoken of the Baptist when he bluntly said, *It is not lawful for thee to have her,* but the sentence cost him dearly. Herod Antipas could bear to do the deed, but he could not bear to be told that he had committed an unlawful act. John did not mince matters, or leave the question alone. What was a king to him if that king dared to trample on the Law of God? He spoke out pointedly and Herod knew that he did so. *Herod laid hold on John* because John's word had laid hold on Herod.

The power of evil love comes out in the words, *for Herodias' sake.* This fierce woman would tolerate no rebuke of her licentiousness. She was a very Jezebel in her pride and cruelty, and Herod was as a puppet in her hands.

5. And when he would have put him to death, he feared the multitude, because they counted him as a prophet.

Neither he nor his lover could bear such plain dealing, and so he would have silenced forever the rebuking tongue if he had not been restrained by a helpful dread of the populace. Herod was already a murderer in intent, but fear halted his cruel hand. The people held John in high esteem as a servant of God and the tyrant dared not incur the wrath of *the multitude.* What slaves to fear bad princes may become. It is well that they should be so, for thus a temporary check is put upon their tyranny. Alas! it is not often a restraint for long, for they soon break loose again and for a favorite's sake risk the anger of the nation.

6. But when Herod's birthday was kept, the daughter of Herodias danced before them, and pleased Herod.

There is no harm in keeping birthdays, but there is great harm in lewd dances or in any other sports that suggest evil. Salome was a true *daughter of Herodias.* She forgot her rank and danced before the court after the lewd fashion of the age, so as to gratify a probably drunken monarch. She *pleased Herod,* her mother's lover, and we can readily guess the kind of dancing that would please him.

In these days, mothers too often encourage their daughters in clothing that is scarcely decent and introduce them to dances that are not commendable for purity. No good can come of this. It may please the Herods, but it displeases God. In this case, dancing led to a cruel crime and it is to be feared that in many instances gross immoralities have taken their rise in dances that suggested uncleanness.

7. Whereupon he promised with an oath to give her whatsoever she would ask.

A foolish *promise* and a wicked *oath.* Men of Herod's order are always free with oaths. Men should know what they are at when they promise, and never set their signature to a blank that another may fill up, for they may thus sign away their all. Besides, a mere piece of immodest posturing could never deserve so large a compensation. Herod was surely as much a fool as a scoundrel. Had wine and lust taken away his heart?

8. And she, being before instructed of her mother, said, Give me here John Baptist's head in a charger.

The whole thing was planned between this shameless mother and daughter, who both knew Herod's weak points and how to handle him. The mother set her daughter dancing and then put the request into her mouth. She was of her mother's nature and readily carried out that wicked woman's instructions. No doubt Herodias was more incensed than Herod at what John the Baptist had dared to say, for it is usually the case that the female offender is most angered by a rebuke of such sin. Sad that from noble Maccabean blood such a female monster should have sprung! She must have *John Baptist's head* upon a dish. The mention of the details shows the cold-blooded character of the demand. As if it were a dainty dish for her mouth, the prophet's head must be served up *in a charger* (a platter).

9. And the king was sorry: nevertheless for the oath's sake, and them which sat with him at meat, he commanded it to be given her.

Pretty sorrow! A crocodile is said to shed tears over those it snaps in two. The king was afraid of the consequences. Poor king! He may have felt a dying struggle of conscience, for Herod had some sort of reverence for John, yet his grief could not have been very deep, for he had already purposed to kill him. The king feared that his courtiers and comrades at the drinking event would think him weak and perhaps jeer at him for being too religious to touch a prophet. Such fear of being thought weak proved that he was weak indeed. In addition to this, Herodias would consider him to be by no means so fond of her as he had professed to be, and how could he endure her passionate grief? Moreover, he was a man of honor, and *for the oath's sake* he must not run back. With the regret that a wolf feels because he must eat the lamb, he gave orders for the murder of John and the handing of his head to the young girl. Rash promises and even oaths are no excuse for doing wrong. The promise was in itself null and void, because no man has a right to promise to do wrong. Wicked oaths ought to be repented of and not acted out, but this cruel tyrant commanded the murder and so went through with his horrible promise.

10. And he sent, and beheaded John in the prison.

Herod *sent, and beheaded John.* By a word a precious life is ended. How lightly tyrants think of murder! No miracle was worked for John's deliverance. Why should there be? It was well for the Baptist to go to his reward, for his work was done. He was not left to languish in solitude. The man of God left his prison for paradise by one sudden stroke of the sword. It was a foul murder, but to the Baptist it was a happy release. He was no longer in the power of Herod or Herodias. He received his crown in heaven though he had lost his head on earth.

Herod is said to have *beheaded John,* for what he ordered to be done is set to his account and in his conscience he knew it. We do ourselves what we do by others. Men may sin by proxy, but they will be guilty in person.

11. And his head was brought in a charger, and given to the damsel: and she brought it to her mother.

What a present for a young lady! It was *given to the damsel.* The girl is not ashamed to lift the dainty dish and give it to her fiendish mother so that she may satisfy her malice by the sight of the head of her faithful reprover. What a mother and daughter! Two bad women can do a world of mischief. What a fate for such a head! Did it even from the charger charge the foul adulteress with her crime?

12. And his disciples came, and took up the body, and buried it, and went and told Jesus.

The good man's followers did not desert their murdered leader: *His disciples came.* The mangled corpse was surrendered to them. They reverently *took up the body, and buried it.* They were his disciples still and his death was not the death of their faith. They did the only act of kindness then in their power to him whom they had followed. They regarded the headless trunk as being the last relic of John, and so they gathered around it and gave it an honorable burial. But it is not said by the evangelist that they buried John, but that *they took up the body, and buried **it*** (emphasis added), not *him.* The real John no man could bury, and Herod soon found that, being dead, he still spoke.

What remained for John's disciples but to go to their leader's Friend and Master and tell Him all the circumstances, and await further orders? John had taught them well, since they went at once to Jesus when their teacher was dead.

When we are in a great trouble, we shall be wise to do our best, and at the same time tell the Lord Jesus all about it so that He may direct us further as to what we are to do. What a relief to tell Jesus! It was a painful story for Him to hear, but He would be sure to impart consolation to these mourners, and in our case also He will send comfort.

Matthew 14:13-22

Our King Gives a Great Banquet

13. When Jesus heard of it, he departed thence by ship into a desert place apart: and when the people had heard thereof, they followed him on foot out of the cities.

Our Lord could not allow so sad an event as the death of His forerunner to pass without special devotion; perhaps also He judged it wise to be out of the dominions of Herod just at this time. When such a tiger once tastes blood, he is apt to thirst for more. Moreover, rest was needed both for Himself and for the little band of men that attended Him, and our Lord was no hard taskmaster, overdriving His servants. As soon, therefore, as *Jesus heard of [John's death],* He went with His followers to a lone spot beyond Herod's jurisdiction, *a desert place apart.* He went there by ship, to put the sea between Him and the crowd. It was difficult for Him to get into seclusion, but He used commonsense ways of obtaining it. He knew the absolute need of privacy and He strove for it. The discreet use of solitude has yet to be learned by many workers.

The multitude would not permit Him to be at rest. They were curious, anxious, and needy, and so they were soon *on foot* after Him. While He sailed by sea, they hurried along the shore. It is a happy sign when there is an eagerness to hear the Word of God. May the Lord send us more of it in these days of religious indifference.

14. And Jesus went forth, and saw a great multitude, and was moved with compassion toward them, and he healed their sick.

When He left the boat and *went forth,* our Lord found a congregation waiting for Him. In the most emphatic sense, He saw the people, and at the sight of them He was burdened. He was not angry at the *great multitude,* nor did He show disappointment at being balked in His pursuit of quietness, but He was *moved with compassion.* The original word is very expressive. His whole being was stirred to its lowest depth and therefore He proceeded at once to work miracles of mercy among them. They came unasked, He received them tenderly, He blessed them graciously, and at length He fed them bountifully. He was as a deer that fled from the hunters, but they had overtaken Him and He yielded Himself to them. To those who needed Him most He attended first; *He healed their sick.* Lord, heal me, for I am sick in soul, if not in body!

15. And when it was evening, his disciples came to him, saying, This is a desert place, and the time is now past; send the multitude away, that they may go into the villages, and buy themselves victuals.

The disciples had the compassion of men who see the need, but to their human thought there seemed but one poor way out of it, namely, in effect to shirk the difficulty by *send[ing] the multitude away.* The short way out of a perplexity is generally a very poor affair. To this day, many Christians get no further than leaving the masses to themselves or to some unknown influences that may turn up. One thing was wise in the disciples – they did bring the matter to Jesus: *When it was evening, his disciples came to him.* They described the place as barren, the time as late, the people as many, their needs as great. They were well versed in all discouraging matters. The proposed course of action was the one weak point in the representation. Our schemes are for the most part wretched affairs. It is almost a wonder that we dare to state them. Do we forget that our Lord Jesus hears our sorry proposals?

Note the disciples' words: *The time is now past.* We usually think the times are unpromising for large attempts. As for the position, it is hopeless: *This is a desert place.* What can be done here? As for the disciples' proposal, it was of a kind that is common enough: "Don't let the people die under our noses. Pull down the rookery in the next street. Clear out the bad houses from our district." *Send the multitude away.* Or better still, show the people the dignity of self-help! Talk to them about thrift and emigration. Urge them to *go into the villages, and buy themselves victuals.* This is a favorite remedy at this time with those who want to save their own loaves and fishes. Our Lord has nobler thoughts than theirs. He will display His royal bounty among the hungry crowd.

16. But Jesus said unto them, They need not depart; give ye them to eat.

Glorious word! *They need not depart.* We are able, when He is with us, to meet any cases of need that may arise. We never need to send the multitude away to be dealt with by the state, by the parish, or by laborers. If we will but set to work, we shall find that the Lord makes us competent for every emergency. *Give ye them to eat.* You talk of their buying for themselves, but they are penniless and cannot buy. Everything must be free or they will starve. You are the men to feed them freely. Get at it. Begin at once.

17. And they say unto him, We have here but five loaves, and two fishes.

See how they overhaul their provisions, and they report, *We have here but five loaves.* With what a gloomy *but,* they show how lean is the pantry! Those two sardines make the stock seem positively ridiculous. It is a good thing for us to know how very poor we are and how far from being able to meet the needs of the people around us. It is for our good to be made to confess this in so many words to our Lord.

Truly, he who writes this comment has often felt as if he had neither loaf nor fish, and yet for some forty years and more he has been a full-handed waiter at the King's great banquets.

18. He said, Bring them hither to me.

He will have us yield up what we have. We are to make no reserve. We must hand all over to Jesus: *Bring them hither to me.* He will accept what we bring. This is implied in the command to bring it. He will make a little go a long way. That which gets to Jesus will reach the needy by the surest route. The shortest way to procure provisions for perishing souls is to go to Jesus about them.

19. And he commanded the multitude to sit down on the grass, and took the five loaves, and the two fishes, and looking up to heaven, he blessed, and brake, and gave the loaves to his disciples, and the disciples to the multitude.

He had prepared both carpet and seats for His guests, by making *grass* to grow in His open-air banquet hall. At the bidding of their great Host, all the crowds sat down. *He commanded* and they obeyed – a proof of the unique power of the personality of our Lord to produce obedience even in simple matters. One would have thought that they might have answered, "What is the use of sitting down? How shall a table be furnished in this wilderness?" But our Lord's presence awed unbelief into silence and obedience. The King of men is immediately obeyed when He commands in the fullness of His majesty. *Where the word of a king is, there is power* (Ecclesiastes 8:4).

Now that all is in order, the divine Lord takes the meager provision into His blessed hands. By a simple sign He teaches the people from where to expect gracious supplies: *Looking up to heaven.* Not without a blessing does the *alfresco* meal begin: *He blessed.* God's blessing must be sought even when Jesus is there. He will not act without the Father. Our Lord Jesus did all in the provision of the feast: *He blessed, and brake, and gave to his disciples.* All is with Him. The disciples come in to take their subordinate position after He has displayed His divine creatorship. They are the waiters. They serve and distribute. They can do no more. They are glad to do *that.* In haste, but yet in order, they divide the food among the throng, much wondering and adoring as they do so. It was bread and a relish with it, good food and agreeable, sufficient, but not luxurious. Some would give the poor only the barest necessities – bread only. Our Lord adds fish. What a feast was this! Christ for Master of the feast, apostles for butlers, thousands for numbers, and miracles for supplies! What a far more glorious feast is that which the gospel spreads for hungry souls! What a privilege to be fed by the Son of God!

20. And they did all eat, and were filled: and they took up of the fragments that remained twelve baskets full.

No one was neglected, no one refused, no one was too faint, no one left off till he was satisfied, no one needed anything else, and no one found that the food did not suit him, for indeed they were all hungry, *and they did all eat.* No one limited himself or was limited; all *were filled.* Ours is a filling Benefactor and He provides filling food.

After the feast, *twelve baskets* were needed to hold *the fragments.* It was impossible to exhaust the store. The baskets were *full* as well as the people. There was more provision after the feeding than before it. By feeding others our stock increases. That which was left had been blessed as well as that which was eaten, and therefore it was fine food for the disciples. They gave plain bread and fish, and they received more in quantity and a blessing to improve the quality. Those who wait upon others at Christ's bidding shall have a fair portion for themselves. Those who fill others' mouths shall have their own baskets filled. Everybody is satisfied when Jesus makes the feast.

21. And they that had eaten were about five thousand men, beside women and children.

Women and children are usually more numerous at a sermon than men, but as the people had come on foot, perhaps the men outnumbered the women and children on this occasion, as they generally do at feeding times.

From many a great banquet women and children are shut out, but in Christ Jesus there is no exclusion because of sex or youth.

Five thousand men is no small dinner party. Think of five thousand fed with five loaves! A loaf among a thousand! Never let us fear that our consecrated supplies will not hold out or that we have not talent or ability enough if the Lord is pleased to use us. Our King will yet feed all the nations on that gospel that is today so little thought of. Amen! So let it be.

22. And straightway Jesus constrained his disciples to get into a ship, and to go before him unto the other side, while he sent the multitudes away.

Straightway is a business word. Jesus loses no time. No sooner is the banquet over than He sends off the guests to their homes. While they are well-fed, He bids them make the best of their way home. He who made the multitude sit down was able also to *[send] the multitude away;* but they needed sending, for they were reluctant to go.

The sea must be crossed again or Jesus cannot find seclusion. How He must run the gauntlet to get a little rest! Before He starts again across the sea, He performs another act of self-denial, for He cannot leave till He sees the crowd happily dispersed. He attends to that business Himself, giving the disciples the opportunity to depart in peace. As the captain is the last to leave the ship, so is the Lord the last to leave the scene of labor. The disciples would have chosen to stay in His company and to enjoy the thanks of the people, but *Jesus constrained [them] to get into a ship.* He could not get anyone to go away from Him at this time without sending and constraining. This loadstone has great attractions. He evidently promised His disciples that He would follow them, for the words are: *To go before him unto the other side.* How He was to follow He did not say, but He could always find a way of keeping His appointments. How considerate of Him to wait amid the throng while the disciples sailed away in peace. He always takes the heavy end of the load Himself.

Matthew 14:23-36

The King Ruling Winds and Waves

23. And when he had sent the multitudes away, he went up into a mountain apart to pray: and when the evening was come, he was there alone.

Now that the crowd is gone, He can take His rest and He finds it in prayer. *He went up into a mountain apart,* in a place where He might speak aloud and not be overheard or disturbed. He communed with the Father *alone.*

This was His refreshment and His delight. He continued therein till the thickest shades of night had gathered and the day was gone. *Alone,* yet not alone, He drank in new strength as He communed with His Father. He must have revealed this private matter to the recording evangelist and surely it was with the intent that we should learn from His example.

We cannot afford to be always in company, since even our blessed Lord felt that He must be *alone.*

24. But the ship was now in the midst of the sea, tossed with waves: for the wind was contrary.

While Jesus was alone, they, in *the ship,* were in the same condition, but not occupied with the same spiritual exercise. When they first left the shore, it was fair sailing in the cool of the evening, but a storm gathered hastily as night covered the sky. On the Sea of Galilee, the wind rushes down from the gullies between the mountains and causes serious peril to little boats, sometimes fairly lifting them out of the water and immediately submerging them beneath the waves. That deep lake was peculiarly dangerous for small craft. They were far from land, for they were *in the midst of the sea,* equally distant from either shore. The sea was furious and their ship was *tossed with waves.* The hurricane was terrible. *The wind was contrary,* and would not let them go to any place that they sought. It was a whirlwind and they were whirled about by it, but could not use it for reaching either shore. How much did their case resemble ours when we are in painful distress! We are tossed about and can do nothing. The blast is too furious for us to bear up against it or even to live while driven before it.

One happy fact remains: Jesus is pleading on the shore though we are struggling on the sea. It is also comfortable to know that we are where He *constrained* us to go (see verse 22), and He has promised to come to us in due time, and therefore all must be safe, though the tempest rages terribly.

25. And in the fourth watch of the night Jesus went unto them, walking on the sea.

Jesus is sure to come. The night wears on and the darkness thickens; *the fourth watch of the night* draws near, but where is He? Faith says, "He must come." Though He should stay away till almost the break of day, He must come. Unbelief asks, "How can He come?" Ah, He will answer for Himself. He can make his own way. *Jesus went unto them, walking on the sea.* He comes in the teeth of the wind and on the face of the wave. Never fear that He will fail to reach the storm-tossed ship. His love will find out the way. Whether it be to a single disciple, or to the church as a whole, Jesus will appear in His own chosen hour and His time is sure to be the most timely.

26. And when the disciples saw him walking on the sea, they were troubled, saying, It is a spirit; and they cried out for fear.

Yes, the disciples *saw him,* saw Jesus their Lord, and derived no comfort from the sight. Poor human nature's sight is a blind thing compared with the vision of a spiritual faith. They saw, but knew not what they saw.

What could it be but a ghost? How could a real man walk on those foaming billows? How could He stand in the teeth of such a hurricane? They were already at their wits' end, and the apparition put an end to their courage. We seem to hear their shriek of alarm: *They cried out for fear.* We read not that *they were troubled* before. They were old sailors and had no dread of natural forces, but *a spirit* – ah, that was too much of a terror. They were at their worst now, and yet, if they had known it, they were on the verge of their best. It is noteworthy that the nearer Jesus was, the greater was their fear. Lack of discernment blinds the soul to its richest consolations. Lord, be near and let me know You! Let me not have to say with Jacob, *Surely the* Lord *is in this place; and I knew it not* (Genesis 28:16).

> *27. But straightway Jesus spake unto them, saying, Be of good cheer; it is I; be not afraid.*

He did not keep them in suspense: *Straightway Jesus spake unto them.* How sweetly sounded that loving and majestic voice! Above the roar of waves and the howling of winds, they heard the voice of the Lord. This was His old word also: *Be of good cheer.* The most conclusive reason for courage was His own presence: *It is I; be not afraid.* If Jesus be near, if the spirit of the storm be, after all, the Lord of love, then all room for fear is gone. Can Jesus come to us through the storm? Then we shall weather it and come to Him. He who rules the tempest is not the devil, not chance, not a malicious enemy, but Jesus. This should end all fear.

> *28. And Peter answered him and said, Lord, if it be thou, bid me come unto thee on the water.*

Peter must be the first to speak. He is impulsive, and besides, he was a sort of foreman in the company. The first speaker is not always the wisest man. Peter's fears have gone, except for one *if,* but that *if* was working him no good, for it seemed to challenge his Master: *Lord, if it be thou.* What a test to suggest: *Bid me come unto thee on the water.* What did Peter want by walking on the waters? His name might have suggested that like a stone he would go to the bottom. It was an unwise request. It was the swing of the pendulum in Peter from despair to a careless venturing. Surely, he knew not what he said. Yet we, too, have put our Lord to tests almost as improper. Have we not said, "If You have ever blessed me, give me this and that"? We, too, have had our water-walking and have ventured where nothing but special grace could uphold us. Lord, what is man?

29. And he said, Come. And when Peter was come down out of the ship, he walked on the water, to go to Jesus.

When good men are unwise and presumptuous, it may be for their lasting good to learn their folly by experience. *He said, Come.* Peter's Lord is about to teach him a practical lesson. He asked to be bidden to come. He may come. He does come. He leaves the boat. He treads the wave. He is on the way towards his Lord. We can do anything if we have divine authorization and courage enough to take the Lord at His word. Now there were two on the sea, two wonders! Which was the greater? The reader may not find it easy to reply. Let him consider.

30. But when he saw the wind boisterous, he was afraid; and beginning to sink, he cried, saying, Lord, save me.

But – a sorrowful *but* for poor Peter. His eye was off his Lord and on the raging of the wind: *He saw the wind boisterous.* His heart failed him and then his foot failed him. Down he began to go – an awful moment is this *beginning to sink,* yet it was only a *beginning;* he had time to cry to his Lord, who was not sinking. Peter cried and was safe. His prayer was as full as it was short. He had brought his eye and his faith back to Jesus, for he cried, *Lord.* He had come into this danger through obedience and therefore he had an appeal in the word *Lord.* Whether in danger or not, Jesus was still his Lord. He is a lost man and he feels it, unless his Lord will save him – save him altogether, save him now. Blessed prayer: *Lord save me.* Reader, does it not suit you? Peter was nearer his Lord when he was sinning than when he was walking. In our low estate, we may be drawn nearer to Jesus than in our more glorious seasons.

31. And immediately Jesus stretched forth his hand, and caught him, and said unto him, O thou of little faith, wherefore didst thou doubt?

Our Lord delays not when our peril is imminent and our cry is urgent: *Immediately Jesus stretched forth his hand.* He first *caught him* and then taught him. Jesus saves first and rebukes afterwards, when He needs to do so. When we are saved is the suitable time for us to chasten ourselves for our unbelief. Let us learn from our Lord that we may not reprove others till we have first helped them out of their difficulties.

Our doubts are unreasonable: *Wherefore didst thou doubt?* If there be reason for little faith, there is evidently reason for great confidence. If it be right to trust Jesus at all, why not trust Him altogether? Trust was Peter's strength, doubt was his danger. It looked like great faith when Peter walked on the water, but a little wind soon proved it to be *little faith*. Till our faith is tested, we can form no reliable estimate of it.

After his Lord had taken him by the hand, Peter sank no farther, but resumed the walk of faith. How easy to have faith when we are close to Jesus!

Lord, when our faith fails, come You to us and we shall walk on the waves.

32. And when they were come into the ship, the wind ceased.

So Peter's walk and his rescue had happened in the face of the tempest. He could walk the water well enough when his Lord held his hand and so can we. What a sight! Jesus and Peter, hand in hand, walking upon the sea! The two headed for the ship at once. Miracles are never spun out to undue length. Was not Peter glad to leave the tumultuous element, and at the same time to perceive that the gale was over? *When they were come into the ship, the wind ceased.* It is well to be safe in a storm, but more pleasant to find the calm return and the hurricane end. How gladly did the disciples welcome their Lord and their brother Peter, who though wet to the skin, was a wiser man for his adventure!

33. Then they that were in the ship came and worshipped him, saying, Of a truth thou art the Son of God.

No wonder that Peter *worshipped him,* nor that his comrades did the same. The whole of the disciples, who had been thus rescued by their Lord's coming to them on the stormy sea, were overwhelmingly convinced of His Godhead. Now they were doubly sure of it by unquestionable evidence, and in lowly reverence they expressed to Him their adoring faith, saying, *Of a truth thou art the Son of God.*

34-36. And when they were gone over, they came into the land of Gennesaret. And when the men of that place had knowledge of him, they sent out into all that country round about, and brought unto him all that were diseased; and besought him that they might only touch the hem of his garment: and as many as touched were made perfectly whole.

The ship so lately tempest-tossed is soon at the desired haven and now other scenes of wonder meet our eyes. Land where He may, the Great Physician is sure to find patients. Some of *the men of that place had knowledge of him,* and these were as sparks to set the rest of the people on fire by wonderful accounts of what Jesus had done. Many became eager advertisers of His skill and either went themselves or *sent out [others] into all that country round about.* Very busy those people were.

They sent out; they *brought unto him;* they *besought him;* they touched *his garment;* they *were made perfectly whole.* The sentences follow each other without a break. The people asked little – they begged *that they might only touch the hem of his garment* – but they received much, for they *were made perfectly whole.* In no case was there any failure. In every instance the work was complete. Their humble request was founded upon a precedent, was urged by earnest spirits, and was accompanied by practical sympathy; therefore, it was not refused. How glad that whole region was made! *All that were diseased* had become happy witnesses of the Lord's healing power.

Our King is Master both on land and water. Whether it is on the sea of Gennesaret or in *the land of Gennesaret,* His supreme power and majesty are infallibly proven. He stills tempests and alleviates fevers. He touches waves with His foot and they grow firm. He touches sick bodies with His hand and they return to health. He imparts to His servant Peter and to the hem of His own garment marvelous power.

Matthew 15

Matthew 15:1-20

Our King Combating Formalists

1-2. Then came to Jesus scribes and Pharisees, which were of Jerusalem, saying, Why do thy disciples transgress the tradition of the elders? for they wash not their hands when they eat bread.

When our Lord was busiest, His enemies attacked Him. These clergymen *of Jerusalem* were probably the cream of the crop, and from their great reputation they reckoned upon an easy victory over the rustic Preacher. Perhaps they were a delegation from headquarters, sent to confound the new Teacher. They had a question to raise, which to them may have seemed important, or possibly they pretended to think it so to answer their own purposes. *Traditions of the elders* were great things with them. To transgress these must be a crime indeed. Washing of the hands is a thing proper enough. One could wish it were more often practiced, but to exalt it into a religious rite is a folly and a sin. These *scribes and Pharisees* washed their hands, whether they needed washing or not, out of a supposed zeal to be rid of any particle that might render them ceremonially unclean. Our Lord's disciples had so far entered into Christian liberty that they did not observe the rabbinical tradition: *They wash not their hands when they eat bread.* Why should they wash if their hands were clean? Tradition had no power over their consciences. No man has any more right to institute a new duty than to neglect an old one. The issuing of commands is for the King alone. Yet these religionists ask why the Lord's disciples break a law that was no law. It will be well if our opponents are unable to bring against us any worse charge than this.

3. But he answered and said unto them, Why do ye also transgress the commandment of God by your tradition?

He answered their question by asking them another. This was a very usual way with our Lord, and we may often imitate Him in discussions with judgmental persons. Our Lord turns a blaze of light upon them by the question, *Why do ye also transgress the commandment of God by your tradition?* What is a *tradition* when compared with a *commandment*?

What is a tradition when it is in conflict with a commandment? What are *elders* in comparison with *God*? Our Lord knew best how to handle these messengers of the evil powers. His question carried the war into their own territory and turned their boastful assault into utter defeat.

4-6. For God commanded, saying, Honour thy father and mother: and, He that curseth father or mother, let him die the death. But ye say, Whosoever shall say to his father or his mother, It is a gift, by whatsoever thou mightest be profited by me; and honour not his father or his mother, he shall be free. Thus have ye made the commandment of God of none effect by tradition.

Our Lord explains His question and lays home His accusation. *God* had bound the son and daughter to honor the parent, and this unquestionably included rendering to father and mother such help as they might need. From this duty, there could be no escape without breaking the plain command of God. It was always right, by the law of nature, to be grateful to parents, and by the law of Moses it was always a deadly sin to revile them. In Exodus 21:17, we read, *And he that curseth his father, or his mother, shall surely be put to death.* Father and mother are to be held in reverence and cherished with love, and the precept that ordains this is called *the first commandment with promise* (Ephesians 6:2). There could be no mistake as to the meaning of the divine law, yet the corrupt teachers of the period had invented a method of excusing men from the performance of so obvious a duty.

These wretched tradition-lovers taught that if a man cried, *Corban! a gift,* and thus nominally set apart for God what his parents sought of him, he must not afterwards give it to them. If in anger or even in arrogance he placed what was requested by father or mother under a ban, he became *free* from the obligation to aid his parents. It is true that he was not required by the rabbis to carry out his vow and actually give the money or the goods to God, but as he had compromised the sacred name, he must on no account hand over the gift to his parents, so that a hasty word would loosen any child from his duty to aid his father or his mother and then he might pretend that he was very sorry for having said it, but that his conscience would not permit him to break the ban. Vile hypocrites! Advocates of the devil! Was ever a device more shallow? Yet thus they *made the commandment of God of none effect.*

7-8. Ye hypocrites, well did Esaias prophesy of you, saying, This people draweth nigh unto me with their mouth, and honoureth me with their lips; but their heart is far from me.

Right well did they deserve the name that the indignant Savior fixed upon them: *Ye hypocrites.* They were agitated about hands unwashed and yet laid their foul hands upon God's most holy law. The prophetic words of Isaiah were indeed descriptive of them. He had pictured them to the life. Theirs was mouth-religion, lip-homage, and that only. *Their heart* never approached the Lord at all.

Thus, our Lord gave His opponents Scripture instead of tradition. He broke their wooden weapons with the sword of the Spirit. Holy Scripture must be our weapon against the church of traditions. Nothing will overthrow Rome but the Word of the Lord.

When quoting from the prophecy of Isaiah, our blessed Lord not only used a translation, but He also gave the sense freely, thus rebuking the mere word-chopping of the rabbis. They could count the letters of a sacred book and yet utterly miss its meaning. He gave the soul and spirit of the inspired utterance. Jesus insisted upon heart-worship and said nothing as to the matter of washing or not washing the hands before eating bread. That was too trivial a point for Him to dwell upon.

9. But in vain they do worship me, teaching for doctrines the commandments of men.

Religion based on human authority is worthless. We must worship the true God in the way of His own appointing or we do not worship Him at all. Doctrines and ordinances are only to be accepted when the divine Word supports them, and they are to be accepted for that reason only. The most formal form of devotion is *vain worship*, if it is regulated by man's ordinance apart from the Lord's own command.

10. And he called the multitude, and said unto them, Hear, and understand.

He turns to the common throng, among whom He had worked His miracles of love. *He called the multitude* and instructed them, *Hear, and understand.* It looks as if He would say by His actions that He would rather teach the ignorant peasants than those falsehearted scribes and Pharisees. He had more hope of being understood by the ignorant multitude than by educated men who had so wretchedly enslaved their judgments by following worthless traditions. The appeal of the gospel is from the doctors to the people. These last have more common sense and honesty than the former, yet even these need the exhortation, *Hear, and understand.*

11. Not that which goeth into the mouth defileth a man; but that which cometh out of the mouth, this defileth a man.

Here is something for the crowd to think over and for the Pharisees to chew upon. It would be a riddle to many and a surprise to all. Preeminently it would be a staggering statement for formalists. Religionists of the day placed the chief point of morals in meats and drinks, but the Lord Jesus declared that it lay in thoughts and acts. The Pharisees had now a string to harp upon, and harp they would. This saying would afford a text for malicious comment for many a day. They had sought to lay hold upon a sentence that they could use as an accusation, and in this case He gave them one that they might quote with that purpose if they dared to do so. It was diametrically opposed to their teaching and yet it was not easy to meet its keen edge or withstand its singular force.

12. Then came his disciples, and said unto him, Knowest thou that the Pharisees were offended, after they heard this saying?

The disciples evidently thought more of offending the Pharisees than their Master did. He knew that they would be *offended* and thought it no calamity that they should be. He placed His remarkable saying in their way so that they might find themselves hindered and baffled by it. They had come to Him in a fawning manner, desiring to catch Him in His speech. He was disgusted with their hypocrisy and by this staggering statement He unmasked them, and they came out in their true colors. They could not further conceal their hate. Henceforth they could not entrap the disciples by their professions of friendliness.

13. But he answered and said, Every plant, which my heavenly Father hath not planted, shall be rooted up.

If men are themselves an offense, they deserve to be offended. If these professed teachers of God's mind fuss at God's Son, they deserve no mercy, but it is right and wise to treat them to truth that shall annoy them. A good gardener is careful to uproot weeds as well as to water plants. Our Lord's instructive utterance operated like a hoe to uproot these men from their religious profession, and He meant that it should do so. But what a solemn word is this! If our religion is not wholly of God, it will come to an end and that end will be destruction. No matter how fair the flower, if the *Father hath not planted* it, its doom is sealed. It shall not be pruned, but *rooted up.* Those whom the truth uproots are uprooted indeed.

14. Let them alone: they be blind leaders of the blind. And if the blind lead the blind, both shall fall into the ditch.

He turned from them as unworthy of further notice, saying, *Let them alone.* There was no need for the disciples to combat the Pharisees; they would be uprooted in the natural order of things by the inevitable consequences of their own course. Both they and their fools would *fall into the ditch* of error and absurdity and ultimately come to utter destruction. In every case it is so. When the bigoted teacher leads the ignorant disciple, they must both go wrong. The same is the case with every form of spiritual blindness in those who lead the thought of an age, and in those who follow their erroneous guidance. The philosophic unbelief of this age is blind with self-conceit, and fearful is the ditch towards which it is hastening. Alas! its teachers are carrying precious souls with them into the ditch of atheism and anarchy.

O Lord, permit us not to be despairing as to the present ascendancy of false doctrine. In patience may we possess our souls! We cannot make either the blind leaders or their blind followers see the ditch before them, but it is there all the same and their fall is certain. You alone can open the eyes of the blind and we trust that this miracle of grace will be worked by You.

15. Then answered Peter and said unto him, Declare unto us this parable.

The saying, which Peter calls a parable, was spoken to the multitude and they were bidden to understand it, but assuredly they did not comprehend it, for even the College of Apostles failed to grapple with it. Peter, as spokesman, did well to go at once to the fountainhead and humbly say, *Declare unto us this parable.* He that uttered the dark saying could best interpret it.

16. And Jesus said, Are ye also yet without understanding?

Of course the Pharisees would hate the light and so refuse to see the spiritual truth that our Lord had set before them in so forcible a fashion. Nor was it wonderful that the crowd should be too ignorant to see the divine meaning of the compact sentence. But should not the chosen twelve have had clearer insight? After all their Lord's teaching, were they *yet without understanding?* Should they not have reached the inner sense of their Lord's utterance? Alas, how often have we been in a similar state! How importantly might the question be put to us, *Are ye also yet without understanding?*

17. Do not ye yet understand, that whatsoever entereth in at the mouth goeth into the belly, and is cast out into the draught?

After years of the Master's teaching, are we still unable to grasp an elementary truth? Can we not discern between physical and spiritual defilement? Food does not touch the soul. It passes through the body, but it does not enter the affections or the understanding, and therefore it does not defile a man. That which is eaten is material substance and does not come into contact with the moral sense. This is clear enough to any unprejudiced mind. Meat passes through every passage of the bodily frame, from its entrance *at the mouth,* its passage through the bowels, to its ultimate expulsion, but it bears no relation to the mental and spiritual part of our being, and it is there only that real defilement can be caused.

18. But those things which proceed out of the mouth come forth from the heart; and they defile the man.

The outcomings of the mind have sprung from the heart of the man and have a moral character about them: *Things which proceed out of the mouth come forth from the heart.* Words and the thoughts that wear words as their garments, and the acts that are the embodiment of words – these are of the man himself and these *defile* him. If the mind or heart had nothing to do with an act, it would no more pollute a man than the food that he swallows and ejects. Because acts and words come not from the mouth only, but also from the heart, they are of far more importance than meats and drinks. Of course, defilement comes to a man when he is guilty of gluttony and drunkenness, yet this is not because of the mere meat or drink, but because the taking of them to excess is the exercise of unbridled appetite, and this also grows by that which gratifies it.

19. For out of the heart proceed evil thoughts, murders, adulteries, fornications, thefts, false witness, blasphemies.

What a list! What must that heart be out of which so many evils pour forth! These are the bees – what must the hive be! *Evil thoughts,* or reasonings, such as these Pharisees had been guilty of – *modern thought* is a specimen of these evils. It comes from the heart rather than from the head. *Murders* begin not with the dagger, but with the malice of the heart.

Adulteries and *fornications* are first gloated over in the heart before they are enacted by the body. The heart is the cage from where these unclean birds fly forth. *Thefts* also are born in the heart. A man would not wrongfully take with the hand if he had not wrongfully desired with the heart. *False witness,* or lying and slander – this, too, first ferments in the heart and then its venom is spit out in the conversation. He that utters *blasphemies* against his Maker shows a very black heart. How could he fall into such a needless, useless vice, unless his inmost soul had been steeped in rebellion against the Lord? These dreadful evils all flow from one fountain, from the very nature and life of fallen man.

20. These are the things which defile a man: but to eat with unwashen hands defileth not a man.

They not only come from a defiled nature, but they also still further *defile a man.* Thus had the Savior proved His saying. The things from within, evidently, are of a most defiling character and make a man unfit for communion with God and for the performance of holy duties, but the neglect of having water poured on the hands cannot be in the least comparable thereto. Yet those who had no repentance of polluting sins were struck with horror at a man's eating a piece of bread *with unwashen hands.*

Blessed Master, wash me within and save me from the defilements of corrupt nature! Permit me not to make outward forms my trust, but in the hidden parts purify me Yourself!

Matthew 15:21-28

Our King and the Woman of Canaan

21. Then Jesus went thence, and departed into the coasts of Tyre and Sidon.

He left the loathsome company of the Pharisees and *went thence,* going as far away as He could without leaving His own country. The great Bishop went to the very borders of His diocese. An inward attraction drew Him where He knew that a believing heart was yearning for Him. He was sent to the house of Israel as a preacher, but He interpreted His commission in its largest sense, and went *into the coasts of Tyre and Sidon.* When those at the center prove incorrigible, the Lord goes to those who can only be reached from the circumference. Let us always plough to the very end of the field and serve our day and generation to the extreme limits of our sphere.

22. And, behold, a woman of Canaan came out of the same coasts, and cried unto him, saying, Have mercy on me, O Lord, thou son of David; my daughter is grievously vexed with a devil.

Behold – here is something worth beholding, good for eyes and hearts.

Just as Jesus went to the coasts of Tyre and Sidon, *a woman came out of the same coasts* to meet Him. Sooner or later, a meeting will come about between Christ and seeking souls. This *woman of Canaan* had no claim on account of her nationality. She was a Gentile of the worst sort, of a race long before condemned to die. She came from the narrow strip of land on which the Tyrians dwelt and like Hiram, of Tyre, she knew the name of David, but she went further, for she had faith in the *son of David.* Love to her daughter led her to travel, to cry, to petition, to implore mercy. What will not a mother's love achieve? Her need had abolished the barrier between Gentile and Jew. She appealed to Jesus as though she were of the same country as His disciples. She asked for the healing of her child as a mercy to herself: *Have mercy on me.* She asked it of Jesus as Lord. She asked it of One greater than Solomon, the *son of David,* the wisest and most powerful of wonder-workers. She put the case briefly and pathetically, and pleaded for her daughter with all a mother's loving anxiety.

Her need taught her how to pray. Until we also know what we require and are full of hopeful longings, we shall never plead prevailingly. Do we pray for our children as this woman pleaded for her daughter? Have we not good reason to take her for our example?

23. But he answered her not a word. And his disciples came and besought him, saying, Send her away; for she crieth after us.

Silence was a hard answer, for it is translatable by fear into something worse than the harshest speech. *Not a word,* not a word from Him whose every word is power! This was a heavy discouragement. Yet she was not silenced by the Lord's silence. She increased her pleas. The disciples were mistaken when they said, *She crieth after us.* No, no, she cried after *Him.* Should this have afflicted them? Oh, that all men would cry after Him! Such a blessed annoyance should be longed for by compassionate hearts among the Lord's servants. The disciples were, however, driven to appeal to their Master, and though that was something, it was not much. Possibly they meant for their complaint to help the woman by obtaining an answer for her one way or another, but their words have a cold look: *Send her away.* May we never be so selfish as to feel troubled by inquirers! May we never send them away ourselves by cold looks and harsh words!

Still the disciples were not able to neglect her. They were forced to plead with Jesus about her. They *came and besought him.* If Christian people are apparently unsympathetic, let us warm them into feeling by our persistent fervency.

24. But he answered and said, I am not sent but unto the lost sheep of the house of Israel.

When Jesus did speak, it was not to her, but to His disciples. She heard the word and felt it to be a side blow that struck heavily at her hopes. She was not *of the house of Israel.* She acknowledged that she could not number herself among the *sheep.* He was *not sent* to her. How could He go beyond His mission? It would have been small wonder if she had withdrawn in despair. However, she redoubled her pleading.

25. Then came she and worshipped him, saying, Lord, help me.

Instead of withdrawing, she came nearer and she *worshipped him.* It was well done. She could not solve the problems of the destiny of her race and of the Lord's commission, but she could pray. She knew little about the limitations of messiahship, but she knew that the Lord had boundless power. If, as a shepherd, He may not gather her, yet, as Lord, He may *help* her. The divine nature of Christ is a wellspring of comfort to troubled hearts.

Her petition was brief, yet comprehensive. It came hot from her heart and went straight to the point. Her daughter's case was her own, and so she cried, *Lord, help me.* Lord, help us to pray as she did.

26. But he answered and said, It is not meet to take the children's bread, and to cast it to dogs.

At length He turns and gives a reply to her pleading, but it is not a cheering one. How hard its language! How unlike our Lord's usual self! And yet how true! How unanswerable! Truly, *It is not meet to take the children's bread, and to cast it to dogs.*

Of course privileges must not be given to those who have no right to them, nor must reserved blessings be wasted upon the unworthy. The blessing sought is as bread for children, and the Canaanites were no more members of the chosen family than so many dogs. Their heathen character made them like dogs as to uncleanness. For generations they had known no more of the true God than the dogs that roam the streets. Often they and other Philistine tribes had snapped as dogs at the heels of the Lord's people. The woman had probably heard such phrases as this from proud Jewish bigots, but she had not expected it from the Lord.

27. And she said, Truth, Lord: yet the dogs eat of the crumbs which fall from their masters' table.

It was humbly spoken: *Truth, Lord.* It was bravely spoken, for she found food for faith in the hard crusts of our Lord's language. Our Lord had used a word that should be rendered *little dogs,* and she caught it. Little dogs become the playmates of the children. They lie under the table and pick up the fragments *which fall* to the ground from the table of their little masters. The householder so far takes the little dog under his care as to allow him to be under the table. If, Gentile dog as she is, she may not be shepherded as one of the flock, she will be content to be tolerated as one of the household in the character of a little dog, for then she will be allowed *the crumbs which fall* from the children's bread, from the dogs' little *masters' table.* Great as was the blessing that she sought, it was but a crumb to the Lord's bounty, and to Israel's portion, and therefore she begged to have it, dog as she acknowledged herself to be.

Let us accept the worst character that the Scripture gives us and still find in it an argument for hope.

28. Then Jesus answered and said unto her, O woman, great is thy faith: be it unto thee even as thou wilt. And her daughter was made whole from that very hour.

Our Savior loves great faith and grants to it whatever it desires. Her faith was great comparatively for a heathen woman, and for one who knew so little of the Savior, she was surpassingly strong in faith. But her faith was not only great comparatively, it was also great positively. To believe in a silent Christ, in one who treats her with a rebuff, in one who calls her a dog, is exceedingly great faith, measure it how you will. Few of us have a tenth as much faith in our Lord as this woman had.

To believe that He can cure her daughter at once and to cling to Him for that blessing is faith that sets even the Lord a-wondering, and He cries, *O woman, great is thy faith.* How splendid the reward: *Be it unto thee even as thou wilt.* According to her will, her daughter's cure was immediate, perfect, and enduring. Oh, for like precious faith, especially for such faith in reference to our sons and daughters! Why should we not have it? Jesus is the same, and we have even more reasons for trusting in Him than the Canaanitess could have had. Lord, we believe; help our unbelief and make our children whole.

Matthew 15:29-39

The King Gives Another Banquet

29. And Jesus departed from thence, and came nigh unto the sea of Galilee; and went up into a mountain, and sat down there.

He was always on the move. He *went about doing good* (Acts 10:38). He had gone to the border of the land. He was soon back again to headquarters. He wastes not a moment. He does not stay to be congratulated upon His success, but hastens to other work, and so we often read, *And Jesus departed from thence.*

How He loved the mountains and the sea! By the Sea of Galilee, He again chooses out a rising knoll, selects a standing place with ground around it for an assembly, and opens another session of His ministry of mercy. He *sat down there,* for He had set His heart upon blessing the people in that convenient spot. In imagination, we see Him taking His seat and then speaking *ex cathedra,* from the rising ground, *nigh unto the sea of Galilee.* The mountain's side was free to all and none could complain of trespassing, and it was far enough from busy towns to escape the noise of necessary labor. See how the people crowd! Our Lord's presence will not long be unnoticed, though no sound of a churchgoing bell gave notice of a service. As a preacher, He never lacked a congregation. Where He sat down, the people came. If He *went up into a mountain,* they climbed after Him. If we preach Jesus in the most out-of-the-way village, in a region almost inaccessible, we shall not be left without hearers.

> *30-31. And great multitudes came unto him, having with them those that were lame, blind, dumb, maimed, and many others, and cast them down at Jesus' feet; and he healed them: insomuch that the multitude wondered, when they saw the dumb to speak, the maimed to be whole, the lame to walk, and the blind to see: and they glorified the God of Israel.*

Still the same story. The magnet always attracts. The crowd has increased in volume. *Great multitudes came unto him.* They seem to spring up from the earth and swarm from the sea. They are so soon around our Lord that there is no interval during which He might rest. The sickness that they bring before Him is still more varied than in former times. What a list of patients! What a gathering of miseries to one spot! The expectation of the people remains at flood tide. They have the sick with them and they *cast them down at Jesus' feet,* leaving them with Him in full confidence. The healing power continues to flow in full force. That one sentence is a grand summary of His marvelous cures: *He healed them.* This time the result is a greater degree of wonder among the crowd, attended by a gracious savor of praise to Israel's God: *They glorified the God of Israel.* It was evident to them that Jehovah had remembered and visited His people, and was healing their sicknesses, and so for the moment they gave Him glory. What must it have been like to be an eyewitness of such a scene of healing and of worship! What an education for the apostles! What support for their faith in hard days after their Master was taken from them!

Lord, when we experience a revival of true religion, we behold the greatness of Your healing power in the spiritual world, and we therefore glorify the God of Israel – the God of the covenant, the God of wrestling prayer, the God of all grace.

> *32. Then Jesus called his disciples unto him, and said, I have compassion on the multitude, because they continue with me now three days, and have nothing to eat: and I will not send them away fasting, lest they faint in the way.*

History repeats itself. We shall be wise to note the variations. What Jesus has done once He can and will do again and again, should need arise. In fact, one mercy is the promise of another. Our Lord is here the first to speak upon the way of dealing with the vast famishing crowd. The disciples do not come to Him about the business, but *He* begins the conversation. In every case, His heart is first and in this case His speech is so. *Then Jesus called his disciples unto him.* They are to be coworkers and so He consults them, making them members of His private council. He has all tenderness and can truly say, *I have compassion on the multitude.*

Whether He moves in a matter of distress or not, His heart is always compassionate, and He thinks of the people's present fasting and possible fainting. His compassion is the spring that sets His power in motion. The crowds had continued to follow Him and He could not but pity the need that arose out of their perseverance in listening to His teaching. These people had endured a *three days'* fast, or at least scantiness of food, to hear Him preach. What preaching it must have been! But the great Teacher cares for their bodies as well as for their souls and will not feel content to feed their minds only. From the usual point of view, their lack of provision was their own concern. They had gathered of their own accord, and they could not reasonably look to Him to give them both provision and instruction for nothing, but His great heart could not consent to let them faint. He would not even innocently be the cause of injury to one of them. He solemnly declares, *I will not send them away fasting.* He would not have His servants be indifferent to the sufferings of the poor, even as to the bread that perishes. We may be doubly sure that He will not for long allow any earnest hearer to faint through spiritual hunger. He may make us wait to awaken our appetite, but He will not in the end dismiss us unfed. He does not love to let the hungry famish. He fears *lest they faint in the way.* If any of us are coming near to that state, He perceives it and will intercede. Let us cultivate an appetite for heavenly food and Jesus will supply its cravings.

33. And his disciples say unto him, Whence should we have so much bread in the wilderness, as to fill so great a multitude?

On this second occasion, we might have hoped for better things from the disciples, but they are in the old rut, as doubtful as ever and as much guilty of forgetting their Lord's power. He said, *I will not send them away fasting,* and they answer His gracious declaration with a hard and chilling question. Note how they forget what *He* would do and dote upon what *they* cannot do. *Whence should we have so much bread?* Who said anything about *we?* The only good point in their speech is their associating themselves with their Lord at all, but even there they take too prominent a place. They think of their own poverty, of the wilderness, of the *so much bread,* and of the *so great a multitude,* and they forget their *so great* Lord. Are we not too much like them? Are we sure that we are even as wise as they were?

34. And Jesus saith unto them, How many loaves have ye? And they said, Seven, and a few little fishes.

The Lord accepts their cooperation and says, *How many loaves have ye?* Small as their supply was, and utterly insignificant for the work proposed, He allows them to contribute it towards His grand design. They make a rapid inventory and they speak of it in mournful tones: *Seven, and a few little fishes.* This is much like our own poor stock-in-trade for holy service. The loaves were by no means such masses of food as we intend by the English word; they were merely thin cakes. The fishes were *few* and *little,* more bones than anything else. So are our abilities meager and marred with many disabilities, yet we must put all that we have into the common stock and it will be enough in the hands of Him who works all things.

35. And he commanded the multitude to sit down on the ground.

The people are prepared for the festival by their willingness to obey. What they had seen of our Lord's miraculous power awakened expectation and created readiness to follow His lead. There is generally a preparedness of mind when Jesus is about to work His wonders of grace. Lord, cause our people to be ready *to sit down on the ground* at Your feast of grace!

36. And he took the seven loaves and the fishes, and gave thanks, and brake them, and gave to his disciples, and the disciples to the multitude.

He did as formerly. His way is perfect and so there was no need for altering it. *He took the seven loaves and the fishes.* They only made one handful for Him. This shows us that our meager abilities must be placed at His disposal and in His wonder-working hands. He does not scorn carrying the bread and the fish, though He bears up both heaven and earth. His *giving thanks* at an outdoor meal should teach us not to eat without thanksgiving. The *breaking* teaches us that there must be an expenditure of talent and that there should be a crumbing down of truth to suit human mouths. His giving the provision into many hands shows that nothing is to be retained in store, but all must be distributed among the many. Our Lord Jesus again honored *his disciples* by making them the servants by whom He reached the multitude. Lord, use us, for if we have neither loaf nor fish, we have willing hands.

37. And they did all eat, and were filled: and they took up of the broken meat that was left seven baskets full.

The feast was carried out in a manner so orderly and with provision so bountiful, that all ate to satisfaction; even little children had their bread and fish. The remainder, *the broken meat,* was too good to waste and so it was taken up in baskets for future use. The God of abundance is yet the God of frugality. We lack not, but also we waste not. *Baskets* are always to be had – the difficulty is in filling them. Here the baskets corresponded to the number of the loaves, whereas in the former banquet they corresponded to the number of the apostles. The blessing that rewards service may bear a relation to the workers or to the original supply that they contributed, according to the manner of comparison. In both cases of feeding the multitude, that which was in store after use was greater than that which was at first possessed. The more we give, the more we have. May not some of us be poor because we have given so little away? Might not the most gifted have had more gifts by this time if they had unselfishly laid out what they have for the good of others?

38. And they that did eat were four thousand men, beside women and children.

Here is no desire to increase the number in order to make the wonder greater. In some religious statistics, the tale would be soon told if the *women and children* were left out, for they are the bulk of the attendants. In the Bible we find the people counted by the number of the males, and

Matthew, when he took taxes, was accustomed so to levy them. That plan is followed here. There is no reason why the women and children should be omitted in our counting nowadays, since the whole method of census-taking has been altered and both sexes are now included. As the men were the greatest eaters, and the most conspicuous persons, they are counted, and though the rest of the guests were not numbered, they were all nourished, which is the main matter.

39. And he sent away the multitude, and took ship, and came into the coasts of Magdala.

Our Lord was ever earnest to send the crowds home. He desired not to detain them from their daily labor. He does not want them to accompany Him as a guard of honor or as enthusiastic persons who take part in a procession. He speeds away from their praises. He *took ship.* Like a shuttle through the loom, He crosses and recrosses the lake. He comes *into the coasts of Magdala.* Was He seeking out Mary of Magdala? He had some errand of mercy there. It was soon accomplished, for He was off to sea again. Our Lord was largely a seafaring man. Let sailors run up Christ's colors and sail under His command. O Lord Jesus, I would cross the sea of life with You as my pilot, owner, and captain!

Matthew 16

Matthew 16:1-4

The King and His Chosen Sign

1. The Pharisees also with the Sadducees came, and tempting desired him that he would shew them a sign from heaven.

The King is again met by His foes. Two sects, which were violently opposed to each other, unite their forces against Him. It is the way of the wicked to become friends when seeking the overthrow of the kingdom of heaven.

On this occasion they come not with a question, but with the old demand for a sign. This time it must be *a sign from heaven,* possibly a marvel in the sky. What right had they to test Him in such a way as their notion might suggest? What need for more signs when His miracles were so many? Were not all His miracles *signs from heaven*? Did not this demand cast a slur on all that He had already done? Was it not a practical ignoring of all His previous works of power? Too often we also have fallen into the weakness of asking for a new token of divine love, thus undervaluing former favors. If the evidence we have already received of our Lord's grace and power is not enough, when will our doubts be ended?

In this demand for a sign, our Lord's foes were *tempting him.* Did the temptation lie in urging Him to seek His own glory by some flamboyant display of power, for which there would be no real need? Whatever it was, our Lord passed unscathed through this ordeal, for there was no pride in Him. Pharisees and Sadducees will tempt us also. From their schemes and smiles may the Lord deliver us! From the desire to stand well with men may we be happily freed by our love to Jesus!

2-3. He answered and said unto them, When it is evening, ye say, It will be fair weather: for the sky is red. And in the morning, It will be foul weather to day: for the sky is red and lowering. O ye hypocrites, ye can discern the face of the sky; but can ye not discern the signs of the times?

They could predict the weather by certain signs, and our Lord Jesus mentions the weather-tokens of Palestine; yet they could not read the plainer and more plentiful warnings of the near future. Weather-signs are doubtful, but there were moral and spiritual tokens around them that could hardly be misunderstood if they would only consider them. Each country has its own sky warnings, and those of Palestine differ from those of England, but the signs of the times are the same in all lands. Our Lord singled out an instance of their supposed weather-wisdom. The same sign which, in the evening, was a token of *fair weather,* was, in the morning, a mark of *foul weather.* They were able to draw nice distinctions on the variable condition of *the face of the sky;* why could they not *discern the signs of the times?* They could have seen, if they had chosen to do so, that all the prophecies were one in declaring that the date of Messiah's appearing had arrived, and they could also have observed that every event was fulfilling those prophecies; but they were false at heart and would not see, and yet cried out for a sign. Signs were all around them and yet they repeated the parrot-cry, "Show us a sign." Most justly our Lord was indignant with them and rebuked them, using the justly severe words, *O ye hypocrites.* Today the men who want more evidences of the supernatural deserve a similar denunciation.

Lord, do not allow any of us to be blind to the heavenly signs – Your cross, Your resurrection, Your Word, Your Spirit, and Your work of grace. Teach us carefully to *discern* these things as being in very deed the abiding *signs of the times.* Even in the growing coldness of the church and the abounding iniquity of the world, let us see the tokens of Your Advent, and stand waiting and watching for Your long-promised appearing.

4. A wicked and adulterous generation seeketh after a sign; and there shall no sign be given unto it, but the sign of the prophet Jonas. And he left them, and departed.

It was not lack of evidence, but the sad depravity of their minds that set them upon *seeking after a sign,* and therefore the Lord would not satisfy their unhealthy craving. They were *wicked* in morals and *adulterous* in heart in their forsaking the one true God, and then they turned around and justified their unbelief in the Son of God by pleading a need of proof, demanding more miracles to enable them to come to a right conclusion. Such is the deceit of man's heart.

Our Lord repeats His former answer. He will give them no other sign. In the scope of the Old Testament, there is no fuller sign of our Lord than Jonah. Our Lord knew that He would fulfill the type of Jonah even in its details, and therefore He points them to that prophet's life. This is a subject that deserves our careful meditation, but we cannot enlarge upon it here. Our Lord looks to His death and resurrection and gives *the prophet Jonas* as His sign. Jesus will be buried, and will rise on the third day, and in the power of His resurrection will win the Gentiles to repentance. In this He will be the antitype of Jonah, and this shall be the sign that He is indeed the Christ of God. This our Lord had said before and here He repeated it, because it was a sufficient reply and there was no need to study variety with a set of people who themselves harped perpetually upon one string.

Our Lord left such persons, for there was nothing to be done with them. *He left them, and departed,* and that place saw Him no more. Lord, do not leave any one of us, for that would be a sure sentence of death to us.

Matthew 16:5-12

The King Misunderstood by His Own

5. *And when his disciples were come to the other side, they had forgotten to take bread.*

They had *forgotten* to supply their boat with food. This they seem to have found out for themselves as soon as they *were come to the other side.* They seldom forgot such worldly matters. Perhaps they trusted each other and what was every man's business was nobody's business.

They did not notice the omission while they were crossing the sea, but mealtime came and their minds were quickly brought to think of the loaves. Controversy had for a while engrossed their minds with religious matters, but lack of bread and consequent hunger soon recalled them to the things of earth.

6. Then Jesus said unto them, Take heed and beware of the leaven of the Pharisees and of the Sadducees.

He used a parabolic expression, which they would readily have understood, had not their minds been already absorbed by their lack of bread. He saw that in them, too, there would soon be a desire for a sign, now that they needed bread, and He feared the influence of both the ritualism of the Pharisee and the rationalism of the Sadducee upon His little church. Thus, His double warning: *Take heed and beware.* The warning is needed today as much as in our Lord's time; perhaps it is even more required and will be less regarded. *Pharisees and Sadducees* are both inoculating the churches, and the spirit of the one is as bad as that of the other. Everywhere we see the one evil force, operating in two opposite ways, but rapidly leavening the meal of nominal Christendom. Lord, save Your people from this souring and corrupting influence!

7. And they reasoned among themselves, saying, It is because we have taken no bread.

Their thoughts ran along the low material level from leaven to *bread.* Did they imagine that He forbade their borrowing leaven from the Pharisees when they began to make a batch of bread? How could they have found any meaning in the literal sense of leaven as applied to Sadducees? They were earthbound by anxiety or they could not have blundered so foolishly. When a number of hungry men are together is it not very natural that they should look at everything with hungry eyes? Yes, it is natural and it is not natural for men to be spiritual. We need to pray that we may not *reason among ourselves* after the same cringing fashion, when we come into a little need.

8-10. Which when Jesus perceived, he said unto them, O ye of little faith, why reason ye among yourselves, because ye have brought no bread? Do ye not yet understand, neither remember the five loaves of the five thousand, and how many baskets ye took up? Neither the seven loaves of the four thousand, and how many baskets ye took up?

Lack of faith made them thus dull and carnal. Lack of bread would not have troubled them if they had possessed more grace. Our Lord as good as says to them, "Why begin raising questions as to what can be done under this small difficulty? Have I not dealt with far greater necessities? Have not your own personal needs been richly supplied? Has your store been exhausted even when all your thoughts have gone out towards the multitude and all your store of bread and fish has been given up to them? What occasion can there be for anxiety in My presence, when I have always supplied your needs?"

How foolish they were, but how like we are to them! We seem to learn nothing. After years of experience, our Lord has to say, *Do ye not yet understand, neither remember?* Two stupendous miracles had not lifted those disciples to that plane of thought that is suitable in believers, and after all our experiences and deliverances, we, alas! are much as they were. How our mind dwells on the bread that we are lacking and how readily it forgets former times when all such needs were abundantly supplied! The *many baskets* that were so amply filled by former providences were the disciples' own share and store, and therefore they ought not to have forgotten the miraculous festivals. Even the empty baskets should have refreshed their memories and reminded them of how they had twice been filled. If it were not for our wretched *little faith* and our *reasoning* among ourselves, the memory of our former deliverances would lift us beyond all tendency to mistrust our God.

O sacred Spirit, teach us or we shall never learn! Make us wise or we shall still continue in the folly of carnal reasoning!

11. How is it that ye do not understand that I spake it not to you concerning bread, that ye should beware of the leaven of the Pharisees and of the Sadducees?

Basically, it was unbelief that clouded their understanding. Jesus may well say to doubters, *Ye do not understand.* Truly, nothing more effectively blunts spiritual perception than an overpowering anxiety for the bread that perishes. When a doctrine is not understood, it may not always be the fault of the teacher. Very plain speaking is frequently misunderstood when the mind is absorbed in pressing needs. It was sad to see the apostles taking our Lord literally and failing to see the obvious parable of His words. How could *the leaven of the Pharisees* be a term used *concerning bread?*

> *12. Then understood they how that he bade them not beware of the leaven of bread, but of the doctrine of the Pharisees and of the Sadducees.*

The *doctrine* of the members of these sects had a secret, insinuating, and souring influence, and the disciples must carefully watch lest even a little of their spirit and teaching should get into their minds and then spread throughout their whole nature. Both of these leavens may be at work at once in the same community. In fact, they are only one leaven. The two sets of opponents attacked the Lord Jesus at the same time, for they had a common ground of opposition against Him. To this day, these two forms of evil are ever working, either secretly or openly, and we have need to beware of them at all times. It is well to understand this and both purge out the old leaven of Pharisaism and keep out the new leaven of Sadduceeism. Self-righteousness and carnal reasoning must alike be cast out. Faith will find them both to be her deadly foes. Many are amusing themselves with the evil leaven, and before they are aware, the unholy thing will defile them. To be evangelical and yet to be superstitious or rationalistic at the same time is next to impossible. Certain of our contemporaries are trying to bake with this leaven, but their bread will be sour. *Beware!*

Matthew 16:13-28

The King Alone with His Friends

> *13. When Jesus came into the coasts of Caesarea Philippi, he asked his disciples, saying, Whom do men say that I the Son of man am?*

Our Lord knew well enough what the people thought of Him, but He asked His disciples the question so that He might instruct them after the method of Socrates by drawing out their own minds. Our Lord was about to inform them as to His death, and it was well that they should have very clear ideas as to who He was. He begins by asking, *Whom do men say that I the Son of man am?* Human opinions about heavenly things count for little, yet it is as well to know them so that we may be prepared to withstand them.

14. And they said, Some say that thou art John the Baptist: some, Elias; and others, Jeremias, or one of the prophets.

These were all conjectures and far from the mark, yet was there some likeness to truth in them all. Herod's notion that Jesus was *John the Baptist,* newly risen from the dead, seemed a probable one to many, since our Lord had like courage and fidelity with John. *Elijah,* too, seemed to live again in our Lord's words of fire. *Jeremiah* was revived in His constant sorrow, and *the prophets* were repeated in His memorable teachings and marvelous life. Since many of these were types of Him, it is small wonder that He should seem to be identical with them. Yet men make no discovery of the Lord's true character by their own guesswork. Only those to whom He reveals Himself will ever know Him.

Error has many voices. Truth alone is one and abiding. Men say differing things concerning our Lord, but His Spirit alone bears effective witness to the one true Christ of God.

15. He saith unto them, But whom say ye that I am?

This is a far more searching question. Our personal thoughts of Jesus touch a vital point. Our Lord presupposes that His disciples would not have the same thoughts as men had. They would not follow the spirit of the age and shape their views by those of the cultured persons of the period. They would have formed a judgment, each one for himself, by what they had heard and seen while in His company. Therefore, He inquired, *But whom say ye that I am?* Let each reader answer the question before he goes further.

16. And Simon Peter answered and said, Thou art the Christ, the Son of the living God.

Peter, as usual, was spokesman for the rest and he spoke right well.

He had perceived the messiahship and the divine sonship of his Lord, and in outspoken words he uttered his inward belief. It was a simple but satisfactory confession of faith. We should always be ready to give an answer to those who would know what we believe on a matter so central as the person and nature of our Lord. A mistake on this point would involve all our religion in failure. If He is not to us *the Christ*, the Lord's Anointed and *the Son of the living God*, we know not Jesus aright.

> *17. And Jesus answered and said unto him, Blessed art thou, Simon Bar-jona: for flesh and blood hath not revealed it unto thee, but my Father which is in heaven.*

His old name is mentioned to bring out the distinction between what he was by nature and what grace had made him. *Simon Bar-Jona*, the fluttering son of a dove, has now become Peter, a rock. He was a happy man to be taught of God on the central truth of revelation. He had not arrived at his belief by mere reason; *flesh and blood* had not worked out the problem. There had been a revelation to him from the *Father which is in heaven.* To know the Lord in a mere doctrinal statement, no such divine teaching is required, but Peter's full assurance of his Lord's nature and mission was no theory in the head. The truth had been written on his heart by the heavenly Spirit. This is the only knowledge worth having as to the person of our Lord, for it brings a blessing with it – a blessing from the mouth of the Lord Jesus: *Blessed art thou.*

> *18. And I say also unto thee, That thou art Peter, and upon this rock I will build my church; and the gates of hell shall not prevail against it.*

Thou art Peter, a piece of rock, and on that rock of which you are a piece, *I will build my church.* He had, by the revelation of the Father, come to know the Son and to be identified with Him. Thus, he was a stone of the one Rock. Christ is the Rock and Peter has become one with Him, *and upon this rock* is the church founded. If there had been no Roman Catholics to twist this passage, it would have presented no difficulty. Jesus is the Builder and He and His apostles make up the first layer of stone in the great temple of the church, and this first layer is one with the eternal Rock on which it rests. In the first twelve layers or foundations are *the names of the twelve apostles of the Lamb* (Revelation

21:14). We *are built upon the foundation of the apostles and prophets, Jesus Christ himself being the chief corner stone* (Ephesians 2:20). Apostles are not the foundation of our confidence meritoriously, but they underlie us as to date, and we rest upon their testimony concerning Jesus and His resurrection.

The assembly that Christ gathers, He builds together, for He says, *I will build my church.* He builds on a firm foundation: *Upon this rock I will build.* What Jesus builds is His own, *my church.* He makes His rock-founded building into a stronghold, against which the powers of evil lay continual siege, but all in vain, for *the gates of hell shall not prevail against it.*

> 19. And I will give unto thee the keys of the kingdom of heaven: and what-
> soever thou shalt bind on earth shall be bound in heaven: and whatsoever
> thou shalt loose on earth shall be loosed in heaven.

The new kingdom would not be all-comprehensive, like Noah's ark, but would have its dove and its keys. For practical purposes, the people of God would need discipline and the power to receive, refuse, retain, or exclude members. Of these keys our Lord says to Peter, *I will give unto thee the keys of the kingdom of heaven.* Foremost among the apostles, Peter used those keys at Pentecost, when he led three thousand into the church in Jerusalem; when he shut out Ananias and Sapphira; and at the house of Cornelius, when he admitted the Gentiles. Our Lord committed to His church the power to rule within herself for Him, not to set up doors, but to open or shut them; not to make laws, but to obey them and see them obeyed. Peter, and those for whom he spoke, became the stewards of the Lord Jesus in the church and their acts were endorsed by their Lord. Today the Lord continues to back up the teaching and acts of His sent servants, those Peters who are pieces of the one Rock. The judgments of His church, when rightly administered, have His sanction so as to make them valid. The words of His sent servants, spoken in His name, shall be confirmed of the Lord, and shall not be, either as to promise or threatening, a mere piece of rhetoric. When He was here on earth, our Lord Himself personally admitted men into the select circle of disciples, but on the eve of His departure, He gave to their leading spirit, and thus to them also, the power to admit others to their number or to dismiss them when found unworthy. Thus was the church (or assembly) constituted and endowed with internal administrative authority. We cannot legislate, but we may and must administer the ordinances and statutes of the Lord, and what we do rightly in carrying out divine law in the church on earth is ratified by our Lord in heaven. A church would be a mere sham and its acts a solemn farce if the great head of the church did not sanction all that is done according to His statute-book.

We need not at any length deal with the claims of the pope of Rome. Even if Peter had been made the head of the church, how would that affect the bishop of Rome? We may as well say that the Cham of Tartary is the successor of Peter, as to make that claim for an Italian pontiff. No unsophisticated reader of his Bible sees any trace of Roman Catholicism in this passage. The wine of Roman Catholicism is not to be pressed out of this cluster.

20. Then charged he his disciples that they should tell no man that he was Jesus the Christ.

As yet they were to be silent as to our Lord's highest claims, for fear the people would in rash zeal set Him up as king by force of arms. It was dangerous to tell such an ill-instructed multitude what they would be sure to misunderstand and misuse. The command to *tell no man* must have sounded very strangely in the disciples' ears. It was no business of theirs to discover the reason for their Lord's orders. It was enough for them to do as He told them. We are under no such prohibition, and therefore we will tell to all that our Lord is the Savior, the Anointed of God, or as He has Himself worded it, *Jesus the Christ.*

21. From that time forth began Jesus to shew unto his disciples, how that he must go unto Jerusalem, and suffer many things of the elders and chief priests and scribes, and be killed, and be raised again the third day.

With the church (or assembly) being now actually arranged and treated as a fact, our Lord began to prepare His disciples for the time when, as an associated body, they would have to act alone, because He would be taken from them. Their first great trial would be His death, of which He had spoken darkly before. *From that time forth began Jesus to shew unto his disciples* His death more plainly. There is a fit time for painful disclosures and our Lord is wise in selecting it. He mentions the gathering together of His foes, *elders and chief priests and scribes,* who will eagerly unite. Their fury will show itself in multiplied cruelties. He will *suffer many things.* He declares that they will push their enmity to the bitter end. He will *be killed.* He foretells that He will *be raised again* and He specifies the time, namely, *the third day.* All this must have fallen sadly on the ears of men who still indulged visions of a kingdom of a very different sort. Most of them were wisely silent in their sadness, yet there was one who had far too bold a tongue.

22. Then Peter took him, and began to rebuke him, saying, Be it far from thee, Lord: this shall not be unto thee.

Peter could not be trusted as a steward or a butler. He takes too much upon himself. See how great he is! He half imagines that he is the master.

He loved his Lord so well that he could not bear to hear of His being killed, and he would gladly stop Him from talking upon a subject so terribly sad. He thinks the Lord is morbid and is attaching more importance to the opposition of the Pharisees than it deserves. Therefore, he gets the Lord alone and chides Him. The words are very strong: *Peter took him, and began to rebuke him.* He meant to be his Lord's candid friend and at the same time to maintain towards Him that respectful demeanor that would be suitable in His follower, but evidently he took too much on himself when he ventured to rebuke his Lord. He could see in our Lord's death nothing but ruin to the cause and therefore he felt it must not be. He implored the mercy of heaven to forbid so dire a catastrophe. *Be it far from thee, Lord.* It must not, cannot fall out as Jesus had prophesied. *This shall not be unto thee.* He would even drive such an idea out of our Lord's mind. Would we not have done the same, had we been there, if we had been as much concerned for the honor of our Lord as Peter was? Would we not have been horror-stricken at the idea that such a one as He should be put to a cruel death? Might we not have vowed in terrible earnest, *This shall not be unto thee*?

23. But he turned, and said unto Peter, Get thee behind me, Satan: thou art an offence unto me: for thou savourest not the things that be of God, but those that be of men.

Our Lord was superior to the temptation that grew out of the very love of His friend. He would remain no longer aside with Peter; *he turned* away from him. Seeing the devil using Peter as his instrument, He addresses Satan himself, and Peter too, so far as he was identified with the evil suggestion: *Get thee behind me, Satan.* The attempt was made to put a stumbling block in that path of self-sacrifice that our Lord intended to pursue, even to the bitter end. He spied out the hindrance and said, *Thou art an offence unto me.* His dearest friend was His most oppressive foe when he would put Him off from His lifework. The devil thought to succeed through our Lord's newly appointed foreman, but Jesus made short work of the temptation. He threw the stone out of the road and cast it behind Him, so that He could not be stumbled. The crux of the error was that Peter looked at things from the point of view of human honor and success, and not from that grand standpoint in which the glory of God in the salvation of men swallows up everything.

A marvel is here. A man may know what only the Father can reveal, and yet he may not *savourest the things that be of God.* Unless he accepts the sacrifice of the Lord Jesus, he has no taste for divine things. He who does not heartily rejoice in the atonement does not discern that sweet savor of rest that the Lord God perceives in the great sacrifice, and therefore he has no fellowship in the things that be of God. He knows not the taste, the aroma, or the essence of spiritual things, and however much he may honor Jesus in words, he is an enemy, yes, a real Satan towards the true Christ, whose very substance is His work as our atoning sacrifice. Those who in this day revile the substitutionary sacrifice of our Lord are fonder of the things *that be of men* than those *that be of God.* They are loud in their claim to be great philanthropists, but sound theologians they are not. Humanitarians they may be, but preachers they cannot be. They may be the friends of man, but they are not the servants of God. How sorrowfully do we write these words when we think of the many preachers to whom they apply!

24. Then said Jesus unto his disciples, If any man will come after me, let him deny himself, and take up his cross, and follow me.

As our Lord, to fulfill His destiny, must sacrifice Himself, so also must everyone who would be His follower. To keep close to our Lord (which He intends by the words *come after me*), we must have no further concern with self, for He denied Himself to redeem His people. We must not know self, nor assent to it, but we must each one *deny himself*. Doing this, each man must cheerfully shoulder his own personal burden of sorrow and service and carry it with self-sacrifice, as Jesus carried His cross.

He had told them of *his cross*, and now He tells them of their own crosses. They might now choose again whether they could and would follow Him. With their increased information as to His destiny, the question was again set before them, whether they would follow or forsake Him. If they did continue to be His followers, it must be as cross-bearers and self-deniers.

Nor are the terms altered in these days. Do we accept them? Can we keep in step in the long procession of cross carriers or will we fall in with the spirit of the age, and say fine things about Jesus, while we deny His substitutionary sacrifice and shirk the personal self-denial that He demands? Our own wisdom, if it leads us to think lightly of *the precious blood* (1 Peter 1:19), must be utterly denied and even abhorred.

25. For whosoever will save his life shall lose it: and whosoever will lose his life for my sake shall find it.

Now they were to practice the doctrine He had taught them before. They could only save their real selves by the loss of this present life, but if they settled it in their own minds that they must first and foremost save their outer life, it would be at the expense of their truest being. To tell them plainly of this was honest dealing on our Lord's part, and it argued well for the disciples that they still remained faithful to Him. Alas! there was one even of the chosen twelve who probably at this very moment was scheming how he could continue to keep the bag and yet could ultimately escape from the consequences of His Master's demand.

26. For what is a man profited, if he shall gain the whole world, and lose his own soul? or what shall a man give in exchange for his soul?

If he loses his real life, how can he profit, even if the world be his? The true gain or loss is a gain or loss of life. All external things are trifles compared with that life. Even now, *What is a man profited?* He has no real life in Christ and what is all else that he may possess? What but a painted pageantry with which he is amusing his soul upon the brink of hell? As to the world to come, there is no question. To lose eternal life is overwhelming loss indeed.

Nothing can be compared with eternal life. The soul's value cannot be estimated by ordinary reckonings. Worlds on worlds were a poor price. *What shall a man give in exchange for his soul?* Bartering is out of the question. His soul is so much a man's sole inheritance that if he has lost it, he has lost all.

27. For the Son of man shall come in the glory of his Father with his angels; and then he shall reward every man according to his works.

There will come a day when Christ, from the judgment seat, will make it appear who was wise in his way of life, for then shall the reward or the punishment throw its light on the past conduct of men. He who was Himself despised shall be the Rewarder of those who laid down their lives for the sake of His cause. In that day, the crucified *Son of man shall come* in glory. That glory will be seen to be *the glory of his Father.* That divine glory will be illustrated by hosts of attendant *angels.* In all the pomp of heaven, He shall distribute the rewards of the last judicial inquest. The righteous shall through divine grace have their *works* taken as evidence of their love to God, and the wicked shall with justice have their doom appointed *according to [their] works,* because those works will be the evidence that they had not the faith that produces good works.

Lord, by Your good Spirit, keep me ever in mind of that great day of days, which will make eternity bright with immeasurable bliss or dark with unutterable woe! May I look at everything in the blaze of light that surrounds Your judgment seat!

28. Verily I say unto you, There be some standing here, which shall not taste of death, till they see the Son of man coming in his kingdom.

So near was that reign that would repay the losses of the saints for Christ's sake, that before certain ones of them were dead, the Lord would have held a rehearsal of it in His judgment of Israel, by the siege and destruction of Jerusalem, and would have set up *his kingdom,* of which the judgment seat is a gauge and an instrument.

We have here a difficult passage and this appears to be the simplest way of reading it in its connection. Our Lord seems to say, "Through suffering and death I pass to a throne, and by that fact it shall be seen that loss and death are often the way to true gain and real life. That kingdom of Mine is not far away or unreal. Some of you will see Me in the exercise of My royal power before you die."

Yet it has been thought that it means that some would never really *taste of death,* or know the fullness of its terrible meaning till the judgment day. This is *true,* but it can scarcely be the teaching in this place.

Matthew 17

Matthew 17:1-13

Our King Transfigured in Glory

1-2. And after six days Jesus taketh Peter, James, and John his brother, and bringeth them up into an high mountain apart, and was transfigured before them: and his face did shine as the sun, and his raiment was white as the light.

Were these *six days* a week's quiet interval, in which our Lord prepared Himself for the unique transaction upon the *mountain apart*? Did the little company of three know from one Sabbath to another that such an amazing joy awaited them? The three were elect out of the elect and were favored to see what no one else in all the world might behold. Doubtless our Lord had reasons for His choice, as He has for every choice He makes, but He does not unveil them to us. The same three beheld the agony in the garden; perhaps the first sight was necessary to sustain their faith under the second.

The name of the *high mountain* can never be known, for those who knew the locality have left no information. Tabor, if you please; Hermon, if you prefer it. No one can decide. It was a lone and lofty hill.

While in prayer, the splendor of the Lord shone out. His face, lit up with its own inner glory, became a sun; and all His clothes, like clouds irradiated by that sun, became white as the light itself: He *was transfigured before them*. He alone was the center of what they saw. It was a marvelous unveiling of the hidden nature of the Lord Jesus. Then was, in one way, fulfilled the word of John: *The Word was made flesh, and dwelt among us, (and we beheld his glory)* (John 1:14).

The transfiguration occurred but once. Special views of the glory of Christ are not enjoyed every day. Our highest joy on earth is to see

Jesus. There can be no greater bliss in heaven, but we shall be better able to endure the exceeding bliss when we have laid aside the burden of this flesh.

3. And, behold, there appeared unto them Moses and Elias talking with him.

Thus, the Law and the Prophets, *Moses and Elijah,* communed with our Lord, *talking with him,* and entering into familiar conversation with their Lord. Saints long departed still live – live in their personality, are known by their names, and enjoy near access to Christ. It is a great joy to holy ones to be with Jesus. They find it heaven to be where they can talk with Him. The heads of former dispensations conversed with the Lord as to His death, by which a new economy would be ushered in. After condescending so long to His ignorant followers, it must have been a great relief to the human soul of Jesus to talk with two masterminds like those of Moses and Elijah. What a sight for the apostles, this glorious trio! They appeared unto *them,* but they were talking with *him.* The object of the two holy ones was not to converse with the apostles, but with their Master. Although saints are seen of men, their fellowship is with Jesus.

4. Then answered Peter, and said unto Jesus, Lord, it is good for us to be here: if thou wilt, let us make here three tabernacles; one for thee, and one for Moses, and one for Elias.

The sight spoke to the three beholders and they felt bound to answer to it. Peter must speak: *Then answered Peter.* That which is uppermost comes out: *Lord, it is good for us to be here.* Everybody was of his opinion. Who would not have been? Because it was so good, he would rather stay in this blissful state and get still more good from it. But he has not lost his reverence, and therefore he would have the great ones sheltered suitably. He submits the proposal to Jesus: *If thou wilt.* He offers that, with his brethren, he will plan and build shrines for the three holy ones: *Let us make here three tabernacles.* He does not propose to build for himself and James and John, but he says, *One for thee, and one for Moses, and one for Elias.* His talk sounds rather like that of a bewildered child. He wanders a little, yet his expression is a most natural one. Who would not wish to abide in such society as this?

Moses, and Elijah, and Jesus, what company! But yet how unpractical is Peter! How selfish the one thought: *It is good for us!* What was to be done for the rest of the twelve, and for the other disciples, and for the wide, wide world? A sip of such bliss might be good for the three, but to continue to drink thereof might not have been really good even for them. Peter knew not what he said. The same might be said of many another excited utterance of enthusiastic saints.

> 5. *While he yet spake, behold, a bright cloud overshadowed them: and behold a voice out of the cloud, which said, This is my beloved Son, in whom I am well pleased; hear ye him.*

While he yet spake. Such wild talk might well be interrupted. What a blessed interruption! We may often thank the Lord for stopping our babbling. *A bright cloud overshadowed them.* It was bright and it cast a shadow. They felt that they were entering it and feared as they did so. It was a unique experience, yet we have had it repeated in our own cases. Do we not know what it is to get a shadow out of brightness and *a voice out of the cloud*? This is after the frequent manner of the Lord in dealing with His favored ones.

The voice was clear and distinct. First came the divine attestation of the sonship of our Lord: *This is my beloved Son,* and the Father's declaration of delight in Him: *In whom I am well pleased.* What happiness for us that Jehovah is well pleased in Christ and with all who are in Him! Then followed the accompanying divine requirement: *Hear ye him.* It is better to hear the Son of God than to see saints or to build tabernacles. This will please the Father more than all else that love can suggest.

The good pleasure of the Father in the Lord Jesus is a conspicuous part of His glory. The voice conveyed to the ear a greater glory than the luster of light could communicate through the eye. The audible part of the transfiguration was as wonderful as the visible. In fact, it would seem, from the next verse, to have been all the more so.

> 6. *And when the disciples heard it, they fell on their face, and were sore afraid.*

Yes, the voice overcame them. Deeper impression was produced by the words of the Lord than by the blinding light. *When the disciples heard it, they fell on their face, and were sore afraid.* They were in the immediate presence of God and listening to the Father's voice. Well might they lie prostrate and tremble. Too clear a manifestation of God, even though it related to Jesus, would rather *overpower* than *empower* us. The three disciples said no more about building tabernacles, but as one man, *they fell on their face.* Awe is the end of talk. In this case it looked as if it were the end of consciousness, but this was only a temporary daze, from which they would recover and be all the more joyous.

7. And Jesus came and touched them, and said, Arise, and be not afraid.

Jesus had seemed to go away from them, lost in a cloud of brightness, but now He *came and touched them.* His communings with pure spirits did not make Him disdain the touch of feeble flesh. Oh, the sweet comfort of that gentle touch! It aroused, consoled, and strengthened His amazed and trembling disciples. The touch of the manhood is more reassuring to poor flesh and blood than the blaze of the Godhead. The voice from heaven casts down, but the word from Jesus is, *Arise.* The Father's voice made them sore afraid, but Jesus says, *Be not afraid.* Glorious God, how much we bless You for the Mediator!

8. And when they had lifted up their eyes, they saw no man, save Jesus only.

Closed were their eyes, because of the too transporting light, and they dared not open them till they felt the touch of Jesus. Then *they lifted up their eyes.* What did they see?

Moses and Elijah and the exceeding brightness had all gone, and they had come back to the common places of their life with Jesus. *They saw no man,* but they had lost nothing, since Jesus remained. They had gained by the vanishing of the shining ones, since they could see Jesus all the better and their attention was not divided. The vision of His transfiguration had blinded them, had stunned them, but to see *Jesus only* was to come back to practical life and to have the best of all sights still left to them. Oh, that we also may have the eye of our mind so fixed on the Lord as our one object, that He may fill the whole field of our vision, and we may see Jesus only!

9. And as they came down from the mountain, Jesus charged them, saying, Tell the vision to no man, until the Son of man be risen again from the dead.

What they had seen would confirm their own confidence and remain a secret spring of delight to them, but as it would require great faith in others to believe it, they were to *tell the vision to no man.* The transfiguration would be as hard to believe as the incarnation itself, and there could be no practical use in making demands upon a faith that scarcely existed. Until the greatest confirmation of all was given in our Lord's resurrection, the vision on the Holy Mount would be rather a strain upon faith than a support of it, in the case of those who did not themselves personally see it but only heard the apostles' report of it. It is wise not to overload testimony. There is a time for making known the higher truths, for out of season these may burden, rather than assist, inquiring minds. What a secret these men had to keep! They did keep it, but they never forgot it, nor ceased to feel its influence.

Now that *the Son of Man [is] risen again from the dead,* no doctrine needs to be kept back. In bringing life and immortality to light, our Lord has torn away the veil that had long concealed the higher mysteries of the gospel. His coming out of the grave has set free all buried truth. It is idle, not to say sinful, to be silent about the deep things of God now that *the Lord is risen indeed* (Luke 24:34). Yet some preachers we could name never mention election, the covenant, or final perseverance by the year together.

10. And his disciples asked him, saying, Why then say the scribes that Elias must first come?

One by one the difficulties of the disciples are stated to their Lord and their solution is soon given. One of these concerned Elijah, and as he had been just now before them, they were led to mention it. *Why then say the scribes that Elias must first come?* This is the report of men who have studied our Scriptures, that Elijah comes before the Lord's appearing. No doubt it staggered their minds when they had it put in some such logical fashion as this:

Messiah cannot come till Elijah has appeared,

Elijah has not appeared,

Therefore, Jesus is not the Messiah.

11-12. And Jesus answered and said unto them, Elias truly shall first come, and restore all things. But I say unto you, That Elias is come already, and they knew him not, but have done unto him whatsoever they listed. Likewise shall also the Son of man suffer of them.

Jesus answered. He has an answer for all questions, and we shall do well to bring our difficulties to Him to hear His replies. Our Lord admits that Elijah must come before the Messiah – *Elias truly shall first come* – but He asserts that the person intended by the prophecy *is come already,* and that the evil ones *have done unto him whatsoever they listed.* This cleared up the doubt at once. Then Jesus went on to say that what had been done to the true Elijah would also be done to Himself, the Messiah. Jesus Himself must die by a cruel death: *Likewise shall also the Son of man suffer of them.* How simple the explanation of the difficulty! How often has it happened that we have been looking for that which has already come, or have been perplexed by a doctrine which, when it has been opened to us by the Holy Spirit, has proved full of instruction and comfort. Without divine teaching, we drown in the shallows, but with it, we swim the fathomless deeps.

13. Then the disciples understood that he spake unto them of John the Baptist.

Then the disciples understood. Our Lord's instructive word opened their understandings. When He teaches, the stupidest scholars learn. Now they see that John the Baptist was "Elijah reborn." He was a stern admonisher of kings and preached repentance to Israel. He had come to restore all things and so the Messiah had not appeared without being preceded by the true Elijah. This was plain enough to them when once their Lord had made them understand. Lord, evermore, not only speak with us, but also cause us to comprehend Your Word!

Matthew 17:14-21

The King Returning to the Field of Conflict

14-16. And when they were come to the multitude, there came to him a certain man, kneeling down to him, and saying, Lord, have mercy on my son: for he is lunatick, and sore vexed: for ofttimes he falleth into the fire, and oft into the water. And I brought him to thy disciples, and they could not cure him.

After communion with saints and the confirmation of His claims by the Father's voice, our Lord comes to give battle to the devil. Our Moses descends from the mount and finds evil triumphant in *the multitude* below.

During His absence, the Enemy had triumphed over His feeble followers. In the midst of jeering adversaries, the disciples had tried in vain to cast out an evil spirit from a youth who had been rendered a *lunatic* by its horrible possession. The poor disappointed father appeals to the Lord at once most humbly, states the case clearly, and pleads most suitably. His epileptic son was a *lunatic, sore vexed* with pain, and in severe peril through sudden falls. The case was a shocking one to have in one's presence. The cries and contortions that accompany epilepsy are frequently terrible to hear and see. The disciples had evidently done their very best and as they had on other occasions cast out devils, they were surprised to find themselves defeated; but defeated they were, for the despairing father truthfully cried, *I brought him to thy disciples, and they could not cure him.* Alas, poor man, you did but speak as all have done since, when they have trusted in disciples and not alone in their Master! Wise was it on your part to hasten to Jesus, *kneeling down to him, and saying, Lord, have mercy on my son.*

How often does sin drive men to one extreme or the other! *Ofttimes he falleth into the fire, and oft into the water.* Certain men are moonstruck and pained at one time, yet hard and callous at another, for a season raving with excitement and soon afterwards dead as a stone. When sin reveals itself in connection with wildness of mind, it is hard to deal with. How often have anxious soul winners been obliged to confess concerning a certain individual that *they could not cure him!* We have been defeated by a person of a unique temperament, and the passion that possessed him has been peculiarly uncontrollable. Possibly he had no link towards better things but an aged parent, whose pleadings pitifully held us in deep anxiety for the half-lunatic and completely depraved young man. Willing as we were to reform and restore the wretched rebel, we were completely unable to help. It was necessary in our case that Jesus should come, even as in the narrative before us. Lord, do not leave us, for if apostles could do nothing without You, poor weaklings are we!

17. Then Jesus answered and said, O faithless and perverse generation, how long shall I be with you? how long shall I suffer you? bring him hither to me.

The whole *generation* among whom He lived caused the Savior suffering by their lack of faith and the absence of that straightforward confidence in God that would have secured them the greatest blessings. This was true of His own disciples – He had been with them and yet they had not learned to have faith in Him. This was true of the scribes and Pharisees – He had suffered from them many times already, and now they must make a poor lunatic the center of conflict with Him. He had been in fellowship with heaven, and it was a terrible jolt to His heart to come down among such an unruly and unbelieving company. They were both *faithless and perverse*; the two things commonly go together. Those who will not believe will not obey.

What a trial was all this to our Lord's holy and gracious mind! "*How long shall I be with you?* Must I continue in such unworthy company? *How long shall I suffer you?* Must I always be thus tested by your ill manners?" It was a moment when His triumphant foes and unbelieving friends alike deserved rebuke. But with the word once spoken, Jesus will not leave the poor sufferer before Him to endure the malicious attacks of the evil spirit.

See how our royal Captain turns the tide of battle with a word! He transferred the fight from the disciples to Himself: *Bring him hither to me.* Once in the circle of our Lord's own power, all is done. *Bring him hither to me.* Never let us forget this precept. When most self-despairing, let us be Christ-confiding.

18. And Jesus rebuked the devil; and he departed out of him: and the child was cured from that very hour.

Jesus rebuked the devil; and he departed. One word from Christ and the devil flees. Mark calls this evil spirit *dumb and deaf* (Mark 9:25), but he heard Jesus and answered to His voice with a cry, and tearing the child terribly, came out of him, never to return.

The child was cured from that very hour, that is to say, at once and forever. God grant us faith to bring our boys and girls to the Lord Jesus with confidence in His power to cure them, and cure them for all future life!

Even though young people may have become violent in temper and premature in sin, the Lord can at once subdue the evil power. There was no need for the boy to wait till he grew up. He was under the power of the devil while a child and he was cured as a child. Let us seek the salvation of children as children.

19. Then came the disciples to Jesus apart, and said, Why could not we cast him out?

This was a very proper question. When we fail, let us acknowledge that we have failed, take the blame for it to ourselves, and appeal to our Lord for His gracious intervention. When we are beaten, let it be said of us, *Then came the disciples to Jesus.* Let us make a private, personal matter of it: They came to Jesus *apart.* Let us sit humbly at our Lord's feet to receive rebuke or instruction as He sees fit.

20. And Jesus said unto them, Because of your unbelief: for verily I say unto you, If ye have faith as a grain of mustard seed, ye shall say unto this mountain, Remove hence to yonder place; and it shall remove; and nothing shall be impossible unto you.

Lack of faith is the great cause of failure among disciples, both as to themselves and their work for others. There may be other specific maladies in certain cases, but this is the great and main cause of all failure: *Because of your unbelief.* If there had been true faith, of the real and living kind, the disciples could have worked any miracle, even to the moving of a mountain. Our faith may be as small *as a grain of mustard seed,* but if it be living and true, it links us with the Omnipotent One. *Ye shall say unto this mountain, Remove hence to yonder place; and it shall remove.* Mountains shall move before our faith by means as sure as if they were miraculous, perhaps by means even more wonderful than if the course of nature had been changed. Comparatively speaking, the suspension of natural law is a coarse substitute, but for the Lord to work the same result without violating any of His laws is an achievement not less divine than a miracle. This is what faith obtains of the Lord at the present hour. Her prayer is heard and things impossible to herself are worked by divine power. Spiritually and symbolically, the mountain is removed. Literally, at this hour the mountain stands, but faith finds a way around it, through it, or over it, and so in effect removes it.

In the mission field, mountains of exclusiveness that shut out missionaries have been removed. In ordinary life, insurmountable difficulties are graciously dissolved. In a variety of ways, before real faith, hindrances disappear according to the word of the Lord Jesus: *Nothing shall be impossible unto you.*

21. Howbeit this kind goeth not out but by prayer and fasting.

Though lack of faith was the chief hindrance to the healing of the poor lunatic child, yet the case was one in which special means were needed. Faith would have suggested and supplied these special means, since they were absolutely necessary in this case if the disciples were to succeed in it; faith would have exercised herself in them. With God all things are equally possible, but to us, one devil may be harder to deal with than another. One kind will go out at a word, but of others it may be said, *This kind goeth not out but by prayer and fasting.* He that would overcome the devil in certain instances must first overcome heaven by prayer, and conquer himself by self-denial. The drink-devil is one of the *kind* that may assuredly be conquered by faith, and yet we must generally use much intercession Godward, and total abstinence as an example manward, before we can displace this demon. Our business in the world is to deliver men from the power of the devil, and we must go to Jesus to learn the way. No amount either of prayer or self-denial must be spared if we can thereby deliver one soul from the power of evil, and true faith in God will enable us to put up the prayer and practice the self-denial. It may be that some of us have failed because we are not yet well instructed in the right method of procedure.

Either we are trying faith without using the appointed means, or we are using the means but not exercising simple faith in God; and in either case, we shall make a failure of it. If we go to work by faith in God, in Christ's own way, we shall drive out the evil spirit.

Matthew 17:22-23

Again the King Speaks of His Death

22-23. And while they abode in Galilee, Jesus said unto them, The Son of man shall be betrayed into the hands of men: and they shall kill him, and the third day he shall be raised again. And they were exceeding sorry.

Our Lord returned often to the solemn subject of His death at the hands of men. It was on His own mind and therefore He spoke of it to His disciples. Their minds were far too receptive of other notions in reference to His kingdom, and therefore He set before them the truth again and again, almost in the same words. He would banish all dreams of a worldly monarchy from their souls. His death would be a painful trial to them, and He would prepare them for it. He now speaks of His being *betrayed.* This was ever a bitter drop in His cup of gall. The Son of Man comes to save men and is, by a man, *betrayed into the hands of men.* For man He lived, by man He is betrayed, and by man He died. Full well He foresaw that *they shall kill him.* Oh, suicidal world! Will nothing satisfy you but the blood of God's own Son?

Our Lord would have us preach much about His death now that it is accomplished, for He continually talked of it while it was still in the future. No theme is so vital, so practical, so necessary. His penetrating mind realized death and anticipated that *third day,* when the word would be fulfilled: *He shall be raised again.* This was the light of the morning that would have banished the darkness of despair from the minds of the disciples, if they had understood and believed. An old writer says, "He sugared the bitter pill of His death with the sweetness of His assured resurrection."

Our Lord well knew what He said, and He used plain terms; but speak as He might, His followers could only in part apprehend His meaning, and that part made them *exceeding sorry.* Christ's words, half understood, may cause the heart great grief. Yet, it may be, that this cooling cloud of fear calmed their minds and kept them from that fanaticism that filled the air around them. He knew best what state of mind would be safest for them at that time, and He knows the same as to us at this moment.

Matthew 17:24-27

Our King and the Tribute Money

24. And when they were come to Capernaum, they that received tribute money came to Peter, and said, Doth not your master pay tribute?

The half-shekel *tribute* was a religious payment, based originally on law, but enlarged by a custom that had no support in Scripture. It was ordained by the divine law to be paid by each person to the Lord when the people were counted. From this redemption money there was no exemption, but it was not a tax levied year by year. It had gradually grown into a fashion among professedly religious people to pay this *tribute money* every year, but the payment was entirely optional. Thus, it was established by custom, but it had not been appointed by law and could not be enforced by it. It was a voluntary annual gift and only persons who were professed devotees of the Jewish religion would pay it. Such religionists as these would be very particular, not only to pay the annual tribute, but also to have it known that they paid it. The collectors of half-shekels did not request it at once of Jesus, of whom, it may be, they stood in favorable awe, but they addressed Peter with the somewhat ensnaring question, *Doth not your master pay tribute?* It was as much as to say, "Surely, He does so. We would not suspect Him of neglecting to do so. A person of such preeminence cannot fail to be peculiarly exact as to this customary fee."

25-26. He saith, Yes. And when he was come into the house, Jesus prevented him, saying, What thinkest thou, Simon? of whom do the kings of the earth take custom or tribute? of their own children, or of strangers? Peter saith unto him, Of strangers. Jesus saith unto him, Then are the children free.

Peter was in such a hurry to vindicate his Lord that he compromised Him. *He saith, Yes.* He might have asked his Lord's mind on this or he might have referred the collectors to Jesus Himself, but he was in a hurry and thought himself safe enough in maintaining his Master's reputation. He was quite certain that his Lord would do all that good people did. Our Savior and His cause have often suffered from the zeal of friends. Christ is better known by what He says Himself than by what His friends say for Him.

Peter was out of doors at the time he gave his quick reply, and little did he think that the Lord Jesus would note what he had said, and tell him of it as soon as *he was come into the house;* but so it was.

Our Lord began with Peter upon the subject before he had time to state his action or defend it: *Jesus prevented him.* He knew what His servant had been doing, and He hastened to set him right. As he had been but little of a *Peter* in this case, our Lord calls him *Simon.* He questions him, *What thinkest thou, Simon?* He will make him judge in the case. Do kings take poll tax *of their own children, or of strangers?* Of course, the family of the prince was always free from the levy. The king's subjects, and especially the aliens under his rule, must pay the poll tax, but the princes of the blood royal were free. Should Jesus pay redemption money for Himself to God? Should He, who is Himself the King's Son, come under poll tax to His Father? If tribute money has become a tax to be levied in the kingdom of God, *then are the children free.* Neither Jesus nor Peter was bound to pay. Peter had not seen the matter in this light.

> 27. *Notwithstanding, lest we should offend them, go thou to the sea, and cast an hook, and take up the fish that first cometh up; and when thou hast opened his mouth, thou shalt find a piece of money: that take, and give unto them for me and thee.*

Our Savior would not willingly give ground for offense. He was not bound to pay, but rather than raise a scandal, He would pay both for Himself and for Peter. How gracious were His words: *Notwithstanding, lest we should offend them!* If the question had remained by itself, clear from other circumstances, our Lord might, on principle, have declined to pay the tribute money, but Peter's rash declaration had compromised his Lord and He would not come across as being false to the promise made by His follower. Besides, Peter would be involved in a dispute and Jesus would far rather pay than leave His servant in a difficulty. When the pocket is involved in a matter of principle, we must be careful that we do not even seem to be saving our money by a pretense. Usually, it will be wisest to pay under protest, lest it should appear that we are careful of conscience in a special degree when we can also be careful of our cash.

The manner of payment prevented the act from compromising our Lord. Very interesting was the hooking of the fish that brought the silver in its mouth. *Take up the fish that first cometh up; and when thou hast opened his mouth, thou shalt find a piece of money.* Very remarkable is the providence that caused the shekel to fall into the sea and made the fish first to swallow it, and then to rise to the hook as soon as Peter began his angling. Thus, the great Son pays the tax levied for His Father's house, but He exercises His royal prerogative in the act and takes the shekel out of the royal treasury. As man He pays, but first as God He causes the fish to bring Him the shekel in its mouth.

The piece of money was enough to pay for Peter as well as for his Lord. Thus did our Lord submit to be treated as one who had forfeited life and must have a half-shekel paid as redemption-money for Him. This He has done for our sake and in association with us, and we are redeemed by His act and in union with Him, for He said of the piece of money, *That take, and give unto them for me and thee.* There were not two half-shekels, but one piece of money, paid for Jesus and Peter. Thus, we see that His people are joined with Him in the one redemption.

> "He bore on the tree the sentence for me,
> And now both the Surety and sinner are free."

The obvious moral lesson is: Pay rather than cause offense.

But far greater and deeper truths lie slumbering down below. They are such as these: the glorious freedom of the Son, His coming under tribute for our sakes, and the clearance of Himself and us by the one payment that He Himself provided.

Matthew 18

Matthew 18:1-5

The King Arranges Rank in His Kingdom

1. At the same time came the disciples unto Jesus, saying, Who is the greatest in the kingdom of heaven?

He spoke of His humility, they thought of their own advancement, and that *at the same time.* How different at the same moment the Teacher and *the disciples*! The idea of greatness, and of more or less of it for each one, was interwoven with their notion of a kingdom, even though it might be *the kingdom of heaven.* They came *unto Jesus,* but how could they have the courage to ask their lowly Lord a question so manifestly alien to His thought and spirit? It showed their trustfulness, but also displayed their folly.

2. And Jesus called a little child unto him, and set him in the midst of them.

He did not answer them with words alone, but He made His teaching more impressive by an act. He *called a little child unto him.* The child came at once and Jesus *set him in the midst of them.* That the child came at His call and was willingly placed where Jesus wished him to be was evidence of a sweetness of manner on the part of our Lord. Surely there was a smile on His face when He instructed the little one to come unto Him, and there must have been a charming gentleness in the manner in which He placed the child in the center of the twelve, as His little model. Let us see Jesus and the little child, and the twelve apostles grouped around the two central figures.

Thus, may the whole church gather to study Jesus and the childlike character.

3. And said, Verily I say unto you, Except ye be converted, and become as little children, ye shall not enter into the kingdom of heaven.

The apostles were converted in one sense, but even they needed a further conversion. They needed to *be converted* from self-seeking to humbleness and contentment. A little child has no ambitious dreams. He is satisfied with little things. He trusts. He aims not at greatness. He yields to command. There is no entering *into the kingdom of heaven* but by descending from imagined greatness to real lowliness of mind, and *becom[ing] as little children.*

To rise to the greatness of grace, we must go down to the littleness, the simplicity, and the trustfulness of childhood. Since this was the rule for the apostles, we may depend upon it that we cannot *enter* the kingdom in any less humbling manner. This truth is verified by our Lord's solemnly attesting word: *Verily I say unto you.*

4. Whosoever therefore shall humble himself as this little child, the same is greatest in the kingdom of heaven.

In the kingdom of heaven, the least is the *greatest.* The most humble is the most exalted. He that will fulfill the lowest offices for the brethren shall be highest in their esteem. We have need to use endeavors to make ourselves truly lowly in mind, and if, through almighty grace, we succeed in it, we shall take high degrees in the school of love. What a kingdom is this, in which every man ascends by willingly going down!

It is wisdom for a man to *humble himself,* for thus he will escape the necessity of being humbled. Children do not try to be humble, but they are so, and the same is the case with really gracious persons. The imitation of humility is sickening. The reality is attractive. May grace work it in us!

5. And whoso shall receive one such little child in my name receiveth me.

It is no small thing to be able to appreciate humble and lowly characters. To *receive* one childlike believer in Christ's name is to receive Christ. To delight in a lowly, trustful character is to delight in Christ. If we count it a joy to do service to such persons, we may be sure that we are in that respect serving our Lord. Those who *receive little ones* in Christ's name will grow like them, and so in another way they will *receive Christ* into their own souls.

Matthew 18:6-14

Our King's Warning against Offenses, Especially Those That Injure the Little Ones

6. But whoso shall offend one of these little ones which believe in me, it were better for him that a millstone were hanged about his neck, and that he were drowned in the depth of the sea.

To bless a little one is to entertain the Savior Himself. To set one's self to pervert the simple or to molest the humble will be the sure way to a terrible doom.

Little ones which believe in [Jesus] are specially under His guardian care, and only the desperately malicious will attack them or seek to make them stumble. Such an evil person will gain nothing, even should he win the easy victory he looks for. He will, on the contrary, be preparing for himself a terrible retribution. *It were better for him that* the biggest of millstones, such as would be used in a mill worked by a donkey, *were hanged about his neck,* and that he himself were then hurled overboard and *drowned in the depth of the sea.* He will surely sink infamously, sink never to rise again. The haters of the humble are among the worst of men, for their enmity is unprovoked. They may hope to rise by oppressing or duping the simplehearted, but such conduct will prove their certain destruction sooner or later. It is the lowly Lord of the lowly who pronounces this condemnation, and He is soon to be the Judge of *the quick and the dead* (2 Timothy 4:1; 1 Peter 4:5).

7. Woe unto the world because of offences! for it must needs be that offences come; but woe to that man by whom the offence cometh!

It is a sad world because of stumbling blocks. This is the great misery of every age. Occasions for falling into sin are terribly many, and from the formation of society, it seems as if it must be so. *It must needs be that offences come.* While man is man, his surroundings will be hard and his fellow man will too often become occasions of evil to him. This brings *woe unto the world;* but the center of that woe will be with the guilty cause of the stumbling, be that stumbling what it may. Those who try to be the greatest are great causers of offenses. The humble are the least likely to make others stumble. Woe, therefore, is the sure heritage of the proud, for he is *that man by whom the offence cometh!*

> 8-9. *Wherefore if thy hand or thy foot offend thee, cut them off, and cast them from thee: it is better for thee to enter into life halt or maimed, rather than having two hands or two feet to be cast into everlasting fire. And if thine eye offend thee, pluck it out, and cast it from thee: it is better for thee to enter into life with one eye, rather than having two eyes to be cast into hell fire.*

Here our Lord repeats a passage from the Sermon on the Mount (Matthew 5:29-30). Why should He not? Great lessons need to be often taught, especially lessons that involve painful self-denial. It is well when at the close of a man's ministry he can preach the same sermon as at the beginning. Some in these days change continually. Jesus is *the same yesterday, and to day, and for ever* (Hebrews 13:8).

Temptations and incitements to sin are so dangerous that, if we find them in ourselves, we must at any cost be rid of the causes of them. If escape from these temptations should cause us to be like men who are *halt or maimed,* or have only *one eye,* the loss will be of small consequence so long as we *enter into life.* Better to miss culture through a rigid Puritanism than to gain all the polish and accomplishments of the age at the expense of our spiritual health. Though at our entrance into the divine life we should seem to have been largely losers by renouncing habits or possessions that we felt bound to leave, yet we shall be real gainers. Our main concern should be *to enter into life;* and if this should cost us skill of hand, nimbleness of foot, and refinement of vision, as it may, we must cheerfully deny ourselves so that we may possess eternal life. To remain in sin and retain all our advantages and capacities will be an awful loss when we are *cast into hell fire,* which is the sure portion of all who persevere in sinning. A lame, maimed, half-blinded saint is, even on earth, better than a sinner with every faculty fully developed. It is not necessary that hand, or foot, or eye should make us stumble, but if they do, the surgical process is short, sharp, and decisive – *Cut them off, and cast them from thee,* or, *pluck it out, and cast it from thee.* The half-educated, timid, simpleminded believer who, to escape the snares of false science, worldly cunning, and graceful pride, has cut himself off from what men call *advantages* will, in the end, prove to have been far wiser than those who risk their souls for the sake of what worldlings imagine to be necessary to human perfecting. The man who believes God and so is set down as losing his critical eye is a wiser person than he who by double perception doubts himself into hell. *Two hands or two feet,* and *two eyes* will be of small advantage if *cast into everlasting fire.* Let the reader note that the terrible terms here employed are not the creation of the dark dreams of medieval times, but are the words of the loving Jesus.

> *10-11. Take heed that ye despise not one of these little ones; for I say unto you, That in heaven their angels do always behold the face of my Father which is in heaven. For the Son of man is come to save that which was lost.*

The humble in heart, though judged to be fools among the ungodly, must not be so judged by us. *Take heed that ye despise not one of these little ones.* We must see to it that we never look down on them with the pity that is akin to contempt. They are very dear to God. They are cared for by angels, alas, by the presence of angels who dwell near the eternal throne. *Their angels* are not in the rear rank, but *in heaven do always behold the face of [the] Father.* The highest courtiers of glory count it their honor to watch over the lowly in heart. Those who are servants to poor saints and little children are allowed free entrance to the King. What must He think of His little ones themselves?

No, this is not all. Jesus Himself cares for the poorest and neediest. Yes, He came *to save that which was lost.* How dare we then be proud and despise a child because of their youth, or a man because of his poverty, or his lack of intelligence. The angels and the angels' Lord care for the most despised of our race; shall not we?

> *12. How think ye? if a man have an hundred sheep, and one of them be gone astray, doth he not leave the ninety and nine, and goeth into the mountains, and seeketh that which is gone astray?*

We may not even think harshly of wandering ones. He who would not have us despise the little will not have us neglect the lost. No, the lost are to have special consideration. Is not the owner of a flock for the moment more concerned about the *one astray,* than the *ninety and nine* that are safe? The lost one is not better than any one of the others, but it is brought into prominence by its condition. It is not to the shepherd the object of deserved blame, much less of contempt, but his main thought is sympathy with its danger and the fear that it may be destroyed before he can find it. To save it, he makes a mountain journey, in person, neglecting the large flock in comparison with his care of the one. This is good argument for despising none – not only of the least, but also of the most erring. *How think ye?* You who yourselves were once *gone astray* and have been restored by the Shepherd and Bishop of souls, *how think ye?*

13. And if so be that he find it, verily I say unto you, he rejoiceth more of that sheep, than of the ninety and nine which went not astray.

In the shepherd's case we read, *If so be that he find it;* but our great Shepherd fails not, and is not discouraged. He brings back all the sheep that his Father gave him.

That sheep which, after wandering, is found, gives the shepherd more immediate joy than all the rest, just because it had caused him more present concern. Its rescue brought it to the front in his mind. He was forced to do more for it than for the ninety and nine, and therefore, estimating its value by what it has cost him, *he rejoiceth more of that sheep, than of the ninety and nine which went not astray.* He is not vexed by his loss of time, nor angry because of his extra labor, but his joy is undiluted and overflowing. Evidently the Good Shepherd does not despise the little one because of its straying, for having restored it, He allots it a chief place in His thoughts of joy; yes, He gets from it, though it be but one, more than from ninety and nine others of the best of His flock.

14. Even so it is not the will of your Father which is in heaven, that one of these little ones should perish.

We may ourselves complete the parallel as to the Shepherd of souls. It is too obvious to need the Savior to rehearse it. In the words before us, our Lord further declares that *our Father which is in heaven* desires not that any *one of these little ones should perish.* Therefore, we may not despise any of them, nor, indeed, despise any because of their being lowly and of a contemptible condition. Humble in their own estimate of themselves, and lightly esteemed among men, as the Lord's people often are, and surrounded by cruel foes, as is frequently the case, the heavenly Father desires not their destruction, nor can they be destroyed. We must not treat the poor, the obscure, the little-gifted, as though we thought they would be better out of our way, or as if they were of no consequence whatsoever and could be most properly ignored. This is in a certain sense to make them *perish,* for those whom we regard as nothing become to us as if they were nothing. He who sits in the highest heavens seeks out those who are lowly in heart and of a contrite spirit because of their wanderings, and He sets great store by them. Our Father in heaven will not have us despise those who are precious in His eyes.

Matthew 18:15-35

The King's Law concerning Offenses

15. Moreover if thy brother shall trespass against thee, go and tell him his fault between thee and him alone: if he shall hear thee, thou hast gained thy brother.

So far from despising any, we are to seek their good, even when they have done us wrong. Here is a case of personal offense. We are to endeavor to make peace with our *brother who has trespassed against us.* The offended is to seek the offender. We must not let the trespass rage in our bosom by maintaining a sullen silence, nor may we go and publish the matter abroad. We must seek out the offender and tell him his fault as if he were not aware of it, as perhaps he may not be. Let the complaint be between *thee and him alone.* It may happen that he will at once rectify the wrong and then we have *gained,* not our appeal, but something worth far more – our *brother.* We might have lost him. Happily, an honest word has won him. God be praised!

16. But if he will not hear thee, then take with thee one or two more, that in the mouth of two or three witnesses every word may be established.

If the brother has trespassed very badly, he will probably be sullen or impertinent, and *he will not hear thee.* Do not, therefore, give him up. Persevere in seeking peace. Give your own pleadings the support of companionship: *Take with thee one or two more.* Possibly the offender may notice what is said by the other brethren, although he may be prejudiced against you, or he may attach weight to united complaining that he might not feel if the complaint came from one only. By calling in worthy arbitrators, you give the offender a fairer opportunity to set himself right. This time, let us hope, the brother will be won. But if not, you will have secured yourself against misrepresentation, *that in the mouth of two or three witnesses every word may be established.* It is by misquotation of words that quarrels are aroused, and it is a great thing to have the means of rectifying erroneous reports. Although it is a very unwise thing to interfere in quarrels, yet from this text it is clear that we should be willing to be one of the two or three who are to assist in settling a difference.

17. And if he shall neglect to hear them, tell it unto the church: but if he neglect to hear the church, let him be unto thee as an heathen man and a publican.

Men capable of injuring their fellows are often so hardened that they reject the kindest objection. If a brother acts in this way, shall we give him up? No, we must make a filial effort: *Tell it unto the church.* The whole assembly of the faithful must at last hear the case and they must plead with him. He is to have an opportunity of hearing the judgment and advice of the whole brotherhood. Should this last attempt fail, *if he neglect to hear the church,* then he must be left as incorrigible. No pains and penalties are affixed. The brother is left to himself. He is regarded as being like the rest of the unbelieving world. This is the utmost stretch of our severity. He is one who needs converting, like the Gentiles outside, but towards even *an heathen man and a publican* we have kind feelings, for we seek their salvation and we seek that of the excommunicated brother in the same way. In all probability, the obstinate friend will ridicule the action of the community, and yet there is some possibility that he will be impressed thereby, and be led to a better mind. At any rate, from the first personal visit of the injured brother down to the last act of disownment, nothing has been done vindictively, but all has been affectionately carried out, with the view of setting the brother right. The trespasser who will not be reconciled has incurred much guilt by resisting the attempts of love, made in obedience to the command of the great head of the church.

18. Verily I say unto you, Whatsoever ye shall bind on earth shall be bound in heaven: and whatsoever ye shall loose on earth shall be loosed in heaven.

Our Lord had inaugurated the church by handing its keys to Peter as representing the whole brotherhood, and now He distinctly recognizes those keys as being in the hands of the whole church. *Verily I say unto you, Whatsoever ye shall bind.* Those who bind are all the disciples or the whole of the church that had been called in to make peace between the two brethren. Each church has the keys of its own door. When those keys are rightly turned by the assembly below, the act is ratified above: That which they *bind on earth shall be bound in heaven.* If, by God's grace, erring brethren repent and are freed from the judgment of the assembly, the Lord on high sanctions the deed according to His Word – *Whatsoever ye shall loose on earth shall be loosed in heaven.* This is to be understood with the limitation that it is really a church of Christ that acts, that it acts in His name, and rightly administers His laws. A deep solemnity surrounds the binding and loosing of true Christian assemblies. It is no light thing to act as a church and no little thing to be put forth from it or to be restored again to its fellowship. Our Lord made this clear by commencing with His authoritative preface – *Verily I say unto you.*

19. Again I say unto you, That if two of you shall agree on earth as touching any thing that they shall ask, it shall be done for them of my Father which is in heaven.

Thus, the Savior sets His seal upon assemblies of the faithful, even of the smallest kind, not only in their acts of discipline, but also in their intercessions. Note how tenderly Jesus speaks of His followers: *If two of you.* Poor as you are, *if two of you* agree in prayer *on earth, my Father which is in heaven* will listen to your pleading. Prayer should be a matter for previous consideration, and persons about to join in prayer should *agree as touching any thing that they shall ask.* Then they come together with an intelligent objective, seeking a known blessing, and agreeing to combine their desires and their faith in reference to the one chosen object. *Two* believers united in holy desire and solemn prayer will have great power with God. Instead of despising the verdict of so small a gathering, we ought to respect it, since the Father does so.

Note the power of combined prayer. There is no excuse for giving up prayer meetings while there are two praying people in the place, for two can prevail with God. Of course, more is needed than a cold agreement that certain things are desirable. There must be persistence and faith.

20. For where two or three are gathered together in my name, there am I in the midst of them.

The presence of Jesus is the fixed center of the assembly, the warrant for its coming together, and the power with which it acts. The church, however small, is *gathered in his name.* Jesus is there first: *I am in the midst of them.* We are gathered together by the holy impulses of Christian brotherhood, and our meeting is *in the name of Jesus,* and therefore there He is – near, not only to the leader or to the minister, but also *in the midst,* and therefore near to each worshipper. We meet to do Him honor, to hear His Word, to stir each other up to obey His will, and He is there to aid us. However small the number, we make a quorum, and what is done according to the laws of Christ is done with His authority. Thus it is that there is great power in united prayer from such persons. It is Jesus pleading in His saints. This should prevent Christian men from giving or taking offense, for if Jesus be in our midst, our peace must not be broken by strife.

21. Then came Peter to him, and said, Lord, how oft shall my brother sin against me, and I forgive him? till seven times?

Peter's question was opportune, giving a further opening for our Lord to enlarge upon the removal of offenses. Peter takes it for granted that he would *forgive,* and he only wishes to know how far he may carry this forgiveness. Doubtless he thought that he had given great latitude when he suggested *till seven times.* Probably he felt that he would need great grace to get so far as that in the patient endurance of his brother's sinning against him. It is true that Peter did not go far enough, but do we go as far? Are not some professing persons very mindful of small grievances? Have many of us grace enough even for a sevenfold forgiveness?

22. Jesus saith unto him, I say not unto thee, Until seven times: but, Until seventy times seven.

Our Lord intends to teach us to forgive always and without end. He sets no limit. *I say not unto thee, Until seven times;* measured mercy is not according to the command. We may read the words of our Lord in this verse as *seventy-seven times* or as *seventy times seven,* or four hundred and ninety times. There is no occasion to be very definite about numbers where an indefinite number is meant. We should make too small an account of offenses to occupy time in counting them or in reckoning the number of times that we have overlooked them.

23. Therefore is the kingdom of heaven likened unto a certain king, which would take account of his servants.

The kingdom of heaven is again brought forward. We must not forget that this is the key of Matthew's Gospel. In all kingdoms there must be a king, a tribunal, and a time for judgment of those under rule. The personal servants of a king must expect to give a special account as to how they have used their lord's goods. Our Lord is that *certain king, who would take account of his servants.* Even if He called no one else to give an account, He would assuredly call His own servants to a settlement.

24. And when he had begun to reckon, one was brought unto him, which owed him ten thousand talents.

Ten thousand talents was an immense amount for a servant to owe his king. Some reckon that it was equivalent to two million dollars in our time. It was a debt that could not be paid; it was overwhelming, and almost incalculable. This debt cropped up as soon as the king *had begun to reckon.* It was a matter of notoriety, too vast to be concealed. The debtor was brought bound before his lord, but his vast debt was his strongest bond: *Ten thousand talents!* Yet what is this amount to the burden of our obligations to God? O my soul, humble yourself as you answer the question, *How much owest thou?* (Luke 16:5, 7).

25. But forasmuch as he had not to pay, his lord commanded him to be sold, and his wife, and children, and all that he had, and payment to be made.

The debtor was penniless; *he had not to pay.* The creditor takes possession of the man; *his lord commanded him to be sold. His wife,* his children, *and all that he had* were to be sold also, but all put together, when *payment was to be made,* it came to nothing compared with the enormous debt. The sale of the man and his family was according to Eastern justice. The generous lord here described did not hesitate to exact it, and the debtor himself raised no question about the righteousness of the proceeding. Our Lord does not justify the act of the *lord* in the story; He simply uses the custom as a part of the scenery of His parable. We may be thankful that the spirit of Christianity has utterly abolished a law that made unoffending children suffer for their father's default, by the loss of their liberties. The servant was in a sad plight indeed when nothing remained his own, and even his own personality was sold away from him. *He had not to pay,* yet by royal order payment was to be made. He was wretched indeed.

26. The servant therefore fell down, and worshipped him, saying, Lord, have patience with me, and I will pay thee all.

He could not pay, but he could humble himself before his lord. He *fell down, and worshipped him.* He acknowledged the debt and begged for time: *Have patience with me.* Moreover, he gave a promise to discharge his obligations: *I will pay thee all.* The promise was not worth the breath that spoke it. It is a very usual thing for men who can incur an enormous debt to make light of the payment and imagine that a bill at three months is as good as gold. They dream that time is money and that a promise is a payment. Many a poor sinner is very rich in resolutions. This servant-debtor thought he only needed *patience,* but indeed he needed forgiveness! It seems strange that he did not see this, since the debt was so great and he had nothing with which to pay, but was utterly bankrupt. Yet it is a well-known fact that men do not see their true condition before the Lord God, even when they perceive that in many things they come short.

27. Then the lord of that servant was moved with compassion, and loosed him, and forgave him the debt.

Humility and prayer prevailed, for *the lord of that servant* was such a king as the whole universe cannot rival for pity and grace. The debtor received far more than he dared to ask, for the measure of the gracious deed was not his own sense of need, nor even his own prayers, but the *compassion* of his lord. The heart of the great creditor was touched and his whole being was moved with pity. The penniless debtor was unbound and his debt was forgiven him; his lord *loosed him, and forgave him.* We know what this means. This was kindness indeed! There could be no greater thing done for the debtor, and all was so free, so noble, and so perfect, that it ought to have produced a great effect upon him and led him, in his measure, to imitate the royal example. Hard was the heart that such a fire of love could not soften.

28. But the same servant went out, and found one of his fellowservants, which owed him an hundred pence: and he laid hands on him, and took him by the throat, saying, Pay me that thou owest.

The same servant, but how different his demeanor! A moment ago he was a lowly pleader, but now he is a bullying tyrant. *He went out* from the presence of his gracious lord, scarcely waiting to express his gratitude. He *found one of his fellowservants,* not his servant, nor his inferior, but one who was his equal and his companion in service. This man *owed him an hundred pence,* a mere trifle when compared with the enormous debt that had been forgiven. We expect that he will at once wipe out that little score; but no, *he laid hands on him,* violently seizing him, for fear he should get away for a time. *He took him by the throat* and bullied him with arrogant demands. He would have no patience with his debtor. He would not let him breathe if he did not pay. The debt was very, very small, but the claim was urged with intense ferocity. Our little claims against our fellow man are too apt to be pressed upon them with unsparing severity. The claimant had not even patience for an hour, but he took his fellow servant *by the throat* with the rough demand, *Pay me that thou owest.* What right had he to be choking his lord's servant? He was injuring one who belonged to his own king. Our fellow servant is our Lord's servant, and not ours to bully and oppress as we please.

29. And his fellowservant fell down at his feet, and besought him, saying, Have patience with me, and I will pay thee all.

It ought to have startled the tyrant when he heard his own prayer addressed to himself. It was word for word what he had said, and the pleader's posture was just what his own had been when before his lord, *he fell down at his feet.* That poor promise too, *I will pay thee all,* was repeated in his ear and with much more likelihood of its being fulfilled.

Surely he would give the same answer as his lord had granted him! Not he. He was in a low state and of an evil spirit. His lord was a king and acted royally.

30. And he would not: but went and cast him into prison, till he should pay the debt.

Not he *could* not, but *he **would** not* (emphasis added). He gave no time, proposed no terms of agreement, and promised no mercy. He used the law of his own generous king as a means of treading down his poor fellow servant. He personally attended to the debtor's arrest: *He went and cast him into prison.* He sees him sentenced to a debtor's dungeon, without hope of coming out again unless by payment. It was his lord's own prison, too. He was making use of his generous sovereign's lockup to gratify his own malice. He vowed that his fellow servant should lie there *till he should pay the debt.* Cruel conduct this! As common as it is cruel!

31. So when his fellowservants saw what was done, they were very sorry, and came and told unto their lord all that was done.

Others could see the evil of his conduct, if he could not. *His fellowservants saw what was done.* He was a notable character and what he did was sure to be observed. Much had been forgiven him and much was expected from him. His fellow servants *were very sorry* for the imprisoned debtor and sorry that any fellow servant of theirs should degrade himself by acting in a manner so opposite to the treatment that he had received from his lord. They were right in reporting the transaction to headquarters, for such a foul offense ought to be known where right could be done. Instead of carrying out lynch law, they *told unto their lord all that was done.* This was a very sensible course of conduct on their part. Let us adopt this plan if we are ever in similar circumstances, instead of indulging in foolish gossip and angry denunciation.

32-33. Then his lord, after that he had called him, said unto him, O thou wicked servant, I forgave thee all that debt, because thou desiredst me: shouldest not thou also have had compassion on thy fellowservant, even as I had pity on thee?

The wretch was not condemned unheard; *his lord* only judged him *after that he had called him.* His lord and king set the matter before him very clearly and appealed to his own judgment upon the case. He reminded him of what he appeared to have forgotten, or at least, he had acted as if it had never happened. His lord addressed him in words of burning indignation: *O thou wicked servant.* It was atrocious wickedness of heart that had permitted him to indulge in such unworthy conduct. *I forgave thee all that debt.* What an *all* it was! How freely was the debt removed! *I forgave thee.* The reason given was *because thou desiredst me.* Not because you had deserved such leniency or could ever repay it. The inference from such abounding generosity was clear, strong, and unanswerable. The last words of the verse are forcible in the highest degree: *Shouldest not thou also have had compassion on thy fellowservant?* How readily should we forgive the little offenses from which we suffer, since our Lord has pardoned our severe transgressions! No offense of a fellow servant can be compared with our sins against our Lord. What a model for our compassion is set before us in those words: *Even as I had pity on thee.*

The culprit made no defense. What could he say? He was unable even to make another appeal to mercy. He had refused mercy and now mercy refused him.

34. And his lord was wroth, and delivered him to the tormentors, till he should pay all that was due unto him.

His lord was wroth. He who could be so compassionate was necessarily a man of warm feelings and therefore he could be angry. Naturally, he was compassionate towards the poor debtor in prison, and this made him indignant with the wretch who had imprisoned him. It was righteous wrath that gave up the unforgiving servant to terrible punishment and *delivered him to the tormentors,* the proper executioners of justice. His punishment would be without end, for it was to last *till he should pay all that was due,* and the debtor could never pay the ten thousand talents. Things must take their course with malicious spirits. They have put themselves beyond the reach of mercy. Love's own greatness necessitates great indignation at the malice that insists upon revenging its little wrongs. The sovereignty of God is never unjust. He only delivers to the tormentors those whom the law of the universe necessarily condemns.

35. So likewise shall my heavenly Father do also unto you, if ye from your hearts forgive not every one his brother their trespasses.

This is the great moral lesson. We incur greater wrath by refusing to forgive than by all the rest of our indebtedness. We cannot escape from condemnation if we refuse to pardon others. If we forgive in words only, but not *from our hearts,* we remain under the same condemnation.

Continued anger against our brother shuts heaven's gate in our own faces. *The heavenly Father* of the Lord Jesus will be righteously wrathful against us and will deliver us to the tormentors if we do not from our hearts *forgive everyone his brother's trespasses.*

Lord, make me of a meek, forgiving spirit! May my heart be as ready to pardon offenses as it is to beat!

Matthew 19

Matthew 19:1-12

The King and the Marriage Laws

1-2. And it came to pass, that when Jesus had finished these sayings, he departed from Galilee, and came into the coasts of Judaea beyond Jordan; and great multitudes followed him; and he healed them there.

He had *finished these sayings* upon forgiveness, and so He hastened to other work that was not finished. He was ever on the move and *he departed from Galilee,* which had received so much of His care that other regions might enjoy His ministry. He now turned more to the south, *into the coasts of Judaea beyond Jordan,* and He did good at every turn. When He had finished speaking to the disciples, He began working deeds of grace in a new district and *great multitudes followed him.* The crowd was always at His heels, held both by His word and by His work. He was drawing near to Jerusalem and His foes were on the watch, but He did not restrain His works of mercy because of their jealous scrutiny; *he healed them there.*

The place of our Lord's gracious work is worthy to be remembered. Where the need was, there the help was given.

3. The Pharisees also came unto him, tempting him, and saying unto him, Is it lawful for a man to put away his wife for every cause?

Here are these vipers again! What perseverance in malice! They cared little for instruction, yet they assumed the air of inquirers. In truth, they were upon the catch and were ready to dispute with Him whatever He might say. The question is cunningly worded, *Is it lawful for a man to put away his wife for every cause?* The looser the terms of a question, the more likely it is to entangle the person interrogated. Their own consciences might have told them that the marriage bond is not to be severed for any and every reason that a man likes to mention. Yet it was a question much disputed at the time, whether a man could send away his wife at pleasure, or whether there must be some serious reason alleged. Whatever Jesus might say, the Pharisees meant to use His verdict against Him.

> *4-6. And he answered and said unto them, Have ye not read, that he which made them at the beginning made them male and female, and said, For this cause shall a man leave father and mother, and shall cleave to his wife: and they twain shall be one flesh. Wherefore they are no more twain, but one flesh. What therefore God hath joined together, let not man put asunder.*

In His reply, Jesus challenges their knowledge of the law: *Have ye not read*? It was a forcible mode of appealing to their own boasted acquaintance with the books of Moses. Our Lord honors Holy Scripture by drawing His argument from it. He chose specially to set His seal upon a part of the story of creation – that story that modern critics speak of as if it were a fable or a myth. He took His hearers back to *the beginning when God made them male and female,* and made them sons. *In the image of God created he* **him;** *male and female created he* **them** (Genesis 1:27, emphasis added). The woman was taken out of man and Adam truly said, *This is now bone of my bones, and flesh of my flesh* (Genesis 2:23). By marriage this unity is set forth and embodied under divine sanction. This oneness is of the most real and vital kind: *They are no more twain, but one flesh.* All other ties are feeble compared with this. Even father and mother must stand second to the wife: *For this cause shall a man leave father and mother, and shall cleave to his wife.* Being divinely appointed, this union must not be broken by the whim of men: *What therefore God hath joined together, let not man put asunder.* Our Lord thus decides for the lifelong perpetuity of the marriage bond, in opposition to those who allowed divorce *for every cause* (Matthew 19:3), which very frequently meant for no cause whatsoever.

> *7. They say unto him, Why did Moses then command to give a writing of divorcement, and to put her away?*

Every reader of the passage in the books of Moses that is here referred to will be struck with the Pharisees' unfair rendering of it. In Deuteronomy 24:1-2, we read, *When a man hath taken a wife, and married her, and it come to pass that she find no favour in his eyes, because he hath found some uncleanness in her: then let him write her a bill of divorcement, and give it in her hand, and send her out of his house. And when she is departed out of his house, she may go and be another man's wife.* Moses *commanded* nothing in this instance, but barely tolerated and greatly limited a custom then in vogue. To set Moses against Moses is not a new device, but the Pharisees would hardly venture to set Moses against God and make Him command an alteration of a divine law ordained from the beginning. Yet our Lord made them see that they would have to do this to maintain the theory of easy divorce. The fact is that Moses found divorce in existence to an almost unlimited extent, and he wisely commenced its overthrow by curtailing the custom rather than by absolutely forbidding it at once. They were not allowed to send away a wife with a hasty word, but must make a deliberate, solemn ceremonial of it by preparing and *giving a writing of divorcement,* and this was only allowed in a special case: *Because he hath found some uncleanness in her.* Although many of the Pharisees spirited away this last limitation and considered that the enactment in Deuteronomy sanctioned almost unlimited divorce, they were not unanimous in the matter and were perpetually disputing over it. Therefore, there were many ways in which our Lord's decision could be turned against Him, whatever it might be.

8. He saith unto them, Moses because of the hardness of your hearts suffered you to put away your wives: but from the beginning it was not so.

Moses tolerated and limited an evil custom which he knew that such a people would not relinquish after its having been established among them for so long a time. They could not bear a higher law, and so he treated them as persons diseased with *hardness of heart,* hoping to lead them back to an older and better state of things by possible stages. As impurity ceased, and as the spirit of true religion would influence the nation, the need for divorce, and even the least desire for it, would die out. There was no provision in paradise for Adam's putting away Eve; there was no desire for divorce in the golden age. The enactment of the Mosaic law of divorce was modern and temporary; and in the form into which a loose interpretation of Scripture had distorted it, it was not defensible.

9. And I say unto you, Whosoever shall put away his wife, except it be for fornication, and shall marry another, committeth adultery: and whoso marrieth her which is put away doth commit adultery.

Fornication makes the guilty person a fit subject for just and lawful divorce, for it is a breaking of the marriage bond. In a case of fornication, upon clear proof, the tie can be loosed, but in no other case. Any other sort of divorce is by the Law of God null and void, and it involves the persons who act upon it in the crime of adultery. *Whoso marrieth her which is put away doth commit adultery,* since she is not really divorced, but remains the wife of her former husband. Our King tolerates none of those enactments that, in certain countries, trifle with the bonds of matrimony. Nations may make what laws they dare, but they cannot alter facts – persons once married are, in the sight of God, married for life, with the one exception of proven fornication.

10. His disciples say unto him, If the case of the man be so with his wife, it is not good to marry.

They had come to look upon the ease of slipping the marriage-knot as a sort of relief, and on marriage itself, without the power of escaping from it by divorce, as an evil thing, or at least as very likely to prove so. Better not marry if you marry for life. This seemed to be their notion. Even *his disciples,* looking at the risks of unhappy married life, concluded that it was better to remain single. They said, *It is not good to marry,* and there was a measure of truth in their declaration.

11. But he said unto them, All men cannot receive this saying, save they to whom it is given.

It may be better in some respects not to marry, but *all men cannot receive this saying* and put it into practice. It would be the end of the race if they could. A single life is not for all, nor for many – nature forbids. To some, celibacy is better than marriage, but such situations are peculiar in nature or in circumstances. Abstinence from marriage is to a few a choice gift, answering high purposes; but to the many, marriage is as necessary as it is honorable.

12. For there are some eunuchs, which were so born from their mother's womb: and there are some eunuchs, which were made eunuchs of men: and there be eunuchs, which have made themselves eunuchs for the kingdom of heaven's sake. He that is able to receive it, let him receive it.

Some have but feeble desires concerning marriage and they *were so born.* They will find it good to remain as they are. Others subdue the desires of nature, for holy and commendable reasons, *for the kingdom of heaven's sake;* but this is not for all, nor for many. It is optional with individuals to marry or not. If they marry, nature commends, but grace is silent. If they abstain for Christ's sake, grace commends and nature does not forbid. Enforced celibacy is a seedbed of sins. *Marriage is honourable in all* (Hebrews 13:4). Violations of purity are abominable in the sight of the Lord. In this matter, we need guidance and grace if we follow the usual way, and if we choose the less frequented road, we shall need grace and guidance even more. As to a resolve to persevere in a single life, *he that is able to receive it, let him receive it.*

Matthew 19:13-15

The Great King among the Little Children

13. Then there were brought unto him little children, that he should put his hands on them, and pray: and the disciples rebuked them.

From questions of marriage to the subject of children was an easy and natural step, and providence so arranged events that our Lord was led to proceed from the one to the other.

We see how gentle was our King in the fact that anyone thought of bringing boys and girls to Him. Their friends *brought unto him little children, that he should put his hands on them* and bestow a blessing, and also lift up His hands to God *and pray* for them. This was a very natural desire on the part of devout parents and it showed much faith in our Lord's condescension. We feel sure that the mothers brought them, for holy women are still doing the same. The disciples, jealous for their Lord's honor, instructed the mothers and nurses to refrain from doing so. They judged that it was too childish an act on the mothers' part and it was treating the great Teacher too familiarly. Were not the disciples the more childish of the two in imagining that their Lord would be unkind to babes?

14. But Jesus said, Suffer little children, and forbid them not, to come unto me: for of such is the kingdom of heaven.

The Lord is more lowly than His servants. He bids them cease to hinder the little children. He calls them to Himself. He declares that they are the very kind of people of whom His heavenly kingdom is made up. *Of such is the kingdom of heaven* – this is the banner of the Sunday school. Children, and those like them, may freely come into the kingdom of the Lord of heaven. Yes, these are the characters who alone can enter into that kingdom.

15. And he laid his hands on them, and departed thence.

He did not baptize them, but He did bless them. The touch of *his hands* meant more than a pen can write. Happy were the children who shared that laying on of hands, for those hands were neither empty nor feeble!

Jesus did not delay even with this lovely company, but hastened on to His appointed work *and departed thence.* Yet He had said so much in the two sentences of the former verse that earth and heaven will never cease to be the richer for them.

Matthew 19:16-30

The King Settles the Order of Precedence

16. And, behold, one came and said unto him, Good Master, what good thing shall I do, that I may have eternal life?

Here was one who thought himself first, yet he had to go last, yes, and even had to go away sorrowful.

He was a self-sufficient gentleman. He seemed to feel that one *good thing* from him would be enough, and that he could and would do it at once. He had some misgivings or he would not have asked the question, *What good thing shall I do?* Perhaps, even in so admirable a life as his own, something might yet be lacking. But if it should turn out to be so, he could readily supply the lack.

He was very respectful and addressed the Lord Jesus as *Good Master.* So far, so good. His question was of great personal importance. *What shall I do, that I may have eternal life?* Oh, that more young men would ask a similar question! It was a very suitable inquiry for an earnest person, such as he undoubtedly was. He sought *eternal life* and could not be content with the honors of the hour. He only wanted to know what to do to win that eternal life and he would set about doing it at once.

This is a hopeful inquirer. Surely he will be a grand convert! Let us wait a little and we shall see.

17. And he said unto him, Why callest thou me good? there is none good but one, that is, God: but if thou wilt enter into life, keep the commandments.

Our Lord cared not for empty compliments, and so He asks, *Why callest thou me good?* Many modern heretics praise Jesus, and their commendations are such an insult to His glorious person that He might well say, *Why callest thou me good?* Did this man really mean it? If so, the Lord Jesus would let him know by a hint that He to whom he spoke was more than man. The argument is clear – either Jesus was *good* or he ought not to have called Him good, but as there is *none good but God,* Jesus who is good must be God.

As for the question of having eternal life through a good work, Jesus answers him on his own ground. Life by the law comes only by keeping its commands: *If thou wilt enter into life, keep the commandments.* No one has ever fulfilled them so as to be good. Did this young man think that he could do so? Yet, on the ground of law, if he would deserve eternal life as a reward, he must be as good as God and keep the commandments to perfection. Thus, the rugged way of works was set before him, not that he might attempt to win eternal life thereby, but that he might perceive his own shortcomings and so feel his weakness as to look for salvation by some other method.

18-19. He saith unto him, Which? Jesus said, Thou shalt do no murder, Thou shalt not commit adultery, Thou shalt not steal, Thou shalt not bear false witness, Honour thy father and thy mother: and, Thou shalt love thy neighbour as thyself.

The questioner ventures to ask, *Which?* Did he suppose that certain ceremonial laws would be mentioned? Probably he did, for he felt himself quite sure upon all the points of the moral law. Our Lord, however, gives him nothing new, but turns to the Ten Commandments. He quotes the second table of the law first and begins with commands that would appear to the young man to be the mere truisms of morality. The last-quoted command summarized the rest, and it ought to have opened the questioner's eyes to his shortcomings, for who has *loved his neighbor as himself?* The young aristocrat was not, however, convicted of sin. He pressed his inquiry as to salvation by works because he thought himself on the road to winning it.

20. The young man saith unto him, All these things have I kept from my youth up: what lack I yet?

Perhaps he spoke the truth, as he understood the law. He had maintained an excellent moral character from his early boyhood. He felt that in act and deed he had kept all those commands without a fault of any consequence. He was no bragger, but he could honestly claim to have led a commendable life. He was, no doubt, a very exemplary person and so amiable that Jesus looked on him very lovingly. We know some who are like him and may be described *as touching the law, . . . blameless* (Philippians 3:5-6). But he was not all he thought himself to be. He did not love his neighbor as himself, as he would soon be made to see. *What lack I yet?* is an inquiry few would dare to put forth. He felt that if there was anything lacking in him, he was altogether ignorant as to what it could be. His self-esteem needed no increasing.

21. Jesus said unto him, If thou wilt be perfect, go and sell that thou hast, and give to the poor, and thou shalt have treasure in heaven: and come and follow me.

Our Lord brings him to the test of the first table of the law: *Thou shalt love the Lord thy God with all thy heart* (Matthew 22:37). If he did this, he would be willing, at a divine command, to part with his property, even as Abraham was ready to offer up his son. Our Lord Jesus, as God, claimed from him an unusual sacrifice. Did he love God sufficiently to make the sacrifice? The command of our Lord was a challenge to self-righteousness to prove its own profession. We may also regard it as putting on its trial his profession to have loved his neighbor as himself. Did he love *the poor* as well as himself? If so, it would be no hardship to sell his possessions *and give to the poor.* We must not infer that Jesus would have all His followers part with all that they have. It was a test for this one man: *If thou wilt be perfect.* Still, if we love our possessions more than we love God, we are idolaters; and if we hug our property so as to let the poor go hungry, we cannot be said to love them as ourselves. We have heard of persons claiming to *be perfect,* and yet retaining possession of hundreds of thousands of pounds, and we have doubted their perfection. Was there not a cause? Compassion for poverty, zeal for the truth, and love of doing good will hardly allow any Christian to own enormous riches. At any rate, such wealthy ones will find it hard to render an account at the last great day. We must love Jesus and His great cause better than our wealth or else we are not His true followers. If our religion were ever put to the great test of fierce persecution and we had to part with all our property or part with Christ, hesitation would be fatal.

22. But when the young man heard that saying, he went away sorrowful: for he had great possessions.

He could not go the whole length of his own plan. He would be saved by works, yet he would not carry out his works to the full extent of the law's demand. He failed to observe the spirit both of the second and the first table. He loved not his poor brother as himself. He loved not God in Christ Jesus with all his heart and soul. He thought of himself first, but he soon stood behind the last, for *he went away sorrowful.* Thus, the Savior tests character. That which glittered so much is not found to be gold. This man's *great possessions* so possessed him that he failed to possess his own soul.

23. Then said Jesus unto his disciples, Verily I say unto you, That a rich man shall hardly enter into the kingdom of heaven.

Worldly possessions, apart from divine grace, have a deadening, hardening, and hampering influence upon the soul. Some rich men do *enter into the kingdom of heaven,* but it is hard for them, very hard indeed. The temptation is to let riches rule the mind, and when that is the case, the kingdom of this world opposes the kingdom of heaven. Houses and land, and gold and silver act as birdlime to the soul and prevent its rising towards heaven. This is especially the case in persecuting times, but it is sufficiently a fact in all periods of human history. It is worthy of notice that this hard sentence was intended for Christians, for it is written, *Then said Jesus unto his disciples, Verily I say **unto you*** (emphasis added).

24. And again I say unto you, It is easier for a camel to go through the eye of a needle, than for a rich man to enter into the kingdom of God.

Weighty words are introduced with the authoritative formula, *Again I say unto you.* Into this statement our Lord throws the full weight of His personality. He uses an expressive proverb that means precisely what the words convey to the common reader. There is no sense in hunting up profound metaphors where the proverbial teaching is as plain as possible. He would show that wealth is far more a hindrance than a help to those who would *enter into the kingdom of God.* In fact, it is such a hindrance as to render the matter practically impossible without divine interposition. *A camel* is not only large, but it also has humps, and how can it *go through* so small an opening as *the eye of a needle?* It could not make such a passage except by a strange miracle, nor can *a rich man enter into the kingdom of God* except by a marvel of grace. How few of the rich even hear the gospel! They are too great, too fine, too busy, and too proud to regard the lowly preacher of the gospel of the poor. If, perhaps, they do hear the heavenly message, they have not the necessities and tribulations that drive men from the present world to seek consolation in the world to come, and so they feel no need to accept Christ. "Gold and the Gospel seldom do agree." Those who are rich in this world, in the vast majority of instances, scorn to become subjects of the kingdom in which faith is riches and holiness is honor.

Should the rich begin the divine life, how hard it is for them to persevere amid the cares, the luxuries, and the temptations of a wealthy position! The difficulties are enormous when we think of the pride of life, the flattery of rank, the danger of power, and the risk of carnal security. Yet, blessed be God, we have seen rich men become poor in spirit! We have seen camels go through this needle's eye, humps and all! We hope to see many more such miracles of almighty grace.

25. When his disciples heard it, they were exceedingly amazed, saying, Who then can be saved?

No common astonishment filled them. Much astounding truth they had already heard from their Master, but this exceeded all and *they were exceedingly amazed.* They had previously thought that wealth was an advantage, and now they judged that if those who had riches could only be saved with surpassing difficulty, poor workingmen like themselves could have no hope whatever. They were ready to despair and therefore they put to their Lord the very natural question, *Who then can be saved?* Even our Lord's disciples felt themselves bewildered by His plain utterance, so hard is it to get rid of prejudices in favor of wealth.

26. But Jesus beheld them, and said unto them, With men this is impossible; but with God all things are possible.

Jesus beheld them. He looked on them with pity and with love, and told them that God could do that which, apart from Him, would never come to pass. To enter the kingdom is impossible to man unaided – one sin or another blocks the way. The cares of this world and the deceitfulness of riches are a sadly effective barrier to the soul when it attempts to enter the city of holiness, but God can cause those barriers to yield and enable the soul to enter by the narrow way. He is mighty to save. *With God all things are possible.* What a joyful truth for the writer and the reader! Our salvation, when we view our own weakness and the power of sin, *is impossible with men.* Only when we turn to God and His grace, does salvation range among the possibilities.

The rich man is set by our Lord, not at the head, but at the foot of the line of candidates for the kingdom.

Lord, my hope of being found in Your kingdom lies in Your power and grace, and not in my possessions!

27. Then answered Peter and said unto him, Behold, we have forsaken all, and followed thee; what shall we have therefore?

Here is another claimant for a front place. Peter answered, adding, as he seemed to think, a question necessary for the full discussion of the subject. Peter speaks for his brethren: *Behold, we have forsaken all, and followed thee.* We have done what the rich young man refused to do; *What shall we have therefore?* He spoke as the representative of a number who had become poor for the kingdom's sake. Surely these must have a large reward. Little as these first believers had to leave, it was their *all,* and they had forsaken it to follow Jesus. Peter would rather hear what their recompense would be. What Peter said was true, but it was not wisely spoken. It has a selfish, grasping look, and it is worded so barely that it ought not in that fashion to have come from a servant to his Lord. After all, what have any of us to lose for Jesus compared with what we gain by Him? *What shall we have?* is a question that we need not raise, for we ought rather to think of what we have already received at our Lord's hands. Our Lord is reward enough to the soul that has Him.

28. And Jesus said unto them, Verily I say unto you, That ye which have followed me, in the regeneration when the Son of man shall sit in the throne of his glory, ye also shall sit upon twelve thrones, judging the twelve tribes of Israel.

Our Lord regards Peter as spokesman for them all and He therefore answered them all: *Jesus said unto them.* Seeing their questioning state of mind, He begins with, *Verily I say unto you.* He condescendingly meets their somewhat-selfish inquiry. They needed not to doubt but what there would be a large and full reward for those who had followed Him. His first adherents would have high rank and should sit as assessors with the great Judge in the day of His exaltation. Those who share His humiliation shall share His glory also.

When our Lord *shall sit in the throne of his glory,* all things will have been made new. That dispensation will be called the regeneration. Then shall the highest honors among their fellows of *the twelve tribes of Israel* await the twelve who followed Jesus, even to the loss of all things.

> 29. *And every one that hath forsaken houses, or brethren, or sisters, or father, or mother, or wife, or children, or lands, for my name's sake, shall receive an hundredfold, and shall inherit everlasting life.*

No man shall be a loser by the Lord Jesus in the long run. *Every one that has bravely forsaken the comforts of this life for Christ shall receive an hundredfold recompense.* Our Lord makes up to the persecuted all that they part with for His sake. Exiles for the truth have found a father and a brother in every Christian, a mother and a sister in every holy woman. Our Lord, by giving us His own love and the love of our fellow Christians, supplies *an hundredfold* compensation to those who have to leave wife or children for His sake. In being entertained hospitably by loving brethren, saints in banishment have had their *houses* and *lands* in a sense restored to them. To be at home everywhere is a great gain, even though for *Christ's name's sake* we should be exiled from our native shores. Above all, in God we have a hundredfold recompense for all that we can possibly lose for His cause, and then there is the eternal life given to us, which no mansions and estates could have procured for us. In faith of this we look forward to the reign of the saints, when even here they shall inherit the earth and rejoice themselves in the abundance of peace. Beyond this, when time ceases, there remains endless bliss, for we *shall inherit everlasting life.* Oh, that we may never hesitate to be glad losers for Jesus! They who lose all for Christ will find all in Christ and receive all with Christ.

> 30. *But many that are first shall be last; and the last shall be first.*

Thus, our Lord sums up His deliverance as to rich men and gives us the saying now before us, which He has already illustrated and means to repeat further on in the sixteenth verse of the next chapter. Our King is here seen arranging human positions as they appear from His throne. To His eye, *many first* are *last* and *many last* are *first,* and He will in His kingdom place men according to the divine order.

Matthew 20

Matthew 20:1-16

A Parable of the Kingdom

1-2. For the kingdom of heaven is like unto a man that is an householder,
which went out early in the morning to hire labourers into his vineyard.
And when he had agreed with the labourers for a penny a day, he sent them
into his vineyard.

The kingdom of heaven is all of grace and so is the service connected
with it. Let this be remembered in the exposition of this parable. The
call to work, the ability, and the reward are all on the principle of
grace, and not upon that of merit. This was no common *man that is*
an householder, and his going out *to hire labourers into his vineyard*
was not after the usual manner of men, for they will have a full day's
work for a full day's wage. This householder considered *the labourers*
rather than himself. He was up before the dew was gone from the grass,
and he found laborers, and *sent them into his vineyard.* It was a choice
privilege to be allowed to begin holy service so *early in the morning.*
They *agreed* with the householder and went to work on his terms. They
might well be content, since they were promised a full day's hire, and
were sure to get it; *a penny a day* represented the usual and accepted
wage. *The householder* and *the labourers agreed* upon the amount and
this is the point that has to be noted further on. Young believers have
a blessed prospect. They may well be happy to do good work, in a good
place, for a good Master, and on good terms.

3-4. And he went out about the third hour, and saw others standing idle in the marketplace, and said unto them; Go ye also into the vineyard, and whatsoever is right I will give you. And they went their way.

Hating laziness and grieving that he *saw others standing idle in the marketplace,* he hired more workers *about the third hour.* They would work only three-quarters of a day, but it was for their good to cease from loafing at the street corner. These are like persons whose childhood is past, but who are not yet old. They are favored to have a good part of their day of life available for holy service. To these the good householder said, *Go ye also into the vineyard, and whatsoever is right I will give you.* He pointed to those already in the field and said, *Go ye also,* and he promised them, not a definite sum as he did those whom he first hired, but he said, *Whatsoever is right I will give you. They went their way* to their labor, for they did not wish to remain idlers, and as right-minded men, they could not quarrel with the householder's agreement to give them whatsoever was right. Oh, that those around us, who are in their rising manhood, would at once take up their tools and begin to serve our great Lord!

5. Again he went out about the sixth and ninth hour, and did likewise.

Had it been wholly and only a business transaction, the householder would have waited to begin a new day and would not have given a whole day's wage for a fraction of a day's work. The entire matter was solely of grace, and therefore, when half the day was gone, *about the sixth hour,* he called in laborers. Men of forty and fifty years old are bidden to enter the vineyard. Yes, and *about the ninth hour* men were hired. At sixty years old, the Lord calls a number by His grace! It is wrong to assert that men are not saved after forty. We know to the contrary and could mention instances.

God in the greatness of His love calls into His service men from whom the exuberance of useful vigor has departed. He accepts the waning hours of their day. He has work for the weak as well as for the strong. He allows none to labor for Him without the reward of grace, even though they have spent their best days in sin. This is no encouragement to procrastination, but it should induce old sinners to seek the Lord at once.

6-7. And about the eleventh hour he went out, and found others standing idle, and saith unto them, Why stand ye here all the day idle? They say unto him, Because no man hath hired us. He saith unto them, Go ye also into the vineyard; and whatsoever is right, that shall ye receive.

The day was nearly over, only a single hour remained, yet *about the eleventh hour he went out.* The generous householder was willing to take on more workmen and give them wages, even though the sun was going down. He found a group lingering at the loafers' corner – *standing idle.* He wished to clear the whole town of sluggards and so he said to them, *Why stand ye here all the day idle?* His question to them may be read by making each word in its turn emphatic, and then it yields a fullness of meaning. Why are you *idle?* What is the good of it? Why do you stand *here* idle where all are busy? Why *all the day* idle? Will not a shorter space suffice? Why are *you* idle? You have need to work, you are able to do it, and you should set about it at once. Why is any one of *us* remaining idle towards God? Has nothing yet had power to engage us to sacred service? Can we dare to say, *No man hath hired us?* Nearly seventy years of age and yet unsaved! Let us rouse ourselves to action. It is time that we went, without delay, to kill the weeds and prune the vines and do something for our Lord in His vineyard. What else but rich grace could lead Him to take on the eleven o'clock lingerers? Yet He invites them as earnestly as those who came in the morning, and He will as surely give them their reward.

8. So when even was come, the lord of the vineyard saith unto his steward, Call the labourers, and give them their hire, beginning from the last unto the first.

Days soon end and to all the laborers evening was come. This was pay time, and *the lord of the vineyard* did not forget his agreements with the laborers, nor tell them to wait for their wages. Our Lord will rob no man of his reward. The householder in the parable sees to everything personally. His is the hiring and the order for the paying. Promptly he *saith unto his steward, Call the labourers, and give them their hire.* We shall be called each one to receive our reward when our day is over.

Happy are we to have been already first called into the vineyard. Thus, the second call to receive the wages becomes a welcome one.

The lord of the vineyard, whose transactions in hiring had been of no ordinary kind, was equally peculiar in the manner of payment. He chose to arrange it so that those who came first were served last, which is not often the manner of men. It was not a transaction of a mercenary sort, but a display of free favor, and so the great quality of sovereignty comes in as to the very order of payment – *beginning from the last unto the first.* The Lord will take care that in the transactions of His grace His sovereignty as well as His goodness shall be conspicuous.

> *9. And when they came that were hired about the eleventh hour, they received every man a penny.*

Our Lord's pay is not a wage of deservings, but a gift of bounty. He paid on the scale of grace and not at the rate of merit. He commenced in superb style, and to those who began to work at *the eleventh hour,* he gave *every man a penny.* Here was a full day's pay for one hour's work. Herein was displayed the boundless bounty of the lord of the vineyard. That some, who have served the Lord but for a very brief time, have equaled and even excelled those who have been for many years believers is clear, for many short-but-blessed lives attest to it. Converted late in life, they have been singularly diligent, specially consecrated, and memorably holy, and thus they have obtained the full result of grace at a speedy rate. God will place in heavenly glory those who turn to Christ even at the last. Did not our Lord say even to the dying thief, *Today shalt thou be with me in paradise* (Luke 23:43)? To what better place could any revered saint have been taken? Oh, the riches of the grace of God!

> *10. But when the first came, they supposed that they should have received more; and they likewise received every man a penny.*

Possibly *the first* felt their vanity wounded by being paid after the others. They used their waiting time in considering their own superiority to the latecomers. Filled with legal principles, they kicked at the sovereignty of grace and virtually in this matter rebelled against justice also. Those who are not friends to any one attribute of God are not in love with the others. Sooner or later, those who rage at sovereignty resist justice also. They had what was promised them. What more would they have? A fair wage was given: *They received every man a penny.* What more could they expect? But *they supposed* – there was the difficulty. They had a theory to support, a supposition to justify, and so they were displeased because their supposition did not develop into a fact. God will not be bound by our supposings, and we do but deceive ourselves if we think He will.

> *11-12. And when they had received it, they murmured against the goodman of the house, saying, These last have wrought but one hour, and thou hast made them equal unto us, which have borne the burden and heat of the day.*

As soon as the penny was in their hand, a murmur was in their mouth. It was a fair wage and it was what they agreed to take; but yet, *when they had received it, they murmured against the goodman of the house.* His only supposable fault was that, as a good man, he was too good to the short-timers. The Lord does often greatly bless men whose working lives are short, and even those who are saved late in life. He does not measure up work as we do, by the rod or by the hour. He has His own gracious ways of estimating service, and the reckonings of grace are not like those of law.

At the sight of great grace, envious hearts grow sour. The murmurers said, not that the generous lord had lowered them, but that he had advanced others *who had wrought but one hour.* Their complaint was, *Thou hast made them equal unto us.* In this he had used his own money as he pleased, even as God dispenses grace as He wills. He is never unjust to any, but in gifts of bounty He will not be bound by our ideas of equity. Had they been of the right sort, they would have rejoiced that they had been able to give to him a fair day's work, since they had *borne the burden and heat of the day.*

At any rate, it is a great privilege to be serving the Lord throughout a long life, and those who have enjoyed this high favor are deeply indebted to the grace of God. Blessed be our heavenly Father, for some of us have been His servants from our youth and have endured no little labor for His name's sake, but in this we rejoice greatly and magnify His love.

13. But he answered one of them, and said, Friend, I do thee no wrong: didst not thou agree with me for a penny?

He did not fall into a dispute with the whole company, *but he answered one of them,* which was quite enough. They had been individually hired, and individually he argues with them. It is a calm and reasonable reply: *Friend, I do thee no wrong.* If the Lord rewards us graciously for what we do, we are not wronged because another, who has done less, has a similar compensation. The quiet personal question is one to which there is no answer: *Didst not thou agree with me for a penny?* Yet the legal spirit will come in even concerning work that is all of grace. Even among the Father's true sons, the elder brother gets touched with this alien spirit.

None of us are quite free from it. It seems bred in the bone of our proud nature, yet nothing is more unlovely or unreasonable.

14-15. Take that thine is, and go thy way: I will give unto this last, even as unto thee. Is it not lawful for me to do what I will with mine own? Is thine eye evil, because I am good?

The good man stands to his determination of generosity. He will not be driven from liberality by envious tongues. What he gives is his own and he maintains his right to do as he pleases with it. This is a fine illustration of the sovereignty of divine grace. Each man shall have all he can claim. *Take that thine is,* and having it, let him rest content: *Go thy way.* The Lord will not be ruled by our regulations, but declares, *I will give unto this last, even as unto thee.* It is condescending on his part to say a word in defense of his most fit and fair position. *Is it not lawful for me to do what I will with my own?* If mercy be the Lord's own, He may give it as He pleases, and if the reward of service be wholly of grace, the Lord may render it according to His own pleasure. Be sure that He will do so. In words of thunder He says, both under the law and under the gospel, *I will have mercy on whom I will have mercy, and I will have compassion on whom I will have compassion* (Romans 9:15).

That was a pointed question for each of the grumblers to answer: *Is thine eye evil, because I am good?* Does it make you jealous to see others enjoy my bounty? Because I am good to these who deserved so little, does this deprive you of the good that I have granted to you?

Let us never envy late converts their joy or their usefulness, but applaud the sovereignty that blesses them so largely. We share the mercy with them. Let us give them an equal portion of our joy.

16. So the last shall be first, and the first last: for many be called, but few chosen.

Here our Lord repeats His famous saying, which we noted in chapter 19, verse 30, and lets us know that precedence in the kingdom of heaven is according to the order of grace. The King will rule in His own courts and who shall question His will? As He is King, it is His right to rule. Loyal subjects are ever ready to support their sovereign. Our King reigns by right divine and cannot do wrong. It was said of David, *Whatsoever the king did pleased all the people* (2 Samuel 3:36). Let this be true of David's Son and His people. Jesus tells us that while *many* men are *called* to service, few reach the standard of choice men. Some of *the last shall be first,* for abounding grace is seen in their brief hour of work; but some of *the first shall be last,* for they are not always diligent throughout their longer day and so fall back in the race, or their legal notions put them far behind those who were called later in life, but who are better instructed in the principles of divine grace.

Matthew 20:17-28

The King on His Way to the Cross

17-19. And Jesus going up to Jerusalem took the twelve disciples apart in the way, and said unto them, Behold, we go up to Jerusalem; and the Son of man shall be betrayed unto the chief priests and unto the scribes, and they shall condemn him to death, and shall deliver him to the Gentiles to mock, and to scourge, and to crucify him: and the third day he shall rise again.

Marching *up,* towards the guilty capital, with resolute and vigorous step, Jesus outwalked the trembling disciples, who foresaw that some dire tragedy would transpire. They went with Him, and that was something; and it showed that, if timid, they were sincere. His words were true and significant: *Behold, we go up to Jerusalem.* He thought it wise to tell them yet again of the dark future that was now drawing very near, so He *took the twelve disciples apart in the way.* That is the best communion when Jesus Himself takes us apart. He knows the fittest seasons for fullest revelations. Possibly, in this, His human soul was seeking fellowship, but how little of it He found among His feeble followers! Lord, when You do take me apart, prepare me for full communion, lest I miss a golden opportunity!

The heart of Jesus was full of His sacrifice. Mark how He dwells on the details from the beginning to the end of His sufferings, death, and resurrection. He uses very much the same terms as when *they abode in Galilee* (Matthew 17:22). We noticed that statement while reading in chapter 17, verse 22, and this is very much like a repetition of it. It was a subject too grave to be set forth with a variety of expressions. He calls their attention to the fact that they were going up *to Jerusalem,* the place of sacrifice. The journey of His utmost grief was now beginning. The end was hastening on. What a pang shot through His heart as He said, *The Son of man shall be betrayed.* This He said in the hearing of the disciple who would act as the traitor. Did no remorse visit his corrupt heart? The twelve knew that Jesus had no more cruel foes than *the chief priests and the scribes,* the men of the Sanhedrin. These, by a mock trial, would *condemn him to death,* but as they could not carry out the sentence themselves, they would *deliver him to the Gentiles.* How accurately the Lord traces the line of action! He omits none of the shameful details. He says that they would deliver Him to the Romans, *to mock, and to scourge, and to crucify him.* Here were three sharp swords. One scarcely knows which one had the sharpest edge. Our hearts ought to melt as we think of this threefold sorrow – scorn, cruelty, and death. Our blessed Master, however, added a word that overpowered the bitterness of the death-dose. Here was the bright lining of the black cloud: *The third day he shall rise again.* This poured a flood of light on what otherwise had been a sevenfold midnight.

Did our Lord thus dwell on His passion and should not we? Yes, it should be our lifelong theme. They say, in this hour of defection, "Think of His life rather than of His death," but we are not to be duped by them. *We preach Christ crucified* (1 Corinthians 1:23). *God forbid that I should glory, save in the cross of our Lord Jesus Christ* (Galatians 6:14).

> *20-21. Then came to him the mother of Zebedee's children with her sons, worshipping him, and desiring a certain thing of him. And he said unto her, What wilt thou? She saith unto him, Grant that these my two sons may sit, the one on thy right hand, and the other on the left, in thy kingdom.*

While the mind of Jesus was occupied with His humiliation and death, His followers were thinking of their own honor and ease. Alas, poor human nature! *The mother of Zebedee's children* only spoke as others felt. She, with a mother's love, sought renown, and even preeminence, for her sons, but the fact that the other disciples were displeased showed that they were ambitious also. Doubtless, they wanted to fill the positions that the mother of James and John craved for them. She approached the Savior reverently, *worshipping him.* Yet there was too much familiarity in her request to be granted an unnamed thing, *desiring a certain thing of him.*

Our Lord here sets us the example of never promising in the dark. *And he said unto her, What wilt thou?* Know what you promise before you promise. Great was this woman's faith in the Lord's ultimate victory and occasion to the throne, since she regards His enthronement as so certain that she prays that her two sons should sit in His courts on His right and left hand. Was she aware of what our Lord had told His disciples? We half think so, for the words are: *Then came to him the mother of Zebedee's children.* If she knew and understood all that went before, she was willing that her sons should share the lot of Jesus, both as to His cross and His crown, and this sets her petition in a bright light. Still, there was a good deal of a mother's partiality in the request. See how she speaks of *these my two sons* with a touch of pride in her action. How grandly she describes the desired situation: *May sit, the one on thy right hand, and the other on the left, in thy kingdom.* She had evidently very elegant notions of what the kingdom would ultimately become. In any case, her request had in it much of trust and much of loyal union to Christ, though somewhat also of self. We need not judge her, but we may question ourselves as to whether we think as much of our Lord as she did.

22. But Jesus answered and said, Ye know not what ye ask. Are ye able to drink of the cup that I shall drink of, and to be baptized with the baptism that I am baptized with? They say unto him, We are able.

The petition of the mother was that of the sons also, for *Jesus answered and said, Ye know not what ye ask.* As from the mother, the request was probably of better quality than as from the sons, for our Lord speaks to them rather than to her. They had asked through the mother, but they may have asked in greater ignorance than she, and had they known what their request included, they might never have presented it. At any rate, our Lord treats the petition as theirs rather than their mother's, and since it was about themselves, He questions them as to how far they were prepared for the consequences. To be near to the throne of the King would involve fellowship with Him in the suffering and self-sacrifice by which He set up His spiritual kingdom. Were they ready for this? Had they strength to endure to the end? *Are ye able to drink of the cup that I shall drink of, and to be baptized with the baptism that I am baptized with? They say unto Him, We are able.* Perhaps this was too hasty an answer, and yet it may under the aspect have been the best they could give. If they were looking alone to their Lord for strength, they were, through His grace, quite able to bear anything. But, when they thought of His *throne,* had they remembered *the cup* and *the baptism,* without which there would be no enjoying the kingdom?

23. And he saith unto them, Ye shall drink indeed of my cup, and be baptized with the baptism that I am baptized with: but to sit on my right hand, and on my left, is not mine to give, but it shall be given to them for whom it is prepared of my Father.

Hearing their professed willingness to have fellowship with Himself in all things, our Lord assures them that He does not refuse to be associated with them, but He points them to the immediate and certain result of that fellowship. Our practical, present business is not to aim at eminence in the kingdom, but submissively to drink the cup of suffering and plunge into the depths of humiliation that our Lord appoints for us. It is a great honor to be allowed to *drink of His cup* and to *be baptized with His baptism.* This He grants to His believing disciples.

This fellowship is the essence of the spiritual kingdom. If our cup be bitter, it is His cup. If our baptism be overwhelming, it *is the baptism that He is baptized with,* and this sweetens the one and prevents the other from being a death-plunge. Indeed, that the cup and the baptism are His makes our share in them to be an honor bestowed by grace.

Other rewards of the kingdom are not arbitrarily granted, but fittingly bestowed. Jesus says that the high places in the kingdom *shall be given to them for whom it is prepared of his Father.* He has no hesitation in speaking of what his Father has *prepared.* Everything about our Lord's kingdom is divinely arranged and fixed; nothing is left to chance or fate.

Even Jesus will not interfere with the divine appointment concerning His kingdom. As a friend, He may not be solicited to use a supposed private influence to alter the arrangements of infinite wisdom. Eternal purposes are not to be changed at the request of ill-advised disciples. In a sense, Jesus gives all things, but as Mediator, He comes not to do His own will, but the will of Him that sent Him, and so He correctly says of rank in His kingdom, *It is not mine to give.* How thoroughly did our Lord take a lowly place for our sakes! In this laying aside of authority, He gives a silent rebuke to our self-seeking. It may be that He intended to reprove not only the mother of Zebedee's children, but also all of the disciples, who were constantly seeking great things for themselves.

> *24-26. And when the ten heard it, they were moved with indignation against the two brethren. But Jesus called them unto him, and said, Ye know that the princes of the Gentiles exercise dominion over them, and they that are great exercise authority upon them. But it shall not be so among you: but whosoever will be great among you, let him be your minister.*

Naturally, the other ten apostles did not relish the attempt of the sons of Zebedee to steal a march upon them. We never hear that they resented our Lord's preference of Peter, James, and John, but when two of these sought precedence for themselves, they could not bear it. Peter was with them in this, for we read, *When the ten heard it.* Unanimously they were angry with the upstarts. That *they were moved with indignation* was a proof that they were ambitious themselves, or at least that they were not willing to take the lowest place. Because they were guilty of the same fault, *they were moved with indignation against the two brethren.*

Here was a sad division in the little camp. How could it be healed? *Jesus called them unto him.* He personally dealt with this rising evil and ordered the twelve to come aside and listen to something meant only for their private ears. They were confounding His kingdom with the ordinary government of men, and therefore they dreamed of being great and exercising dominion in His name, but He wished them to correct their ideas and turn their thoughts another way. It was true, that to be His followers was a highly honorable thing, and made them partakers of a kingdom; but it was not like earthly kingdoms. In the great Gentile monarchies, princes ruled by authority, force, and pomp, but in His kingdom the rule would be one of love, and the dignity would be that of service. He who could serve most would be the greatest. The lowliest would be the most honored. The most self-sacrificing would have the most power. Whenever we see the nobles of earth contending for precedence, we should hear our Master say, *But it shall not be so among you.* We must forever quit seeking after honor, office, power, and influence. If we aim at greatness at all, it must be by being great in service, becoming the minister or servant of our brethren.

27. And whosoever will be chief among you, let him be your servant.

To rise in Christ's kingdom, we must descend. He who would *be chief,* or first, among saints, must *be their servant,* bondsman, or slave. The lower we have stooped, the higher we have risen. In this kind of rivalry, we shall be allowed to excel without exciting the indignation of the brethren.

28. Even as the Son of man came not to be ministered unto, but to minister, and to give his life a ransom for many.

Assuredly, He who is greatest and chief among us has set us the example of the utmost love-service. No servants waited on Him. He was Master and Lord, but He washed His servants' feet. *He came not to be served, but to serve.* He received nothing from others. His was a life of giving and the giving of a life. For this purpose, He was *the Son of man.* With this purpose *he came,* and to this end He gave *his life a ransom for many.* No service is greater than to redeem sinners by His own death, and no ministry is lowlier than to die in the place of sinners.

Matthew 20:29-34

The King Opening the Eyes of the Blind

29-30. And as they departed from Jericho, a great multitude followed him. And, behold, two blind men sitting by the way side, when they heard that Jesus passed by, cried out saying, Have mercy on us, O Lord, thou son of David.

On *Jericho* a curse had rested, but the presence of Jesus brought it a blessing. We suppose He must of necessity go through Jericho as once before He needed to go through Samaria. Our Lord *departed from Jericho* and a vast crowd accompanied Him, for His fame had spread far and wide. Nothing striking is noted concerning His doings till two beggars come upon the scene. Mercy needs misery to give it an occasion to work. *Behold, two blind men sitting by the way side.* They could not behold Jesus, but we are asked to *behold* them. They had taken up a hopeful position *by the way side,* for there they would be likely to hear any good news and there they would be seen by the compassionate One. They had ears if they had not eyes, and they used their hearing well. On inquiry, they learned *that Jesus passed by,* and believing that He could restore their sight, they grew earnest in prayer to Him: *They cried out.* Their plea was for pity: *Have mercy on us.*

Their appeal was to the royal heart of Jesus: *O Lord, thou son of David.*

Our Lord's sermon was interrupted by the repeated outcries of these two blind beggars of Jericho, but this never displeased Him. Neither would true preachers of the gospel be disconcerted if some of their hearers were to cry out with similar eagerness for salvation.

31. And the multitude rebuked them, because they should hold their peace: but they cried the more, saying, Have mercy on us, O Lord, thou son of David.

The crowd desired to hear Jesus, but could not do so because of the shouts of the blind men; therefore, *the multitude rebuked them.* Did they scold them for ill manners, or for noise, or for harshness of tone, or for selfishly wishing to monopolize Jesus? It is always easy to find a stick when you wish to beat a dog. The people wanted them to be quiet and *hold their peace,* and they found plenty of arguments as to why they should do so. This was all very well for those who were in possession of their faculties, but men who have lost their sight cannot be quieted if there is an opportunity for obtaining sight, and as that opportunity was rapidly passing away from these poor men, they became vehement in their earnestness. Unhindered by the threats of the crowd, *they cried the more.* Some men are urged onward by all attempts to pull them back. When we are seeking the Lord, we shall be wise to make every hindrance into a stimulus. We may well bear rebukes and rebuffs when our great aim is to obtain mercy from Jesus.

Unvarying was the blind beggars' cry: *Have mercy on us, O Lord, thou son of David.* Variety of words they had no time to study. Having asked for what they needed, in words that leaped from their hearts, they repeated their prayer and their plea, and it was no vain repetition.

32. And Jesus stood still, and called them, and said, What will ye that I shall do unto you?

Jesus stood still. At the voice of prayer, the Sun of Righteousness paused in His progress. Believing cries can hold the Son of God by the feet. *He called them,* and this was because they had called Him. What comfort that call yielded them! We are not told that they came to Him. There is no need to tell us that. They were at His feet as soon as the words were uttered. How sadly blind are those who, being called a thousand times by the voice of mercy, still refuse to come!

Our Lord enlightened minds as well as eyes, and so He would have the blind men intelligently feel and express their needs. He puts to them the personal inquiry: *What will ye that I shall do unto you?* It was not a hard question, yet it is one that many an attendant at our places of worship would find it difficult to answer. You say you "wish to be saved." What do you mean by those words?

33. They say unto him, Lord, that our eyes may be opened.

Just so. They needed no time for second thoughts. Oh, that our people were as quick to pray, *Lord, that our eyes may be opened.* They went straight to the point. There is not a word to spare in their explanatory prayer. No book was needed, no form of words. The desire clothed itself in simple, natural, and earnest speech.

34. So Jesus had compassion on them, and touched their eyes: and imme-diately their eyes received sight, and they followed him.

So, that is, since they thus stated their desire and had so great a need, *Jesus had compassion on them,* pitying their loneliness in the dark, their deprivation of enjoyment, their loss of power to follow a vocation, and their consequent poverty. *He touched their eyes.* What hands were those that undertook such lowly fellowship with human flesh and worked such deeds of power! *Immediately their eyes received sight.* Only a touch, and light entered. Time is not necessary to the cures of Jesus. Proof of their sight came at once, for *they followed him.* We best use our spiritual sight when we look to Jesus and keep close to His heel.

Oh, that the reader, if he be spiritually blind, may ask for the touch of Jesus and receive it at once, for immediately he will receive sight! An inward light will in an instant shine forth upon the soul, and the spiritual world will become apparent to the enlightened mind. The Son of David still lives and still opens the eyes of the blind. He still hears the humble prayer of those who know their blindness and their poverty. If the reader fears that he, too, is spiritually blind, let him cry unto the Lord at this very instant, and he will see what he shall see, and he will forever bless the hand that gave sight to the eyes of his soul.

Matthew 21

Matthew 21:1-11

The King Rides Triumphantly into His Capital

1-3. And when they drew nigh unto Jerusalem, and were come to Bethphage, unto the mount of Olives, then sent Jesus two disciples, saying unto them, Go into the village over against you, and straightway ye shall find an ass tied, and a colt with her: loose them, and bring them unto me. And if any man say ought unto you, ye shall say, The Lord hath need of them; and straightway he will send them.

The time was come for our Lord to finish His great work on earth, and His going up to Jerusalem was with this intent. He now determines to enter His capital city openly and there to reveal Himself as King. To this end, when He came near to the city, *Jesus sent two disciples* to bring Him the foal of a donkey on which He should ride. His orders to the two disciples whom He commissioned, *when they were come to Bethphage,* are worthy of our serious attention. He directed them to the place where they should find the animal: *Go into the village over against you.* The Lord knows where that which He requires is to be found.

Perhaps it is nearer to us than we dream: *Over against you.* He told them that they would not have to search, but that *straightway ye shall find.* When the Lord sends us on an errand, He will speed us on our way. He described the condition of the creatures: *An ass tied, and a colt with her.* Our Lord knows the position of every animal in the world, and He counts no circumstance to be beneath His office.

Nor did He leave the disciples without orders as to how they were to proceed: *Loose them, and bring them.* Protest and debate there would be none. They might act at once. To stand questioning is not for the messengers of our King. It is their duty to obey their Lord's orders and to fear nothing. The two animals would be willingly yielded up by their owner when the disciples said, *The Lord hath need of them.* No, he would not only give them up, but also *straightway he will send them.* Either the owner was himself a secret disciple, or some awe of the Lord Jesus was on his mind, but he would very joyfully consent to lend the donkey and its foal for the purpose for which they were required.

What a singular conjunction of words is here: *The Lord* and *hath need*! Jesus, without laying aside His sovereignty, had taken on a nature full of needs, yet being in need, He was still the Lord and could command His subjects and request their property. Whenever we have anything of which the Lord's cause has need, how cheerfully should we hand it over to Him! The owner of the donkey and her colt regarded it as an honor to furnish Jesus with a creature to ride upon. How great is the power of Jesus over human minds, so that by a word He quietly moves them to do His bidding!

We have here the record of two disciples being sent to fetch a donkey. Those who do little things for Jesus are honored thereby. Their errand appeared strange, for what they did might seem like robbery; but He who sent them took care to protect them from the least shade of suspicion. The messengers raised no question, offered no objection, and met with no difficulty. It is ours to do what Jesus bids us, just as He bids us, and because He bids us, for His command is our authority.

4-5. All this was done, that it might be fulfilled which was spoken by the prophet, saying, Tell ye the daughter of Sion, Behold, thy King cometh unto thee, meek, and sitting upon an ass, and a colt the foal of an ass.

Matthew is always reminding us of the Old Testament, as well, indeed, he may, for our Lord is always fulfilling it. Every point of detail is according to prophetic model: *All this was done, that it might be fulfilled which was spoken by the prophet.* The Old and New Testaments dovetail into each other. Men have written "Harmonies of the Gospels," but God has given us a harmony of the Old and New Testaments. The passage referred to is in Zechariah 9:9. It represents Zion's King as meek and lowly, even in the hour of His triumphant entrance into His metropolis, riding, not upon a warhorse, but upon a young donkey, on which no man had sat. He had before said of Himself, *I am meek and lowly in heart* (Matthew 11:29), and now He gives one more proof of the truth of His own words, and at the same time, of the fulfillment of prophecy: *Tell ye the daughter of Sion, Behold, thy King cometh unto thee, meek, and sitting upon an ass.* He did not, like Solomon, fetch horses out of Egypt to minister to His pride, but He who was greater than Solomon was content with *a colt the foal of an ass,* and even that humble creature was borrowed, for He had none of His own. The tenderness of Jesus comes out in the fact of His having the donkey brought with her foal so that they might not be parted. He was, as a King, all gentleness and mercy. His grandeur involved no pain, even for the humblest living thing. How blessed is it for us to be ruled by such a King!

6-7. And the disciples went, and did as Jesus commanded them, and brought the ass, and the colt, and put on them their clothes, and they set him thereon.

This should be an accurate description of the conduct of all Christians: *The disciples went, and did as Jesus commanded them.* They did not question or criticize their King's commands. They obeyed them, which was much better. What a church would we see on earth if this were universally true! They carried out their King's bidding in every detail.

The disciples also *brought the ass, and the colt,* in no way deviating from the orders that they had received. They added actions that naturally grew out of their King's orders. There must be suitable adornment for the steeds that are to be employed for such a royal procession, so they *put on them their clothes.* This was done of their own accord. Many are ready to fetch other men's donkeys, but are slow to lend *their own clothes.* These disciples were willing and eager to bear their share in the triumphal procession of the Lord Jesus. From first to last, there was no forced contribution or greedy service. All was most voluntary. The donkey and the colt were cheerfully loaned, and the garments were spontaneously placed on them. All was simple and natural, full of truth and heartiness. How different from the artificial ceremonials of ordinary monarchs!

They set him thereon. When men previously had tried to take Jesus by force, to make Him a king in earthly fashion, He withdrew Himself from them, but the hour for His public entry into Jerusalem had arrived, and He therefore allowed His disciples to set Him upon the lowly beast that was to carry Him into the city. Gladly they put the Lord in the place of honor and joyfully they walked at His side.

> *8. And a very great multitude spread their garments in the way; others cut down branches from the trees, and strawed them in the way.*

The people were so numerous that they are described as *a very great multitude.* Unusual unanimity prevailed among the populace. They all gathered to Jesus. The patriarch Jacob had foretold, concerning the Shiloh, *Unto him shall the gathering of the people be* (Genesis 49:10). This was fulfilled many times during the Savior's earthly ministry and it is still continually being fulfilled.

The crowd was in a state of great excitement and came marching along with Jesus in high enthusiasm. Carpeting the road, they *spread their garments in the way,* and as if this were not enough, *others cut down branches from the trees, and strawed them in the way.* Our first parents, in their shame, made clothes of the leaves of trees, but now both clothes and leaves are at the feet of man's Redeemer. John says that the people *took branches of palm trees, and went forth to meet him* (John 12:13). The long, feathery fronds of the palms would be suitable either for waving in the air or casting upon the ground before the King. The common people, in the simplest but most effective manner, prepared a royal welcome for the Son of David. What an unusual sight! They were on the tiptoe of expectation, looking for a Kingly Deliverer, and they vaguely hoped that *Jesus the prophet of Nazareth* (verse 11) might prove to be the Promised One. He had excited their wonder, raised their hopes, and earned their reverence. For the time, they held Him in high honor. Do we wonder at it when we think how He had healed their sick and had fed them by thousands when they fainted?

> *9. And the multitudes that went before, and that followed, cried, saying, Hosanna to the son of David: Blessed is he that cometh in the name of the Lord; Hosanna in the highest.*

Numbers still flocked together till there was not only a multitude, but also *multitudes,* some *that went before,* and others *that followed.* The crowds preceding and following the Lord were of one mind concerning

Him, and indeed, they seemed to have but one voice. Scarcely knowing what they did, probably dreaming of an earthly kingdom, they lifted up one and the same loyal shout of *Hosanna to the son of David: Blessed is he that cometh in the name of the Lord; Hosanna in the highest.* They quoted an ancient psalm (118) and applied it to Jesus, and in every way expressed their delight and expectation. Alas! how soon this gleam of sunlight gave place to black darkness. The day of palms was closely followed by the day of crucifixion. Thus fickle are the sons of men. *Vox populi* ("the voice of the people") is anything but *Vox Dei* ("the voice of God").

10. And when he was come into Jerusalem, all the city was moved, saying, Who is this?

He had been there before, but not in this manner. Never had such enthusiastic multitudes surrounded Him with acclamations. Quiet citizens, who had not left their homes, wondered at the crowd. Great numbers had been moved by some uncontrollable impulse to go out to meet Jesus, *and when he was come into Jerusalem,* still greater crowds were attracted – *all the city was moved.* There is nothing that can *move* mankind like the coming of Christ. Everyone inquired, *Who is this?* It may have been in some of them an idle curiosity and in others a fleeting interest, but it was far better than the dull indifference that cares for none of these things. Where Jesus comes, He makes a stir and raises inquiry. *Who is this?* is a proper, profitable, personal, and pressing question. Let our reader make this inquiry concerning Jesus and never rest till he knows the answer.

11. And the multitude said, This is Jesus the prophet of Nazareth of Galilee.

Everyone who had entered the city in the royal procession was prepared to inform inquiring citizens. *The multitude said,* that is to say, the answer was unanimous: *This is Jesus the prophet of Nazareth of Galilee.* The answer was true, but not all the truth. Seldom is a multitude so well informed as in this instance. Christ's name, His office, His early abode, and His lowly race are all indicated. Those who wished to know more about Him had in the answer of the multitude the keys of all that was necessary for them to discover. Oh, that our teeming populations knew as much of Jesus as the multitudes of Jerusalem knew! And yet it may be that, if they did, they might act as badly as did these sinners of Jerusalem, when their Hosannas were so soon changed into cruel cries of, *Away with him, away with him, crucify him* (John 19:15).

Matthew 21:12-14

The King Cleanses the Temple

12-13. And Jesus went into the temple of God, and cast out all them that sold and bought in the temple, and overthrew the tables of the moneychangers, and the seats of them that sold doves, and said unto them, It is written, My house shall be called the house of prayer; but ye have made it a den of thieves.

Jesus went into the temple of God again, as He did at the beginning of His ministry. Then the reforming Prophet announced what was needed, and now the King proceeds to carry it out. A temple dedicated to God must not become a place of merchandise and robbery. *Jesus cast out all them that sold and bought in the temple.* The sellers were the more permanently obstructive and the more constantly offensive, so they were driven out first, but as there would have been no sellers if there had not been buyers, they must be cast out also. Those who kept *the tables of the moneychangers* might have pleaded that they were there for the public convenience, since they supplied shekels and other moneys of the sanctuary in lieu of Roman coins. *The seats of them that sold doves* seemed licensed, since they dealt in young pigeons and turtledoves for the sacrifices. But these traders were not serving God in this, but making profit for themselves, and therefore our Lord *overthrew* all their arrangements and cleared the Holy Place.

What an awe must have surrounded this one Man, that the whole tribe of traffickers should flee before Him while they endured the overturning of their tables and their seats! Neither the temple guard nor the Roman soldiers appear to have interfered in any way. When Jesus takes to Himself power, opposition ceases. What a prophecy this incident affords of the sense with which, in His Second Advent, He will purge His floor with the fan in His hand (see Matthew 3:12)!

Our Lord, while He drives out the profaners of the temple, vindicates His holy violence by saying, *It is written.* Whether He was contending with the archenemy or with wicked men, He used but one weapon, *the sword of the Spirit, which is the word of God* (Ephesians 6:17). In this, as in everything else, let us follow His example. Isaiah had penned those words (Isaiah 56:7): *Mine house shall be called an house of prayer for all people.* This prophecy had a special relation to the court of the Gentiles, which was being so grossly desecrated by these dealers. Our Savior likened His Father's house, when occupied by these buyers and sellers, to those caves in the mountains where robbers were accustomed to lurking in His day: *Ye have made it a den of thieves.* The words spoken by the King were strong, but not more so than the case before Him required. It is a king's business to break up the hiding places of bandits, and Jesus did so. He could not bear to see His Father's *house of prayer* made into a haven of robbers.

14. And the blind and the lame came to him in the temple; and he healed them.

The coming into the temple of blind beggars and limping beggars was no defilement to the Holy Place. *The blind and the lame came to him.* To whom else should they come? Was He not the good Physician? They came to Him *in the temple.* Where else should they come? Was it not the house of mercy? Jesus, in His Father's name, welcomed the motley band and *healed them.* Some people seem to think that if the very poor come into places of worship, they are out of place, but this is the vain notion of a wicked pride. The poorest and the most sinful may come to Jesus. We, too, came into the assembly of the saints at one time, spiritually blind and lame, but Jesus opened our eyes and healed us of our lameness. If He sees anything amiss with us now, we are sure He will not drive us away from His courts, but He will heal us at once. Let all the blind and lame come to Him now.

Matthew 21:15-16

The King Acknowledges the Children's Acclamations

15-16. And when the chief priests and scribes saw the wonderful things that he did, and the children crying in the temple, and saying, Hosanna to the son of David; they were sore displeased, and said unto him, Hearest thou what these say? And Jesus saith unto them, Yea; have ye never read, Out of the mouth of babes and sucklings thou hast perfected praise?

Chief priests and scribes are ever on the watch. Nothing that glorifies the Lord Jesus will escape their eyes. Expect no less in these days. If the gospel prevails, formalists will be enraged. Praise rendered to Jesus was gall and wormwood to the religious leaders whose abuses He rebuked. His actions in the temple, which were self-evidently right, they dared not attack, but they were nonetheless full of wrath because of *the wonderful things that he did.* More and more they nursed their indignation. At last the enthusiastic shouts of *the children crying in the temple, and saying, Hosanna to the son of David* gave them an occasion to vent their contempt. How could a real prophet allow boys and girls to be shouting at His heels at that rate? Yet their contempt was only assumed. In truth they feared Jesus and dreaded the effect of the popular enthusiasm, and so *they were sore displeased.* As soon as they could find an opportunity, they would spit their venom upon the Lord.

They boldly speak to Jesus about this rabble of juveniles. *They said unto him,* "Hearest thou what these say? They salute You as if You were a king. These silly children cry to You, 'Hosanna.' Why do You allow them to say it? Bid the youngsters cease their boisterous noise. How can You as a man bear with such childish cries?" Our Savior's answer was complete. In answer to their question, *Hearest thou what these say? Jesus saith unto them, Yea; have ye never read?* "You chief priests and scribes, have you not read the Psalms, of which you profess to be such diligent students? If you have read them, then remember the words of David in Psalm 8:2: *Out of the mouth of babes and sucklings thou hast perfected praise.*" Our Lord gives the sense of the passage rather than the exact words. God's praise is *perfected* out of children's mouths. In them His glory is seen, and frequently by them it is declared. When others are silent, these shall speak out, and in their simple truthfulness they shall give forth the praise of the Lord more fully than grown-up men and women will.

Matthew 21:17-22

The King Gives a Token of the Judgment of Jerusalem And of the Power of Prayer

17. And he left them, and went out of the city into Bethany; and he lodged there.

Jesus did not love complaining priests. *He left them.* He gave them a scriptural answer to their inquiry, and then, knowing that further argument with them was useless, *he left them.* A wise example for us to follow. He desired quiet and so *he went out of the city.* He loved the villages and therefore He turned aside from the busy havens of men and entered *into Bethany.* In that place there lived a well-beloved family, always delighted to entertain Him, *and he lodged there.* There He was at home, for He loved Mary and Martha and Lazarus. A day of excitement was followed by an evening of retreat in a country home. He spent the night of that most eventful day with His faithful friends. What a contrast between His entry into Jerusalem and His visit to His friends at Bethany! Lord, lodge with me! Make my house Your home!

18. Now in the morning as he returned into the city, he hungered.

He hungered. Wonderful words! The Lord of heaven hungered! We cannot imagine that His kind hosts had neglected to provide for Him; probably He was so absorbed in thought that He forgot to eat bread. It may be that, according to His habit, *in the morning* He had risen while all others in the house were still sleeping, so that He might hold communion in private with His Father, and receive from heaven strength for the work that lay before Him. At least, this was no unusual thing with Him. *He returned into the city.* He shirked not the work that He had yet to do, but this time the King came hungering to His capital city. He was about to begin a long day's work without breaking His fast, yet

His hand had fed thousands at one time. Surely all heaven and earth will be eager to wait upon His need.

19. And when he saw a fig tree in the way, he came to it, and found nothing thereon, but leaves only, and said unto it, Let no fruit grow on thee henceforward for ever. And presently the fig tree withered away.

Looking for food, a *fig tree* in full leaf promised Him a little refreshment. This fig tree was, apparently, no one's property. It stood *in the way,* it was growing in the public highway, all by itself. Its position was conspicuous and its appearance striking, so that *he saw* it at once. It was not the time for figs, but the fig tree has this peculiarity, that the fruit comes before the leaves. If, therefore, we see leaves fully developed, we naturally look for figs fit to be eaten. This tree had put forth leaves out of season, when other fig trees were bare and had not begun to put forth their early figs. It, so to speak, outran its fellows, but its premature growth was all deception. Our Lord, when *he came to it, found nothing thereon, but leaves only.* It had overleaped the necessary first stage of putting forth green figs and had rushed into a fruitless verdure. It was great at wood and leaf, but worthless for fruit. In this it sadly resembled Jerusalem, which was lush with religious claims, and extreme with a vain enthusiasm, but it was destitute of repentance, faith, and holiness, which are far more important than pious formalities. The Lord Jesus used this green but barren and disappointing tree as an object lesson. He came to it as He came to the Jews. He found nothing but leaves. He condemned it to perpetual fruitlessness: *Let no fruit grow on thee henceforward for ever,* and He left it under a sentence that was very speedily executed, even as Jerusalem would soon be destroyed.

And presently the fig tree withered away. This has been styled the one miracle of judgment worked by our Lord, but surely that which is done to a tree cannot be called vindictive. To fell a whole forest has never been considered cruel, and to use a single barren tree as an object lesson can only seem unkind to those who are sentimental and idiotic. It was kindness to the ages to use a worthless tree to teach a helpful lesson.

20. And when the disciples saw it, they marvelled, saying, How soon is the fig tree withered away!

The Lord's word was so very quickly fulfilled, that the disciples wondered. We marvel that *they marvelled.* By this time, they should have grown accustomed to deeds of power and to the rapidity with which they were performed. Even to this day, some doubt a work if it is speedy, and thus imitate the cry, *How soon is the fig tree withered away!* Whatever the Lord does, He does perfectly and completely. The fig tree was *presently* destroyed.

> 21. *Jesus answered and said unto them, Verily I say unto you, If ye have faith, and doubt not, ye shall not only do this which is done to the fig tree, but also if ye shall say unto this mountain, Be thou removed, and be thou cast into the sea; it shall be done.*

To the first disciples, the power of absolutely working miracles was given by our Lord and given in connection with a simple, unwavering confidence: *If ye have faith, and doubt not.* God may not work miracles for us, but He will do all that we need in accordance with our faith, doing it in a way of providence, according to the spirit of the present dispensation. But here also the faith that we exercise in Him must be free from doubt.

Before a living faith, barren systems of religion will wither away, and by the power of undoubting confidence in God, *mountains* of difficulty shall *be removed* and *cast into the sea.* Have we ever spoken in Christ's name to barren fig trees and obstructing mountains, bidding them to depart out of our way? If not, where is our faith? If we have faith and doubt not, we shall know the truth of this promise: *It shall be done.* Apart from the actual possession of unwavering faith, the words of our Lord will seem fabulous.

> 22. *And all things, whatsoever ye shall ask in prayer, believing, ye shall receive.*

This gives us a grand checkbook on the Bank of Faith, which we may use without limitation. How wide are the terms: *All things, whatsoever ye shall ask in prayer, believing*! If we are enabled to pray the prayer of faith, we shall gain the blessing, be it whatever it may. This is not possible concerning things unpromised or things not according to the divine will.

Believing prayer is the shadow of the coming blessing. It is a gift from God, not a dream of the human will, nor an anomaly of idle wishing. *Believing, ye shall receive*; but too often the believing is not there.

Matthew 21:23-32

The King Confounds and Warns His Enemies

23. And when he was come into the temple, the chief priests and the elders of the people came unto him as he was teaching, and said, By what authority doest thou these things? and who gave thee this authority?

Jesus returned to His Father's house and there He was again met by His old antagonists. *When he was come into the temple, the chief priests and the elders of the people came unto him.* They had rallied their forces and taken time to recall their courage. They interfered with Him *as he was teaching,* and demanded His *authority* for what He said and did. He had taken their breath away by His daring purge of the temple, unarmed and unaided, and only after a night's interval dared they question His right to act as He had done. Now they put Him to the question: *By what authority doest thou these things? and who gave thee this authority?* That He did marvelous things was admitted, but in what official capacity did He act and who placed Him in that office? This was carrying the war home. They struck out fiercely at their assailant. They hoped to wound Him in this point and to overcome Him. Poor fools! They were not worthy of an answer from Him.

24. And Jesus answered and said unto them, I also will ask you one thing, which if ye tell me, I in like wise will tell you by what authority I do these things.

Yes, *Jesus answered.* His answers are always complete, but are seldom what His foes expect. The quarrelers of our day need not be in too great a hurry to call their statements unanswerable. Jesus will answer for Himself in due time. He says to these chief priests and elders, *I also will ask you one thing.* Their question was met by another question, even as the rods of the Egyptian magicians, when turned into serpents, were met by Aaron's rod, which, as a serpent, swallowed up their rods.

Frequently it will be wise not to reply to the complaints of the enemies of the gospel, but to pose them with some mystery too deep for them.

Our Lord's conditions were fair and reasonable: *If ye tell me, I in like wise will tell you by what authority I do these things.* Apparently, the questioners raised no objection, for Jesus at once stated His question to them.

> *25-27. The baptism of John, whence was it? from heaven, or of men? And they reasoned with themselves, saying, If we shall say, From heaven; he will say unto us, Why did ye not then believe him? But if we shall say, Of men; we fear the people; for all hold John as a prophet. And they answered Jesus, and said, We cannot tell. And he said unto them, Neither tell I you by what authority I do these things.*

The question our Lord put to the chief priests and elders was simple enough had they been honest men, but as they had a game to play, they could not reply without great difficulty.

Men-pleasers are obliged to be politicians and see which way the land lies. Our Lord put His questioners on the horns of a dilemma. If John the Baptist was sent *from heaven,* why had they rejected him? That John was *of men* they dared not assert, for their *fear [of] the people* silenced them. They were in a corner and saw no way of escape, and therefore they pleaded ignorance: *They answered Jesus, and said, We cannot tell.*

This answer was really no answer *from* them, but it supplied Him with a just and crushing reply *to* them: *Neither tell I you by what authority I do these things.* They could have told Jesus from what source John's baptism was, but they would not, and He could have told them all about His divine authority, but He knew that no useful end would be answered, and therefore He declined to say more. It is a solemn thing when love itself grows weary and refuses further conversation. Our Lord's tone to these questioners is that of one who is dealing with hopeless creatures who deserve no mercy, since they would make no use of leniency. They could not be won by gentleness. They must be shaken off exposed and dethroned from the seat of power, before the eyes of those who had been misled by them.

> *28-29. But what think ye? A certain man had two sons; and he came to the*

first, and said, Son, go work to day in my vineyard. He answered and said,
I will not: but afterward he repented, and went.

By two parables the Lord Jesus deals with the religious leaders who
had opposed Him.

In the first parable, that of the two sons, He exposes their fair but
false dealings with God. *A certain man had two sons.* Both were bound to
serve upon the family estate and ought to have felt it a pleasure to do so.
The first son was willful and wayward, but he was truthful, outspoken,
and aboveboard in all that he did. His father said to him, *Son, go work*
to day in my vineyard – a command that contains the father's claim,
the son's duty, the immediate character of that duty, and the sphere of
it. The command was plain enough and so was the reply: *He answered*
and said, I will not. It was rude, rebellious, ungrateful, and unfilial,
but it was hasty, and when a little interval had elapsed, quiet reflection
brought the wayward boy to a better mind. *Afterward he repented, and*
went. This was true repentance, for it led to practical obedience. He did
not offer a verbal apology or make a promise of future good behavior.
He did far better, for he went about his father's business without further
ado. Oh, that many, who have yet refused to obey the gospel might now
be changed in mind, listen to the voice of God, and enter His service!

30. And he came to the second, and said likewise. And he answered and
said, I go, sir: and went not.

The second was of milder mood and blander manner. To him the
father spoke as to the elder, and the reply was verbally all that he could
desire: *I go, sir.* As if it were a matter of course, with exemplary polite-
ness, he told his father to consider that he was fully at his disposal. He
agreed and consented. He was polite and precise. He had an easy, natural
religiousness, which strongly contrasted with the blunt ungodliness of
his brother. But note those words: *And went not.* His fine phrases and
fair promises were deceit and falsehood. He never went to the vineyard,
much less lifted a pruning knife or spade. His father's vineyard might
go to ruin for all he cared, yet all the while he was bowing and scrap-
ing, and promising what he never meant to perform.

31-32. Whether of them twain did the will of his father? They say unto him,

The first. Jesus saith unto them. Verily I say unto you, That the publicans and the harlots go into the kingdom of God before you. For John came unto you in the way of righteousness, and ye believed him not: but the publicans and the harlots believed him: and ye, when ye had seen it, repented not afterward, that ye might believe him.

Jesus made the hypocritical religious leaders judges in a case that was indeed their own. He asked them, *Whether of them twain did the will of his father?* Only one reply was possible: *They say unto him, The first.* It was clear that the first son, despite his rough refusal when he first heard his father's command, was after all the doer of the father's will. Then Jesus pointed out that *the publicans and the harlots* were like the first son, while the chief priests and elders of the people, with all their pretty claims, were deceitful and disobedient like the second son. They had professed great reverence for the divine Word, but when it came by John, *they did not repent that they might believe him.* Open sinners, who had seemed to refuse the voice of God, did actually believe him, and so by heeding John's ministry *of righteousness,* they went *into the kingdom of God before* the more likely classes. What must these self-satisfied priests and elders have thought when they heard *publicans* and *harlots* placed before them? Gnashing their teeth, they planned murder in their hearts.

Matthew 21:33-44

The King Makes His Enemies Judge Themselves

33. Hear another parable: There was a certain householder, which planted a vineyard, and hedged it round about, and digged a winepress in it, and built a tower, and let it out to husbandmen, and went into a far country.

In this parable, *a certain householder* did all that could be done for his *vineyard*: it was well *planted* and *hedged round about,* and it was provided with *a winepress digged* in the rock and guarded by a tower built for the purpose. Even so the Jewish church had been created, trained, guarded, and fully furnished by the Lord: *For the vineyard of the* LORD *of hosts is the house of Israel, and the men of Judah his pleasant plant* (Isaiah 5:7). Everything was in good order for the production of fruit, so that the Lord was able to say, *What could have been done more to my vineyard, that I have not done in it?* (Isaiah 5:4).

The owner *went into a far country* and committed the estate to *husbandmen* who were to take care of it for him and yield to him a certain share of the produce as the rent. Thus, the great Lord of Israel left the nation under the care of priests, and kings, and men of learning, who should have cultivated this heritage of Jehovah for Him and yielded up to Him the fruit of this choice vineyard. God for a while seemed gone from His chosen people, for miracles had ceased; but this should have made the scribes and priests the more watchful, even as good servants are the more awake to guard the estate of their master when he is away.

34. And when the time of the fruit drew near, he sent his servants to the husbandmen, that they might receive the fruits of it.

The householder waited till near the full time in which he could expect a return. The *time of the fruit drew near,* and as the husbandmen sent him none of the produce of the vineyard, *he sent his servants* to *receive the fruits of it,* and bring them to him. These servants, as the lord's representatives, ought to have been received with due honor, but they were not. The leaders of the Jewish nation for a long time rendered to the Lord no homage, love, or service. Prophets were sent of God to Israel, but their message was refused by the rulers of the people.

35. And the husbandmen took his servants, and beat one, and killed another, and stoned another.

The husbandmen, the persons in charge and authority, kings, priests, and teachers – these united in doing evil to the owner's *servants.* They were not themselves his *servants.* They deserved not so honorable a title. Beating, killing, and stoning are put for various forms of mistreatment, which the Lord's prophets received at the hands of Israel's husbandmen, the religious rulers of the nation. Those to whom the vineyard was leased were traitors to the chief landlord and did violence to his messengers, for in heart they desired to keep the vineyard for themselves.

36. Again, he sent other servants more than the first: and they did unto them likewise.

The lord of the vineyard was patient and gave them further opportunities to mend their ways: *Again, he sent other servants.* Failure to bring back the fruit was not the fault of the first messengers, for other servants were rejected even as they had been. The householder was very anxious to get the husbandmen to a better state of mind, for he increased the number of his representatives, sending *more than the first,* trusting that the evil men would yield to repeated calls. No good came of this effort of kindness, for the badly disposed husbandmen only continued their murderous cruelty: *They did unto them likewise.* It was evidently a bad case. The Jewish people would not listen to the voices of the Lord's servants, and their rulers set them the example of persecuting the men whom God had sent to them.

37. But last of all he sent unto them his son, saying, They will reverence my son.

The sending of *his son* was the householder's last resort. Luke represents him as saying, *What shall I do?* (Luke 20:13). He might have resolved at once to punish the evildoers, but his action proved that mercy had triumphed over wrath. *Last of all he sent unto them his son.* The sending of Jesus to Jerusalem was God's ultimatum. If He should be rejected, judgment must fall upon the guilty city. It seemed impossible that His mission could fail. In sending His beloved Son, the Father seemed to say, "Surely, *they will reverence my son.*" Can they go the length of treating with contempt the Heir of all things? Will not His own beauty and majesty overawe them? Heaven adores Him. Hell trembles at Him. Surely, *they will reverence my son.*

38. But when the husbandmen saw the son, they said among themselves, This is the heir; come, let us kill him, and let us seize on his inheritance.

Things turned not out as a loving heart might have hoped. Evil worked itself to its consummation. *When the husbandmen saw the son,* that is to say, as soon as the chief priests and Pharisees perceived that the true Messiah was come, *they said among themselves* what they dared not say openly. The very sight of the heir of all things fired them with malice.

In their hearts they hated Jesus, because they knew that He really was the Messiah. They feared that He would dismiss them and assume possession of His own inheritance, and therefore they would make an end of Him: *This is the heir; come, let us kill him.* Once they got Him out of the way, they hoped to keep the nation in their own hands and use it for their own purposes. Therefore, they inwardly said, *Let us seize on his inheritance.* They knew that He was *the heir,* and that it was *His inheritance,* but their knowledge did not prevent them from seeking to snatch the vineyard away from its rightful owner. Our Lord resembled exactly what was passing in the minds of the proud religious leaders around Him, and He did not hesitate to do this to their faces. No names were mentioned, but this was personal preaching of the best kind.

39. And they caught him, and cast him out of the vineyard, and slew him.

The Lord Jesus becomes prophetic, as by the parable He foretells the success of their malice. The husbandmen were hasty in carrying out their wicked plot. No sooner said than done. Three acts were in that drama and they followed quickly upon each other. We will drop the figures of speech and unveil the facts. *They caught him* in the garden of Gethsemane. *They cast him out* in their council in the hall of Caiaphas, and when He was led outside the gate of Jerusalem, *they slew him* at Calvary, for theirs was the crime, though the Romans did the deed. Thus the Heir was slain, but the murderers did not long retain the vineyard. Swift justice overtook them.

40. When the lord therefore of the vineyard cometh, what will he do unto those husbandmen?

Jesus puts the matter before them. Out of their own mouths shall the verdict proceed. There is a time *when the lord of the vineyard cometh.* To those chief priests that hour was drawing very near. The question for them to think of was, *What will he do unto those husbandmen?* As a class, the religious leaders of the Jews were guilty of the blood of a long line of prophets, and they were about to crown their long career of crime by the murder of the Son of God Himself. In the destruction of Jerusalem, the God of heaven visited them and dealt out just punishment to them.

The siege of the city and the massacre of the inhabitants was a terrible avenging of the innocent blood that the people and their rulers had shed.

41. They say unto him, He will miserably destroy those wicked men, and will let out his vineyard unto other husbandmen, which shall render him the fruits in their seasons.

Their reply was probably made complete and full of details, so that they might hide their own shame by a parade of justice in a case that they would have men think was no concern of theirs. In very deed, they pronounced upon themselves the sentence of being *wicked men,* to be *miserably destroyed,* and to have their offices given to better men: *He will let out his vineyard unto other husbandmen.* They could not or would not give an opinion as to the mission of John the Baptist, but it seems that they could form a judgment as to themselves. The Lord's vineyard passed over to other husbandmen, and the apostles and the first preachers of the gospel were found faithful to their trust.

Just now there are many professed ministers of Christ who are abandoning the truth that He has committed to His stewards as a sacred trust, and are setting up a doctrine of their own. Oh, that the Lord may raise up a race of men who *shall render him the fruits in their seasons!* The hallmark of a faithful minister is his giving to God all the glory of any work that he is enabled to do. That which does not magnify the Lord will not bless men.

42-43. Jesus saith unto them, Did ye never read in the scriptures, The stone which the builders rejected, the same is become the head of the corner: this is the Lord's doing, and it is marvellous in our eyes? Therefore say I unto you, The kingdom of God shall be taken from you, and given to a nation bringing forth the fruits thereof.

Our Lord reminds them of David's language in Psalm 118:22-23. They were professedly the builders and they had *rejected* Him who was the chief cornerstone. Yet the Lord God had made the despised one to be *the head of the corner.* He was the most conspicuous and honored stone in Israel's building. Against the will of scribe and priest this had been accomplished, for it was *the Lord's doing.* They might rage, but holy minds adored and said, *It is marvellous in our eyes.* The sufferings and glory of Christ are the wonder of the universe, *which things the angels desire to look into* (1 Peter 1:12). All that relates to Him is marvelous in the eyes of His people.

The doom of the unfaithful religious builders was the result of their sin: *Therefore say I unto you.* They were to lose the blessings of the gospel: *The kingdom of God shall be taken from you.* All portion in the honors and offices of that kingdom would be refused them. That loss would be aggravated by their seeing it *given to a nation bringing forth the fruits thereof.* What a warning is this to our own country! We, too, are seeing the sacrifice and deity of our Lord questioned, and His sacred Word attacked by those who should have been its advocates. Unless there is a speedy amendment, the Lord may take away the candlestick out of its place and find another race that will prove more faithful to Him and to His gospel than our own has been.

44. And whosoever shall fall on this stone shall be broken: but on whomsoever it shall fall, it will grind him to powder.

Those who stumble over Christ, the chief cornerstone of the church, are injured. They suffer severe bruising and breaking, but He remains unhurt. Opposition to Jesus is injury to ourselves. Those upon whom He falls in wrath are *ground to powder,* for the results of His anger are overwhelming, fatal, and irretrievable. Oppose Him and you suffer, but when He arises in His might and opposes you, destruction has already come to you.

Matthew 21:45-46

The King's Enemies Plot against Him

45. And when the chief priests and Pharisees had heard his parables, they perceived that he spake of them.

They had tried to turn aside the point of His parables, but they had tried in vain. The likenesses were striking, the parallels were perfect, and they could not help knowing *that he spake of them.* Such parables

– so true, so cutting, so pertinent – how could they escape them or endure them?

46. But when they sought to lay hands on him, they feared the multitude, because they took him for a prophet.

Since they could not answer Him, they would arrest Him. Fortunately, *the multitude* thought too well of Jesus to allow them to lay their hands on Him, though they sought to do so. These great religionists were as cowardly as they were cruel: *They feared the multitude, because they took him for a prophet.*

They dared not tell the truth concerning John because they feared the people, and that fear restrained their anger against John's Lord. It was arranged, in the order of providence, that religious malice should be held in check by popular feeling. This was an instance of the way in which many times the earth has helped the woman (Revelation 12:16), and the will of the masses has screened the servants of God from priestly cruelty. He who rules all things sets in motion a high order of politics in the affairs of men in reference to His church. At times, princes have saved men of God from priestly hostility, and immediately the multitude has preserved them from aristocratic hate. One way or another, Jehovah knows how to preserve His Son and all those who are with Him, until the hour comes when by their deaths they can glorify His name and enter into glory themselves.

Matthew 22

Matthew 22:1-14

Parable of the Marriage of the King's Son

1. And Jesus answered and spake unto them again by parables, and said.

And Jesus answered and spake unto them again. This was His reply to the hatred of the chief priests and Pharisees. He answered them by going on with His ministry. For them, and for the people also, He spoke again by parables. They came to Him with complaints. He replied *by parables.* In the previous chapter, we noticed that *they perceived that he spake of them.* This perception did not, however, lead them to repentance, but only increased their hatred against the Savior. Their partly concealed anger was all the greater because, through fear of the multitude, they could not yet lay hands on Jesus and put Him to death. They had willfully closed their eyes to the light, yet it continued to shine upon them. If they would not receive it, perhaps some of the people, whom they had been misleading, might accept it. Therefore, once more the King would give them a parable concerning His kingdom and concerning Himself. This parable must be distinguished from the one recorded in Luke 14:16-24, which was spoken on another occasion and with a different object. It would be worthwhile to compare the two parables and to note their resemblances and their differences.

2. The kingdom of heaven is like unto a certain king, which made a marriage for his son.

A certain king made a marriage for his son. Thus does the King of Glory celebrate the union of His Son with our humanity. The divine Son of God condescended to be united with our human nature, in order that

He might redeem the beloved objects of His choice from the penalty due to their sins, and might enter into the nearest conceivable connection with them. The gospel is a glorious festival in honor of that wonderful marriage, by which God and man are made one. It was a grand event and grandly did the King propose to celebrate it by a wedding feast of grace. The marriage and the marriage festivities were all arranged by the King. He took such delight in His only begotten and well-beloved Son that everything that was for His honor and joy afforded infinite satisfaction to the great Father's heart. In addition to the Son's equal glory with the Father as Creator, Preserver, and Provider, by His marriage He was to be crowned with fresh honors as Savior, Redeemer, and Mediator.

3. And sent forth his servants to call them that were bidden to the wedding: and they would not come.

The set time had arrived, and the Jews, who as a nation *were bidden to the wedding,* were invited to come and partake of the royal bounty. They had been *bidden* long before by the prophets whom the King had continued to send to them, and now that the festive day had dawned, the King *sent forth his servants to call them that were bidden to the wedding.* This was in accordance with the Eastern custom of sending a second invitation to those who had favorably received the first. John the Baptist and our Lord's apostles and disciples plainly told the people that the long looked-for event was drawing near. Indeed, the appointed hour had already struck, the set time to favor Zion had come, and all that was needed was that the guests should come to the wedding.

The Jews were highly honored in being chosen out of all the nations of the earth to attend the wedding of the King's Son, but alas! they did not prize their privileges: *They would not come.* They were instructed, entreated, and warned, but all to no purpose: *They would not come.* Our Lord was very near the end of His sojourn on earth, and He summed up all that He had seen of Israel's conduct towards Himself in this short sentence: *They would not come.* It is not said, They *could* not come, but, They *would* not come. Some for one reason, and some for another, and perhaps some without any reason at all, but without exception, *they would not come.* They thus manifested their disloyalty to the King, their disobedience to His command, their dislike to His Son, their distaste for the royal banquet, and their disregard for the messengers sent to them by the King.

Note that it was the king who made this wedding feast; therefore, to refuse to be present, when the invitation implied great honor to those who received it, was as distinct an insult as could well be perpetrated against both the king and his son. If an ordinary person had invited them, they might have pleased themselves about accepting the invitation, but a royal invitation is a command that will be disobeyed at the refuser's peril. Let this be remembered by those who are now refusing the invitation of the gospel.

> 4. Again, he sent forth other servants, saying, Tell them which are bidden, Behold, I have prepared my dinner: my oxen and my fatlings are killed, and all things are ready: come unto the marriage.

The king was patient and gave the disloyal people a further opportunity of coming to the wedding feast: *Again, he sent forth other servants.* He wished to make every allowance for those who had refused his invitation so that they might be left without excuse if they persisted in their refusal. Possibly there may have been something in the servants that repelled instead of attracted them, or they may not have put the king's message in the best possible form. Perhaps the invitation was not given clearly enough, or perhaps, on thinking over the matter, those who *would not come* might regret their hasty decision and long for another invitation to the feast.

So the king *sent forth other servants,* and lest there should be any mistake about the message they were to deliver, he said to them, *Tell them which are bidden, Behold, I have prepared my dinner: my oxen and my fatlings are killed, and all things are ready: come unto the marriage.*

Jesus here seemed to glance into the near future and to foretell what would happen after His death. The apostles and the immediate disciples of our Lord went throughout the land, declaring the gospel in all its fullness, freeness, and readiness. At first, they kept to the Jews, according to the King's word: *Tell them which are bidden.* At Antioch, in Pisidia, Paul and Barnabas said to the Jews who contradicted and blasphemed them, *It was necessary that the word of God should first have been spoken to you* (Acts 13:46). The apostles at first seemed to have regarded their mission as restricted to the Jews, but they certainly did preach the gospel to *them.* They told them that, by the death of Jesus, the preparation of salvation for men was fully made, according to the King's words: *Behold, I have prepared my dinner.* They preached a present salvation and one that displayed the riches of divine grace: *My oxen and my fatlings are killed.*

Indeed, they proclaimed grace all-sufficient, meeting every need of the soul: *All things are ready.* And then they uttered the King's proclamation: *Come unto the marriage.* In His name they invited, urged, and even commanded the *bidden* ones to come. They began at Jerusalem and called to the feast the favored seed of Abraham, whose honor it was to be the first invited to the royal banquet.

5. But they made light of it, and went their ways, one to his farm, another to his merchandise.

The bulk of the Jewish race gave small heed to apostolic preaching: *They made light of it.* They counted it of less importance than the worldly affairs in which their hearts were engrossed. In making light of the gospel, they really were making light of the great King Himself, treading underfoot the Son of God and treating with contempt the Spirit of grace. The doctrine of the cross was a stumbling block to them. The spiritual kingdom of the crucified Nazarene was despicable in their eyes: *They made light of it.*

And went their ways. They did not go in the way the King would have had them go. They despised His way and went their own ways, *one to his farm, another to his merchandise. His farm* and *his merchandise* are set up against the King's dinner: *My oxen and my fatlings.* The rebel seemed to say, "Let the King do as he likes with *his* oxen and *his* fatlings; I am going to look after my farm, or to attend to my merchandise." Worldly men love worldly things and *make light of* spiritual blessings. Alas, that the seed of Abraham, the friend of God, should thus have become as earthbound as those whom the Jews contemptuously called *sinners of the Gentiles* (Galatians 2:15)!

6. And the remnant took his servants, and entreated them spitefully, and slew them.

The religious remnant among the Jews, who clung to external forms with a ferocious bigotry, rose against the first preachers of the gospel and subjected them to cruel persecutions. They cared nothing for the incarnation of Emmanuel, that mysterious marriage of Godhead and manhood. They cared nothing for the Lord God Himself, but *took his servants*, and by scourging, stoning, slander, and imprisonment, *entreated them spitefully*. Their cruel conduct toward the Lord's servants proved that they were full of spite, malice, and anger. Saul of Tarsus, before his conversion, was a type of the fanatical Pharisees and religious rulers who were, as he confessed to King Agrippa, *exceedingly mad* (Acts 26:11) against Christ's followers.

In many cases, they not only spitefully treated the King's servants, but they even *slew them*. Stephen was the first martyr of the truth after his Lord's crucifixion, but he was by no means the last. If "the blood of the martyrs is the seed of the Church," the Holy Land was plentifully sown with it in the early days of Christianity. This was Israel's answer to the King, who told the long-favored nation to unite in doing honor to His well-beloved Son. The Jews said, in effect, "We defy the King. We will not have His Son to reign over us and in proof of our rebellion against Him, we have killed His servants."

7. But when the king heard thereof, he was wroth: and he sent forth his armies, and destroyed those murderers, and burned up their city.

In these terrible words, the siege of Jerusalem, the massacre of the people, and the destruction of their capital city are all described. *When the king heard thereof, he was wroth.* The king had reached the utmost limit of his tolerance and long-suffering patience. *The cup of the wine of the fierceness of his wrath* (Revelation 16:19) overflowed when he heard how his servants had been mistreated and killed, and *he sent forth his armies.* The Roman emperor thought that he was sending *his* armies against the Jews, but he was, unconsciously, working out the eternal purposes of the Most High God, even as the kings of Assyria and Babylon had been, in the olden time, the instruments by which the Lord had punished His rebellious people (see Isaiah 10:5; Jeremiah 25:9).

The cruel executioners did their terrible work in the most thorough manner. Read Josephus and see how the Romans *destroyed those murderers, and burned up their city.* The words are remarkable in their awful force and accuracy. Only Omniscience could foresee and foretell so fully and faithfully the woes that were to come upon the murderers and their city.

The divine retribution that fell upon Jerusalem ought to convey a solemn warning to us in these days when so many are making light of the gospel in our highly favored land. No nation ever yet refused the gospel without having some overwhelming judgment as the consequence of its daring criminality. France is to this day suffering the effects of the massacres of St. Bartholomew. If England should reject the truth of God, then its light, as a nation, will be quenched in seas of blood. May God prevent such an awful calamity by His almighty grace!

> *8-9. Then saith he to his servants, The wedding is ready, but they which were bidden were not worthy. Go ye therefore into the highways, and as many as ye shall find, bid to the marriage.*

Then, when the king was angry, even then he was gracious. In wrath, he remembered mercy. Judgment is God's strange work, but *he delighteth in mercy* (Micah 7:18). *Then saith he to his servants.* The king still had servants left, though his enemies were destroyed. Christian preachers remained when chief priests and Pharisees were extinct and Jerusalem was in ruins. The royal Host gathered His servants together and put before them the exact position of affairs: *The wedding is ready.* Gospel provision was made in abundance. There was no lack on the king's part. His son's wedding must be celebrated by a feast, and a feast requires guests, *but they which were bidden were not worthy.* This is the last we hear of those who were bidden. Seeing that they judged themselves unworthy of eternal life, others must be called. Salvation is not a matter of worthiness, or none would be saved. These men were too proud, too self-sufficient, too high-minded to be worthy recipients of the king's favor. They preferred their farms and their merchandise to doing honor to the king and his son, for at heart they were traitors.

What was to be done? Should the wedding be canceled and the provision for the feast be destroyed? Not so. The king said to his servants, *Go ye therefore into the highways, and as many as ye shall find, bid to the marriage.* Glorious was the outburst of grace that bade the apostles to turn to the Gentiles. Up to this time they had not been instructed, but when the Jews finally rejected the Messiah, He gave to His disciples their wider commission: *Go ye into all the world, and preach the gospel to every creature* (Mark 16:15). In the parable, highwaymen, vagrants, travelers, tramps, and all sorts of people are mentioned, and thus is Jesus to be preached to men in every condition, but especially to those who are *out of the way* (Romans 3:12). It is not after the manner of men to invite to a wedding banquet those who stray in the highways, but Jesus was setting forth the glorious freeness of the gospel invitation: *As many as ye shall find, bid to the marriage.* This indicates no limited call, no preaching to gracious character. Restrictions there rightly were at the first, but after the death of Christ, they were all removed. Even our Lord said, *I am not sent but unto the lost sheep of the house of Israel* (Matthew 15:24), and when He first sent forth His twelve apostles, His command to them was, *Go not into the way of the Gentiles, and into any city of the Samaritans enter ye not* (Matthew 10:5). But the time had come for the universal proclamation of the gospel. After His resurrection, Jesus said to His disciples, *All power is given unto me in heaven and in earth. Go ye therefore, and teach all nations* (Matthew 28:18-19).

> 10. *So those servants went out into the highways, and gathered together all as many as they found, both bad and good: and the wedding was furnished with guests.*

So those servants went out into the highways. They did as they were told. This was the disciples' warrant for doing what must at first have seemed very strange to them. They themselves belonged to the favored race that had been told first, but God's grace overcame their prejudices and they *went out* among the heathen, proclaiming the marriage of the Son of God and urging men to come to the wedding feast. The servants went in different directions *into the highways.* The word is in the plural: "the partings of the highways." *The Amplified Bible, Classic Edition* renders it *the crossroads,* where most people might be expected to be gathered together. Wherever the people are, there should the preachers of the gospel go with their God-given message.

The king's servants were so earnest and diligent, and their master's grace worked so effectively through them, that their efforts were very successful. They *gathered together all as many as they found.* The message that had been despised by the Jews was welcomed by the Gentiles, and from the great heathen highways of the world – Rome, Athens, Ephesus, etc. – many were gathered to the gospel feast. All ranks, classes, and conditions of men came to the banquet of love. These people were manifestly willing to come, for the king's servants *gathered together all as many as they found.* Characters who were outwardly very different united in obeying the summons, *both bad and good,* and were collected at the table. The best gathering into the visible church will be sure to be a mixture in the present imperfect state of humanity. There will be some admitted who ought not to be there. Tares will grow among the wheat. Corn and chaff will lie on the same floor. Dross will be mingled with precious gold. Goats will get in among the sheep. The gospel net will enclose fish of every kind, *both bad and good.*

And the wedding was furnished with guests. Happy, willing, wondering, enthusiastic guests found themselves lifted from the highways into royal company. The beggar was taken from the dunghill to sit with princes in the presence of the king. Hallelujah! Thus the king was happy, the prince was honored, the festive hall was filled, and all went merry as a marriage bell. What shouts of joy would go up from these outcasts as they sat at the royal table! Everything was ready for the feast before them, and nothing was lacking except guests to partake of the king's bounty. Now that they had come, surely all would go well. We shall see.

11. And when the king came in to see the guests, he saw there a man which had not on a wedding garment.

The success of the servants in filling the banqueting hall was not altogether so great as it appeared to be at first sight; at least it was not so perfect as to be without a mixture. The guests continued to pour into the palace, putting on the robes provided by the king, and sitting down with honest delight to enjoy the good things prepared for them. But there was one among them who hated the king and his son, and who resolved to come into the festive assembly without wearing the robe of gladness, and thus to show, even in the royal presence, his contempt for the whole proceedings. He came because he was invited, but he came only in appearance. The banquet was intended to honor the king's son, but this man meant to do nothing of the kind. He was willing to eat the good things set before him, but in his heart there was no love either for the king or his well-beloved son.

His presence was tolerated till a certain solemn moment, *when the king came in to see the guests.* Then the eye, which looks over all things, but overlooks nothing, spied out the daring intruder: *He saw there a man which had not on a wedding garment.* The wedding garment represents anything that is indispensable to a Christian, but which the unrenewed heart is not willing to accept. The man who did not have on the wedding garment was out of sympathy with the assembly, out of harmony with its object, devoid of loyalty to the king, and yet he brazened it out and thrust himself in among the wedding guests. It was a piece of defiant insolence, which could not be allowed to pass unnoticed and unpunished. In some respects, he was worse than those who refused the invitation, for while he professed to accept it, he only came so that he might insult the king to his face. He would not put on the garment that was freely provided, because by doing so he would have been honoring the prince, whose marriage was to him an object of contempt and scorn.

It is well to remember that there are foes of the heavenly King, not only outside the professing church of Christ, but also within its borders. Some altogether refuse to come to His Son's wedding, but others help to fill the banqueting hall, yet all the while they are enemies to the great Founder of the feast. This man without the wedding garment is the type of those who, in these days, pretend to be Christians, but do not honor the Lord Jesus, nor His atoning sacrifice, nor His Holy Word. They are not in accord with the purpose of the gospel feast, namely, the glory of the Lord Jesus in His saints. They come into the church for gain, for honor, for fashion, or for the purpose of undermining the loyal faith of others. The godly can often see them. This man must have been conspicuous among the wedding guests. The traitors within the church, however, have most to fear from the coming of the King. He will detect them in a moment, even as the royal host in the parable, as soon as he came in to see the guests, saw there the man who *had not on a wedding garment.*

12. And he saith unto him, Friend, how camest thou in hither not having a wedding garment? And he was speechless.

The king addressed him kindly enough: *He saith unto him,* **Friend** (emphasis added). Perhaps, after all, he did not intend to insult the king; therefore, he called him *Friend.* He pretended to be a friend; therefore the king addressed him as such. Still, it was a grave outrage that he had committed and he must account for it: "*How camest thou in hither not having a wedding garment?* Was it by accident or design? Did not the keeper of the wardrobe tell you about the garments provided for all my guests? Did you not feel like a speckled bird as you saw all your companions in wedding array, while your own clothes badly suited this festive hall? If you are an enemy, how did you come into this place? Was there no other place in which to defy me than in my own palace? Was there no other time for this insult than my son's wedding day? What have you to say as an explanation or excuse for your strange conduct?" Notice how personal the question is. The king addresses him as though he had been the only one present.

And he was speechless. He had a fair opportunity of excusing himself if he could, but he was awed by the king's majesty and convicted by his own conscience. No evidence needed to be given against him. He stood before the whole company, self-condemned, guilty of open and undeniable disloyalty. The original says, "He was muzzled." He may have talked glibly enough before the king came in, but he had not a word to say afterwards. Eloquent silence that! Why did he not even then fall on his knees and seek forgiveness for his daring crime? Alas! pride made him incapable of repentance. He would not yield even at the last moment.

There is no defense for a man who is in the church of Christ, but whose heart is not right towards God. The King still comes in to see the guests who have accepted His royal invitation to His Son's wedding. Woe be to any whom He finds without the wedding garment!

13. Then said the king to the servants, Bind him hand and foot, and take him away, and cast him into outer darkness, there shall be weeping and gnashing of teeth.

He had, by his action, if not in words, said, "I am a free man and will do as I like." So *the king said to the servants, Bind him.* Let him never be free again. He had been made too free with holy things. He had actively insulted the king. He had lifted up his hand in rebellion and dared to set his foot within the king's palace. Bind him *hand and foot.* Prepare the criminal for execution. Let there be no possibility of the rebel's escape. He is where he ought not to be. *Take him away.* The king's palace is no place for traitors. Sometimes this sentence of excommunication is executed by the church, when deceivers are put out of the ranks of the Lord's people by just discipline; but it is more fully carried out in the hour of death. It is worthy of note that the word for *servants* in this verse is not the same as that used in verses 3-4, 6, 8, and 10. There it is *douloi,* here it is *diakonoi,* "ministers," meaning the angels, whose business it is especially to gather out of Christ's kingdom *all things that offend, and them which do iniquity* (Matthew 13:41), *and sever the wicked from among the just* (Matthew 13:49).

The man in the parable had refused the robe of light, so the king says to his servants, *Cast him into outer darkness.* Cast him away, as men throw weeds over the garden wall or shake off vipers into the fire. Cast him far away from the banquet hall where torches flame and lamps are bright, *into outer darkness.* It will be all the darker to him now that he has seen the light within. His daring insolence deserves the most notable punishment. He is appointed to a place where *there shall be weeping and gnashing of teeth.* It will be no place of repentance, for the tears shed there will not be those of godly sorrow for sin, but hot, scalding streams from eyes that flash with the fire of rebellion and envy burning in unsubdued hearts. The *gnashing of teeth* shows the character of the *weeping.* The outcast from God would gnash his teeth in all the fury of disappointed hatred, which had been foiled in its attempt to bring dishonor upon the King in connection with his Son's wedding. Those who are professedly Christian, and yet really are unbelieving and disobedient, will have such a doom as is here described. May the Lord in mercy save all of us from such a fearful fate!

14. *For many are called, but few are chosen.*

Many are called. The limit lies not there. We preach no restricted gospel. All who hear that gospel are called, but it does not come with power to every heart: *But few are chosen.* The result goes to show that, one way or another, the mass miss the wedding feast and a few choice spirits find it, by the choice of God's grace.

These words, of course, relate to the whole parable. Those who were *called* included the rejectors of the king's invitation, who, by their refusal, proved that they were not *chosen.* Even among those who accepted the invitation, there was one who was not *chosen,* for he insulted the king in his own palace and showed his enmity by his disobedience to the royal requirements. There were, however, *chosen* ones, and sufficient in number to fill the festive hall of the great king and to render due honor to the wedding of his son. Blessed are all they that shall sit down at the marriage supper of the Lamb! May the writer and all his readers be among that chosen company and forever adore the distinguishing grace of God that has so highly favored them!

Matthew 22:15-22

The King's Enemies Try to Ensnare Him

15. Then went the Pharisees, and took counsel how they might entangle him in his talk.

Then went the Pharisees. They must have perceived that the parable of the wedding feast, like that of the wicked husbandmen, was spoken against them. Our Lord's words, however, did not move them to repentance, but only increased their malice and hatred against Him. Their hearts were hardened and their consciences seared, so they *took counsel how they might entangle him in his talk.* They would not acknowledge that Christ was the wisdom of God and the power of God. Had they done so, they would not have attempted their impossible task. They saw that to ensnare Jesus in His talk was a difficult undertaking and therefore they *took counsel* as to how they might accomplish it. If He had been as faulty as we are, they might have succeeded, for men who wish to entrap us in our talk need not consult much about how to do it.

This incident teaches us that men who can be as precise and formal as these Pharisees were, can yet deliberately set themselves to entangle an opponent. Great outward religiousness may consist with the meanest spirit.

> 16. And they sent out unto him their disciples with the Herodians, saying, Master, we know that thou art true, and teachest the way of God in truth, neither carest thou for any man: for thou regardest not the person of men.

They sent out unto him their disciples. They were probably ashamed to appear again in the presence of Christ, after His exposure of their conduct towards Himself as the King's Son. So they dispatched a select detachment of their disciples, in the hope that the scholars might succeed where their teachers had failed. *With the Herodians.* The disciples of the Pharisees were to be reinforced by a company from an opposite section of the enemies of Christ. The united band could operate against Jesus from different sides. The Pharisees hated the rule of a foreign power, while the Herodians advocated the supremacy of Caesar. Differing as these two sects did, even to mutual hate, they for the time laid aside their own disputes, so that they might in one way or another ensnare our Lord.

They began with fair speeches. They addressed Jesus by a title of respect: *Master.* They only used the word in hypocrisy, but they professed to regard Him as a teacher of the Law and an authority on disputed points of doctrine or practice. They also admitted His sincerity and truthfulness: *We know that thou art true, and teachest the way of God in truth.* They further praised Him for His fearlessness: *Neither carest thou for any man.* They then lauded Him for His impartiality: "*For thou regardest not the person of men.* You will speak without any regard for what Caesar, or Pilate, or Herod, or any of us may think, or say, or do." Thus did they try to throw Him off His guard by what they uttered in sheer flattery. All that they said was true, but they did not mean it. From their lips it was mere cajolery. Let us take note that when evil men are very loud in their praises of us, they usually have some wicked design against us. They curry favor and flatter so that they may deceive and destroy.

17. Tell us therefore, What thinkest thou? Is it lawful to give tribute unto Caesar, or not?

"*Tell us therefore.* Because You are true, because You teach the way of God in truth, because You care not for any man's opinion when You are Yourself in the right, and because You regard not the person of men, but dare to speak the truth whether they will hear or whether they will avoid it, *tell us therefore, What thinkest thou?* We are very anxious to have Your opinion upon this important point, on which some teach one thing, some another. It is a matter of great public interest and everybody is talking about it. It must have been considered in all its relevance by such a learned teacher as You are, and we would like to know Your thoughts upon it. *What thinkest Thou?*" Dear innocents! Much they wanted instruction from Him! All the while that they were speaking, they were inwardly gloating over the triumph that they felt sure would be theirs, when by any answer that He might give or even by His silence, He must provoke the animosity of one portion of the people or the other.

Here is the question they put to our Lord: *Is it lawful to give tribute unto Caesar, or not?* They referred to the annual poll tax, imposed by the Romans, which was the cause of great indignation among the Jews and led to frequent insurrections. Judas of Galilee (Acts 5:37), one of the many pretended messiahs, had taught that it was not lawful to give tribute unto Caesar, and he had perished in consequence of his rebellion against Rome. Christ's questioners may have hoped that some such fate would come upon Him.

Their question was a delicate and difficult one in many ways. Any answer whatever would bristle with points by which His enemies hoped to entrap Him. If He said, "It is lawful," then they would denounce Him as being in league with the oppressor of His people and a traitor to the theocracy of which they boasted, even though they had virtually cast off the divine rule over them. If He said, "It is not lawful," they could accuse Him to the Roman governor as provoking the multitude to rebellion. This was, in fact, one of the false accusations brought against Jesus when He was before Pilate: *We found this fellow perverting the nation, and forbidding to give tribute to Caesar, saying that he himself is*

Christ a King (Luke 23:2). If He remained silent, they would taunt Him with being a coward who did not dare to say what He thought, lest He should offend His hearers. Very cleverly was the net spread, but those who had so cunningly made it and laid it, little thought that they were only setting a snare in which they themselves would be caught. Thus does it often happen, as David said, *The wicked is snared in the work of his own hands* (Psalm 9:16).

18. But Jesus perceived their wickedness, and said, Why tempt ye me, ye hypocrites?

Our great thought-reading King was not to be deceived either by their flattery or their crafty questioning. *But Jesus perceived their wickedness,* for it was that, with a vengeance. Malice and deceit designed His overthrow, but He saw through the cunning of His enemies and perceived the wickedness that prompted them thus to attack Him. Onlookers may not have perceived their wickedness, and our Lord's disciples may have been puzzled as to how He would reply, but as in all other trying circumstances, Jesus Himself knew what He would do.

Probably even His enemies did not expect such a question as He now put to them: *Why tempt ye me, ye hypocrites?* They hoped that they had disguised their real purpose so cleverly that they must have been surprised to have the mask so quickly torn from their faces and to be exposed to public gaze in their true character as *hypocrites.* Jesus compared them to stage-players, dissemblers, men acting a false part with intent to deceive. Rightly did He name them and wisely did He say to them, *Why tempt ye me?* It is as if He had said, "You see that I am not deceived by your false and flattering speeches. I can read the malice that is written in your hearts; you are just powerless before Me if I choose to treat you as I can do. What can poor, puny creatures, such as *you* are, do against *Me? Why tempt ye Me?*" There is infinite scorn in our Savior's question, yet there is an undertone of pity even for those who deserved it not. "*Why tempt ye Me?* Have I given you any cause why you should seek to entrap Me? Why are you so foolish as to ask questions that must be to your own hurt?"

Whenever men pretend great reverence for Jesus and then seek, by their erroneous teaching or their science falsely so-called, to overthrow His gospel, they are corrupt hypocrites.

19. Shew me the tribute money. And they brought unto him a penny.

Having exposed their folly and hypocrisy, Jesus proceeds to put them publicly to shame. He said to them, *Shew me the tribute money.* This request on His part, and their compliance with it, would make the whole matter more vivid and impressive to the bystanders. When there is something to see and handle, a lesson becomes the more striking. Our Lord asked them to show Him a specimen of the coin usually paid for the poll tax, *and they brought unto him a penny,* a *denarius.* This coin represented the daily pay of a Roman soldier, and in the parable of the vineyard, it was said to be the daily wage of the laborer. Had these men guessed the use to which Jesus would put the denarius, they would not have so quickly procured one for Him. They bought their own confusion with that coin. They would never afterwards be able to look upon the tribute money without remembering how they were foiled in their attempt to entangle the hated Nazarene.

20-21. And he saith unto them, Whose is this image and superscription? They say unto him, Caesar's. Then saith he unto them, Render therefore unto Caesar the things which are Caesar's; and unto God the things that are God's.

He asked another question so that they might themselves assist in replying to themselves: *He saith unto them, Whose is this image and superscription?* Or rather, *inscription.* Before them were the image and inscription of the Roman emperor on the piece of money, but He would make them say as much, so He asks, *Whose is this?* The Jewish rabbis taught that "If a king's coin is current in a country, the men of the country do thereby evidence that they acknowledge him for their lord."

When we are dealing with ungodly men, it is well if we can make them to be their own accusers.

They say unto him, Caesar's. No other answer was possible. This tribute money was not a shekel of Jewish coinage, but money of the Roman empire. This was a plain proof that, whether they liked it or not, they were Roman subjects and Caesar was their ruler. What then must follow but that they should pay to their acknowledged ruler his due? *Then saith he unto them, Render therefore unto Caesar the things which are Caesar's.* Whatever belongs to Caesar is to be rendered to him. Jesus did not say what was Caesar's; the coin itself settled the question of paying tribute. His reply covered all the duties of loyal subjects to the ruler under whose jurisdiction they lived, but this did not touch the sovereignty of God. Jehovah held rule over consciences and hearts, and they must see to it that, as Caesar had his own, the Lord had His own also. *Render therefore unto God the things that are God's.* This was not an evasive reply on Christ's part. It was full of meaning and very much to the point, and yet it was so put that neither Pharisees nor Herodians could make anything out of it for party purposes or for their wretched purpose of entangling Jesus in His talk. Neither of the two sects turned a penny by their penny.

To us the lesson of this incident is that the state has its sphere and we must discharge our duties to it, but we must not forget that God has His throne and we must not allow the earthly kingdom to make us traitors to the heavenly kingdom. Caesar must keep his place and by no means go beyond it, but God must have the spiritual dominion to Himself alone.

22. When they had heard these words, they marvelled, and left him, and went their way.

They had some sense left even if they had no feeling. They saw that their plot had disgracefully failed; *they marvelled* at the wisdom with which Christ had baffled their cunning. They knew that it was hopeless to continue the conflict, so they *left him, and went their way.* Their way was not His way. They had already admitted, in their flattering speech, that He was a true teacher of God's way, and now they completed their own condemnation by leaving Him and going their own way.

Lord, save us from following their evil example! Rather, may we cleave to Christ and go His way!

Matthew 22:23-33

The King and the Sadducees

23. The same day came to him the Sadducees, which say that there is no resurrection, and asked him.

The same day. There was no rest for Jesus. As soon as one set of enemies was driven away, another company marched up to attack Him. He had silenced the Pharisees and the Herodians; now there *came to him the Sadducees,* the broad churchmen, the rationalists of our Savior's day, *which say that there is no resurrection.* They rejected a great deal more of the teaching of the Scriptures than this one point of the resurrection, but this is specially mentioned here as it was the subject on which they hoped to entrap or confuse the Savior. The Sadducees *say that there is no resurrection,* yet they came to Christ to ask what would happen, in a certain contingency, *in the resurrection* (Matthew 22:28). They evidently thought that they could state a case that would bring into contempt the doctrine of the resurrection of the dead. They might have taken warning from the experience of the Pharisees and the Herodians, but doubtless they felt so sure of their own position that they expected to succeed though the others had so conspicuously failed.

24. Saying, Master, Moses said, If a man die, having no children, his brother shall marry his wife, and raise up seed unto his brother.

Master. They came with pretended respect for the great *Teacher* (John 3:2). They were as polite as the previous company of assailants, but like them, though the words of their mouth were smoother than butter, war was in their hearts. Though their words *were softer than oil, yet were they drawn swords* (Psalm 55:21).

Moses said. They gave the substance, though not the exact words recorded in Deuteronomy 25:5. The law of Moses, in this as in many other matters, recognized existing customs and imposed certain regulations upon them. For a man to die without leaving a child to bear his name, and enter upon his inheritance, was regarded as so great a calamity that the Jews judged that every possible means must be taken to prevent it. The practice described here prevails among various Eastern nations even to this day.

> *25-28. Now there were with us seven brethren: and the first, when he had married a wife, deceased, and, having no issue, left his wife unto his brother: likewise the second also, and the third, unto the seventh. And last of all the woman died also. Therefore in the resurrection whose wife shall she be of the seven? for they all had her.*

These Sadducees may have known such a case as they stated, though it is extremely unlikely. More probably this was one of the stock stories they were in the habit of telling in order to cast ridicule upon the resurrection.

They had no belief in spiritual beings; therefore, they supposed that if there were a future state, it would be similar to the present. Having stated their case, they put to the Savior this perplexing question: *In the resurrection whose wife shall she be of the seven? for they all had her.*

They doubtless thought that this question would puzzle Christ, as it had puzzled others to whom it had been put, but He had no more difficulty in answering this than He had with the previous inquiries.

> *29. Jesus answered and said unto them, Ye do err, not knowing the scriptures, nor the power of God.*

Jesus answered and said unto them, Ye do err. The error was not with Him, but with them. Their supposed argument was based on their own erroneous notions about the unseen world, and when the light of God's Word was poured upon their seven men of straw, they vanished into thin air. The answer to objectors, skeptics, and infidels today may be given in our Lord's words, *Ye do err, not knowing the scriptures, nor the power of God.* These Sadducees thought that they had found a difficulty in the Scriptures, but their error arose from their *not knowing the scriptures.*

This is the root of almost all error: ignorance of the inspired Word of God. These men were acquainted with the letter, but they did not really know the Scriptures, or they would have found there abundant revelations concerning the resurrection.

Their error arose, also, from ignorance of *the power of God.* The resurrection of the dead is one of the greatest proofs of the power of God, with whom all things are possible. These Sadducees limited the Holy One of Israel in their ignorance or denial of His power. What is there about the resurrection that is incredible to the man who knows *the power of God*? Surely, He, who created all things by the word of His power, can, by that same power, raise the dead in His own appointed time.

> *30. For in the resurrection they neither marry, nor are given in marriage, but are as the angels of God in heaven.*

In the resurrection. Our Lord implied that there is a resurrection. He did not even stay to prove that truth, but went on to speak of the resurrection life as being of a higher order than our present natural life: *They neither marry, nor are given in marriage, but are as the angels of God in heaven.*

Our Savior's answer struck at another Sadducean error. His questioners did not believe in angels. Jesus did not attempt to prove the existence of angels, but took that fact also for granted by saying that *in the resurrection* men *are as the angels of God in heaven.* He did not say that they are changed into angels, but as Luke records His words, *They are equal unto the angels* (Luke 20:36). They are spiritual beings, as Paul explains in 1 Corinthians 15.

> *31-32. But as touching the resurrection of the dead, have ye not read that which was spoken unto you by God, saying, I am the God of Abraham, and the God of Isaac, and the God of Jacob? God is not the God of the dead, but of the living.*

Our Savior now gives these Sadducees further instruction *as touching the resurrection of the dead.* He used the formula He so often employed in speaking to those who professed to read the Scriptures: "*Have ye not read?* You reject the oral traditions that the Pharisees accept and teach in place of the commandments of God; have you not read *that which was spoken unto you by God?*" Jesus always manifested the utmost reverence for the revealed Word of God. He here showed that the truth made known in the Scriptures is a very personal matter. This message was spoken unto these Sadducees, although they knew it not; it was spoken by God, yet they received it not.

How necessary it is that we should search the Scriptures, lest there should be divinely revealed truths that we have not even read! How necessary, also, is the teaching of the Holy Spirit, lest we should read, as these Sadducees did, and yet not know the Scriptures!

Jesus might have referred to many passages in the Old Testament about the resurrection, but as the Sadducees regarded the Pentateuch with special honor, he quoted what Moses had recorded in Exodus 3:6: *I am the God of Abraham, the God of Isaac, and the God of Jacob,* and then added His own comment and exposition: *God is not the God of the dead, but of the living.* Abraham, Isaac, and Jacob had long been dead when the Lord spoke to Moses out of the burning bush. His words implied that the patriarchs were still living. His covenant was made with those who still existed.

There is much teaching in this truth, that *God is not the God of the dead, but of the living.* Some suppose that, until the resurrection, the saints are virtually nonexistent, but this cannot be. Though disembodied, they still live. Jesus does not argue about it, but He states the fact as beyond all question. The living God is the God of living men, and Abraham, Isaac, and Jacob are still alive and identified as the same persons who lived on the earth. God is the God of Abraham's body as well as of his soul, for the covenant seal was set upon his flesh. The grave cannot hold any portion of the covenanted ones. God is the God of our entire being: spirit, soul, and body.

33. And when the multitude heard this, they were astonished at his doctrine.

Our Lord's reply to the Sadducees was so complete that they were *put to silence* (verse 34). They did not attempt any further assault upon Him, for they must have been convinced of their own weakness. Those who had stood by as listeners, *the multitude* that had gathered, as crowds delight to do when there is a public discussion, *were astonished at his doctrine.* They were *astonished* both at the matter and the manner of Christ's teaching.

This is an expression that we often find in the life of our Lord, but apparently those who were *astonished* did not accept His teaching. They talked to one another about the marvelous way in which He answered all questions, but they did not admit that such a Teacher could be none other than the long looked-for Messiah. Even the scribes, who complimented Christ upon His answer (Luke 20:39), saying, *Master, thou hast well said,* did not follow up that confession by becoming His disciples.

Matthew 22:34-40

The King Tested by a Lawyer

34. But when the Pharisees had heard that he had put the Sadducees to silence, they were gathered together.

The multitude that had listened to Christ, and had been *astonished* at His answers to the Sadducees, would soon publish the tidings of their defeat.

When the Pharisees had heard that he had put the Sadducees to silence, they doubtless felt pleased that their natural enemies had been routed, but grieved that Jesus had again proved victorious in argument. He had, in one day, baffled the chief priests and elders of the people, Pharisees and their disciples, Herodians, and Sadducees. If He continued to prevail, all the people would be won over to His side. So once more they met in consultation: *They were gathered together.* They must think of some fresh device, some new plan for His overthrow. How persevering wicked men are in their evil strategies! While we deplore their wickedness, let us imitate their persistency.

35. Then one of them, which was a lawyer, asked him a question, tempting him, and saying.

Apparently, the result of their conference was that they selected one of their number to put to Jesus another inquiry: *One of them, which was a lawyer, asked him a question.* Mark says that this man was one of the scribes, one of those constantly engaged in copying the Law, and also one who explained its meaning to the people. He was a gentleman learned in the Law. He came, either as the representative of the Pharisees or on his own account, and asked Jesus a question, *tempting him* (Mark 8:11). Putting the mildest meaning on the word *tempting,* it conveys the idea of testing and trying in an unfriendly sense. Probably he was a man of clearer light and greater discernment than his associates, for he was evidently only half-hearted in the work of *tempting* Christ. Mark says that he had heard our Lord's words to the Sadducees, *and perceiving that he had answered them well* (Mark 12:28), he put his own question to Jesus. He was evidently a man of honesty, possessing a considerable amount of spiritual knowledge. This may help to explain the reason for his question.

36. Master, which is the great commandment in the law?

According to the rabbis, there were many commandments that were secondary, and others that were of first importance. They often put commands that really were comparatively small on a par with those that were greatest. One of them even ventured to say that the commands of the rabbis were more important than the commands of the Law, because the commands of the Law were little and great, but *all* the commands of the rabbis were great. Some of them regarded eating with unwashed hands as being as great a crime as murder, and they would classify the rubbing of ears of corn together on the Sabbath day with adultery, so that they caused great confusion as to the real order of moral precepts. It was, therefore, most desirable to get from this wise Teacher, whom the scribe addressed as *Master,* an authoritative answer to the question, *Which is the great commandment in the law?* The inquiry was one that would be sure to entangle the Savior if He did not answer it wisely, and in that respect the lawyer tempted, tested, tried, and proved Him.

Blessed be His dear name, He can stand any test to which He may be put! Satan tempted, tested, and tried Him to the uttermost of his power, but even he never found any flaw, or fault, or failing in Him.

37-38. Jesus said unto him, Thou shalt love the Lord thy God with all thy heart, and with all thy soul, and with all thy mind. This is the first and great commandment.

These were very familiar words to our Lord's hearers, for all devout Jews were in the habit of repeating them every morning and evening. Deuteronomy 6:4-9, from which our Savior quoted, was one of the four passages that were worn as *phylacteries* (Matthew 23:5). *Jesus said unto him, Thou shalt love the Lord thy God with all thy heart.* Because He is our God, Jehovah claims our heart's love. As our Creator, Preserver,

Provider, and Judge, He commands us to yield to Him all our heart's affection, to love Him first, best, and heartiest – out of all comparison to the love we have for any fellow creature or for ourselves.

And with all thy soul. We are to love God with all our life, to love Him more than our life, so that, if necessary, we would give up our life rather than give up our love to God.

And with all thy mind. We are to love God with our intellect, with all the powers of our mind, bringing memory, thought, imagination, reason, judgment, and all our mental powers as willing subjects to bow at God's feet in adoration and love.

This is the first and great commandment. It is *first* in point of time, for it was binding upon the angels before man was created. It was binding upon Adam from the hour of his creation in the image of God. It is *first* in importance, for there is no love to a creature worthy of comparison with love to the Creator. This commandment is also *great,* because it encompasses all others and because its demands are so great, namely, the whole love of our heart, and soul, and mind.

Who *can* render to God this perfect love? None of our fallen race can. Salvation by the words of the Law is clearly an impossibility, for we cannot obey even the first commandment. There is One who has obeyed it, and the obedience of Christ is reckoned as the obedience of all who trust Him. Being free from legal condemnation, they seek ever after to obey this *great and first commandment* (RSV) by the power of the Holy Spirit who dwells within them.

39. And the second is like unto it, Thou shalt love thy neighbour as thyself.

The answer is wider than the question. The lawyer asked about *the great commandment.* Christ answered his inquiry and then added, *And the second is like unto it, Thou shalt love thy neighbour as thyself.* Who of us has really loved his neighbor as himself? Under the gospel, this commandment is certainly not less binding than under the Law.

40. On these two commandments hang all the law and the prophets.

The teaching of Moses and all the prophets might be summarized in *these two commandments.* The duty of loving God and loving our neighbor as we love ourselves is the supreme subject of the divine revelation. On this, as on a great peg, *hang all the law and the prophets.* Remove the peg, and what have you left as a support for the teaching given by the Lord through the holy men of old who wrote as they were moved by the Holy Spirit?

Matthew 22:41-46

The King Asking Questions

41-42. While the Pharisees were gathered together, Jesus asked them, saying, What think ye of Christ? whose son is he? They say unto him, The son of David.

The King now carried the war into the enemy's country. He had answered all the questions put to Him. It was His turn to propound some to those who had come to examine Him. *While the Pharisees were gathered together,* that is, while they still lingered near Him, disappointed and defeated, yet watching for any opportunity of attacking Him, *Jesus asked them, saying, What think ye of Christ?* Our Lord here sets His servants the example of how they should deal with complainers, nitpickers, and objectors. Having wisely answered all their questions, He pressed home upon them the question of questions: *What think ye of Christ?* They had tried to puzzle Him with their inquiries about church and state, the future life, and the relative value of the commandments, but He put to them the much more vital question: *What think ye of Christ?*

Jesus also pressed upon His hearers further inquiry about *the Christ* (RSV), for the words used evidently mean the Messiah: *Whose son is he? They say unto him, The son of David.* They knew that the promised Deliverer would be descended from David, but they either did not know or would not confess that He had a divine as well as a human origin. This the Savior brings out by further questions.

43-45. He saith unto them, How then doth David in spirit call him Lord, saying, The LORD said unto my Lord, Sit thou on my right hand, till I make thine enemies thy footstool? If David then call him Lord, how is he his son?

These questions of our Lord themselves contain the answers to the present-day critics who deny the divine inspiration of the Scriptures, and the Davidic authorship, and the messianic application of certain Psalms. *He saith unto them, How then doth David in spirit call him Lord?* Quoting from Psalm 110:1, *saying, The LORD said unto My Lord, Sit thou on my right hand, till I make thine enemies thy footstool,* our Savior declared that these were the words of David, speaking *by the Holy Spirit* (see Mark 12:36), concerning the Christ, the Messiah. This ought forever to settle the question about the inspiration, authorship, and application of that psalm at least. *The LORD said unto my Lord –* Jehovah said unto my Adonai. David, by the Holy Spirit, learned what the Father said unto the Son and thus he was brought into connection with the whole sacred Trinity. *Sit thou on my right hand.* The Messiah was told to rest after His great mediatorial work was accomplished, and to sit on His Father's right hand, in the place of honor, power, and majesty. *Till I make thine enemies thy footstool.* Jesus is to keep His seat till His foes are all prostrate at His feet.

This was the problem the Pharisees had to solve: If the Messiah was David's Son, how was it that David, by the Holy Spirit, called Him his Lord? The Christ must be something more than mere man, otherwise the psalmist's words would have been unsuitable and even blasphemous. He was higher than the angels, for unto none of them did Jehovah ever say, *Sit on my right hand, until I make thine enemies thy footstool* (Hebrews 1:13).

> 46. *And no man was able to answer him a word, neither durst any man from that day forth ask him any more questions.*

If the Pharisees could have denied that the psalm had reference to the Messiah, it would have been easy for them to reply to Christ's question; but *no man was able to answer him a word.* The rabbis of our Savior's day admitted that this was one of the messianic psalms, without recognizing what their admission involved; in later times, as at the present day, false teachers sought to wrest it from its proper meaning.

Christ's questions silenced His adversaries in a double sense. First, they could not *answer him a word,* and next, *neither durst any man from that day forth ask him any more questions.* He remained Master of the field. They could not entrap or entangle Him in His talk. If they would put Him to silence, they must do it by putting Him to death.

Matthew 23

Matthew 23:1-12

The King's Warning against False Teachers

1-3. Then spake Jesus to the multitude, and to his disciples, saying, The scribes and the Pharisees sit in Moses' seat: all therefore whatsoever they bid you observe, that observe and do; but do not ye after their works: for they say, and do not.

Then spake Jesus to the multitude. The King commenced His final address to the people. He was soon to withdraw Himself from them, but first He would put them on their guard against their false teachers. They had heard what He had said *to* the scribes and Pharisees; now they would hear what He said *of* them *and to his disciples.* According to Luke, Jesus spoke to His disciples *in the audience of all the people* (Luke 20:45). His theme was one that concerned the whole population as well as His own disciples. He knew that He would shortly be taken away from them; therefore, He warned them against those who would seek their ruin, *saying, The scribes and the Pharisees sit in Moses' seat: all therefore whatsoever they bid you observe, that observe and do.* It was the duty of Moses to expound to the people the Law of God. The scribes and Pharisees occupied his place, but alas! the Spirit that guided him was not in them. They spoke as from the chair of Moses, *ex cathedra,* as we say, and as far as they really filled his seat and followed his sayings, their words were to be obeyed. Our Savior could not have intended the people to heed their false comments and foolish commentaries upon the law of Moses, for He had already declared that by their traditions they had transgressed the commandment of God and made it of no effect.

At this time, however, our Lord was speaking of another severe fault in the scribes and Pharisees, namely, that they said one thing and did another. *But do not ye after their works: for they say, and do not.* Sad indeed is the state of that religious teacher of whom the Searcher of hearts has to say, "Do as he says, and not as he does." Many such as these are with us still, preaching one thing and practicing another. May the Lord preserve the people from following their evil example!

> *4. For they bind heavy burdens and grievous to be borne, and lay them on men's shoulders; but they themselves will not move them with one of their fingers.*

The contrast between the true Teacher and the false ones is clearly brought out by this verse: *They bind heavy burdens and grievous to be borne, and lay them on men's shoulders.* Their regulations as to moral and ceremonial observances were like huge bundles of sticks or crushing burdens bound together and made into a weight intolerable for any man to carry. Many of these rules by themselves were harsh enough, but all together they formed a yoke that neither the people nor their fathers could bear. The scribes and Pharisees piled the great load upon them, but they neither helped them to sustain it, nor offered to relieve them of any portion of it: *They themselves will not move them with one of their fingers.* How different was Christ's teaching: *Come unto me, all ye that labour and are heavy laden, and I will give you rest* (Matthew 11:28). Taking their burdens of sin and sorrow and care upon His own shoulders, He exchanges them for His easy yoke, which itself gives rest to all who wear it.

> *5-7. But all their works they do for to be seen of men: they make broad their phylacteries, and enlarge the borders of their garments, and love the uppermost rooms at feasts, and the chief seats in the synagogues, and greetings in the markets, and to be called of men, Rabbi, Rabbi.*

This was the fatal flaw in their character: *But all their works they do for to be seen of men.* So long as they stood well in the sight of their fellow creatures, they cared little or nothing about how they appeared to the eye of God. They were very particular about the literal observance of certain Mosaic injunctions, although they completely missed the spiritual meaning of them: *They make broad their phylacteries, and enlarge the borders of their garments.* Four passages from the Law – Exodus 13:3-10, 11-16; Deuteronomy 6:4-9; 11:13-21 – were written on strips of parchment and worn on the forehead and the hand or arm as amulets or preservatives. These the scribes and Pharisees made especially prominent, yet all the while the Word of the Lord was not hidden in their hearts, nor obeyed in their lives. The Lord commanded the children of Israel to make fringes in the borders of their garments and to put upon the fringe a ribbon or thread of blue, that they might look upon it *and remember all the commandments of the LORD, and do them* (Numbers 15:38-39). These ritualists of our Savior's day were very scrupulous about having deep fringes or large tassels on their garments, but they remembered not the commandments of the Lord to do them. Many keep the laws of God to the eye, but violate them in the heart. From such deceit may the Spirit of truth preserve us!

Jesus next put together four things that the scribes and Pharisees loved: *The uppermost rooms at feasts, and the chief seats in the synagogues, and greetings in the markets, and to be called of men, Rabbi, Rabbi.* Whether they met with their fellow man for feasting, for worship, for business, or for instruction, they loved to be first and foremost. This is a common sin and one into which we may easily fall. Our Lord felt it necessary to warn even His disciples against that evil, for His next words were evidently spoken specially to them.

> *8-10. But be not ye called Rabbi: for one is your Master, even Christ; and all ye are brethren. And call no man your father upon the earth: for one is your Father, which is in heaven. Neither be ye called masters: for one is your Master, even Christ.*

In the church of Christ, all titles and honors that exalt men and give occasion for pride are here forbidden. In the Christian commonwealth, we should seek to realize a truer "Liberty, Equality, and Fraternity" than that for which the world clamors in vain. He who is called Rabbi robs Christ of His honor as the only Master or Teacher of His disciples, *for one is your Master, even Christ.* He also takes from His fellow Christians the privilege that they share equally with Him: *And all ye are brethren.*

Those who use such titles as *Holy Father* and *Right Reverend Father in God* would have a difficulty in explaining away our Savior's words,

Call no man your father upon the earth: for one is your Father, which is in heaven. In the tenth verse, our Lord's words might be rendered, *Neither be ye called leaders* [guides, instructors]: *for one is your Leader* [Guide, Instructor], *even the Christ* [the Messiah]. If we follow Him, we cannot go wrong.

> *11-12. But he that is greatest among you shall be your servant. And whosoever shall exalt himself shall be abased; and he that shall humble himself shall be exalted.*

This is nearly the same lesson that is recorded in chapter 20, verse 27. Our Lord had to repeat many times this law of His kingdom: *He that is greatest among you shall be your servant.* You are all equal, but if there is one among you who claims to be the greatest, he shall be the servant of all. Where our King rules, any one of His disciples who exalts himself shall be humiliated, while, on the other hand, the one who humbles himself shall be exalted. The way to rise is to sink self. The lower we fall in our own esteem, the higher shall we rise in our Master's estimation.

Matthew 23:13-33

The King Pronouncing Woes

> *13. But woe unto you, scribes and Pharisees, hypocrites! for ye shut up the kingdom of heaven against men: for ye neither go in yourselves, neither suffer ye them that are entering to go in.*

While our Savior was speaking to the people and His disciples, the scribes and Pharisees may have again drawn near. At any rate, His next words were addressed to them: *Woe unto you, scribes and Pharisees, hypocrites!* This is the first of eight *woes,* in which the Lord Jesus both foretells the doom of the hypocrites gathered before Him and reveals the depth of His pity even for them. In seven of the eight *woes,* He calls them hypocrites, and in one He addresses them as *blind guides.* This first *woe* was pronounced against them because, as far as they could, they *shut up the kingdom of heaven against men.* This was a terrible charge to be brought against them by Him who could read their hearts and who could truthfully say to them, *for ye neither go in yourselves, neither suffer ye them that are entering to go in.* They ought to have helped men into the kingdom; instead of doing so, they hindered those who were entering. Are there not false teachers nowadays who put stumbling stones instead of stepping stones in the way of those who are entering the kingdom of heaven?

> *14. Woe unto you, scribes and Pharisees, hypocrites! for ye devour widows' houses, and for a pretence make long prayer: therefore ye shall receive the greater damnation.*

The second *woe* was supported by two most serious accusations, which our Lord would not have uttered if they had not been true: *Ye devour widows' houses, and for a pretence make long prayer.* Either of these sins by themselves would have been very harsh, and the two together were sufficient to sink those who were guilty of them to the lowest hell. The men who had defrauded widows would have to answer for their misdeeds to the widows' *judge* (Psalm 68:5). Those who had sought to cover their crimes with the cloak of superior holiness deserved to be stripped before the people they had deceived and to hear the King's righteous sentence, *Therefore ye shall receive the greater damnation.* These words prove that there are degrees of punishment, as there are series of degrees in glory. All the ungodly will be judged and condemned by the Righteous Judge, but *the greater damnation* will be reserved for the hypocrites who have *for a pretence [made] long prayer[s],* while behind the mask, they have been devouring the property of widows and the fatherless.

> *15. Woe unto you, scribes and Pharisees, hypocrites! for ye compass sea and land to make one proselyte, and when he is made, ye make him twofold more the child of hell than yourselves.*

The third *woe* related to the unholy zeal of the scribes and Pharisees in gaining adherents to Judaism and their own party, and in the process making them even worse than themselves. They freely gave time and trouble to the work with the prospect of a very slight return: *Ye compass sea and land to make one proselyte.* They would, as it were, drag the Great Sea with a seine, in the hope of entangling one proselyte in its meshes, or they would go over all the land in order to persuade one Gentile to be circumcised so as to become a Jew outwardly (see Romans 2:28). The result to the proselyte was only evil: *When he is made, ye make him twofold more the child of hell than yourselves.* Perverts usually become bigots. The proselyte would naturally imitate the vices of his hypocritical teachers, without having that knowledge of the Scriptures that might to some extent exercise a wholesome restraint upon them. The circumcised heathen would be a Judas rather than a Jew, a true *son of perdition* (see John 17:12).

> *16-19. Woe unto you, ye blind guides, which say, Whosoever shall swear by the temple, it is nothing; but whosoever shall swear by the gold of the temple, he is a debtor! Ye fools and blind: for whether is greater, the gold, or the temple that sanctifieth the gold? And, Whosoever shall swear by the altar, it is nothing; but whosoever sweareth by the gift that is upon it, he is guilty. Ye fools and blind: for whether is greater, the gift, or the altar that sanctifieth the gift?*

The form of the fourth *woe* differs from all the rest. In the other seven, our Savior said, *Woe unto you, scribes and Pharisees, hypocrites!* In this case, His words were, *Woe unto you, ye blind guides!* They were nominally the religious guides of the Jews, but they were really *blind guides.* Sin, prejudice, bigotry, and hypocrisy had blinded their eyes. They reckoned themselves to be the wise men of the nation, but Jesus addressed them as both *fools and blind.* There are none so stupid as those who will not learn, and none so blind as those who will not see. This was the case with the scribes and Pharisees. They were willfully foolish and willingly blind.

Our Lord here condemned their misleading teaching concerning oaths. They actually taught that if a man swore *by the temple,* his oath was not binding, but if he swore *by the gold of the temple,* he was bound by his oath. And in like manner, they declared that an oath *by the altar* was not binding, but that if a man swore *by the gift that is upon [the altar],* he was bound by his oath! We marvel not at our Savior's indignant exclamation: *Ye fools and blind: for whether is greater, the gold, or the temple that sanctifieth the gold? the gift, or the altar that sanctifieth the gift?* The sanctity lay in the temple and the altar, not in the gold or the gift.

Jesus had forbidden all swearing (chapter 5, verses 34-36), so that He was not exalting one form of oath over another, but rather pointing out the folly and blindness of the scribes and Pharisees in reversing the right order of things. If any swearing had been permissible, an oath *by the temple* must have been more binding than one *by the gold of the temple,* yet these false teachers said, *It is nothing.* When men once abandon the plain teaching of Christ, it is easy for them to go into all manner of heresies and absurdities.

> *20-22. Whoso therefore shall swear by the altar, sweareth by it, and by all things thereon. And whoso shall swear by the temple, sweareth by it, and by him that dwelleth therein. And he that shall swear by heaven, sweareth by the throne of God, and by him that sitteth thereon.*

The Jews invented fantastic forms of swearing in order to evade the use of the divine name. Our Lord therefore next proved the utter failure of all their attempts. Swearing *by the altar* was swearing *by all things thereon.* An oath *by the temple* was really *by him that dwelleth therein.* The binding force of the oath could not lie in the mere building, but in the Most High God, who condescended to dwell therein. Many Jews would swear *by heaven,* although they would not call God to be a witness to their appeal; but Jesus showed that they were doing the very thing they tried to avoid: *He that shall swear by heaven, sweareth by the throne of God, and by him that sitteth thereon.* The only right course for us is to obey our Lord's command: *I say unto you, Swear not at all; neither by heaven; for it is God's throne: nor by the earth; for it is his footstool: neither by Jerusalem; for it is the city of the great King. Neither shalt thou swear by thy head, because thou canst not make one hair white or black. But let your communication be, Yea, yea; Nay, nay: for whatsoever is more than these cometh of evil* (Matthew 5:34-37).

> *23-24. Woe unto you, scribes and Pharisees, hypocrites! for ye pay tithe of mint and anise and cummin, and have omitted the weightier matters of the law, judgment, mercy, and faith: these ought ye to have done, and*

not to leave the other undone. Ye blind guides, which strain at a gnat, and swallow a camel.

In this fifth *woe,* our Lord called the scribes and Pharisees both *hypocrites* and *blind guides.* They were *hypocrites* as to their own character and conduct, and *blind guides* as the religious leaders of the nation. Jesus first spoke of their painstaking attention to certain minor matters: *Ye pay tithe of mint and anise and cummin.* Some of them were so meticulous about paying tithes that they even gave to the temple service the tenth of the herbs they bought in the market, as well as of those they grew in their gardens. Although they were so particular about things that were of secondary importance, they *omitted the weightier matters of the law, judgment* [or, *justice*], *mercy, and faith.* Their hearts were not right in the sight of God; therefore, their minds were unbalanced. They counted the lesser requirements of the Law as of first importance, while they *omitted the weightier matters* altogether. Our Lord did not blame them for paying the tithes, but He showed that they ought first to have exercised *judgment, mercy, and faith. These ought ye to have done, and not to leave the other undone.* No commandment of God is nonessential, but that which relates to the condition of the heart and the life in the sight of the Lord Jehovah must receive our first and best attention.

Jesus used a very expressive simile to set forth the inconsistency of the scribes and Pharisees: *Ye blind guides, which strain at* [or, *out*] *a gnat, and swallow a camel.* They rewarded trifles as if they were of first importance and so, as it were, strained out gnats from their wine, lest they should be choked; but they committed great sins without any guilt of conscience and thus, in effect, swallowed a camel, an unclean animal, equal in size to an almost innumerable quantity of gnats. There are gnat-strainers among us still, who apparently have no difficulty in swallowing a camel, "hump and all."

25-26. Woe unto you, scribes and Pharisees, hypocrites! for ye make clean the outside of the cup and of the platter, but within they are full of extortion and excess. Thou blind Pharisee, cleanse first that which is within the cup and platter, that the outside of them may be clean also.

The sixth *woe* is uttered against the scribes and Pharisees with regard to their eating and drinking: *Ye make clean the outside of the cup and of the platter, but within they are full of extortion and excess.* They had frequent washings, both of themselves and of their vessels for eating and drinking. They did well to *make clean the outside of the cup and of the platter.* The evil consisted in the method of filling and emptying the vessels. They were filled by *extortion,* and used for *excess;* therefore, all the outside washing was of no avail. Singling out one of the evildoers, our Lord said, "*Thou blind Pharisee, cleanse first that which is within the cup and platter,* get rid of *extortion* in gathering and *excess* in consuming, and then the clean cup and platter will be in harmony with that which is within them."

> *27-28. Woe unto you, scribes and Pharisees, hypocrites! for ye are like unto whited sepulchres, which indeed appear beautiful outward, but are within full of dead men's bones, and of all uncleanness. Even so ye also outwardly appear righteous unto men, but within ye are full of hypocrisy and iniquity.*

The reason given for the seventh *woe* reveals what the scribes and Pharisees really were like in Christ's sight: *Ye are like unto whited sepulchres, which indeed appear beautiful outward, but are within full of dead men's bones, and of all uncleanness.* The annual whitewashing of the sepulchers had recently taken place, so the burial places looked at their best, but inside the tombs corruption was doing its deadly work. They were whitewashed, not only for sanitary purposes, but also mainly to keep people away from them, lest they should become defiled. Our Lord certainly did not flatter the scribes and Pharisees by this comparison, but the more closely it is examined, the more appropriate to their abominable character will it be proved to be. However much they might *outwardly appear righteous unto men, within [they were] full of hypocrisy and iniquity.* Well might the holy Jesus cry, "Woe!" unto such foul sinners.

> *29-31. Woe unto you, scribes and Pharisees, hypocrites! because ye build the tombs of the prophets, and garnish the sepulchres of the righteous, and say, If we had been in the days of our fathers, we would not have been partakers with them in the blood of the prophets. Wherefore ye be witnesses unto yourselves, that ye are the children of them which killed the prophets.*

The eighth *woe* referred to their false professions of reverence for "the goodly fellowship of the prophets" and "the noble army of martyrs": *Ye build the tombs of the prophets, and garnish the sepulchres of the righteous.* They pretended to have such regard for the holy men of the past that, being unable to honor them in person, they would set up monuments to their memory and adorn their resting places with tokens of respect. They also testified as to what they would have done if they had lived in the days of their fathers: *We would not have been partakers with them in the blood of the prophets.* What bitter irony there was in such language from the lips of men who were even then plotting the death of the Lord of the prophets and of the righteous of all ages! Thus do men still speak with seeming horror of the dark deeds of past persecutors, whose linear descendants they are, not only according to the flesh, but also after the spirit.

Out of their own mouth our Lord condemned the hypocrites: *Wherefore ye be witnesses unto yourselves, that ye are the children of them which killed the prophets.* In effect, Jesus said to them, "You confess that you are the sons of the murderers of the prophets. That admission carries with it far more than you imagine. You are their sons, not only by birth, but also by resemblance. You are true children of those who killed the prophets. If you had lived in their day, you would have committed the crimes you pretend to condemn."

32. Fill ye up then the measure of your fathers.

This is one of the most terrible sentences that ever fell from Christ's lips. It is like His message to Judas: *That thou doest, do quickly* (John 13:27). The *measure* of Israel's iniquity was almost full. The Savior knew that the scribes and Pharisees were determined to put Him to death and so to complete their own condemnation. This crowning sin would fill up the measure of their fathers' guilt and bring down upon them the righteous judgment of God.

33. Ye serpents, ye generation of vipers, how can ye escape the damnation of hell?

Our Lord spoke very severely, but faithfulness required such language as this. A good surgeon cuts deep; so did Jesus. Our modern preachers would not talk like this, even to scribes and Pharisees who were crucifying Christ afresh and putting Him to an open shame (see Hebrews 6:6). He is not the most loving who speaks the smoothest words. True love often compels an honest man to say that which pains him far more than it affects his callous hearers.

Matthew 23:34-39

The King's Farewell to His Capital City

34-36. Wherefore, behold, I send unto you prophets, and wise men, and scribes: and some of them ye shall kill and crucify; and some of them shall ye scourge in your synagogues, and persecute them from city to city: that upon you may come all the righteous blood shed upon the earth, from the blood of righteous Abel unto the blood of Zacharias son of Barachias, whom ye slew between the temple and the altar. Verily I say unto you, All these things shall come upon this generation.

Our great King knew that His earthly life was soon to end. He was, in fact, about to utter His final farewell to the people gathered in the temple. But before leaving them, He delivered a royal and prophetic message: *Behold, I send unto you prophets, and wise men, and scribes.* None but the King of Kings could speak thus without blasphemy. These *prophets, and wise men, and scribes* would be Christ's ascension gifts to the church and the world. He foretold what kind of reception His servants would have from the Jews: *And some of them ye shall kill and crucify; and some of them shall ye scourge in your synagogues, and persecute them from city to city.* All of this was literally fulfilled.

The object of the King in sending His last representatives was that the guilty city should be left forever without excuse when its measure of iniquity should be full and its awful doom be sealed. *That upon you may come all the righteous blood shed upon the earth, from the blood of righteous Abel unto the blood of Zacharias son of Barachias, whom ye slew between the temple and the altar.* The destruction of Jerusalem was more terrible than anything that the world has ever witnessed, either before or since. Even Titus seemed to see in his cruel work the hand of an avenging God. Truly, the blood of the martyrs slain in Jerusalem was amply avenged when the whole city became a veritable *Aceldama*, or *field of blood* (Acts 1:19).

The Kingly Prophet foretold the time of the end: *Verily I say unto you, All these things shall come upon this generation.* It was before that generation had passed away that Jerusalem was besieged and destroyed. There was a sufficient interval for the full proclamation of the gospel by the apostles and evangelists of the early Christian church and for the gathering out of those who recognized the crucified Christ as their true Messiah. Then came the awful end, which the Savior foresaw and foretold, and the prospect of which wrung from His lips and heart the sorrowful lament that followed His prophecy of the doom awaiting His guilty capital city.

> 37. *O Jerusalem, Jerusalem, thou that killest the prophets, and stonest them which are sent unto thee, how often would I have gathered thy children together, even as a hen gathereth her chickens under her wings, and ye would not!*

What a picture of pity and disappointed love the King's face must have presented when, with flowing tears, He uttered these words! What an exquisite emblem He gave of the way in which He had sought to woo the Jews to Himself: *How often would I have gathered thy children together, even as a hen gathereth her chickens under her wings.* What familiar tenderness! What a warm Elysium ("bliss") of rest! What nourishment for the feeble! What protection for the weak! Yet it was all provided in vain: *How often would I have gathered thy children together, and ye would not!* Oh, the awful perversity of man's rebellious will! Let all the readers of these lines beware lest the King should ever have to utter such a lament as this over them.

> 38-39. *Behold, your house is left unto you desolate. For I say unto you, Ye shall not see me henceforth, till ye shall say, Blessed is he that cometh in the name of the Lord.*

Nothing remained for the King but to pronounce the solemn sentence of death upon those who would not come unto Him that they might have life: *Behold, your house is left unto you desolate.* The whole *house* of the Jews was left desolate when Jesus departed from them, and the temple, the holy and beautiful *house*, became a spiritual desolation when Christ finally left it. Jerusalem was too far gone to be rescued from its self-sought doom.

Amid all this gloom there was one gleam of light: *For I say unto you, Ye shall not see me henceforth, till ye shall say, Blessed is he that cometh in the name of the Lord.* After His death and resurrection, the Lord Jesus appeared many times to His disciples, but not once to the unbelieving Jews. His personal ministry to them was at an end, but it would be renewed when He would come to them a second time, without a sin-offering unto salvation, and then they would say, *Blessed is he that cometh in the name of the Lord.* Long ages have passed since the King went away into the far country. The signs of the times all tell us that His coming *draweth nigh* (James 5:8). Oh, that Christians and Jews alike were on the lookout for the true Messiah, whose message to all is, *Behold, I come quickly!*

Matthew 24

Matthew 24:1-2

The King and His Father's House

1-2. And Jesus went out, and departed from the temple: and his disciples came to him for to shew him the buildings of the temple. And Jesus said unto them, See ye not all these things? verily I say unto you, There shall not be left here one stone upon another, that shall not be thrown down.

The King, having finished His final discourse in the temple, left it, never to return: *Jesus went out, and departed from the temple.* His ministry there was ended. As His disciples moved away with Him towards the Mount of Olives, they called His attention to the great stones of which *the temple* was constructed and the costly adornments of the beautiful building. To them the appearance was glorious, but to their Lord it was a sad sight. His Father's house, which ought to have been *an house of prayer for all people* (Isaiah 56:7), had become *a den of thieves* (Matthew 21:13), and soon would be utterly destroyed. *Jesus said unto them, See ye not all these things? verily I say unto you, There shall not be left here one stone upon another, that shall not be thrown down.* Josephus tells us that Titus at first tried to save the temple, even after it was set on fire, but his efforts were of no avail, and at last he gave orders that the whole city and temple should be leveled, except a small portion reserved for the garrison. This was so thoroughly done that the historian says, "There was left nothing to make those that came thither believe it had ever been inhabited."

We sometimes delight in the temporal prosperity of the church as if it were something that must certainly endure; but all that is external will pass away or be destroyed. Let us only reckon that to be substantial which comes from God and is God's work. *The things which are seen are temporal* (2 Corinthians 4:18).

Matthew 24:3-31

The King Answers Difficult Questions

3. And as he sat upon the mount of Olives, the disciples came unto him privately, saying, Tell us, when shall these things be? and what shall be the sign of thy coming, and of the end of the world?

The little procession continued ascending *the mount of Olives* until Jesus reached a resting place from which He could see the temple (Mark 13:3). There He sat down and *the disciples came unto him privately, saying, Tell us, when shall these things be? and what shall be the sign of thy coming, and of the end of the world?* These are the questions that have been asked in every age since our Savior's day. There are two distinct questions here, perhaps three. The disciples inquired first about the time of the destruction of the temple, and then about the sign of Christ's coming, and then about *the consummation of the age* (Amplified Bible). The answers of Jesus contained much that was mysterious and that could only be fully understood as that which He foretold actually occurred. He told His disciples some things that related to the siege of Jerusalem, some that concerned His Second Advent, and some that would immediately precede *the end of the world.* When we have clearer light, we may possibly perceive that all our Savior's predictions on this memorable occasion had some connection with all three of these great events.

4-6. And Jesus answered and said unto them, Take heed that no man deceive you. For many shall come in my name, saying, I am Christ; and shall deceive many. And ye shall hear of wars and rumours of wars: see that ye be not troubled: for all these things must come to pass, but the end is not yet.

Jesus was always practical. The most important thing for His disciples was not that they might know when *these things* would be, but that they might be preserved from the peculiar evils of the time. Therefore, *Jesus answered and said unto them, Take heed that no man deceive you.*

For many shall come in my name, saying, I am Christ; and shall deceive many. They were to beware lest any of the pretended messiahs should lead them astray, as they would pervert many others. A large number of impostors came forward before the destruction of Jerusalem, declaring that they were the anointed of God. Almost every page of history is blotted with the names of such deceivers; and in our own day, we have seen some come in Christ's name, saying that they are Christs. Such men seduce many, but they who heed their Lord's warning will not be deluded by them.

Our Savior's words, *Ye shall hear of wars and rumours of wars,* might be applied to almost any period of the world's history. Earth has seldom had a long spell of quiet. There have almost always been both the realities of war and the rumors of war. There were many such before Jerusalem was overthrown. There have been many such ever since, and there will be many such until that glorious period when *nation shall not lift up sword against nation, neither shall they learn war any more* (Micah 4:3).

See that ye be not troubled is a timely message for the disciples of Christ in every age. *For all these things must come to pass;* therefore, let us not be surprised or alarmed at them, *but the end is not yet.* The destruction of Jerusalem was the beginning of the end, the great type and anticipation of all that will take place when Christ shall stand at the latter day upon the earth. It was an end, but not *the* end. *The end is not yet.*

> 7-8. *For nation shall rise against nation, and kingdom against kingdom: and there shall be famines, and pestilences, and earthquakes, in divers places. All these are the beginning of sorrows.*

One would think that there was sorrow enough in *famines, and pestilences, and earthquakes, in divers places,* but our Lord said that *all these* were only *the beginning of sorrows;* they are the first birth pangs of the torment that must precede His coming, either to Jerusalem or to the whole world. If famines, pestilences, and earthquakes are only *the beginning of sorrows,* what may we not expect the end to be? This prophecy ought both to warn the disciples of Christ of what they may expect and wean them from the world where all these and greater sorrows are to be experienced.

9. Then shall they deliver you up to be afflicted, and shall kill you: and ye shall be hated of all nations for my name's sake.

Our Lord foretold not only the general trial that would come upon the Jews and upon the world, but also the special persecution that would be the portion of His chosen followers: *Then shall they deliver you up to be afflicted, and shall kill you: and ye shall be hated of all nations for my name's sake.* The New Testament gives abundant proof of the fulfillment of these words. Even in Paul's day, *this sect [was] every where spoken against* (Acts 28:22). Since then, has there been any land unstained by the blood of the martyrs? Wherever Christ's gospel has been preached, men have risen up in arms against the messengers of mercy and afflicted and killed them wherever they could.

10. And then shall many be offended, and shall betray one another, and shall hate one another.

This would be a bitter trial for the followers of Christ, yet this they have always had to endure. Persecution would reveal the traitors within the church as well as the enemies without. In the midst of the chosen ones, there would be found successors of Judas, who would be willing to betray the disciples as he betrayed his Lord. Saddest of all is the betrayal of good men by their own relatives, but even this have many of them had to bear for Christ's sake.

11-12. And many false prophets shall rise, and shall deceive many. And because iniquity shall abound, the love of many shall wax cold.

What could not be accomplished by persecutors outside the church, and traitors inside, would be attempted by teachers of heresy: *Many false prophets shall rise, and shall deceive many.* They have risen in all ages. In these modern times, they have risen in clouds, till the air is thick with them, as with an army of devouring locusts. These are the men who invent new doctrines and who seem to think that the religion of Jesus Christ is something that a man may twist into any form and shape that he pleases. Alas, that such teachers should have any disciples! It is doubly sad that they would be able to lead astray *many.* Yet, when it so happens, let us remember that the King said that it would be so.

Is it any wonder that where such *iniquity abound[s]* and such law-lessness is multiplied, *the love of many shall wax cold*? If the teachers deceive the people and give them another gospel, which is not another gospel, it is no wonder that there is a lack of love and zeal. The wonder is that there is any love and zeal left after they have been subjected to such a chilling and killing process as that adopted by the advocates of the modern *destructive criticism.* Truly, it is rightly named *destructive,* for it destroys almost everything that is worth preserving.

13. But he that shall endure unto the end, the same shall be saved.

Again our Savior reminded His disciples of the personal responsibility of each one of them in such a time of trial and testing as they were about to pass through. He would have them remember that it is not the man who starts in the race, but the one who runs to the goal who wins the prize: *He that shall endure unto the end, the same shall be saved.* If this doctrine were not supplemented by another, there would be but little good tidings for poor, tempted, tested, and struggling saints in such words as these. Who among us would persevere in running the heavenly race if God did not preserve us from falling and give us per-severing grace? But blessed be His name, that *the righteous also shall hold on his way* (Job 17:9). *He which hath begun a good work in you will perform it until the day of Jesus Christ* (Philippians 1:6).

14. And this gospel of the kingdom shall be preached in all the world for a witness unto all nations; and then shall the end come.

The world is to the church like a scaffold is to a building. When the church is built, the scaffold will be taken down. The world must remain until the last elect one is saved, and *then shall the end come.* Before Jerusalem was destroyed, *this gospel of the kingdom* was prob-ably *preached in all the world,* so far as it was then known, but there is to be a fuller proclamation of it *for a witness unto all nations* before the great consummation of all things, *and then shall the end come,* and the King shall sit upon the throne of His glory and decide the eternal destiny of the whole human race.

15-18. When ye therefore shall see the abomination of desolation, spoken of by Daniel the prophet, stand in the holy place, (whoso readeth, let him understand:) then let them which be in Judaea flee into the mountains: let him which is on the housetop not come down to take any thing out of his house: neither let him which is in the field return back to take his clothes.

This portion of our Savior's words appears to relate solely to the destruction of Jerusalem. As soon as Christ's disciples saw *the abomination of desolation,* that is, the Roman ensigns, with their idolatrous emblems, *stand in the holy place,* they knew that the time for them to escape had arrived and they did *flee into the mountains.* The Christians in Jerusalem and the surrounding towns and villages *in Judaea* availed themselves of the first opportunity for eluding the Roman armies, and fled to the mountain city of Pella, in Perea, where they were preserved from the general destruction that overthrew the Jews. There was no time to spare before the final siege of the guilty city; the man *on the housetop* could *not come down to take any thing out of his house,* and the man *in the field* could not *return back to take his clothes.* They must flee to the mountains in the greatest haste the moment that they saw *Jerusalem compassed with armies* (Luke 21:20).

19-21. And woe unto them that are with child, and to them that give suck in those days! But pray ye that your flight be not in the winter, neither on the sabbath day: for then shall be great tribulation, such as was not since the beginning of the world to this time, no, nor ever shall be.

It must have been a peculiarly trying time for the women who had to flee from their homes just when they needed quiet and rest. How thoughtful and tender was our compassionate Savior in thus sympathizing with suffering mothers in their hour of need! *Flight in the winter* or *on the sabbath day* would have been accompanied by special difficulties, so the disciples were exhorted to *pray* that some other time might be available. The Lord knew exactly when they would be able to escape, yet He told them to pray that their flight might not be in the winter, nor on the Sabbath day. The wise men of the present day would have said that prayer was useless under such conditions. Not so the great Teacher and Example of His praying people. He taught that such a season was the very time for special petition.

The reason for this injunction was thus stated by the Savior: *For then shall be great tribulation, such as was not since the beginning of the world to this time, no, nor ever shall be.* Read the record written by Josephus of the destruction of Jerusalem and see how truly our Lord's words were fulfilled. The Jews irreverently said, concerning the death of Christ, *His blood be on us, and on our children* (Matthew 27:25). Never did any other people invoke such an awful curse upon themselves and upon no other nation did such a judgment ever fall. We read of Jews crucified till there was no more wood for making crosses; of thousands of the people slaying one another in their fierce faction fights within the city; of so many of them being sold for slaves that they became a drug in the market, and all but valueless; and of the fearful carnage when the Romans at length entered the doomed capital; and the blood-curdling story exactly bears out the Savior's statement uttered nearly forty years before the terrible events occurred.

22. And except those days should be shortened, there should no flesh be saved: but for the elect's sake those days shall be shortened.

These were the words of the King as well as of the Prophet, and as such they were both authentic and authoritative. Jesus spoke of what *should be,* not only as the Prophet who was able to gaze into the future, but also as the sovereign Disposer of all events. He knew what a fiery trial awaited the unbelieving nation, and that *except those days should be shortened, there should no flesh be saved.* If the horrors of the siege were to continue long, the whole race of the Jews would be destroyed. The King had the power to cut short the evil days, and He explained His reason for using that power: *For the elect's sake those days shall be shortened.* Those who had been hated and persecuted by their own countrymen became the means of preserving them from absolute annihilation. Thus has it often been since those days and for the sake of His elect that the Lord has withheld many judgments and shortened others. The ungodly owe to the godly more than they know or would care to acknowledge.

23-26. Then if any man shall say unto you, Lo, here is Christ, or there; believe it not. For there shall arise false Christs, and false prophets, and shall shew

361

great signs and wonders; insomuch that, if it were possible, they shall deceive the very elect. Behold, I have told you before. Wherefore if they shall say unto you, Behold, he is in the desert; go not forth: behold, he is in the secret chambers; believe it not.

It is a grand thing to have such faith in Christ that you have none to spare for impostors. It is important not to distribute your faith too widely. Those who believe a little of everything will, in the end, believe nothing of anything. If you exercise full faith in that which is sure and steadfast, *false Christs and false prophets* will not be able to make you their fools. In one respect, the modern teachers of heresy are more successful than their Judean prototypes, for they do actually *deceive the very elect,* even though they cannot *shew great signs and wonders.* One of the saddest signs of the times in which we live is the ease with which *the very elect* are deceived by the smooth-tongued *false Christs and false prophets* who abound in our midst. Yet our Savior expressly forewarned His followers against them: *Behold, I have told you before.* Forewarned is forearmed. Let it be so in our case. Our Savior's expressive command may be appropriately applied to the whole system of *modern thought,* which is contrary to the inspired Word of God: *Believe it not.*

27. For as the lightning cometh out of the east, and shineth even unto the west; so shall also the coming of the Son of man be.

When He comes, we shall know who He is and why He has come. There will be no longer any mystery or secret about *the coming of the Son of man.* There will be no need to ask any questions then. No one will make a mistake about His appearing when it actually takes place. *Every eye shall see him* (Revelation 1:7). Christ's coming will be sudden, startling, universally visible, and terrifying to the ungodly, *as the lightning cometh out of the east, and shineth even unto the west.* His first coming to judgment at the destruction of Jerusalem had terrors about it that till then had never been realized on the earth. His last coming will be more dreadful still.

28. For wheresoever the carcase is, there will the eagles be gathered together.

Judaism had become a *carcase,* dead and corrupt, fit prey for the vultures or carrion-kites of Rome. By and by, there will arrive another day when there will be a dead church in a dead world and *the eagles* of divine judgment *will be gathered together* to tear in pieces those whom there shall be none to deliver. The birds of prey gather wherever dead bodies are to be found, and the judgments of Christ will be poured out when the body politic or religious becomes unbearably corrupt.

> *29-30. Immediately after the tribulation of those days shall the sun be darkened, and the moon shall not give her light, and the stars shall fall from heaven, and the powers of the heavens shall be shaken: and then shall appear the sign of the Son of man in heaven: and then shall all the tribes of the earth mourn, and they shall see the Son of man coming in the clouds of heaven with power and great glory.*

Our Lord appears to have purposely mingled the prophecies concerning the destruction of Jerusalem and His own second coming, so that there should be nothing in His words to satisfy idle curiosity, but everything to keep His disciples always on the watch for His appearing. These verses must apply to the coming of the King at the last great day. There may have been a partial fulfillment of them in *the tribulation* that came upon His guilty capital city, and the language of the Savior might have been taken metaphorically to set forth the wonders in *the heavens* and the woes on *the earth* in connection with that awful judgment. But we must regard Christ's words here as prophetic of the final manifestation of *the Son of man coming in the clouds of heaven with power and great glory.* There will be no further need of *the sun and the moon and the stars* when He who is brighter than the sun shines forth in all the glory of His Father and of His holy angels.

Christ's coming will be the source of untold joy to His friends, but it will bring unparalleled sorrow to His foes: *Then shall all the tribes of the earth mourn.* When Jesus comes, He will find the nations still unsaved, and horror will be their eternal portion.

> *31. And he shall send his angels with a great sound of a trumpet, and they shall gather together his elect from the four winds, from one end of heaven to the other.*

Our Lord's first concern when He comes again will be the security of *his elect.* He has gone to prepare a place for them, and when the place is ready and the time for their glorification has come, *he shall send his angels with a great sound of a trumpet, and they shall gather together his elect from the four winds, from one end of heaven to the other.*

> "East and west, and south and north,
> Speeds each glorious angel forth,
> Gathering in with glittering wing
> Zion's saints to Zion's King."

What a contrast between the gathering together of the eagles to devour the rotting carcass and the gathering together of Christ's elect at the great trumpet-summons of His holy angels! May every reader of these lines be in the latter company! Such will look forward with joy to the time of the King's appearing.

Matthew 24:32-41

The King Speaks of the Time of His Coming

32-35. Now learn a parable of the fig tree; When his branch is yet tender, and putteth forth leaves, ye know that summer is nigh: so likewise ye, when ye shall see all these things, know that it is near, even at the doors. Verily I say unto you, This generation shall not pass, till all these things be fulfilled. Heaven and earth shall pass away, but my words shall not pass away.

Our Lord here evidently returns to the subject of the destruction of Jerusalem and in these words gives His apostles warning concerning the signs of the times. He had recently used the barren fig tree as an object lesson; He now bids His disciples to *learn a parable of the fig tree and all the trees* (Luke 21:29). God's great book of nature is full of illustrations for those who have eyes to perceive them; and the Lord Jesus, the great Creator, often made use of its illuminated pages in conveying instruction to the minds of His hearers. On this occasion, He used a simple simile from the parable of the fig tree: *When his branch is yet tender, and putteth forth leaves, ye know that summer is nigh.*

They could not mistake so plain a token of the near return of summer, and Jesus would have them read quite as quickly the signs that were to herald the coming judgment on Jerusalem: *So likewise ye, when ye shall see all these things, know that it is near, even at the doors.* The Revised Standard Version has the words, *You know that he is near,* the Son of man, the King. His own nation rejected Him when He came in mercy, so His next coming would be a time of terrible judgment and retribution to His guilty capital city. Oh, that Jews and Gentiles today were wise enough to learn the lesson of that fiery trial and to seek His face, whose wrath they cannot bear!

The King left His followers in no doubt as to when these things would happen: *Verily I say unto you, This generation shall not pass, till all these things be fulfilled.* It was just about the ordinary limit of a generation when the Roman armies surrounded Jerusalem, whose measure of iniquity was then full and overflowed in misery, agony, distress, and bloodshed such as the world never saw before or has ever seen since. Jesus was a true prophet. Everything that He foretold was literally fulfilled. He confirmed what He had already said and what He was about to say, by a solemn affirmation: *Heaven and earth shall pass away, but my words shall not pass away.*

The word of the Lord endureth for ever (1 Peter 1:25), and though that Lord appeared in form as a man, and was shortly to be crucified as a criminal, His words would endure when heaven and earth would have fulfilled the purpose for which He had created them, and passed away.

Christ's promises of pardon are as sure of fulfillment as His prophecies of punishment. No word of His shall ever *pass away.*

36. But of that day and hour knoweth no man, no, not the angels of heaven, but my Father only.

There is a clear change in our Lord's words here, which clearly indicates that they refer to His last great coming to judgment: *But of that day and hour knoweth no man.* Some would-be prophets have wrested this verse from its evident meaning by saying, "Though we do not know the day and the hour of Christ's coming, we may know the year, the month, and even the week." If this method of treating the words of Jesus is not blasphemous, it is certainly foolish, and it reveals disloyalty to the King.

He added that, not only does no man know of that day and hour, but it is hidden from angelic beings also: *No, not the angels of heaven, but my Father only.* We need not therefore be troubled by idle prophecies of hairbrained fanatics, even if they claim to interpret the Scriptures, for what the angels do not know has not been revealed to them. Even Christ, in His human nature, so voluntarily limited His own capacities that He knew not the time of His Second Advent (Mark 13:32). It is enough for us to know that He will surely come. Our great concern should be to be ready for His appearing whenever He shall return.

> *37-39. But as the days of Noe were, so shall also the coming of the Son of man be. For as in the days that were before the flood they were eating and drinking, marrying and giving in marriage, until the day that Noe entered into the ark, and knew not until the flood came, and took them all away; so shall also the coming of the Son of man be.*

Though the King did not reveal the time of *the coming of the Son of man,* He declared plainly that history would repeat itself, and that *that day* would be *as the days of Noe were.* When He comes, He will find many unprepared, even as the antediluvians were when *the flood came, and took them all away.* Yet in both cases, sinners will have had ample warning. Noah was *a preacher of righteousness* (2 Peter 2:5) to the men of his day: *And this gospel of the kingdom shall be preached in all the world for a witness unto all nations; and then shall the end come* (Matthew 24:14). Christ's coming, like the flood, will be sudden, unexpected, universal in its effects, and terrible to the ungodly, although they will be utterly unconcerned, *eating and drinking, marrying and giving in marriage, until the day.*

That which is lawful and right, under other circumstances, becomes a positive evil when it takes the place of preparation for the coming of the Son of Man. Woe unto those whose eating and drinking do not include the bread and the water of life, and who marry or are given in marriage, but not to the heavenly Bridegroom! That *Dies Irae* ("Day of Wrath") will be a dreadful day for sinners.

"Day of judgment, day of wonders!
Hark, the trumpet's awful sound,
Louder than a thousand thunders,
Shakes the vast creation round!
How the summons will
The sinner's heart confound!"

40-41. Then shall two be in the field; the one shall be taken, and the other left. Two women shall be grinding at the mill; the one shall be taken, and the other left.

The division between the godly and the ungodly, at the coming of Christ, will be very precise. Companions in labor will be separated forever in *that day*: *Then shall two be in the field,* ploughing, sowing, reaping, or resting; *the one shall be taken, and the other left.* The believing laborer shall be taken by the angels to join the hosts of the redeemed, while his unbelieving fellow workman shall be left to the judgment that will swiftly be poured out upon him. *Two women shall be grinding at the mill.* They may be fellow servants in a rich man's mansion or they may be mother and daughter or two sisters in a poor man's home, but however closely they may have been attached to one another, if one is saved by grace and the other is still under the sentence of condemnation, *the one shall be taken, and the other left.* This separation will be eternal. There is no hint of any future reunion.

Matthew 24:42-51

The King Commands His Servants to Watch

42. Watch therefore: for ye know not what hour your Lord doth come.

This is the practical conclusion of the whole matter. That our Lord is coming is certain. That His coming may be at any moment is a matter of faith, and that we are ignorant of the time of His coming is a matter of fact: *Ye know not what hour your Lord doth come.* Christ's words are in the present tense. He does not say, "Ye know not what hour your Lord *will* come," but, *what hour your Lord **doth** come* (emphasis added), as if to keep us always expecting Him; and lest we should not heed His words, He puts the command in the plainest language: *Watch therefore*. The title that He uses gives additional force to the command to His disciples to watch, for it is our *Lord* who is coming quickly.

> *43-44. But know this, that if the goodman of the house had known in what watch the thief would come, he would have watched, and would not have suffered his house to be broken up. Therefore be ye also ready: for in such an hour as ye think not the Son of man cometh.*

If the householder has reliable information that a thief is coming, but does not know at what hour he will arrive, he will keep awake all night, waiting for his appearance; but if *the goodman of the house* is told *in what watch the thief* will come, he will be specially on the alert at that time. Every little sound will attract his attention. He thinks he hears someone at the back door. No, the thief is trying to enter by a front window! Wherever he comes, he will find that the master's ear is listening, the master's eye is watching, and the master's hand is ready to arrest him, for he had received timely warning of the housebreaker's coming. Men act thus wisely with regard to burglars; what a pity they are not equally wise in watching for the coming of their Lord! We do not know, we cannot even guess, in what watch of earth's long night He will come: *In such an hour as ye think not the Son of man cometh*. There is the present tense again: *The Son of man cometh*; He is coming. His own words are, *Behold, I come quickly* (Revelation 22:12).

Christ's coming to the world will be like that of the thief, when it is not suspected or expected, and therefore when due preparations for His reception have not been made; but His true followers will not let *that day overtake [them] as a thief* (1 Thessalonians 5:4). They ought ever to be looking for His appearing. Our Lord's injunction to His disciples ought to have even greater weight with us who live so much nearer to the time of His Second Advent than it had with those to whom He addressed His warning words, *Therefore be ye also ready*. We ought to be as watchful as if we knew that Christ would come tonight, because, although we do not know when He will come, we do know that He may come at any moment. Oh, to be ready for His appearing, watching and waiting for Him as servants whose Lord has been long away from them and who may return at any hour! This will not make us neglect our daily calling. On the contrary, we shall be all the more diligent in attending to our earthly duties because our hearts are at rest about our heavenly treasures.

45-46. Who then is a faithful and wise servant, whom his lord hath made ruler over his household, to give them meat in due season? Blessed is that servant, whom his lord when he cometh shall find so doing.

The apostles were *stewards of the mysteries of God* (1 Corinthians 4:1) and *good stewards of the manifold grace of God* (1 Peter 4:10). One great qualification for a steward was that he should be found *faithful* both to *his lord* and to all in the *household* over whom he was *made ruler.* It was necessary also that he should be *wise* in his dealings with his fellow servants, for, notwithstanding the honor put upon him, he was still a *servant,* who must give to his lord an account of his stewardship. These words describe the service of a minister, preaching the truth with all his heart and seeking *to give meat in due season* to all over whom the Holy Spirit has made him an overseer. Or they picture a teacher, endeavoring to feed the minds of the young with sound doctrine, or they portray any servant of Christ, whatever his calling may be, doing the work that his Master has appointed for him, just as he would wish to do it if he knew that his Lord was coming at that moment to examine it: *Blessed is that servant whom his lord when he cometh shall find so doing.* Such a servant of Christ is blessed. He is a happy man to be found by his Lord *so doing.* May our Master find us thus occupied when He comes!

47. Verily I say unto you, That he shall make him ruler over all his goods.

His lord had formerly made him *ruler over his household,* the steward who had charge of all the household servants. His faithful and wise conduct in that office won for him promotion to a higher post, so that his lord resolved to *make him ruler over all his goods.* Thus is it among the servants of King Jesus: there are rewards for faithful service not of debt, but of grace; not according to the rule of the Law, but according to the discipline of the house of God and the higher rule of love.

It should be noted that faithfulness in one form of service is rewarded by further service and increased responsibility. The servant, whose pound gained ten pounds, received authority over ten cities (Luke 19:17).

> *48-51. But and if that evil servant shall say in his heart, My lord delayeth his coming; and shall begin to smite his fellowservants, and to eat and drink with the drunken; the lord of that servant shall come in a day when he looketh not for him, and in an hour that he is not aware of, and shall cut him asunder, and appoint him his portion with the hypocrites: there shall be weeping and gnashing of teeth.*

This man was a *servant,* so that we have here a warning, not to the outside world, but to those who are inside the church of Christ and who profess to be servants of God. This is also specially a warning to ministers of the Word, those who are made rulers over God's household. This man, though a servant, was an *evil servant,* a hypocrite, one who had intruded into an office that he had no right to occupy. His thoughts and words were evil: *If that evil servant shall say in his heart, My lord delayeth his coming.* His conduct towards those put under him was evil: *And shall begin to smite his fellowservants.* His own life was evil: *And to eat and drink with the drunken.* His evildoing would be suddenly cut short by his master's appearance: *The lord of that servant shall come in a day when he looketh not for him, and in an hour that he is not aware of.* Immediate and terrible punishment would be meted out to him: *And shall cut him asunder, and appoint him his portion with the hypocrites.* He was one of them. He pretended to be a servant of God when all the while he was a slave of Satan, serving self and sin. Let him go to his own company. He was really cut in two before: outwardly he was a follower of Christ, inwardly he served his own lusts, so to *cut him asunder* will only be a righteous perpetuation of his own double-faced character. Will that be the end of him? No, *there shall be weeping and gnashing of teeth.* What a *portion* for one who was numbered among God's servants! As we read of it, let us in deep humility remember the solemn injunction of the apostle: *Let him that thinketh he standeth take heed lest he fall* (1 Corinthians 10:12).

Matthew 25

Matthew 25:1-13

The King and His Marriage Procession

Our Lord was still seated with His disciples upon the Mount of Olives (see chapter 24, verse 3). The instructive parable that follows was spoken by Him in continuation of the discourse we have been considering. It is evidently intended to set forth, under a familiar figure of speech, the need of preparation for the King's glorious appearing when He comes to claim His bride. To those of us who will not be alive at Christ's Second Advent, the midnight cry, *Go ye out to meet Him* (Matthew 25:6), will sound forth at the hour of death.

> *1-2. Then shall the kingdom of heaven be likened unto ten virgins, which took their lamps, and went forth to meet the bridegroom. And five of them were wise, and five were foolish.*

According to Eastern custom, the bridegroom is represented as having gone to the house of his bride's father, from where he would escort his spouse to her future home. The parable opens at the point where some of his professed friends are waiting to join the procession and go in with him to the marriage feast. Thus is the nominal church of Christ waiting for the coming of the Lord. There did not seem to be much difference in the external appearance of the *ten virgins, which took their lamps, and went forth to meet the bridegroom.* They were all virgins, they all took their lamps, and they all went forth to meet the bridegroom. They all made a profession of attachment to him, which led them to separate themselves from their other companions and acquaintances so that they might go forth to meet him on his wedding night.

There was, however, a vital and essential difference between them: *Five of them were wise, and five were foolish.* Let us be inclined to hope that we are not to gather from our Lord's words that one-half of the professing church is composed of those whom He calls *foolish.* Yet our Savior would not have spoken of so great a proportion if there were not really a very large mixture of foolish professors with the wise possessors of the grace of God.

3. They that were foolish took their lamps, and took no oil with them.

They may have thought that, if they had lamps that were similar to those carried by others, it would be sufficient. Perhaps they judged that the secret store of oil, being unseen, was unnecessary. They were willing to carry a lamp in one hand, but to devote the other hand to the care of an oil flask was more than they were willing to do. It is the lack of the oil of grace that is the fatal flaw in many a professing person's lamp. Many have a name to live, but have not the life of God within their souls. They make a profession of attachment to Christ, but they have not the inward supply of the Spirit of grace to keep it up. There is a glitter or a flash, but there is no permanent light and there cannot be any, for although they have *lamps,* they have *no oil with them.*

4. But the wise took oil in their vessels with their lamps.

They had oil *in* their lamps and oil *with* their lamps. Lamps are of no use without oil, yet the oil needs the lamp or it will not be used. Grace should reveal its presence, faith in Christ should be declared, but it is worse than useless to make a profession of love to Christ unless there is a secret store of grace by which the external part of religion may be maintained even before the all-searching eye of the King Himself. Unless the Spirit of God be in us indeed and certainly, we may for a while make a fair show in the flesh, but the end will be the blackness of darkness forever.

5. While the bridegroom tarried, they all slumbered and slept.

How sadly true it is that in the history of Christ's church, genuine saints and mere professing persons have often *slumbered and slept* side by side! Those who have the oil of grace are not always wide awake to serve their Master and watch for His appearing. In the case of even true believers, the delay in Christ's coming causes disappointment, weariness, and lethargy, and His church falls fast asleep, when she ought to be watching for her Lord. As for the *foolish,* whether self-deceived or hypocrites, and there being no true life of God in the soul, after a while their apparent earnestness disappears and Satan drugs them into a fatal slumber.

> 6. *And at midnight there was a cry made, Behold, the bridegroom cometh; go ye out to meet him.*

That midnight cry, *Behold, the bridegroom cometh,* startled all the sleepers. It would be well if we all thought more of the great truth of our Lord's Second Advent. The more often it is preached, in due proportion with other revealed doctrines, the more likely will it be to arouse both slumbering possessors and sleeping professors of love to Christ. As the midnight of this present evil age approaches, there is increasing need for all to be bidden to listen for the clarion cry, *Go ye out to meet him.*

> 7. *Then all those virgins arose, and trimmed their lamps.*

The suddenness of the alarm made them all jump to their feet and begin to examine and trim their lamps. They could not go to meet the bridegroom without carrying a light, as that was an essential part of their preparation for joining the king's marriage procession. Those virgins who had *oil in their vessels with their lamps* soon finished their trimming and were ready to start, but those who had *lamps,* but *no oil,* were unable to perform the necessary trimming. It is a pity that any should have to be trimming their lamps when they come to die or when the sign of the Son of Man appears in the heavens; but if that work is attempted without the Spirit or the grace of God, it will be an eternal failure.

> 8. *And the foolish said unto the wise, Give us of your oil; for our lamps are gone out.*

They now began to value what they had formerly despised. They had been so foolish as to think that oil was unnecessary, and now they saw that it was the one thing necessary, thus their request to their wiser companions: *Give us of your oil.* They gave a dreadful reason for their request: *For our lamps are gone out,* or *going out.* The dry wick flickered awhile and then died out in darkness, like the snuff of a candle.

Those are terrible words: *Our lamps are gone out.* It is worse to have a lamp that has gone out than never to have had a lamp at all. *Our lamps are gone out.* The foolish virgins seemed to say, "We thought everything was ready for tonight, we even gloried in our lamps, we promised ourselves a bright future, and we thought all was well for our share in the marriage supper; but our lamps are gone out and we have no oil with which to supply them." May no reader of this page ever have to utter this bitter lament!

Those who are putting off their repentance till their dying hour are like these foolish virgins. Their folly has reached its utmost height. When the death-sweat lies cold on the brow, the neglected oil of grace will be valued. Then will come the despairing cry, "Send for a minister to pray for me. Get in some Christian people to see what they can do for me."

9. But the wise answered, saying, Not so; lest there be not enough for us and you: but go ye rather to them that sell, and buy for yourselves.

No believer has more grace than he needs; *the wise* virgins had no oil to give away. They gave the best advice they could under the circumstances, although it was of no avail: *Go ye rather to them that sell, and buy for yourselves.* There is a proper place where the oil can be bought at the right time. We are bidden to *buy the truth* (Proverbs 23:23). Grace is sold in God's market on gospel terms: *Without money and without price* (Isaiah 55:1), but when the midnight cry is heard, the day of grace has closed, and buying and selling are over forever.

10. And while they went to buy, the bridegroom came; and they that were ready went in with him to the marriage: and the door was shut.

Undoubtedly, there are deathbed repentances, but it is to be feared that, in the great majority of cases, people who wake up so late to a true conviction of their condition will find that, while they go to buy the long-despised grace, *the bridegroom* will come. The poor head may be so distracted with pain that the mind may not be able to catch the idea of what faith in Christ is. Mental capacity may wholly fail in that dread hour. The risk is so great that none but the fatally foolish will postpone till then the preparation for the King's coming.

They that were ready went in with him to the marriage. Their readiness consisted in having lighted lamps or flaming torches. Our preparation for death or Christ's coming is the possession of grace in the heart. *And the door was shut.* When that door is once shut, it will never be opened.

There are some who dote and dream about an opening of that door after death, for those who have died unrepentant, but there is nothing in the Scriptures to warrant such an expectation. Any larger hope than that revealed in the Word of God is a delusion and a snare.

> *11-12. Afterward came also the other virgins, saying, Lord, Lord, open to us. But he answered and said, Verily I say unto you, I know you not.*

The other virgins were not *ready* when the bridegroom came, and there is no hint in the parable that they were any more ready when they came and shouted at his closed door, "*Lord, Lord, open to us. We came to meet You; we carried lamps, we were with the other virgins. Lord, Lord, open to us!*" His answer sounded the death knell of any vain hope of admission that they might have cherished: *Verily, I say unto you, I know you not. If any man love God, the same is known of him* (1 Corinthians 8:3). The Good Shepherd says, *I know mine own, and mine own know me* (John 10:14, RSV). Those whom Jesus Christ knows in this sense, He loves, and they love Him because He has first loved them. The foolish virgins had professed to be the bridegroom's friends, yet they were proved to be not even his acquaintances. May none of us ever hear from the blessed lips of the heavenly Bridegroom that terrible death sentence: *I know you not!*

> *13. Watch therefore, for ye know neither the day nor the hour wherein the Son of man cometh.*

Our Lord again teaches His followers about the duty of watchfulness, as in chapter 24, verse 42, and repeats, in a slightly altered form, the reason previously given: *For ye know neither the day nor the hour wherein the Son of man cometh.* It is vain to say that we may find out the year, if not the day and hour, of Christ's coming. The time of the end is hidden and shall not be known until suddenly He shall appear *in the clouds of heaven with power and great glory* (Matthew 24:30). It should be our one great concern to be sure that we shall be ready to meet Him whenever He may come.

Matthew 25:14-30

The Parable of the Talents

14-15. For the kingdom of heaven is as a man travelling into a far country, who called his own servants, and delivered unto them his goods. And unto one he gave five talents, to another two, and to another one; to every man according to his several ability; and straightway took his journey.

Our Savior had been speaking of Himself as the heavenly Bridegroom, and now He compares Himself to *a man travelling into a far country.* The word *travelling* suggests that our Lord has only gone away for a season and that He will return when His purpose in going into the *far country* is accomplished. When He went back from earth to heaven, it was a long journey, but He did not leave His servants without necessary supplies during His absence. He *called his own servants,* his bondservants, his household servants, *and delivered unto them his goods.* The servants were his, and the goods also were his. His slaves could not claim as their own either their persons or their possessions; all belonged to their lord and were to be used for him.

He did not entrust to all the same quantity of goods: *Unto one he gave five talents, to another two, and to another one; to every man according to his several ability.* He was the judge of the ability of each of his servants and he made no mistake in his allotment of the talents to them. We may rest assured, if we are the Lord's servants, that He has bestowed upon us as many talents as we can rightly use and quite as many as we shall be able to account for when He returns. The all-important matter for us is to be faithful to the trust committed to us.

And straightway took his journey. Our Lord knew all that was to happen before He left the earth – His passion, crucifixion, and resurrection – but He calmly talked of it as a man might speak of his preparations for traveling into a foreign country. He has gone and His servants are left behind to make the best use they can of His ascension-gifts while He is absent.

This parable, like that of the ten virgins, has to do with real and nominal Christians, with all who are or who profess to be the servants of Christ. The *talents* are anything and everything that our Lord has given to us for use here as His stewards.

> *16-18. Then he that had received the five talents went and traded with the same, and made them other five talents. And likewise he that had received two, he also gained other two. But he that had received one went and digged in the earth, and hid his lord's money.*

It is very significant that our Savior said that *he that had received one went and digged in the earth, and hid his lord's money.* Many who have *five talents* or *two* have not *traded with the same,* and so gained *other five* or *other two,* but Jesus knew that it was the servant with one talent who was most exposed to the temptation to do nothing because he could only do a little. There are perils connected with the possession of five talents or two, but the man who has only one talent is in equal, if not greater, danger. Let us all remember that, as it is a sin to hide one talent in the earth, it is a greater sin to hide two or five talents. It was *his lord's money* that the slothful servant hid. It would have been wrong to bury what belonged to himself, but he was doubly blameworthy in hiding that which had been entrusted to him by his lord, instead of trading with it so as to increase it. Are any of us thus sinning against our Savior?

> *19. After a long time the lord of those servants cometh, and reckoneth with them.*

There is a reckoning-day coming, even though *a long time* may elapse before *the lord of those servants cometh.* Jesus is coming back from the far country where He has gone. His own word is, *Behold, I come quickly* (Revelation 3:11). We must not leave this great fact out of our reckoning, and as His stewards, we must be prepared at any moment for Him to come and reckon with us as to the talents with which He has endowed each of His servants.

> *20-21. And so he that had received five talents came and brought other five talents, saying, Lord, thou deliveredst unto me five talents: behold, I have gained beside them five talents more. His lord said unto him, Well done, thou good and faithful servant: thou hast been faithful over a few things, I will make thee ruler over many things: enter thou into the joy of thy lord.*

Have all of us, who *received five talents* from our Lord, *gained beside them five talents more*? I think not. Have we double the grace we had at first? Twice the tact with which we began our service for God? Twofold adaptation to the work He has given us to do? It was so with this servant and therefore his lord commended and rewarded him. There was no proportion between his service and its reward: *Thou hast been faithful over a few things, I will make thee ruler over many things.* He who is faithful to his Lord shall have greater opportunities of proving his loyalty and devotion in a higher sphere, and in addition, he shall share the bliss of his Lord's return: *Enter thou into the joy of thy lord.* This is not the servant's portion, but the Master's portion shared with His faithful servants. This will be the consummation of all heavenly delights, not so much that we shall have a joy of our own, as that we shall enter into the joy of our Lord.

> *22-23. He also that had received two talents, came and said, Lord, thou deliveredst unto me two talents: behold, I have gained two other talents beside them. His lord said unto him, Well done, good and faithful servant; thou hast been faithful over a few things, I will make thee ruler over many things: enter thou into the joy of thy lord.*

This servant's commendation and reward are exactly the same as those given to his more highly privileged brother, as if our Savior would teach us that it is not the number of our talents, but the use we make of them, that is the essential matter. He does not expect as much from the man with two talents as from the one to whom He has given five. What He does expect is that they should both be faithful over the few things He has committed to their care. It was so with the two servants mentioned in the parable. The second had doubled the capital received from his lord, even as the first had done with his larger amount of trust-money. Therefore, they were equally praised and blessed.

24-25. Then he which had received the one talent came and said, Lord, I knew thee that thou art an hard man, reaping where thou hast not sown, and gathering where thou hast not strawed: and I was afraid, and went and hid thy talent in the earth: lo, there thou hast that is thine.

At the day of reckoning, the unfaithful as well as the faithful have to give account of their stewardship. This man's words were self-contradictory and his excuse was self-condemnatory. He said that he knew that his lord was a hard man, reaping where he had not sown, and gathering where he had not strawed, yet he confessed that the talent he brought back had been given to him by this master whom he represented as severe and unreasonable. He also admitted that it was his lord's money that he had hidden in the earth: *Thy talent.* It was entrusted to him and yet even the servant acknowledged that it did not belong to him: "*Lo, there thou hast that is thine.* I have not made any addition to thy talent, but I have not lost it, nor given it away. I have brought it back; lo, there it is." He seemed to speak as though this was all that could be rightly expected of him. Yet he was evidently not satisfied with himself, for he said, *I was afraid, and went and hid thy talent in the earth.* See how fear may become the mother of presumption. Faith in God produces holy fear, but humble fear is the parent of doubt, which in its turn has a family of unbelieving rebels.

26-27. His lord answered and said unto him, Thou wicked and slothful servant, thou knewest that I reap where I sowed not, and gather where I have not strawed: thou oughtest therefore to have put my money to the exchangers, and then at my coming I should have received mine own with usury.

His lord took the *wicked and slothful servant* on his own ground and condemned him out of his own mouth. The master did not mean to admit that he was such a one as he had been called by the *malicious and lazy slave,* as the original might be literally rendered, but supposing the servant's words had been true, what ought he to have done? If he was afraid to trade with his lord's talent on his own responsibility, he might have taken it to the bankers, who would at least have kept it secure and added interest to it while it was deposited with them.

If we cannot trade directly and personally on our Lord's account, if we have not the skill or the tact to manage a society or an enterprise for Him, we may at least contribute to what others are doing and join our capital to theirs, so that, by some means, our Master may have the interest to which He is entitled. His talent must not be buried in the earth, but must be invested wherever it will bring to Him the best return at His coming.

> *28-30. Take therefore the talent from him, and give it unto him which hath ten talents. For unto every one that hath shall be given, and he shall have abundance: but from him that hath not shall be taken away even that which he hath. And cast ye the unprofitable servant into outer darkness: there shall be weeping and gnashing of teeth.*

The servant who had gained five talents to his lord's five was allowed to keep them all, for his master spoke of *him which hath ten talents.* The unused talent of the slothful servant was also given to him, for he who uses well that which is entrusted to him shall receive more. He who has faith shall have more faith. He who has a taste for divine things shall develop a greater appetite for them. He who has some understanding of the mysteries of the kingdom shall understand them more fully: *For unto every one that hath shall be given, and he shall have abundance.*

To lose the talent that had remained idle was only a small part of the doom of *the unprofitable servant.* His lord ordered him to be *cast into outer darkness,* and his punishment is indicated by that oft-repeated refrain of our Savior's revelation of the horrors that await lost souls: *There shall be weeping and gnashing of teeth.* If we give any description of the world to come that is at all terrible, we are supposed to have borrowed it from Dante or Milton, but the most awful and painful descriptions of hell that ever fell from human lips do not exceed the language of the loving Christ Himself. He is the true lover of men who faithfully warns them concerning the eternal woe that awaits the unrepentant, while he who paints the miseries of hell as though they were but trivial is seeking to murder men's souls under the claim of friendship.

Matthew 25:31-46

The Royal and Universal Judge

Here we have the King's own description of the day of judgment, and in the solemn silence of our spirits, we may well put off our shoes from our feet as we draw near to this holy ground.

31. When the Son of man shall come in his glory, and all the holy angels with him, then shall he sit upon the throne of his glory.

Our Savior had a wonderful series of contrasts passing before His eye as He uttered this sublime prophecy.

Within three days He was to be crucified, yet He spoke of the time *when the Son of man shall come in his glory.* He had with Him a little company of disciples, one of whom would betray Him, another would deny Him, and all would forsake Him; yet by faith He saw the heavenly entourage that would accompany Him at His coming: *And all the holy angels with him.* Wearied and worn with His labors and saddened because of the hardness of men's hearts and the impending doom of Jerusalem, He sat on the slope of the Mount of Olives, but His thoughts were projected across the ages as He told His hearers of the glorious throne He would occupy in the day when He would return as the royal and universal Judge of mankind: *Then shall he sit upon the throne of his glory.* The great white throne shall be set on high, all pure and lustrous, bright and clear as a polished mirror, in which every man shall see himself and his sins reflected, and on that throne shall sit *the Son of man.* Behind the Kingly Judge, *all the holy angels* shall be grouped, rank on rank, an innumerable and glorious bodyguard, to grace the court of their enthroned Lord on the day of the last great judicial inquest, and at His bidding to remove from His presence all whom He shall condemn.

32-33. And before him shall be gathered all nations: and he shall separate them one from another, as a shepherd divideth his sheep from the goats: and he shall set the sheep on his right hand, but the goats on the left.

In the last great day of the Lord, all nations that have ever existed on the face of the globe shall be gathered before the judgment seat of Christ. The earth, which is now becoming more and more one vast graveyard or *charnel house* ("a building or chamber in which bodies or bones are deposited"), shall yield up her dead, and the sea itself, transformed into a solid pavement, shall bear upon its bosom the millions who lie hidden in its gloomy caverns. All mankind will be assembled before their Judge, *and every eye shall see him, and they also which pierced him: and all kindreds of the earth shall wail because of him* (Revelation 1:7). At first they will be gathered together in one diverse mass, but the myriad multitude will speedily be divided into two companies: *And he shall separate them one from another.* The King will be the divider in that dread day. How He will separate them, no one can tell, except that it will be *as a shepherd divideth his sheep from the goats.* Not one goat will be left among the sheep, nor one sheep with the goats. The division will be very close and personal: *One from another.* They will not be separated into nations, nor even into families, but each individual will be allotted his or her proper place among the sheep or among the goats.

And he shall set the sheep on his right hand, but the goats on the left.

There will be only two companies: one on the right hand of the Judge and the other on His left. The Lord Jesus Christ *shall judge the quick and the dead at his appearing* (2 Timothy 4:1), and all who will be summoned before His dread tribunal will be either alive from the dead or still dead in trespasses and sins. There will be no middle company in that day, as in God's sight there is no third class even now. All our names are either in the Lamb's Book of Life or in the Judge's Book of Death.

Some have taught that the judgment here foretold is that of the professing church and not of the whole world. There may be some ground for their belief, yet it seems impossible to apply the full meaning of our Savior's majestic words to any scene except the general judgment of the whole human race.

34. Then shall the King say unto them on his right hand, Come, ye blessed of my Father, inherit the kingdom prepared for you from the foundation of the world.

Turning first to the chosen company on His right hand, the *great multitude, which no man could number* (Revelation 7:9), the King will say to them, *Come.* They had accepted His previous invitation, *Come unto me* (Matthew 11:28), and now He gives them another and a more glorious *Come,* which was, however, included in the former one, for when He said, *I will give you rest* (Matthew 11:28), heaven itself was promised to them. The King calls His loved ones by a choice name: *Ye blessed of my Father.* We shall not know what bliss that title implies until we hear it from our Savior's lips, and even then we shall only begin to understand what we shall continue to enjoy throughout eternity.

All true believers are joint heirs with Jesus Christ, so the King will next say to them, *Inherit the kingdom prepared for you from the foundation of the world.* The *inheritance incorruptible, and undefiled, and that fadeth not away* (1 Peter 1:4) is the inalienable right of all who are made kings and priests unto God, and that which has been prepared for them from the foundation of the world must be possessed by them when the world itself has answered the end of its creation and has been burned up.

35-36. For I was an hungred, and ye gave me meat: I was thirsty and ye gave me drink: I was a stranger, and ye took me in: naked, and ye clothed me: I was sick, and ye visited me: I was in prison, and ye came unto me.

The King dwells with great delight upon the details of His servants' kindnesses to Himself. Are we then, after all, to be saved by our works? By no means. Yet our works are the evidences of our being saved. If our actions are such as Christ will commend at the day of judgment, they prove that we are saved by grace and that the Holy Spirit has worked effectively in us and through us. The services mentioned by the King were all rendered to Himself: *I was an hungred, and ye gave me meat: I was thirsty and ye gave me drink: I was a stranger, and ye took me in: naked, and ye clothed me: I was sick, and ye visited me: I was in prison, and ye came unto me.* There is no mention of what the righteous had said or of what profession of love to Christ they had made. The commendation was for what the King declared they had actually done by way of ministering unto Him.

37-39. Then shall the righteous answer him, saying, Lord, when saw we thee an hungred, and fed thee? or thirsty, and gave thee drink? When saw we thee a stranger, and took thee in? or naked, and clothed thee? Or when saw we thee sick, or in prison, and came unto thee?

They will bashfully disclaim the praise pronounced by the King. They had no idea that there was anything commendable in what they had done. They never dreamed of being rewarded for it. When the saints stand before the judgment seat, the bare thought of there being any excellence in what they have done will be new to them, for they have formed a very lowly estimate of their own performances. They fed the hungry, clothed the naked, visited the sick, all for Christ's sake, because it was the sweetest thing in the world to do anything for Jesus. They did it because they delighted to do it, because they could not help doing it, because their new nature drove them to do it.

40. And the King shall answer and say unto them, Verily I say unto you, Inasmuch as ye have done it unto one of the least of these my brethren, ye have done it unto me.

Christ has much more to do with His brethren's sorrow than we sometimes think. Are they hungry? He puts it, *I was an hungred.* Do they thirst? He says, *I was thirsty.* The sympathy of Christ is continuous, and down through the ages He will perpetually incarnate Himself in the suffering bodies of His tested and afflicted people, thus, the opportunity of doing Him service so long as we are here.

41. Then shall he say also unto them on the left hand, Depart from me, ye cursed, into everlasting fire, prepared for the devil and his angels.

Every word in the King's sentence upon those on His left hand will strike terror into their hearts. *Depart from me.* To be banished from Christ's presence is hell. *Ye cursed.* They could not plead that they had either kept the Law or obeyed the gospel. They were indeed doubly cursed. They were commanded to depart *into everlasting fire, prepared for the devil and his angels.* They had joined the devil in refusing allegiance to the Lord, so it was only right that, imitating his rebellion, they should share his punishment.

42-43. For I was an hungred, and ye gave me no meat: I was thirsty, and ye gave me no drink: I was a stranger, and ye took me not in: naked, and ye clothed me not: sick, and in prison, and ye visited me not.

Two little words – *no* and *not* – explain the difference between *their* conduct and that of the righteous. To those on His right hand, the King will say, *I was an hungred, and ye gave me meat;* but to those on His left hand, He will say, *Ye gave me no meat.* This omission on their part was no small matter. It was fatal and it was visited with the eternal death sentence: *Depart from me.* Men may think lightly now of their lack of love to Christ and their neglect to care for His poor brethren, but their conduct will appear in another light in the blaze of the last great day. Yet, even then, some will try to justify themselves.

44. Then shall they also answer him, saying, Lord, when saw we thee an hungred, or athirst, or a stranger, or naked, or sick, or in prison, and did not minister unto thee?

What a deceiver is sin! How presumptuous, that even in the presence of the omniscient Judge, it denies its own real character and makes its followers pretend to have attained to the divine standard of holiness!

45. Then shall he answer them, saying, Verily I say unto you, Inasmuch as ye did it not to one of the least of these, ye did it not to me.

Our Lord does not mean to teach that men will be condemned because they have not been charitable to the poor and needy, or that they will be saved if they are generous and openhanded. That would indeed be salvation by works, to be boasted of to all eternity. He does mean that only those who produce such fruit as this prove that *the root of the matter* (Job 19:28) is in them; by ministering to His poor brethren, out of love to Him, they show that they are the subjects of that distinguishing grace that makes them differ from others. All our future depends upon our relationship to the Lord Jesus Christ.

46. And these shall go away into everlasting punishment: but the righteous into life eternal.

Everlasting and *eternal* are different translations of the same Greek word. The one is no more temporary or terminable than the other. In heaven, *the righteous* will be forever anticipating future bliss while enjoying present perfect happiness; and in hell, the unrighteous will be ever looking forward to *the wrath to come* (Matthew 3:7) while enduring what our Savior here describes as *everlasting punishment* in *everlasting fire* (Matthew 25:41). Between heaven and hell there is a great gulf fixed, an awful abyss that cannot be crossed, so that the separation between the sheep and the goats will be eternal and unalterable. God grant that none of us may be on the wrong side of that great gulf!

Matthew 26

Matthew 26:1-5

The King Prophesying – His Enemies Plotting

1-2. And it came to pass, when Jesus had finished all these sayings, he said unto his disciples, Ye know that after two days is the feast of the passover, and the Son of man is betrayed to be crucified.

Our Lord, having finished all these sayings about the destruction of Jerusalem, His own Second Advent, and the great day of judgment, brought back the thoughts of His disciples to His own death. He had often foretold what the end of His life would be. He now states definitely when it would be: *Ye know that after two days is the feast of the passover.* In a sense that they probably did not fully comprehend, the Passover, the one great Passover, was about to be observed. After two days, the Paschal Lamb of God, *Christ our passover* (1 Corinthians 5:7), would be slain. His betrayal was so certain and so near that it might be spoken of as already accomplished: *The Son of man is betrayed to be crucified.* The time for Christ to be delivered up into the hands of sinners had almost arrived, and when once His enemies had Him in their power, they would never rest until He was crucified.

3-5. Then assembled together the chief priests, and the scribes, and the elders of the people, unto the palace of the high priest, who was called Caiaphas, and consulted that they might take Jesus by subtilty, and kill him. But they said, Not on the feast day, lest there be an uproar among the people.

While Jesus was prophesying, His enemies were plotting. Thus was fulfilled Psalm 2:2: *The rulers take counsel together against the LORD, and against his anointed.* Their aim was *that they might kill him,* but they *consulted* on how they might *take Jesus by subtilty.* They decided not to arrest Him *during the feast* (RSV), yet the evil deed was to be postponed, not from any religious regard for the Passover, but *lest there be an uproar among the people.* Their plan was contrary to Christ's prophecy, but the event proved that He was right and they were wrong, for He was crucified at the time He foretold.

Matthew 26:6-13

The King Anointed for His Burial

6-7. Now when Jesus was in Bethany, in the house of Simon the leper, there came unto him a woman having an alabaster box of very precious ointment, and poured it on his head, as he sat at meat.

We do not know who *Simon the leper* was, nor whether this *woman* was Mary, the sister of Lazarus, though I believe she was the one who came to Jesus, *having an alabaster box of very precious ointment, and poured it on his head, as he sat at meat.* The beauty of this woman's act consisted in this: that it was all for Christ. All who were in the house could perceive and enjoy the perfume of the precious ointment, but the anointing was for Jesus only.

8-9. But when his disciples saw it, they had indignation, saying, To what purpose is this waste? For this ointment might have been sold for much, and given to the poor.

When you do the best you can do, from the purest motives, and your Lord accepts your service, do not expect that your brethren will approve all your actions. If you do, you will be greatly disappointed. There was never a more beautiful proof of love to Christ than this anointing at Bethany, yet the disciples found fault with it, and *they had indignation, saying, To what purpose is this waste? For this ointment might have been sold for much, and given to the poor.* According to John's account, it was Judas who asked, *Why was not this ointment sold for three hundred pence, and given to the poor?* (John 12:5). The same evangelist gives the reason for the traitor's question: *This he said, not that he cared for the poor; but because he was a thief, and had the bag, and bare what was put therein* (John 12:6). The complaint having been started by Judas, others of the disciples joined in it. If this devoted and enthusiastic woman had waited for the advice of these wise people, she would neither have sold the ointment, nor poured it out. She did well to take counsel with her own loving heart and then to pour the precious nard upon that dear head that was so soon to be crowned with thorns. She thus showed that there was, at least, one heart in the world that thought nothing was too good for her Lord, and that the best of the best ought to be given to Him. May she have many imitators in every age until Jesus comes again!

10. When Jesus understood it, he said unto them, Why trouble ye the woman? for she hath wrought a good work upon me.

She had been very happy in the act; probably it was the happiest hour in all her life when she gave this costly gift to the Lord she loved so well. But a cloud passed over her bright face as the whispered complaints reached her ears. Jesus perceived that the murmuring of the disciples troubled the woman, so He rebuked them and commended her: *Why trouble ye the woman? for she hath wrought a good work upon me.* She did something we cannot do, for Christ is not now here in person, to be anointed by those who love Him as this woman did. We can perform good works upon others for His sake, and He will accept them as though they were done unto Himself.

11. For ye have the poor always with you; but me ye have not always.

Our Lord always cared for the poor. He was Himself poor. He was the poor people's Preacher. He fed the hungry poor and healed the sick poor. He would always have His people show their love to Him by caring for the poor, but He had reached the one occasion in His life when it was appropriate that something should be done specially for Himself, and this woman, by the intuition of love, did that very thing. Oh, that we might all love Christ as intensely as she did!

12-13. For in that she hath poured this ointment on my body, she did it for my burial. Verily I say unto you, Wheresoever this gospel shall be preached in the whole world, there shall also this, that this woman hath done, be told for a memorial of her.

She probably did not know all that her action meant when she anointed her Lord for His burial. The consequences of the simplest action done for Christ may be much greater than we think. "Go you, my sister, and do what God tells you, and it shall be seen that you have done far more than you know. Obey the holy impulse within your spirit, my brother, and you may do ten thousand times more than you have ever imagined to be possible."

This woman's outburst of affection, this simplehearted act of love to Christ Himself, is one of those things that are to live as long as the gospel lives. The aroma of this loving deed is to continue as long as the world itself endures.

Matthew 26:14-16

The Betrayer's Bargain

14-16. Then one of the twelve, called Judas Iscariot, went unto the chief priests, and said unto them, What will ye give me, and I will deliver him unto you? And they covenanted with him for thirty pieces of silver. And from that time he sought opportunity to betray him.

What a contrast to the incident we have just been considering! The anointing of Jesus is to be the theme of admiration wherever the gospel is preached, but His betrayal by *Judas* will be a subject for condemnation to all eternity. It was *one of the twelve,* who *went unto the chief priests,* to bargain for the price of his Lord's betrayal. He did not even mention Christ's name in his infamous question: *What will ye give me, and I will deliver him unto you?* The amount agreed upon, *thirty pieces of silver,* was the price of a slave, and it showed how little value the chief priests set upon Jesus, and it also revealed the greed of Judas in selling his Master for so small a sum. Yet many have sold Jesus for a lesser price than Judas received; a smile or a sneer has been sufficient to induce them to betray their Lord.

Let us, who have been redeemed with Christ's precious blood, set high importance by Him, think much of Him, and praise Him much. As we remember, with shame and sorrow, these thirty pieces of silver, let us never undervalue Him or forget the priceless preciousness of Him who was reckoned as worth no more than a slave.

Matthew 26:17-30

The Last Passover and the New Memorial

17-18. Now the first day of the feast of unleavened bread the disciples came to Jesus, saying unto him, Where wilt thou that we prepare for thee to eat the passover? And he said, Go into the city to such a man, and say unto him, The Master saith, My time is at hand; I will keep the passover at thy house with my disciples.

How truly royal was Jesus of Nazareth even in His humiliation! He had no home of His own where He could *keep the passover* with His disciples. He was soon to be put to a public and shameful death, yet He had only to send two of His disciples *into the city to such a man,* and the guestchamber, furnished and prepared, was at once placed at His disposal. He did not take the room by arbitrary force, as an earthly monarch might have done, but He obtained it by the more divine compulsion of almighty love. Even in His lowest estate, our Lord Jesus had the hearts of all men beneath His control. What power He has now that He reigns in glory!

19. And the disciples did as Jesus had appointed them; and they made ready the passover.

If Christ's disciples always loyally *did as Jesus appointed them,* they would always succeed well on His errands. There are many more people in the world ready to yield to Christ than some of us think. If we would only go to them as Peter and John went to this man in Jerusalem and say to them what *the Master saith,* we would find that their hearts would be opened to receive Christ even as this man's house was willingly yielded up at our Lord's request.

20-21. Now when the even was come, he sat down with the twelve. And as they did eat, he said, Verily I say unto you, that one of you shall betray me.

Our Lord remained in seclusion until the evening and then went to the appointed place, and sat down, or rather, reclined at the Passover table with the twelve. *And as they did eat, he said, Verily I say unto you, that one of you shall betray me.* This was a most unpleasant thought to bring to a feast, yet it was most appropriate to the Passover, for God's commandment to Moses concerning the first paschal lamb was, *With bitter herbs they shall eat it* (Exodus 12:8). This was a painful reflection for our Lord and also for His twelve chosen companions: *One of you,* and His eyes would glance around the table as He said it: *One of you shall betray me.*

22. And they were exceeding sorrowful, and began every one of them to say unto him, Lord, is it I?

That short sentence fell like a bombshell among the Savior's body-guard. It startled them. They had all made great professions of affection for Him and for the most part, those professions were true. *And they were exceeding sorrowful,* and well they might be. Such a revelation was enough to produce the deepest emotions of sorrow and sadness. It is a beautiful trait in the character of the disciples that they did not suspect one another, but *every one of them* inquired, almost incredulously, as the form of the question implies: *Lord, is it I?* No one said, "Lord, is it Judas?" Perhaps no one of the eleven thought that Judas was cruel enough to betray the Lord who had given him an honorable place among His apostles.

We cannot do any good by suspecting our brethren, but we may do great service by suspecting ourselves. Self-suspicion is near akin to humility.

23-24. And he answered and said, He that dippeth his hand with me in the dish, the same shall betray me. The Son of man goeth as it is written of him: but woe unto that man by whom the Son of man is betrayed! it had been good for that man if he had not been born.

A man may get very near to Christ, alas, may dip his hand in the same dish with the Savior, and yet betray Him. We may be high in office and may apparently be very useful, as Judas was, yet we may betray Christ.

We learn from our Lord's words that divine decrees do not deprive a sinful action of its guilt: *The Son of man goeth as it is written of him: but woe unto that man by whom the Son of man is betrayed!* His criminality is just as great as though there had been no *determinate counsel and foreknowledge of God* (Acts 2:23). *It had been good for that man if he had not been born.* The doom of Judas is worse than nonexistence. To have consorted with Christ as he had done and then to deliver Him into the hands of His enemies sealed the traitor's eternal destiny.

25. Then Judas, which betrayed him, answered and said, Master is it I? He said unto him, Thou hast said.

Judas appears to have been the last of the twelve to ask the question, *Is it I?* Those who are the last to suspect themselves are usually those who ought to be the first to exercise self-suspicion. Judas did not address Christ as *Lord,* as the other disciples had done, but called Him Rabbi, *Master.* Otherwise, his question was like that of his eleven companions. But he received from Christ an answer that was given to no one else: *He said unto him, Thou hast said.* Probably the reply reached his ear alone and if he had not been a hopeless reprobate, this unmasking of his traitorous plan might have driven him to repentance; but there was nothing in his heart to respond to Christ's voice. He had sold himself to Satan before he sold his Lord.

26-28. And as they were eating, Jesus took bread, and blessed it, and brake it, and gave it to the disciples, and said, Take, eat; this is my body. And he took the cup, and gave thanks, and gave it to them, saying, Drink ye all of it; for this is my blood of the new testament, which is shed for many for the remission of sins.

The Jewish Passover was made to melt into the Lord's Supper, as the stars of the morning dissolve into the light of the sun. As they were eating, while the Passover supper was proceeding, Jesus instituted the new memorial that is to be observed until He comes again. How simple was the whole ceremony! *Jesus took bread, and blessed it, and brake it, and gave it to his disciples, and said, Take, eat; this is my body.* Christ could not have meant that the bread *was* His body, for His body was reclining by the table; but He intended that broken bread to *represent* His body that was about to be broken on the cross. Then followed the second memorial, *the cup,* filled with *the fruit of the vine* (Matthew 26:29), of which Christ said, *Drink ye all of it.* There is no trace here of any altar or priest. There is nothing about the elevation or adoration of the host. There is no resemblance between the Lord's Supper and the Roman Catholic Mass. Let us keep strictly to the letter and spirit of God's Word in everything, for if one adds a little, another will add more, and if one alters one point and another alters another point, there is no telling how far we shall get from the truth.

The disciples had been reminded of their own liability to sin, and now their Savior gives them a personal pledge of the pardon of sin, according to Luke's record of His words: *This cup is the new testament in my blood, which is shed for you* (Luke 22:20).

> *29. But I say unto you, I will not drink henceforth of this fruit of the vine, until that day when I drink it new with you in my Father's kingdom.*

Thus Jesus took the great Nazarite vow never to drink of the fruit of the vine till He should drink it new with His disciples in His Father's kingdom. He will keep His appointment with all His followers and they with Him shall hold a greater festival forever.

> *30. And when they had sung an hymn, they went out into the mount of Olives.*

Was it not truly brave of our dear Lord to sing under such circumstances? He was going forth to His last dread conflict, to Gethsemane, and Gabbatha, and Golgotha, yet He went with a song on His lips. He must have led the singing, for the disciples were too sad to start the Hallel with which the Passover feast closed: *And when they had sung an hymn, they went out into the mount of Olives.* Then came that desperate struggle in which the great Captain of our salvation wrestled even to a bloody sweat and prevailed.

Matthew 26:31-35

The King Again Prophesying – Peter Protesting

31-32. Then saith Jesus unto them, All ye shall be offended because of me this night: for it is written, I will smite the shepherd, and the sheep of the flock shall be scattered abroad. But after I am risen again, I will go before you into Galilee.

Observe our Lord's habit of quoting Scripture. He was able to speak words of infallible truth, yet He fell back upon the inspired record in the Old Testament. His quotation from Zechariah (chapter 13, verse 7) does not seem to have been really necessary, but it was most appropriate to His prophecy to His disciples: *All ye shall be offended because of me this night: for it is written, I will smite the shepherd, and the sheep of the flock shall be scattered abroad.* Jesus was the Shepherd who was about to be struck, and He foretold the scattering of the sheep. Even those leaders of the flock that had been first chosen by Christ and had been most with Him, would stumble and fall away from Him on that dread night, but the Shepherd would not lose them; there would be a reunion between Him and His sheep: *After I am risen again, I will go before you into Galilee.* Once again He would resume, for a little while, the character of their Shepherd-King and with them He would revisit some of their old havens in Galilee, before He ascended to His heavenly home. *I will go before you* suggests the idea of the Good Shepherd leading His flock after the Eastern manner. Happy are His sheep in having such a Leader and blessed are they in following Him wherever He goes.

33. Peter answered and said unto him, Though all men shall be offended because of thee, yet will I never be offended.

This was a very presumptuous speech, not only because of the self-confidence it betrayed, but also because it was a flat contradiction of the Master's declaration. Jesus said, *All ye shall be offended because of me this night,* but Peter thought he knew better than Christ, so he answered, *Though all men shall be offended because of thee, yet will I never be offended.* No doubt these words were spoken from his heart, but *the heart is deceitful above all things, and desperately wicked* (Jeremiah 17:9). Peter must have been amazed the next morning as he discovered the deceitfulness and wickedness of his own heart, as manifested in his triple denial of his Lord.

He who thinks himself so much stronger than his brethren is the very man who will prove to be weaker than any of them, as did Peter, not many hours after his boast was uttered.

34. Jesus said unto him, Verily I say unto thee, That this night, before the cock crow, thou shalt deny me thrice.

Jesus now tells his boastful disciple that, before the next morning's cockcrowing, he will three times deny his Lord. Not only would he stumble and fall with his fellow disciples, but he would also go beyond them all in his repeated denials of that dear Master whom he professed to love with more intense affection than even John possessed. Peter declared that he would remain true to Christ if he were the only faithful friend left. Jesus foretold that, of all the twelve, only Judas would exceed the boaster in wickedness.

35. Peter said unto him, Though I should die with thee, yet will I not deny thee. Likewise also said all the disciples.

Here again Peter contradicts his Master straight to His face. It was a pity that he should have boasted once after his Lord's plain prophecy that all the disciples would that night be offended because of Him, but it was shameful that Peter should repeat his self-confident declaration in the teeth of Christ's express prediction concerning him. He was not alone in his utterance, for *likewise also said all the disciples.* They all felt that under no circumstances could they deny their Lord. We have no record of the denial of Christ by the other ten apostles, although they *all forsook him, and fled* (Mark 14:50), and thus practically disowned Him. Remembering all that they had seen and heard of Him and especially bearing in mind His most recent discourses, the communion in the upper room, and His wonderful intercessory prayer on their behalf, we are not surprised that they felt themselves bound to Him forever. But, alas! notwithstanding their protests, the King's prophecy was completely fulfilled, for that night they were all *offended,* or were *caused to stumble* (Revised Version margin note), and Peter three times denied his Lord.

Matthew 26:36-46

The King beneath the Olive Trees

Here we come to the holy of holies of our Lord's life on earth. This is a mystery like that which Moses saw when the bush burned with fire and was not consumed. No man can rightly expound such a passage as this. It is a subject for prayerful, heartbroken meditation more than for human language. May the Holy Spirit graciously reveal to us all that we can be permitted to see of the King beneath the olive trees in the garden of Gethsemane!

> *36. Then cometh Jesus with them unto a place called Gethsemane, and saith unto the disciples, Sit ye here, while I go and pray yonder.*

Our Lord directed eight of His disciples to keep watch either outside or near the entrance of *Gethsemane,* which means "the olive press." This garden had been Christ's favorite place for private prayer and it was well selected as the scene of His last agonizing plea.

> "'Twas here the Lord of life appeared,
>   And sigh'd, and groan'd, and pray'd, and fear'd;
> Bore all incarnate God could bear,
>   With strength enough, and none to spare."

> *37-38. And he took with him Peter and the two sons of Zebedee, and began to be sorrowful and very heavy. Then saith he unto them, My soul is exceeding sorrowful, even unto death: tarry ye here, and watch with me.*

The three disciples who had been with him on the Mount of Transfiguration were privileged to be nearer to Him than the rest of their brethren, but even they could not be actually with Him. His sorrow was so great that He had to bear it alone, and there was also that Scripture to be fulfilled: *I have trodden the winepress alone; and of the people there was none with me* (Isaiah 63:3). Yet He would have His three choicest companions near Him so that He might derive such slight solace from their presence as they could convey to Him. They had never before seen their Lord overwhelmed with Atlantic billows of sorrow like those that rolled in upon Him as He *began to be sorrowful and very heavy.* He was bowed down as if an enormous weight rested on His soul, as indeed it did. This was the soul-agony, the soul-offering for sin, which was completed on the cross, and well might He say, *My soul is exceeding sorrowful, even unto death.* The sorrow of His soul was the very soul of His sorrow. His soul was full of sorrow, until He seemed to reach the utmost limit of endurance and to be at the very gate of death. In such dire distress, He needed faithful friends at hand, so He said to Peter, James, and John, *Tarry ye here, and watch with me.* He must bear alone the awful burden of His people's sin, but His disciples might show their sympathy with Him by watching at a respectful distance and adding their poor prayers to His mighty wrestlings. Alas! they did not prize the privilege Christ gave them. Have not we been too much like them when our Savior has bidden us to watch with Him?

39. And he went a little farther, and fell on his face, and prayed, saying, O my Father, if it be possible, let this cup pass from me: nevertheless not as I will, but as thou wilt.

Was He heard? Yes, truly, and especially in that which was the very core and marrow of His prayer: *Not as I will, but as thou wilt.* This was the vital part of His petition, its true essence, for as much as His human nature shrank from the *cup,* still more did He shrink from any thought of acting contrary to His Father's will. Christ's sense of sonship was clear and undimmed even in that dark hour, for He began His prayer with the filial utterance, *O my Father.*

40. And he cometh unto the disciples, and findeth them asleep, and saith unto Peter, What, could ye not watch with me one hour?

We cannot tell how long He had been wrestling alone in prayer, but it was long enough for the disciples to fall asleep. *Peter* had established himself as the spokesman of the company; therefore, to him our Lord addressed His gentle rebuke, which was meant also for his companions:

What, could ye not watch with me one hour? According to Mark 14:37, the question was put personally to Peter: *Simon, sleepest thou?* It was bad enough for James and John to be slumbering instead of watching, but after all Peter's boasting, it seemed worse in his case. He who had made the loudest protestations of devotion deserved to be the most blamed for his unfaithfulness.

41. Watch and pray, that ye enter not into temptation: the spirit indeed is willing, but the flesh is weak.

It was truly kind on Christ's part to find an excuse for His weak and weary disciples. It was just like Him to say anything that He could in their praise, even though they had slept when they ought to have been watching. Yet He repeated the command, *Watch,* for that was the special duty of the hour, and He added, *and pray,* for prayer would help them to watch, and watching would aid them in praying. Watching and praying were commanded for a special purpose: *That ye enter not into temptation.* He knew what hard temptations were about to attack them, so He would have them doubly armed by *watching unto prayer.*

42. He went away again the second time, and prayed, saying, O my Father, if this cup may not pass away from me, except I drink it, thy will be done.

These calm, simple words scarcely convey to our minds a full idea of the intense agony under which they were uttered. Luke mentions that our Savior, in His second petition, *prayed more earnestly: and his sweat was as it were great drops of blood falling down to the ground* (Luke 22:44). The tension upon His whole frame became so great that His life seemed to be oozing away through every pore of His body, and He was so weak and faint, through the terrible strain, that He might well fear that His human nature would sink under the awful trial and that He would die before His time. Yet even then He recognized His sonship: *O my Father!* and He absolutely surrendered Himself to His Father's will: *Thy will be done.*

43-44. And he came and found them asleep again: for their eyes were heavy. And he left them, and went away again, and prayed the third time, saying the same words.

Great sorrow produces different results in different persons. In the Savior's case, it aroused Him to an awful agony of earnestness in prayer. In the disciples' case, it sent them to sleep. Luke says that they were *sleeping for sorrow* (Luke 22:45). Their Master might find an excuse for their neglect, but oh! how they would blame themselves afterwards for missing that last opportunity of watching with their wrestling Lord! As He could get no comfort from them, *he left them, and went away again, and prayed the third time, saying the same words.* Those who teach that we should pray only once, and not repeat the petition that we present to the Lord, cannot quote our Savior's example in support of their theory, for three times on that dread night He offered the same petition and even used the same language. Paul also, like his Master, *besought the Lord thrice* (2 Corinthians 12:8) that the *thorn in the flesh, the messenger of Satan* (2 Corinthians 12:7) might depart from him.

> 45-46. *Then cometh he to his disciples, and saith unto them, Sleep on now, and take your rest: behold, the hour is at hand, and the Son of man is betrayed into the hands of sinners. Rise, let us be going: behold, he is at hand that doth betray me.*

I do not think Jesus was speaking ironically when he said, *Sleep on now, and take your rest,* but that He allowed them to take a little sleep while He sat by and watched. Not long did He sit or did they sleep, for through the olives He could see the glare of the approaching torches, and the stillness of the night was broken by the trampling and shouting of the rabble throng that had come to arrest Him. He gently wakened His drowsy disciples by saying, *Rise, let us be going,* adding words that must have struck terror to their sorrowing hearts: *Behold, he is at hand that doth betray me.* The crushing in *the olive press* was over. The long looked-for *hour* of betrayal had come, and Jesus went calmly forward, divinely strengthened to meet the terrible trials that yet awaited Him before He could fully accomplish the redemption of His chosen people.

Matthew 26:47-56

The King's Betrayal

47-49. And while he yet spake, lo, Judas one of the twelve, came, and with him a great multitude with swords and staves, from the chief priests and elders of the people. Now he that betrayed him gave them a sign, saying, Whomsoever I shall kiss, that same is he: hold him fast. And forthwith he came to Jesus, and said, Hail, master; and kissed him.

It is a remarkable fact that we do not read in the New Testament that any *one of the twelve*, except *Judas*, ever *kissed Jesus*. It seems as if the most disrespectful familiarity was very near akin to dastardly treachery. This *sign* of Judas was typical of the way in which Jesus is generally *betrayed*! When men intend to undermine the inspiration of the Scriptures, how do they begin their books? Why, always with a declaration that they wish to promote the truth of Christ!

Christ's name is often slandered by those who make a loud profession of attachment to Him and then sin foully as the chief of transgressors. There is the Judas-kiss first and the betrayal afterwards. Thus Judas said, *Hail, master, and kissed Him* **much** (emphasis added, RSV margin), betraying Him by the act that ought to have been the token of firmest friendship.

50. And Jesus said unto him, Friend, wherefore art thou come? Then came they, and laid hands on Jesus and took him.

The meek and lowly Jesus spoke not as any mere man might have done under such circumstances. He did not address Judas as, "Wretch!" or, "Heretic!" but His first word after receiving the traitor's kiss was, *Friend*! He did not denounce him as the vilest of mankind, but quietly said, *Wherefore art thou come?* or, *Do that for which you have come* (Revised Version). Right royally did our King behave in that rough hour. *Then came they, and laid hands on Jesus and took him.* He offered no resistance, although the whole multitude would have been powerless to seize Him unless He had been willing to be taken. They came to take Him, so He shielded His disciples from arrest while He yielded up Himself to His captors, saying, *If therefore ye seek me, let these go their way* (John 18:8). Jesus was always thoughtful of others. He was so in the garden and even when hanging on the cross.

> *51-52. And, behold, one of them which were with Jesus stretched out his hand, and drew his sword, and struck a servant of the high priest's, and smote off his ear. Then said Jesus unto him, Put up again thy sword into his place: for all they that take the sword shall perish with the sword.*

A good man's hand is never more out of place than when it is on the handle of a sword, yet there is always a tendency, even among Christians, to draw the sword from its sheath. It would have been far better if Peter's hands had been clasped in prayer. That act of cutting off the ear of Malchus helped to identify him as one who was with Christ in the garden and directly led to one of his denials of his Lord (John 18:26-27). The sword never helps to establish Christ's kingdom. All that is ever done by it will have to be undone. Brute force will throw down what brute force has built up.

> *53-54. Thinkest thou that I cannot now pray to my Father, and he shall presently give me more than twelve legions of angels? But how then shall the scriptures be fulfilled, that thus it must be?*

How royally our King speaks! He was the true Master of the situation. He had but to pray to His Father and *more than twelve legions of angels* would come flashing down from the court of heaven. Each timid disciple might have found himself captain of an angelic legion, while their Lord might have had as many more as He chose. There was, however, one difficulty in the way: *How then shall the scriptures be fulfilled, that thus it must be?* Jesus thought more of fulfilling the Scriptures than of being delivered from the hands of wicked men. Neither Jewish bands nor Roman ropes could have held Him captive if He had not been under the bond of a mightier force, even that eternal covenant into which He had entered on behalf of His people.

> *55. In that same hour said Jesus to the multitudes, Are ye come out as against a thief with swords and staves for to take me? I sat daily with you teaching in the temple, and ye laid no hold on me.*

Luke says that this question was put to *the chief priests, and captains of the temple, and the elders* (Luke 22:52). Yet even to them Jesus only addressed a mild complaint, instead of the terrible denunciation that their conduct deserved. It did seem a great farce for *multitudes with swords and staves* to go out from Jerusalem, at midnight, to arrest the *man of sorrows* (Isaiah 53:3), who would not allow one of His followers to draw a sword in His defense. Yet even His foes knew that He possessed extraordinary power if He only chose to exert it, and their numbers, arms, and authority were so many unconscious tributes to His royal dignity and might.

> 56. But all this was done, that the scriptures of the prophets might be fulfilled. Then all the disciples forsook him, and fled.

Our Lord's one great concern was that He might finish the work He had come to perform and that so *the scriptures of the prophets might be fulfilled.*

Jesus was not surprised that *all the disciples forsook him, and fled,* for He had foretold that they would do so. He knew them better than they knew themselves, so He prophesied that the flock would be scattered when the Shepherd would be struck. So it was, for when the fierce wolves came and seized Him, the sheep all fled.

It would have been to the eternal honor of any one of the disciples to have kept close to Christ right up to the end, but neither the loving John nor the boastful Peter stood the test of that solemn time. Human nature is such poor stuff, even at the best, that we cannot hope that any of us would have been braver or more faithful than the apostles were.

Matthew 26:57-68

The King before the Jewish High Priest

> 57. And they that had laid hold on Jesus led him away to Caiaphas the high priest, where the scribes and the elders were assembled.

Some of the chief priests and elders were so enraged against Christ that they went to Gethsemane with the Roman cohort that was sent to arrest Jesus. The rest of them met at the house of *Caiaphas the high priest,* waiting for their victim to be brought to them. It was night or early morning, but they were only too willing to sit up to judge the Lord of glory and put the King of Israel to shame.

58. But Peter followed him afar off unto the high priest's palace, and went in, and sat with the servants, to see the end.

Peter was not to be blamed because he *followed afar off,* for at first he and John were the only two disciples who followed their captive Master. John went with Jesus into *the high priest's palace,* and by his influence Peter was also admitted. Attracted by the fire, *Peter sat with the servants,* a dangerous place for him, as it soon proved. When a servant of Christ by his own choice sits with the servants of the wicked, sin and sorrow speedily follow.

59-61. Now the chief priests, and elders, and all the council, sought false witness against Jesus, to put him to death; but found none: yea, though many false witnesses came, yet found they none. At the last came two false witnesses, and said, This fellow said, I am able to destroy the temple of God, and to build it in three days.

The enemies of Jesus wanted *to put him to death.* They must therefore have at least two witnesses against Him, for by the law of Moses the evidence of one witness was not sufficient to convict any person accused of a crime deserving the death penalty. *The chief priests, and elders, and all the council, sought false witness, but found none* until *at the last came two false witnesses,* who wrested Christ's words and misrepresented His meaning, but even they did not agree in their testimony (Mark 14:59), and therefore Jesus could not be condemned.

62. And the high priest arose, and said unto him, Answerest thou nothing? what is it which these witness against thee?

What was the use of answering? There really was nothing to answer except palpable and willful misrepresentation. Our Lord also knew that the council had determined to put Him to death, and besides that, there was another prophecy to be fulfilled: *He is brought as a lamb to the slaughter, and as a sheep before her shearers is dumb, so he openeth not his mouth* (Isaiah 53:7).

> *63-64. But Jesus held his peace, And the high priest answered and said unto him, I adjure thee by the living God, that thou tell us whether thou be the Christ, the Son of God. Jesus saith unto him, Thou hast said: nevertheless I say unto you, Hereafter shall ye see the Son of man sitting on the right hand of power, and coming in the clouds of heaven.*

The time for Christ to speak had come. First, He answered the high priest's solemn adjuration and declared that He was *the Christ, the Son of God.* There was no longer any reason for concealing that fact. Then He uttered a prophecy that must have startled His accusers. He stood there bound, apparently alone and helpless before His powerful enemies, who expected soon to put Him to death, yet the Prophet-King declared that they would be witnesses of His future glory, and would see Him *sitting on the right hand of power, and coming in the clouds of heaven.* His hearers rightly understood Him to claim to be divine, and gladly do we acknowledge the justice of His claim.

> *65-66. Then the high priest rent his clothes, saying, He hath spoken blasphemy; what further need have we of witnesses? behold, now ye have heard his blasphemy. What think ye? They answered and said, He is guilty of death.*

If He had not been God incarnate, He would have been guilty of blasphemy and would have deserved to die. By the law of Moses, a blasphemer was to be stoned to death (Leviticus 24:16). Christ's works had proved that He was God, so His words were not those of a blasphemer, but His confession gave His enemies the opening they were seeking, and they declared Him to be unworthy to live: *They answered and said, He is guilty of death.* He had foretold that He would be crucified, whereas the punishment for blasphemy was death by stoning, so further forms of trial must be gone through before the end would come.

> *67-68. Then did they spit in his face, and buffeted him; and others smote him with the palms of their hands, saying, Prophesy unto us, thou Christ, Who is he that smote thee?*

Put together these two texts: *Then did they spit in his face,* and, I saw a great white throne, and him that sat on it, *from whose face the earth and the heaven fled away; and there was found no place for them* (Revelation 20:11). In the day of His humiliation, they struck Him and mocked Him, *saying, Prophesy unto us, thou Christ, Who is he that smote thee?* Unless they repented of their wickedness, the day will come when the divine Judge will point out each one of them who then abused Him and He will say, *Thou art the man* (2 Samuel 12:7)!

Oh, what shameful indignities and cruelties were heaped upon our precious Savior!

> "See how the patient Jesus stands
> Insulted in His lowest case!
> Sinners have bound the Almighty hands,
> And spit in their Creator's face."

Matthew 26:69-75

The King Denied by His Disciple

69-70. Now Peter sat without in the palace: and a damsel came unto him, saying, Thou also wast with Jesus of Galilee. But he denied before them all, saying, I know not what thou sayest.

While our Lord was in the high priest's house, *Peter sat without in the palace.* In the courtyard overlooked by the rooms of the palace, the servants and officers had lighted a fire to warm themselves while they waited to see what would be done with Jesus.

Peter joined the company, and *a damsel*, who had let him in at John's request, said to him, *Thou also wast with Jesus of Galilee.* Now came the test of his confident boast to his Lord, *Though I should die with thee, yet will I not deny thee. But he denied before them all, saying, I know not what thou sayest.* Whatever the consequences of confessing Christ might have been to Peter, they could not have been as bad as this cruel denial was.

71-72. And when he was gone out into the porch, another maid saw him, and said unto them that were there, This fellow was also with Jesus of Nazareth. And again he denied with an oath, I do not know the man.

There were so many who had seen Peter with Christ that he was easily recognized as one of the companions of the Nazarene. His second denial differed from the first in that he added an oath to the lie, and declared concerning Christ, *I do not know the man.* Perhaps the oath was meant to prove that he was no follower of Him who said, *Swear not at all* (Matthew 5:34), or it may have been a return to Peter's old habit before his conversion. When once a child of God gets on the downward road, no man can tell how fast and how far he will fall unless almighty grace be granted to him.

73. And after a while came unto him they that stood by, and said to Peter, Surely thou also art one of them; for thy speech bewrayeth thee.

Even when Peter swore, there was something of the dialect of Galilee in his utterance, so that these people in Jerusalem detected his provincial dialect, and said to him, *Surely thou also art one of them; for thy speech bewrayeth thee.* If a child of God begins to swear, he will not do it as the ungodly do, and he will be sure to be found out.

74-75. Then began he to curse and to swear, saying, I know not the man. And immediately the cock crew. And Peter remembered the word of Jesus, which said unto him, Before the cock crow, thou shalt deny me thrice. And he went out, and wept bitterly.

Lying led to swearing and swearing to cursing. No one but the Lord knows how much further Peter would have fallen if he had not been divinely caught in his sinful practice. Many men heard the cock crow that morning, but to *Peter* it carried a solemn reminder of his Lord's prophetic warning: *Before the cock crow, thou shalt deny me thrice.* There was something else that affected Peter more than the crowing of the cock. Luke tells us that *the Lord turned, and looked upon Peter* (Luke 22:61). Peter must have looked up at the Lord or he would not have seen that look of sorrow, pity, love, and forgiveness that the Lord gave him, before *he went out and wept bitterly.*

If any one of us has denied the Lord that bought him, let him look up to Him who now looks down from heaven, ready to pardon the backslider who cries with the returning prodigal, *Father, I have sinned against heaven, and in thy sight, and am no more worthy to be called thy son* (Luke 15:21). Even more, this same Peter, when reinstated in his Lord's favor, preached on the day of Pentecost the sermon that led to the conviction and conversion of thousands of his hearers.

Matthew 27

Matthew 27:1-2

The King Taken to Pilate

1. When the morning was come, all the chief priests and elders of the people took counsel against Jesus to put him to death.

They were so full of enmity against *Jesus* that they were eager to seize the first opportunity to *[take] counsel to put him to death.* They had spent the latter part of the night and the earliest moments of the morning in examining, condemning, and abusing their illustrious prisoner. Jesus had foretold that He would be delivered to the Gentiles, so the next act in the terrible tragedy was His appearance before the Roman governor.

2. And when they had bound him, they led him away, and delivered him to Pontius Pilate the governor.

Those who had arrested Jesus had bound Him before they took him to Annas (John 18:12-13). Annas sent him bound unto Caiaphas (John 18:24). Now the Sanhedrin officially *bound him, and delivered him to Pontius Pilate the governor.* As Isaac was bound before he was laid upon the altar, so was the great Antitype bound before He was *brought as a lamb to the slaughter* (Isaiah 53:7) and delivered up to the Roman governor.

Matthew 27:3-10

The Traitor's Remorse and Suicide

3-4. Then Judas, which had betrayed him, when he saw that he was con-
demned, repented himself, and brought again the thirty pieces of silver to
the chief priests and elders, Saying, I have sinned in that I have betrayed the
innocent blood. And they said, What is that to us? see thou to that.

Perhaps *Judas* expected that Jesus would miraculously deliver Himself
from His captors, and *when he saw that he was condemned*, remorse
seized him, and he carried back to his fellow criminals the reward of
his disgrace. There was one good result of his despairing confession: *I*
have sinned in that I have betrayed the innocent blood. Judas had been
with our Lord in public and in private, and if he could have found a flaw
in Christ's character, this would have been the time to mention it; but
even the traitor, in his dying speech, declared that Jesus was *innocent.*
The chief priests and elders had no more pity for Judas than they had
for Jesus. No remorse troubled them; they had secured the Savior, and
they cared nothing for any of the consequences of their action. As for
the traitor, he had made his bargain and he must abide by it.

5. And he cast down the pieces of silver in the temple, and departed, and
went and hanged himself.

Those terrible words – *and went and hanged himself* – reveal the real
character of the repentance of Judas. His was a repentance that needed
to be repented of, not that *godly sorrow [that] worketh repentance to*
salvation (2 Corinthians 7:10). In the history of the church of Christ,
there have been a few instances of remorse like that of Judas, driving
men to despair, if not to actual suicide. May God in mercy preserve us
from any more repetitions of such an awful experience!

6-8. And the chief priest took the silver pieces, and said, It is not lawful
for to put them into the treasury, because it is the price of blood. And they
took counsel, and bought with them the potter's field, to bury strangers in.
Wherefore that field was called, The field of blood, unto this day.

Whether Judas bought the *field* in which he committed suicide (Acts 1:18) or whether *the chief priests,* hearing how he meant to spend *the silver pieces,* carried out his intention, makes no real difference in the result. *The field of blood* became the perpetual memorial of the shame of Judas. When he sold his Lord, he little thought what would be done with the money received as the price of the betrayal. In the fullest sense possible, he was guilty of the blood of the Lord; that blood was upon him, not to seal his pardon, but to confirm his condemnation.

9-10. Then was fulfilled that which was spoken by Jeremy the prophet, saying, And they took the thirty pieces of silver, the price of him that was valued, whom they of the children of Israel did value; and gave them for the potter's field, as the Lord appointed me.

Even the disposal of *the thirty pieces of silver* fulfilled an ancient prophecy. The dark sayings of the prophets as well as their brighter utterances shall all be proved to be true as, one by one, they come to maturity.

The fate of Judas should be a solemn warning to all professing Christians and especially to all ministers. He was one of the twelve apostles, yet he was a *son of perdition* (John 17:12), and in the end he went to his own place. Each of us has his own place, heaven or hell; which is it?

> "Lord! when I read the traitor's doom,
>   To his own place consign'd,
> What holy fear, and humble hope,
>   Alternate fill my mind!
>
> Traitor to Thee I too have been,
>   But saved by matchless grace,
> Or else the lowest, hottest hell
>   Had surely been my place."

Matthew 27:11-26

Jesus – Pilate – Barabbas

11. And Jesus stood before the governor: and the governor asked him, say-ing, Art thou the King of the Jews? And Jesus said unto him, Thou sayest.

Jesus did not look much like a king as He stood before Pilate. There was little enough of the robes of royalty about His simple apparel. Yet even in His humiliation there must have been so much of majesty that even the governor was prompted to ask, *Art thou the King of the Jews?* There was no longer any reason why the King should conceal His true position, so He answered, "*Thou sayest.* It is even as thou sayest – I am the King of the Jews." The Jews rejected their King: *He came unto his own, and his own received him not* (John 1:11). Yet He was their King, even though they refused to bow before His scepter of grace and mercy.

12-14. And when he was accused of the chief priests and elders, he answered nothing. Then said Pilate unto him, Hearest thou not how many things they witness against thee? And he answered him to never a word; insomuch that the governor marvelled greatly.

This was the time for Jesus to be dumb, *like a lamb dumb before his shearer* (Acts 8:32). His silence astonished Pilate, as His speech had before overawed the officers sent to arrest Him (John 7:45-46). Jesus *answered nothing,* for He was there as His people's representative and though He had not sinned, they were guilty of all that was falsely laid to His charge. He might have cleared Himself of every accusation that was brought against Him, but that would have left the load of guilt upon those whose place He came to take, so *he answered him to never a word.* Such silence was sublime.

15-18. Now at that feast the governor was wont to release unto the people a prisoner, whom they would. And they had then a notable prisoner, called Barabbas. Therefore when they were gathered together, Pilate said unto them, Whom will ye that I release unto you? Barabbas, or Jesus which is called Christ? For he knew that for envy they had delivered him.

Pilate was really anxious to deliver Christ from His cruel enemies, but like most wicked men, he was a great coward, so he attempted to gain his end by a crafty trick. *He knew that for envy they had delivered him;* and he may have hoped that Jesus was so popular among the people that an appeal to the masses would result in a verdict in Christ's favor, especially as the choice of one to be released lay between *the King of the Jews* and a notoriously wicked man, *Barabbas.* Surely they would ask for their King to be set at liberty! Pilate little knew the sway the chief priests had over the populace, nor the fickleness of the crowds, whose jubilant cry of, "Hosanna!" would so soon be changed to hoarse shouts of, *Away with him, crucify him* (John 19:15).

> 19. *When he was set down on the judgment seat, his wife sent unto him, saying, Have thou nothing to do with that just man: for I have suffered many things this day in a dream because of him.*

Here was an unlooked-for witness to the innocence of Christ. Whether the dream of Pilate's wife was a divine revelation of Christ's glory or not, we cannot tell, but the message sent by her to the governor must have made him even more anxious than before to release Jesus.

> 20-22. *But the chief priests and elders persuaded the multitude that they should ask Barabbas, and destroy Jesus. The governor answered and said unto them, Whether of the twain will ye that I release unto you? They said, Barabbas. Pilate saith unto them, What shall I do then with Jesus which is called Christ? They all say unto him, Let him be crucified.*

Now the die is cast, the choice of the multitude is made, and *Barabbas* is preferred before *Jesus.* The Lord of glory had been sold by Judas for the price of a slave, and now a robber, a murderer, and a leader in sedition is a greater favorite with the people than the Prince of life. Were there no voices raised in Christ's favor? Were there none out of all that multitude whose sickness He had healed, whose hunger He had satisfied, who would remember Him in that day and ask that He might be spared? No, not one. There were none in the crowd silently sympathizing with the Savior. They *all* said, *Let him be crucified.*

23. And the governor said, Why, what evil hath he done? But they cried out the more, saying, Let him be crucified.

A blind, unreasoning hate had taken possession of the people. They gave no answer to Pilate's wondering inquiry, *Why, what evil hath he done?* for He had done nothing amiss. They only repeated the brutal demand, *Let him be crucified.*

The world's hatred of Christ is shown in similar fashion today. He has done no evil, no one has suffered harm at His hands, all unite to pronounce Him innocent, and yet they practically cry, "Away with Him! Crucify Him!"

24. When Pilate saw that he could prevail nothing, but that rather a tumult was made, he took water, and washed his hands before the multitude, saying, I am innocent of the blood of this just person: see ye to it.

Ah! Pilate, you need something stronger than water to wash *the blood* of that *just person* off your *hands.* You cannot rid yourself of responsibility by that farce. He who has power to prevent a wrong is guilty of the act if he permits others to do it, even though he does not actually commit it himself.

Pilate joined with all the other witnesses in declaring that Jesus was *just* or *righteous.* He even went so far as to declare, *I find in him no fault at all* (John 18:38).

25. Then answered all the people, and said, His blood be on us, and on our children.

All the people willingly took upon themselves the guilt of the murder of our dear Lord: *His blood be on us, and on our children.* This fearful curse must have been remembered by many when the soldiers of Titus spared neither age nor sex and the Jewish capital became the veritable *Aceldama,* "the field of blood." That self-imposed curse still rests upon unbelieving Israel, and till she accepts the Messiah whom she then rejected, the brand will remain upon the dulled nation's brow.

26. Then released he Barabbas unto them: and when he had scourged Jesus, he delivered him to be crucified.

The Roman scourging was one of the most terrible punishments to which anyone could be subjected. The Jewish beating with rods was a mild chastisement compared with the brutal flagellation by the imperial Roman officers, yet even this our Lord endured for our sakes. These were the stripes by which we were healed (1 Peter 2:24). Yet the scourging was but the beginning of the awful end: *When he had scourged Jesus, he delivered him to be crucified.* Knowing Him to be innocent, Pilate first scourged Him and then gave Him up to the fury of His fanatical foes.

Matthew 27:27-31

The King Mocked by the Soldiers

27-30. Then the soldiers of the governor took Jesus into the common hall, and gathered unto him the whole band of soldiers. And they stripped him, and put on him a scarlet robe. And when they had platted a crown of thorns, they put it upon his head, and a reed in his right hand: and they bowed the knee before him, and mocked him, saying, Hail, King of the Jews! And they spit upon him, and took the reed, and smote him on the head.

Ridicule is very painful to bear. In our Savior's case, there was great cruelty mixed with mockery. These Roman *soldiers* were men to whom bloodshed was amusement, and now that there was given up into their hands one who was charged with making Himself a king, we can conceive what a subject for jest the gentle Jesus was in their esteem. They were not touched by the gentleness of His manner, nor by His sorrowful countenance, but they sought to invent all manner of scorn to pour on His devoted head. Surely the world never saw a more astonishing scene than the King of Kings thus derided as a mimic monarch by the meanest of men.

The whole band of soldiers was gathered unto him, for seldom was such sport provided in *the common hall.* Jesus is a king, so He must wear the garb of royalty: *They stripped him, and put on him a scarlet robe,* some old soldier's scarlet or purple coat. The king must be crowned: *When they had platted a crown of thorns, they put it upon his head.* He must wield a scepter: *A reed in his right hand.* Homage must be paid to Him: *And they bowed the knee before him.* Cruel men! Yet probably they knew no better.

Oh, that we were half as inventive in devising honor for our King as these soldiers were in planning His dishonor! Let us render to Christ the real homage that these men pretended to offer Him. Let us crown Him Lord of all and in truest loyalty bow the knee and hail Him, *"King."*

31. And after that they had mocked him, they took the robe off from him, and put his own raiment on him, and led him away to crucify him.

It was divinely overruled that Jesus should go forth with His own raiment on Him, that nobody might say that another person had been substituted for the Savior. As they led Him away, robed in that well-known seamless garment, woven from the top throughout, all who looked upon Him would say, "It is the Nazarene going forth to execution. We recognize His dress as well as His person."

Matthew 27:32-38

The King Crucified

32. And as they came out, they found a man of Cyrene, Simon by name: him they compelled to bear his cross.

Perhaps they were afraid that Christ would die from exhaustion, so they *compelled Simon to bear his cross.* Any one of Christ's followers might have wished to have been this *man of Cyrene,* but we need not envy him, for there is a cross for each of us to carry. Oh, that we were as willing to bear Christ's cross as Christ was to bear our sins on His cross! If anything happens to us by way of persecution or ridicule for our Lord's sake and the gospel's, let us cheerfully endure it. As knights are made by a stroke from the sovereign's sword, so shall we become princes in Christ's realm as He lays His cross on our shoulders.

33-34. And when they were come unto a place called Golgotha, that is to say, a place of a skull, they gave him vinegar to drink mingled with gall: and when he had tasted thereof, he would not drink.

Golgotha was the common place of execution for criminals, the Tyburn or Old Bailey of Jerusalem, outside the gate of the city. There was a special symbolic reason for Christ's suffering *without the gate,* and His followers are bidden to *go forth therefore unto him without the camp, bearing his reproach* (Hebrews 13:11-13).

A shocking drink was given to the condemned to take away something of the agony of crucifixion, but our Lord came to suffer and He would not take anything that would at all impair His faculties. He did not forbid His fellow sufferers from drinking the *vinegar mingled with gall* (*wine mingled with myrrh* [Mark 15:23]), but *he would not drink thereof.* Jesus did not refuse this drink because of its bitterness, for He was prepared to drink even to the last dreadful dregs the bitter cup of wrath that was His people's due.

35. And they crucified him, and parted his garments, casting lots: that it might be fulfilled which was spoken by the prophet, They parted my garments among them, and upon my vesture did they cast lots.

There is a world of meaning in that short sentence – *And they crucified him* – driving their bolts of iron through His blessed hands and feet, fastening Him to the cross, and lifting Him up to hang there upon a gallows reserved for felons. We can scarcely realize all that the crucifixion meant to our dear Lord, but we can join in Faber's prayer:

> "Lord Jesus! may we love and weep,
> Since Thou for us art crucified."

Then was fulfilled all that our Lord had foretold in chapter 20, verses 17 to 19, except His resurrection, the time for which had not arrived.

The criminals' clothes were the executioners' bonus. The Roman soldiers who crucified Christ had no thought of fulfilling the Scriptures when they *parted his garments, casting lots,* yet their action was exactly that which had been foretold in Psalm 22:18. The seamless robe would have been spoiled if it had been torn, so the soldiers raffled for the *vesture* while they shared the other *garments* of our Lord. The dice would be almost stained with the blood of Christ, yet the gamblers played on beneath the shadow of His cross. Gambling is the most hardening of all vices. Beware of it in any form! No games of chance should be played by Christians, for the blood of Christ seems to have splattered them all.

36. And sitting down they watched him there.

Some watched Him from curiosity, some to make sure that He really did die, some even delighted their cruel eyes with His sufferings; and there were some, close to the cross, who wept and mourned, a sword passing through their own hearts while the Son of Man was agonizing even unto death.

37. And set up over his head his accusation written, THIS IS JESUS THE KING OF THE JEWS.

What a marvelous providence it was that moved Pilate's pen! The representative of the Roman emperor was little likely to concede kingship to any man, yet he deliberately wrote, THIS IS JESUS THE KING OF THE JEWS, and nothing would induce him to alter what he had written. Even on His cross, Christ was proclaimed King in the pastoral Hebrew, the classical Greek, and the common Latin, so that everybody in the crowd could read the inscription.

When will the Jews acknowledge Jesus as their King? They will do so one day, looking on Him whom they pierced. Perhaps they will think more of Christ when Christians think more of them; when our hardness of heart towards them has gone, then possibly their hardness of heart towards Christ may also disappear.

38. Then were there two thieves crucified with him, one on the right hand, and another on the left.

As if to show that they regarded Christ as the worst of the three criminals, they put Him between the two thieves, giving Him the place of dishonor. Thus was the prophecy fulfilled: *He was numbered with the transgressors* (Isaiah 53:12). The two criminals deserved to die, as one of them admitted (Luke 23:40-41), but a greater load of guilt rested upon Christ, for *he bare the sin of many* (Isaiah 53:12), and therefore He was rightly distinguished as the King of sufferers, who could truly ask, "Was ever grief like Mine?"

Matthew 27:39-49

Mocking the Crucified King

39-40. And they that passed by reviled him, wagging their heads, and saying, Thou that destroyest the temple, and buildest it in three days, save thyself. If thou be the Son of God, come down from the cross.

Nothing torments a man when in pain more than mockery. When Jesus Christ most needed words of pity and looks of kindness, *they that passed by reviled him, wagging their heads*. Perhaps the most painful part of ridicule is to have one's most solemn sayings turned to scorn, as were our Lord's words about the temple of His body: *Thou that destroyest the temple, and buildest it in three days, save thyself.* He might have saved Himself, He might have *come down from the cross*, but if He had done so, we could never have become the sons of God. It was because He was the Son of God that He did not come down from the cross, but hung there until He had completed the sacrifice for His people's sin. Christ's cross is the Jacob's ladder by which we mount up to heaven.

This is the cry of the Socinians today: "*Come down from the cross.* Give up the atoning sacrifice and we will be Christians." Many are willing to believe in Christ, but not in Christ crucified. They admit that He was a good man and a great teacher, but by rejecting His vicarious atonement, they practically un-Christ the Christ, as these mockers at Golgotha did.

41-43. Likewise also the chief priests mocking him, with the scribes and elders, said, He saved others; himself he cannot save. If he be the King of Israel, let him now come down from the cross and we will believe him. He trusted in God; let him deliver him now, if he will have him: for he said, I am the Son of God.

The chief priests, with the scribes and elders, forgetting their high station and rank, joined the ribald crew in mocking Jesus in His death pangs. Every word was emphatic, every syllable cut and pierced our Lord to the heart. They mocked Him as a Savior: *He saved others; himself he cannot save.* They mocked Him as a King: *If he be the King of*

Israel, let him now come down from the cross, and we will believe him.
They mocked Him as a believer: *He trusted in God; let him deliver him
now, if he will have him.* They mocked Him as the Son of God: *For he
said, I am the Son of God.* Those who say that Christ was a good man
virtually admit His deity, for He claimed to be the Son of God. If He
was not what He professed to be, then He was an impostor. Notice the
testimony that Christ's most bitter enemies bore even as they reviled
Him: *He saved others. He is the King of Israel* (RSV). *He trusted in God.*

44. The thieves also, which were crucified with him, cast the same in his teeth.

The sharers of His misery, the sordid ones who were crucified with
Him, joined in reviling Jesus. Nothing was lacking to fill up His cup of
suffering and shame. The conversion of the repentant thief was all the
more remarkable because he had but a little while before been among
the mockers of his Savior. What a trophy of divine grace he became!

*45. Now from the sixth hour there was darkness over all the land unto the
ninth hour.*

Some have thought that this darkness covered the whole world
and so caused even a heathen to exclaim, "Either the world is about to
expire, or the God who made the world is in anguish." This darkness
was supernatural. It was not an eclipse. The sun could no longer look
upon his Maker surrounded by those who mocked Him. He covered
his face and traveled on in tenfold night, in true shame that the great
Sun of Righteousness would Himself be in such terrible darkness.

*46. And about the ninth hour Jesus cried with a loud voice, saying, Eli, Eli,
lama sabachthani? that is to say, My God, My God, why hast thou forsaken me?*

In order that the sacrifice of Christ might be complete, it pleased the
Father to forsake His well-beloved Son. Sin was laid on Christ, so God
must turn away His face from the Sin-Bearer. To be deserted by His Father
was the climax of Christ's grief, the epitome of His sorrow. See here the
distinction between the martyrs and their Lord. In their dying agonies,
they have been divinely sustained, but Jesus, suffering as the Substitute
for sinners, was forsaken of God. Those saints who have known what it
is to have their Father's face hidden from them even for a brief period of

time can scarcely imagine the suffering that wrung from our Savior the agonizing cry: *My God, My God, why hast thou forsaken me?*

47. Some of them that stood there, when they heard that, said, This man calleth for Elias.

They knew better, yet they mocked the Savior's prayer. Wicked – willfully and scornfully – they turned His death-shriek into ridicule.

48-49. And straightway one of them ran, and took a spunge, and filled it with vinegar, and put it on a reed, and gave him to drink. The rest said, Let be, let us see whether Elias will come to save him.

A person in such agony as Jesus was suffering might have mentioned many pangs that He was enduring, but it was necessary for Him to say, *I thirst* (John 19:28), in order that another Scripture might be fulfilled. *One of them,* more compassionate than his companions, *ran, and took a spunge, and filled it with vinegar* from the vessel probably brought by the soldiers for their own use, *and put it on a reed, and gave him to drink.* It always seems to me very remarkable that the sponge, which is the very lowest form of animal life, should have been brought into contact with Christ, who is at the top of all life. In His death, the whole circle of creation was completed.

As the sponge brought refreshment to the lips of our dying Lord, so may the least of God's living ones help to refresh Him now that He has ascended from the cross to the throne.

Matthew 27:50-54

"It Is Finished"

50. Jesus, when he had cried again with a loud voice, yielded up the spirit.

Christ's strength was not exhausted. His last word was uttered *with a loud voice,* like the shout of a conquering warrior. And what a word it was: *It is finished* (John 19:30). Thousands of sermons have been preached upon that little sentence, but who can tell all the meaning that lies compacted within it? It is a kind of infinite expression for breadth, and depth, and length, and height altogether immeasurable. Christ's life being finished, perfected, and completed, He *yielded up the spirit*, willingly dying, laying down His life as He said He would: *I lay down my life for the sheep. I lay it down of myself. I have power to lay it down, and I have power to take it again* (John 10:15, 18).

> *51-53. And, behold, the veil of the temple was rent in twain from the top to the bottom; and the earth did quake, and the rocks rent; and the graves were opened; and many bodies of the saints which slept arose, and came out of the graves after his resurrection, and went into the holy city, and appeared unto many.*

Christ's death was the end of the Old Covenant. *The veil of the temple was rent in twain from the top to the bottom.* As if shocked at the sacrilegious murder of her Lord, the temple tore her garments, like one stricken with horror at some stupendous crime. The body of Christ being torn, *the veil of the temple was rent in twain from the top to the bottom.* Now was there an entrance made into the holiest of all, by the blood of Jesus, and a way of access to God was opened for every sinner who trusted in Christ's atoning sacrifice.

See what marvels accompanied and followed the death of Christ: *The earth did quake, and the rocks rent; and the graves were opened.* Thus did the material world pay homage to Him whom man had rejected, while nature's convulsions foretold what will happen when Christ's voice *once more shake[s] not the earth only, but also heaven* (Hebrews 12:26).

These first miracles worked in connection with the death of Christ were typical of spiritual wonders that will be continued till He comes again – rocky hearts are torn, graves of sin are opened, those who have been dead in trespasses and sins and buried in sepulchers of lust and evil are revived and come out from among the dead and go unto the holy city, the New Jerusalem.

> *54. Now when the centurion, and they that were with him, watching Jesus, saw the earthquake, and those things that were done, they feared greatly, saying, Truly this was the Son of God.*

These Roman soldiers had never witnessed such scenes in connection with an execution before, and they could only come to one conclusion about the illustrious prisoner whom they had put to death: *Truly this was the Son of God.* It was strange that those men would confess what the chief priests and scribes and elders denied, yet since their day it has often happened that the most abandoned and profane have acknowledged Jesus as the Son of God while their religious rulers have denied His divinity.

Matthew 27:55-61

The King's Faithful Friends

55-56. And many women were there beholding afar off, which followed Jesus from Galilee, ministering unto him: Among which was Mary Magdalene, and Mary the mother of James and Joses, and the mother of Zebedee's children.

We have no record of any unkindness to our Lord from any woman, though we have many narratives of the loving ministry of women at various periods in His life. It was suitable, therefore, that even at Calvary *many women were there beholding afar off.* The ribald crowd and the rough soldiers would not permit these timid yet brave souls to come near, but we learn from John 19:25 that some of them edged their way through the throng till they *stood by the cross of Jesus.* Love will dare anything.

57-58. When the even was come, there came a rich man of Arimathaea, named Joseph, who also himself was Jesus' disciple: He went to Pilate, and begged the body of Jesus. Then Pilate commanded the body to be delivered.

This *rich man of Arimathaea, named Joseph,* a member of the Jewish Sanhedrin, was *Jesus' disciple, but secretly for fear of the Jews* (John 19:38); yet when his Lord was actually dead, extraordinary courage nerved his spirit, and boldly *he went to Pilate, and begged the body of Jesus.* Joseph and Nicodemus are models of many more who have been emboldened by the cross of Christ to do what, without that mighty magnet, they would never have attempted. When night comes, the stars appear. So in the night of Christ's death, these two bright stars shone forth with blessed radiance. Some flowers bloom only at night; such a blossom was the courage of Joseph and Nicodemus.

59-60. And when Joseph had taken the body, he wrapped it in a clean linen cloth, and laid it in his own new tomb, which he had hewn out in the rock: and he rolled a great stone to the door of the sepulchre, and departed.

Our King, even in the grave, must have the best of the best. His body was *wrapped in a clean linen cloth, and laid in Joseph's own new tomb,* thus completing the fulfillment of Isaiah 53:9. Some see in this linen shroud an allusion to the garments in which priests were to be clothed.

Joseph's was a virgin sepulcher, where up to that time no one had been buried, so that when Jesus rose, none could see that another came forth from the tomb instead of Him.

That rock-hewn cell in the garden sanctified every part of God's acre where saints lie buried. Instead of longing to live till Christ comes, as some do, we should rather pray to have fellowship with Jesus in His death and burial.

61. And there was Mary Magdalene, and the other Mary, sitting over against the sepulchre.

Love and faith were both typified by these two Marys *sitting over against the sepulchre.* They will be the last to leave their Lord's resting place and the first to return to it when the Sabbath is past.

Can we cling to Christ when His cause seems to be dead and buried? When truth is fallen in the streets or is even buried in the sepulcher of skepticism or superstition, can we still believe in it and look forward to its resurrection? That is what some of us are doing at the present time. O Lord, keep us faithful!

Matthew 27:62-66

Guarding the King's Sepulcher

62-64. Now the next day, that followed the day of the preparation, the chief priests and Pharisees came together unto Pilate, saying, Sir, we remember

that that deceiver said, while he was yet alive, After three days I will rise
again. Command therefore that the sepulchre be made sure until the third
day, lest his disciples come by night, and steal him away, and say unto the
people, He is risen from the dead: so the last error shall be worse than the first.

These meticulous *priests and Pharisees,* who were so scrupulous
about keeping the Sabbath, did not mind profaning the day of rest
by holding a consultation with the Roman governor. They knew that
Christ was dead and buried, but they still stood in dread of His power.
They called Him a *deceiver,* and they even pretended to *remember* what
he said, *while he was yet alive.* At His trial, their false witnesses gave
another meaning to His words, but they knew all the while that He
was speaking of His resurrection, not of the temple on Mount Zion.
Now they are afraid that, even in the sepulchre, He will bring to nothing all their plans for His destruction. They must have known that the
disciples of Jesus would not *steal him away, and say unto the people,*
He is risen from the dead, so they probably feared that He really would
come forth from the tomb.

Whatever conscience they had made great cowards of them, so they
begged *Pilate* to do what he could to prevent the rising of their victim.

65-66. Pilate said unto them, Ye have a watch: go your way, make it as sure
as ye can. So they went, and made the sepulchre sure, sealing the stone, and
setting a watch.

The chief priests and Pharisees wanted *Pilate* to *make the sepulchre*
sure, but he left them to secure it. There seems to have been a grim sort
of irony about the governor's reply: *Ye have a watch: go your way, make*
it as sure as ye can. Whether he meant it as a taunt or as a command to
secure the sepulcher, they became unconsciously witnesses that Christ's
resurrection was a supernatural act. The tomb in the rock could not
be entered except by rolling away the stone, and they guarded that by
sealing the stone, and setting a watch.

According to the absurd teaching of the rabbis, rubbing ears of corn
was a kind of threshing, and therefore was unlawful on the Sabbath;
yet here were these men doing what, by similar reasoning, might be
called furnace and foundry work, and calling out a guard of Roman

soldiers to assist them in breaking the Sabbath. Unintentionally, they did honor to the sleeping King when they obtained the representatives of the Roman emperor to watch His resting place till the third morning, when He came forth as Victor over sin and death and the grave. Thus, once more was the wrath of man made to praise the King of Glory, and the remainder of that wrath was restrained.

Matthew 28

Matthew 28:1-7

The Empty Sepulcher

1. In the end of the sabbath, as it began to dawn toward the first day of the week, came Mary Magdalene and the other Mary to see the sepulchre.

While the Jewish Sabbath lasted, they paid to it due respect. They did not even go to *the sepulchre* to perform the kindly offices of embalment, but when the old Sabbath was dying away and the new and better Sabbath *began to dawn,* these holy women found their way back to their Lord's tomb. A woman must be first at the sepulcher as she was last at the cross. We may well forget that she was first in the transgression; the honor that Christ put upon her took away that shame. Who but *Mary Magdalene* should be the first at the tomb? Out of her Christ had cast seven devils and now she acts as if into her He had sent seven angels. She had received so much grace that she was full of love to her Lord.

2. And, behold, there was a great earthquake: for the angel of the Lord descended from heaven, and came and rolled back the stone from the door, and sat upon it.

Death was being upheaved and all the bars of the sepulcher were beginning to burst. When the King awoke from the sleep of death, He shook the world. The bedchamber in which He rested for a little while trembled as the heavenly Hero arose from His couch: *Behold, there was a great earthquake.* Nor was the King unattended in His rising, *for the angel of the Lord descended from heaven.* It was not merely one of the angelic host, but some mighty-presence angel, *the angel of the Lord,* who came to minister to Him on that resurrection morning. Jesus was put in the prison of the tomb as a hostage for His people. Therefore, He must not break out of it by Himself, but the angelic sheriff's officer must bring the warrant for His deliverance and set the captive at liberty. When the angel had *rolled back the stone from the door, [he] sat upon it*, as if to defy earth and hell to ever roll it back again. That great stone seems to represent the sin of all Christ's people, which shut them up in prison. It can never be laid again over the mouth of the sepulcher of any child of God. Christ has risen and all His saints must rise too.

3-4. His countenance was like lightning, and his raiment white as snow: and for fear of him the keepers did shake, and became as dead men.

It took a great deal to alarm Roman soldiers. They were toughened to all manner of terrors, but this angel's dashing *countenance and raiment white as snow* paralyzed them with fright, until they swooned away *and became as dead men.* He does not appear to have drawn a flaming sword, nor even to have spoken to *the keepers,* but the presence of perfect purity overawed these rough soldiers. What terror will strike through the ungodly when all the hosts of angels shall descend and surround the throne of the reigning Christ on the last great day!

5. And the angel answered and said unto the women, Fear not ye: for I know that ye seek Jesus, which was crucified.

Let the soldiers tremble, let them lie as if dead through fright, but, *Fear not ye: for I know that ye seek Jesus, which was crucified.* Those who seek Jesus need not fear. These women were mistaken in seeking the living among the dead, yet their seeking ended in finding. They did fear, even though the angel said, *Fear not.* Only Jesus can silence the fears of trembling hearts.

6-7. He is not here: for he is risen, as he said. Come, see the place where the Lord lay. And go quickly, and tell his disciples that he is risen from the dead; and, behold, he goeth before you into Galilee; there shall ye see him: lo, I have told you.

Jesus always keeps His word: *He is risen, as he said.* He said He would rise from the dead and He did. He says that His people also shall rise and they shall *come, see the place where the Lord lay. And go quickly.* The angel would not let the women stay for long, looking into the sepulcher, for there was work for them to do. In this world, we cannot afford to spend all our time in contemplation, however heavenly it may be. Notice the angel's words: first, *See,* and then, *Go.* Make sure about the fact for yourselves and then let others know of it. What you know, tell and do it *quickly.* Swift be your feet, for such good news as you have to carry should not be long on the road. *The king's business required haste* (1 Samuel 21:8).

Tell his disciples that he is risen from the dead; and, behold, he goeth before you into Galilee; there shall ye see him. Matthew wrote the Gospel of the Kingdom, yet in his writings there is much said about that despised region called *Galilee of the Gentiles* (see Matthew 4:15), that borderland that touches us as well as the chosen seed of Abraham. There, in Galilee, is the place where Jesus will hold the first general assembly of His church after His resurrection.

Matthew 28:8-10

The Risen King

8. And they departed quickly from the sepulchre with fear and great joy; and did run to bring his disciples word.

That seems a strange mixture: *Fear and great joy,* awe and delight, doubt and faith; yet the joy was greater than the fear. It was not joy and great fear, but *fear and great joy.* Have we never had that mixture – drops of grief, like April showers, and peace and joy, like sunlight from heaven, making a glorious rainbow reminding us of God's covenant of peace? A holy fear, mingled with great joy, is one of the sweetest mixtures we can bring to God's altar; such were the spices these holy women took away from Christ's sepulcher. Fear and joy would both make them *run to bring his disciples word.* Either of these emotions gives speed to the feet, but when *fear and great joy* are combined, running is the only pace that fits with the messengers' feelings.

9-10. And as they went to tell his disciples, behold, Jesus met them, saying, All hail. And they came and held him by the feet, and worshipped him.

Then said Jesus unto them, Be not afraid: go tell my brethren that they go into Galilee, and there shall they see me.

Saints running in the way of obedience are likely to be met by Jesus. Some Christians travel to heaven so slowly that they are overtaken by follies or by faults, by slumber or by Satan; but he who is Christ's running footman shall meet his Master while he is speeding on his way.

And they came and held him by the feet, and worshipped Him. These holy women were not Unitarians; knowing that Jesus was the Son of God, they had no hesitation in worshipping Him. There must have been a new attraction about Christ after He had risen from the dead: something more sweet about the tones of His voice, something more charming about the countenance that had been so marred at Gethsemane, and Gabbatha, and Golgotha. Perhaps these timid souls clung to their Lord through fear that He might be again taken from them, so *they held him by the feet, and worshipped him,* with fear and faith striving within them for dominion.

Jesus perceived the palpitation of these poor women's hearts, so He repeated the angel's message: *Be not afraid.* He also confirmed the angel's information about *Galilee,* only He spoke of His disciples as *my brethren.* When Christ's servants, angelic or human, speak what He has bidden them, He will endorse what they say.

Matthew 28:11-15

Falsehood and Bribery

11. Now when they were going, behold, some of the watch came into the city, and shewed unto the chief priests all the things that were done.

While good people were active, bad people were active too. *Some of the watch,* having recovered from their fright, came into the city to report the startling scenes they had witnessed. It is noteworthy that they did not go to Pilate. They had been placed at the disposal of *the chief priests,* and therefore, while some of them remained on guard at the sepulcher, others of the soldiers went to their religious employers *and shewed unto [them] all the things that were done,* so far as they knew the particulars. A startling story they had to tell, and one that brought fresh terror to the priests and led to further sin on their part.

12-15. And when they were assembled with the elders, and had taken counsel, they gave large money unto the soldiers, saying, Say ye, His disciples came by night, and stole him away while we slept. And if this come to the governor's ears, we will persuade him, and secure you. So they took the money, and did as they were taught: and this saying is commonly reported among the Jews until this day.

For money Christ was betrayed, and for money the truth about His resurrection was kept back as far as it could be: *They gave large money unto the soldiers.* Money has had a hardening effect on some of the highest servants of God, and all who have to touch the filthy cash have need to pray for grace to keep them from being harmed by being brought into contact with it.

The lie put into the soldiers' mouths was so noticeable that no one ought to have been deceived by it: *Say ye, His disciples came by night, and stole him away while we slept.* A Roman soldier would have committed suicide sooner than confess that he had slept at his post of duty. If they were asleep, how did they know what happened? The chief priests and elders were not afraid of Pilate hearing of their lie, or if he did, they knew that favorable arguments would be as convincing with him as with the common soldiers: *If this come to the governor's ears, we will persuade him, and secure you.*

The soldiers acted just as many men have continued to do from their day to ours: *They took the money, and did as they were taught.*

"What makes a doctrine straight and clear? About five hundred pounds a year" is an *old saw* that can be *reset* today. How much even of religious teaching can be accounted for by the fact that *they took the money!* There are many who make high professions of godliness, who would soon give them up if they did not pay. May none of us ever be affected by considerations of profit and loss in matters of doctrine, matters of duty, and matters of right and wrong!

And this saying is commonly reported among the Jews unto this day. This lie, which had not a leg to stand upon, lived on till Matthew wrote his Gospel, and long afterwards. Nothing lives so long as a lie, except the truth. We cannot kill either the truth or a lie; therefore, let us beware of ever starting a falsehood on its terrible career. Let us never teach even the least error to a little child, for it may live on and become a great heresy long after we are dead.

The modern philosophy, which is thrust forward to cast a slur upon the great truths of revelation, is no more worthy of credence than this lie put into the mouths of the soldiers; yet common report gives it currency and amongst a certain clique it pays.

Matthew 28:16-20

The King's Last Command

16-17. Then the eleven disciples went away into Galilee, into a mountain where Jesus had appointed them. And when they saw him, they worshipped him: but some doubted.

Notice those words: *The eleven disciples.* There were twelve, but Judas, one of the twelve, had gone to his own place, while Peter, who had denied his Lord, had been restored to his place among the apostles. The eleven *went away into Galilee,* to the appointed place their Lord had fixed, *into a mountain where Jesus had appointed them.* Jesus always keeps His appointments, so He met the company that assembled at the selected spot, *and when they saw him, they worshipped him.* Seeing their Lord, they began to adore Him and to render divine honors to Him, for to them He was God, *but some doubted.* Where will not Mr. Doubting and other members of his troublesome family be found? We can never expect to be quite free from doubters in the church, since even in the presence of the newly risen Christ *some doubted.* Yet the Lord revealed Himself to the assembled company, although He knew that some among them would doubt that it was really their Lord who was risen from the dead.

Probably this was the occasion referred to by Paul, when the risen Savior *was seen of above five hundred brethren at once* (1 Corinthians 15:6). It was evidently a meeting for which He had made a special appointment, and His own words to the women, following those of the angel, seem to point this out as the one general assembly of His church on earth before He ascended to His Father. Those who gathered were, therefore, a representative company, and the words addressed to them were spoken to the one church of Jesus Christ throughout all time.

> *18-20. And Jesus came and spake unto them, saying, All power is given unto me in heaven and in earth. Go ye therefore, and teach all nations, baptizing them in the name of the Father, and of the Son, and of the Holy Spirit: teaching them to observe all things whatsoever I have commanded you: and, lo, I am with you always, even unto the end of the world. Amen.*

What a truly royal speech our King made to His loyal subjects! What a contrast was this scene in Galilee to the groans in Gethsemane and the gloom of Golgotha! Jesus claimed omnipotence and universal sovereignty: *All power is given unto me in heaven and in earth.* This is part of the reward of his humiliation (Philippians 2:6-10). On the cross, He was proclaimed King of the Jews, but when John saw Him, in his apocalyptic vision, *on his head were many crowns* (Revelation 19:12). *And he hath on his vesture and on his thigh a name written, KING OF KINGS, AND LORD OF LORDS* (Revelation 19:16).

By virtue of His kingly authority, He issued this last great command to His disciples: *Go ye therefore, and teach,* or, make disciples of *all nations, baptizing them in the name of the Father, and of the Son, and of the Holy Spirit: teaching them to observe all things whatsoever I have commanded you.* This is our commission as well as theirs. From it we learn that our first business is to make disciples of all nations, and we can only do that by teaching them the truth as it is revealed in the Scriptures, and seeking the power of the Holy Spirit to make our teaching effective in those we try to instruct in divine things. Next, those who by faith in Christ become His disciples are to be baptized into the name of the triune Jehovah, and after baptism they are still to be taught all that Christ commanded. We are not to invent anything new, nor to change anything to suit the current of the age, but to teach the baptized believers to observe *all things whatsoever* our Divine King has commanded.

This is the perpetual commission of the church of Christ; and the great seal of the kingdom attached to it, giving the power to execute it, and guaranteeing its success, is the King's assurance of His continual presence with His faithful followers: *Lo, I am with you always, even unto the end of the world. Amen.* May all of us realize His presence with us until He calls us to be with Him, *ever with the Lord* (1 Thessalonians 4:17)! Amen.

Charles H. Spurgeon – A Brief Biography

Charles Haddon Spurgeon was born on June 19, 1834, in Kelvedon, Essex, England. He was one of seventeen children in his family (nine of whom died in infancy). His father and grandfather were Nonconformist ministers in England. Due to economic difficulties, eighteen-month-old Charles was sent to live with his grandfather, who helped teach Charles the ways of God. Later in life, Charles remembered looking at the pictures in *Pilgrim's Progress* and in *Foxe's Book of Martyrs* as a young boy.

Charles did not have much of a formal education and never went to college. He read much throughout his life though, especially books by Puritan authors.

Even with godly parents and grandparents, young Charles resisted giving in to God. It was not until he was fifteen years old that he was born again. He was on his way to his usual church, but when a heavy snowstorm prevented him from getting there, he turned in at a little Primitive Methodist chapel. Though there were only about fifteen people in attendance, the preacher spoke from Isaiah 45:22: *Look unto me, and be ye saved, all the ends of the earth.* Charles Spurgeon's eyes were opened and the Lord converted his soul.

He began attending a Baptist church and teaching Sunday school. He soon preached his first sermon, and then when he was sixteen years old, he became the pastor of a small Baptist church in Cambridge. The church soon grew to over four hundred people, and Charles Spurgeon, at the age of nineteen, moved on to become the pastor of the New Park Street Church in London. The church grew from a few hundred attenders to a few thousand. They built an addition to the church, but still needed more room to accommodate the congregation. The Metropolitan Tabernacle was built in London in 1861, seating more than 5,000 people. Pastor Spurgeon preached the simple message of the cross, and thereby attracted many people who wanted to hear God's Word preached in the power of the Holy Spirit.

On January 9, 1856, Charles married Susannah Thompson. They had twin boys, Charles and Thomas. Charles and Susannah loved each other deeply, even amidst the difficulties and troubles that they faced in life, including health problems. They helped each other spiritually, and often together read the writings of Jonathan Edwards, Richard Baxter, and other Puritan writers.

Charles Spurgeon was a friend of all Christians, but he stood firmly on the Scriptures, and it didn't please all who heard him. Spurgeon believed in and preached on the sovereignty of God, heaven and hell, repentance, revival, holiness, salvation through Jesus Christ alone, and the infallibility and necessity of the Word of God. He spoke against worldliness and hypocrisy among Christians, and against Roman Catholicism, ritualism, and modernism.

One of the biggest controversies in his life was known as the "Down-Grade Controversy." Charles Spurgeon believed that some pastors of his time were "down-grading" the faith by compromising with the world or the new ideas of the age. He said that some pastors were denying the inspiration of the Bible, salvation by faith alone, and the truth of the Bible in other areas, such as creation. Many pastors who believed what Spurgeon condemned were not happy about this, and Spurgeon eventually resigned from the Baptist Union.

Despite some difficulties, Spurgeon became known as the "Prince of Preachers." He opposed slavery, started a pastors' college, opened an orphanage, led in helping feed and clothe the poor, had a book fund for pastors who could not afford books, and more.

Charles Spurgeon remains one of the most published preachers in history. His sermons were printed each week (even in the newspapers), and then the sermons for the year were re-issued as a book at the end of the year. The first six volumes, from 1855-1860, are known as *The Park Street Pulpit*, while the next fifty-seven volumes, from 1861-1917 (his sermons continued to be published long after his death), are known as *The Metropolitan Tabernacle Pulpit*. He also oversaw a monthly magazine-type publication called *The Sword and the Trowel,* and Spurgeon wrote many books, including *Lectures to My Students, All of Grace, Around the Wicket Gate, Advice for Seekers, John Ploughman's Talks, The Soul Winner, Words of Counsel for Christian Workers, Cheque Book of the Bank of Faith, Morning and Evening*, his autobiography, and more, including some commentaries, such as his twenty-year study on the Psalms – *The Treasury of David.*

Charles Spurgeon often preached ten times a week, preaching to an estimated ten million people during his lifetime. He usually preached from only one page of notes, and often from just an outline. He read about six books each week. During his lifetime, he had read *The Pilgrim's Progress* through more than one hundred times. When he died, his personal library consisted of more than 12,000 books. However, the Bible always remained the most important book to him.

Spurgeon was able to do what he did in the power of God's Holy Spirit because he followed his own advice – he met with God every morning before meeting with others, and he continued in communion with God throughout the day.

Charles Spurgeon suffered from gout, rheumatism, and some depression, among other health problems. He often went to Menton, France, to recuperate and rest. He preached his final sermon at the Metropolitan Tabernacle on June 7, 1891, and died in France on January 31, 1892, at the age of fifty-seven. He was buried in Norwood Cemetery in London.

Charles Haddon Spurgeon lived a life devoted to God. His sermons and writings continue to influence Christians all over the world.

www.ingramcontent.com/pod-product-compliance
Lightning Source LLC
Chambersburg PA
CBHW071132130626
46553CB00004B/1339